BROOKINGS–WHARTON

papers
on
URBAN
AFFAIRS
2001

William G. Gale and
Janet Rothenberg Pack
Editors

BROOKINGS INSTITUTION PRESS
Washington, D.C.

BROOKINGS-WHARTON

papers
on
URBAN
AFFAIRS
2001

Symposium on Urban Sprawl

Articles

Purpose   The *Brookings Wharton Papers on Urban Affairs* is an annual publication containing the articles and formal discussant remarks from a conference held at the Brookings Institution and arranged by the editors.

The annual forum and journal are the products of a collaboration between the Brookings Institution Center on Urban and Metropolitan Policy and the Zell Lurie Real Estate Center at the Wharton School of the University of Pennsylvania. All of the papers and discussant remarks represent the views of the authors and not necessarily the views of the staff members, officers, or trustees of the Brookings Institution or the Wharton School of the University of Pennsylvania.

2001 Subscription Rates   Individuals and Institutions $24.95

Standing order plans are available by calling 1-800/275-1447 or 202/797-6258. For international orders add $8.00 surface mail and $16.00 airmail.

Send subscription orders to the Brookings Institution, Department 037, Washington, DC 20042-0037. Or call 202/797-6258 or toll free 1-800/275-1447. Or e-mail bibooks@brook.edu.

Visit Brookings online at www.brookings.edu.

Brookings periodicals are available online through both Online Computer Library Center (contact the OCLC subscriptions department at 1-800/848-5878, ext. 6251) and Project Muse (http://muse.jhu.edu).

Contributors   Richard Arnott   *Boston College*
Dan Black   *Syracuse University*
Jan K. Brueckner   *University of Illinois at Urbana-Champaign*
Gary Burtless   *Brookings Institution*
Janet Currie   *University of California, Los Angeles*
Greg J. Duncan   *Northwestern University*
Edward L. Glaeser   *Harvard University* and *Brookings Institution*
Jeffrey Grogger   *University of California, Los Angeles*
Douglas Holtz-Eakin   *Syracuse University*
Bruce Fallick   *Board of Governors of the Federal Reserve System*
Matthew Kahn   *Tufts University*
Jeffrey Kling   *Princeton University*
Michael Kremer   *Harvard University* and *Brookings Institution*
Helen F. Ladd   *Duke University*
Jens Ludwig   *Georgetown University*
Christopher Mayer   *University of Pennsylvania*
Edwin Mills   *Northwestern University*
Katherine M. O'Regan   *New York University*
Steven Raphael   *University of California, Berkeley*
Stuart Rosenthal   *Syracuse University*
Robert F. Schoeni   *RAND*
Kenneth A. Small   *University of California, Irvine*
Michael A. Stoll   *University of California, Los Angeles*
Clifford Winston   *Brookings Institution*

Conference   Elijah Anderson   *University of Pennsylvania*
participants   Ingrid Gould Ellen   *New York University*
John Goering   *CUNY/Baruch College*
Andrew Haughwout   *Federal Reserve Bank of New York*
Christian Hilber   *University of Pennsylvania*
Lori Kletzer   *Institute for International Economics*
Peter Linneman   *University of Pennsylvania*
Janice Madden   *University of Pennsylvania*
Virginia McConnell   *Resources for the Future*
Kathleen McGarry   *Council of Economic Advisers*
Richard Netzer   *New York University*
Pietro Nivola   *Brookings Institution*
John Quigley   *University of California, Berkeley*
Amy Schwartz   *New York University*
Mark Schroder   *Department of Housing and Urban Development*
Anita Summers   *University of Pennsylvania*
Richard Voith   *Federal Reserve Bank of Philadelphia*
Susan Wachter   *Department of Housing and Urban Development*
Matthew Wilson   *Council of Economic Advisers*

Preface

The *Brookings-Wharton Papers on Urban Affairs* is devoted to bringing cutting-edge research to bear on urban policy issues in an accessible manner. The collaboration between the Wharton School and the Brookings Institution in this endeavor represents an effort to draw on resources and personnel in both academia and the policy community. We hope and expect that the journal itself will be of interest and use to an even wider audience that includes policymakers and their staffs, interested parties in the private sector, journalists, students, and others.

The existence of this journal owes much to the efforts of key people at Brookings and Wharton. At Brookings, President Michael Armacost has been an enthusiastic supporter of this project from the beginning. Robert Litan, director of the Economic Studies Program, has encouraged the project at every turn. Bruce Katz, director of the Center on Urban and Metropolitan Policy, has been a tireless and vocal supporter of the journal and its goals, and has helped provide financial support.

At Wharton, Peter Linneman and Joseph Gyourko, former director and current director of the Samuel Zell and Robert Lurie Real Estate Center, have supported this undertaking intellectually and financially from its inception. The dean's office has made its contribution by freeing some of Janet Rothenberg Pack's time to organize the conference and edit the volume. The Department of Public Policy and Management has in numerous ways encouraged Professor Pack's participation in this endeavor.

Several people made vital contributions to the publication of this volume and the conference on which it is based. Catherine McLoughlin at Brookings organized conference logistics and managed the paper flow with efficiency and good cheer. Amy Liu and Jamaine Tinker provided valuable support at many stages. The authors and discussants deserve special thanks for taking extra efforts to draft their arguments in a clear and accessible manner.

Editors' Summary

THE SECOND VOLUME of the *Brookings-Wharton Papers on Urban Affairs* contains papers and formal discussant remarks from a conference held at Brookings on October 26 and 27, 2000. The symposium for this issue focuses on urban sprawl and decentralization and contains three papers. Edward Glaeser and Matthew Kahn document the enormous decentralization in employment and population that has occurred over the past fifty years and seek to explain these changes. Jan Brueckner sets out a theoretical framework for assessing the claim that the growth of urban areas has been excessive and analyzes several policy options. Steven Raphael and Michael Stoll examine how ownership or access to a car affects employment prospects of minorities in decentralized urban areas. The symposium papers show that although numerous key issues remain unresolved, economists have both the tools and the data to provide important new analyses of what promises to be an increasingly contentious set of issues in the public policy arena.

The other papers in the volume examine current topics of importance to urban economies. Jens Ludwig, Helen F. Ladd, and Greg J. Duncan test for effects of the Moving to Opportunity program on children's educational outcomes. Janet Currie and Jeffrey Grogger explore the determinants of the recent substantial decline in participation in the Food Stamp Program, with a focus on the extent to which changes have been concentrated in urban areas. Dan Black, Douglas Holtz-Eakin, and Stuart Rosenthal examine why minority self-employment rates differ so dramatically across urban areas. These papers are indicative of the broad range of interesting research topics that fall under the "urban" rubric.

Symposium on Decentralization and Urban Sprawl

The enormous decentralization of economic activity has been the central feature of metropolitan development over the past fifty years. Some observers view this trend with alarm and argue that decentralization has led to a series of maladies in central cities as well as to urban sprawl and related problems in the suburbs. Others view decentralization as a positive development, reflecting the preferences of Americans regarding residence, employment, and other factors. A full assessment of decentralization, however, requires facts documenting the extent and nature of the trend, analyses of the causes and consequences of decentralization, and a conceptual framework that integrates these factors. Accordingly, this volume begins with three papers that explore these issues.

Decentralization: Basic Facts and Their Implications

In the traditional view, urban areas have a dense central business district with concentrated employment and production, in order to reduce costs of transportation and information sharing. In such monocentric urban areas, land has the highest value in the city center, where employment density is highest. As distance from the city center increases, land and housing prices fall, lot sizes rise, workers' commute times rise, and the incidence of poverty falls.

This standard view has been increasingly challenged by the trend toward decentralization. Edward L. Glaeser and Matthew E. Kahn document in new ways basic facts of decentralization and analyze the implications for the economic structure of urban areas. They show that in 1940 only one of the ten largest cities had population density below 10,000 people per square mile. By 1990 seven of the ten largest cities had densities below 7,500. Although there is no formal definition of decentralization, urban areas today are highly decentralized: as of 1996, across all metropolitan areas in the United States, only 24 percent of jobs were within three miles of a city center.

Despite the ubiquity of decentralization, there are substantial differences across urban areas. In New York, one of the few cities with concentrated employment patterns, over 45 percent of jobs are within three miles of the city center. In Los Angeles, which is known for its sprawling nature, 45 percent of employment is located within an eleven-mile ring of the city center. The authors also find that the dispersion of employment and population in Chicago, and in most other American metropolitan areas, bears a much stronger resemblance to the spatial patterns in Los Angeles than those in New York.

The authors then examine the causes of these trends. The residential preferences of workers appear to be the driving forces behind this move toward decentralization, according to Glaeser and Kahn. That is, firms have located in the suburbs in large part because that is where the workers choose to locate. In addition, better access to trucking transit routes from suburban locations encourages manufacturing firms to locate in the suburbs. The trend toward decentralization appears to be somewhat less pronounced among cities that are more than 200 years old and somewhat more pronounced among those less than sixty years old. In addition, cities with younger suburbs are associated with greater decentralization of employment. Forces offsetting decentralization include the advantage of urban areas in accelerating the communication of ideas. Idea-intensive or service-based industries (such as commercial banking) are more likely to locate in the central city, whereas manufacturing firms and firms that require more physical infrastructure are more likely to locate in the suburbs.

The implications of these results are striking. The decentralization of employment suggests that the classic stylized facts of urban economics may no longer be empirically valid. Indeed, in contrast to the standard model, Glaeser and Kahn find that cities with more decentralized employment are less likely to see housing prices fall and commute times rise, and in more decentralized urban areas, median incomes are less likely to rise with distance to the city center. Interestingly, the spatial patterns for these factors are still correlated with employment densities, but since employment is no longer concentrated at the city center, the spatial patterns do not follow those suggested by the traditional approach. Thus Glaeser and Kahn present an important set of facts that disputes much traditional thinking on cities and will challenge experts to develop innovative approaches for thinking about urban dynamics.

Systematic Thinking about Urban Sprawl

Extensive decentralization of cities and the resulting development of the urban fringe bring new users to roadways, reduce open space, and require cities or suburbs to extend their utility services farther. All of these factors raise concerns about urban sprawl, which has become an increasingly contentious political issue in recent years. Twelve states have enacted growth management programs, and 240 antisprawl initiatives appeared on local and state ballots in November 1998, with many additional measures proposed in November 2000.

In light of this heated public debate, Jan K. Brueckner provides a framework in which to analyze sprawl issues and the relative merits of alternative remedies. He defines urban sprawl as the *excessive* spatial growth of urban areas. The emphasis on whether growth is excessive is crucial, because the natural growth of urban areas due to increases in income or population or to improvements in transportation efficiency should not be cause for concern.

Brueckner's paper suggests that under current policies, there are reasons to believe that too much new suburban development occurs because developers and new residents are not forced to pay the full costs that they impose on others. He suggests that forcing developers and new residents to face these costs with taxes and fees is the best strategy for controlling growth. He also highlights three such problems and discusses the prospects and pitfalls of the implied policy solutions.

First, each new driver that moves to the suburbs adds to roadway congestion there and consequently imposes costs on others, including increasing the time and fuel costs needed to drive a given distance. Economists have often suggested forcing commuters to realize these costs by assessing congestion tolls. Brueckner points out that technological developments could make assessing such tolls simpler now than it has been previously but notes strong political resistance to such taxes in the past.

Second, suburban development reduces the amount of open space around the perimeter of a city, which reduces the benefits that all area residents can obtain from such spaces. Brueckner discusses the possibility of using development taxes to correct this market failure but warns that identifying the optimal level for such a tax would be extremely difficult in practice, because it is very hard to measure how much value people place on the amenity of undeveloped land outside the city.

Third, cities do not charge developers or new residents the full cost of extending infrastructure, such as water and sewer lines, to new developments. This encourages development beyond optimal levels. Impact fees for service extension could correct this pricing error.

Some metropolitan areas concerned about urban sprawl, such as Portland, Oregon, have tried another policy alternative: urban growth boundaries. These boundaries are set by governments and designate a ring beyond which urban development is either prohibited or very strictly controlled. Brueckner argues that such policies are likely to be difficult to implement effectively and thus are likely to hurt urban residents, especially low-income residents. Moreover, the policies do not specifically target the market failures of road congestion, utility use, and open space. He warns that in some cases a draconian urban growth boundary policy could be worse for society than no government intervention and the resulting sprawl.

Brueckner's findings will not provide solace to staunch advocates on either side of the debate on urban sprawl. Rather, his paper highlights the importance of systematic thinking about the causes and consequences of sprawl and the necessity of matching both the character and the level of policy intervention to the particular problems that sprawl presents.

Employment Opportunities in Decentralized Metropolitan Areas

The exodus of jobs to the suburbs raises the possibility that people who continue to live in cities will find it more difficult to find jobs close to their residence. If so, the ability to travel via public transportation or private automobile will become an increasingly important determinant of people's ability to obtain and retain employment. The issue becomes especially interesting from a policy viewpoint when it is recognized that urban residents are disproportionately minority and lower-income households, and that public transportation often provides poor service for those who live in the city and work in the suburbs.

The importance of car ownership for employment is examined by Steven Raphael and Michael A. Stoll. They document a spatial mismatch between some employment opportunities and available workers. For example, the average black resident of Chicago lives in a zip code where there are only four retail jobs per 100 residents. They also construct dissimilarity indexes between minority groups and job access. The index for blacks and retail jobs in Chicago was 0.74, meaning that 74 percent of blacks would have to move to a different zip code in order be spatially distributed in the same proportion as retail employment opportunities.

The main focus of the paper is an empirical examination of how car ownership affects employment probabilities for the black and Latino population relative to the white population. White families are more likely to have cars; only 5 percent of white households do not own an automobile, compared with 24 percent of black households and 12 percent of Latino households. Among those who own cars, however, the probability of being employed is nearly constant across these groups. The authors find a positive relationship between owning a car and being employed, controlling for other factors. More interestingly, they find that this relationship is stronger for more segregated minority groups. It is much stronger for blacks than for whites, and slightly stronger for Latinos than for whites. This effect is also stronger in cities in which black households are more geographically isolated from employment opportunities.

Raphael and Stoll close by raising issues regarding subsidies for minority car ownership. They show that raising car-ownership rates for minorities to the same rates as for white households would be expected to significantly reduce the employment rate gap between these groups. They note that increased car use would worsen traffic-related externalities such as congestion and air quality, but also that many minority workers with cars would be reverse commuters, traveling from homes in the central city to employment in the suburbs. Furthermore, they expect many minority workers to be employed on night shifts or at other times that would not conflict with rush hour traffic.

Research Papers

The other three papers in this volume provide new evidence on current issues in urban economics and urban policy. They demonstrate the breadth of topics that fall comfortably within the area of urban economics and the important insights that can be gained on urban issues from related fields of research, such as public finance and labor economics.

Do Housing Relocation Programs Help Children to Do Better in School?

The combination of residential segregation by income and race and the suburbanization of high-income households raises many questions about the effects of neighborhood on residents. This is especially true in relation to children and the schools that they attend. To what extent do peer groups influence individuals' educational outcomes? Are children who grow up in high-poverty environments fundamentally different from others? At what point do neighborhood effects become irreversible?

The experimental design of the Department of Housing and Urban Development's Moving to Opportunity program, currently operating in five cities, allows researchers to study overall effects of neighborhood on children's outcomes. Public housing families who volunteer for the program are randomly assigned to one of three groups: a group that is given Section 8 housing vouchers valid only in census tracts with a very low poverty rate; a group that is given Section 8 vouchers valid anywhere; and a group that is given no assistance in finding alternative housing.

The effects of this program on children's educational achievements is the focus of the paper by Jens Ludwig, Helen F. Ladd, and Greg J. Duncan. Exploiting the experimental nature of the program, they find that children aged between five and twelve who moved to low-poverty neighborhoods demonstrated substantial improvement on standardized tests in both reading and math. Only the reading test scores for teenagers whose families moved were available. They do not differ from the scores of those who did not move. However, teens who transferred to lower poverty areas experienced more grade retention and disciplinary action than their peers who did not move. The authors suggest that differences in school standards, rather than actual declines in teens' behavior or abilities, may account for these apparently negative implications.

The authors note that their findings are encouraging but are only one input into a larger debate about whether the expansion of relocation policies would be desirable. Which aspects of the new neighborhoods or schools are leading to the positive effects remains unclear. In some cases, reform of schools in low-income neighborhoods might be as effective as relocation. Also, introducing students from low-income neighborhoods into low-poverty areas might have negative impacts on the educational outcomes of host children. The best policy options for taking advantage of neighborhood effects are uncertain. Nevertheless, the authors do provide important new evidence that should be part of any discussion of the costs and benefits of relocation programs.

Why Did Food Stamp Program Participation Decline?

The Food Stamp Program provides a monthly allotment of coupons or credit for low-income households to purchase food at participating stores and is currently one of the largest transfer programs in the United States. However, participation rates have fallen dramatically in the past decade, from 27 million persons in 1994 to 20 million in 1998, with much of the decline occurring after 1996 and most of it in urban areas. Janet Currie and Jeffrey Grogger examine the causes of the decline in Food Stamp Program enrollment and their implications for public policy and urban areas.

Three alternative (and not mutually exclusive) hypotheses have been suggested to explain falling enrollment in the Food Stamp Program: welfare reform, the strength of the economy, and changes in stigma and transactions costs attached to participation. The Personal Responsibility and Work Opportunity Restoration Act of 1996 allowed states to penalize Food Stamp participants for failure to meet work requirements, which may have substantially reduced the size of the eligible population. Currie and Grogger found that, overall, welfare reform was responsible for almost a third of the decrease. This effect was especially strong among single-head households. The strong economy and corresponding lower unemployment rates explained about one-fifth of the overall decline in participation between 1993 and 1998. Welfare reform, the strong economy, and changes in program rules may have increased transaction costs and stigma associated with participation. More frequent recertification requirements under the new rules impose more costs on households wishing to sign up for the program. Stigma may be a greater factor in states that still provide food stamp coupons, as opposed to the roughly two dozen states using credit card–style electronic balance transfer methods. (All states are required to shift to electronic transfer methods by October 2002.) Currie and Grogger suggest that transaction costs are especially problematic for single parents and rural households, while stigma seems to be more important for married households without children.

The decline in food stamp use is particularly important for urban areas, given the concentration of the poor in cities. Much of the fall in participation rates occurred in cities. This is especially true of the decline due to welfare reform. Currie and Grogger found that implementation of the Temporary Aid for Needy Families (TANF) program had close to no impact on Food Stamp Program rolls in rural areas but was responsible for about 40 percent of the decline in enrollment in central cities. In comparison, decreases in unemployment were responsible for only 18 percent of the decline in central city locations. The fact that TANF implementation seems to play a greater role than falling unemployment in the reduction of Food Stamp Program participation in cities suggests that needy families are experiencing more difficulty in obtaining food stamps, rather than reduced need. Under these circumstances, policy reforms intended to restore benefits to households in need should target families in central cities, especially single-head households.

Why Do Minority Self-Employment Rates Vary across Metropolitan Areas?

The promotion of minority business ownership has been a major thrust of federal and local government policies for some time. The much lower rate of self-employment among minorities contributes to differences in employment rates between minority and white populations and may well restrict the abilities of minority groups to accumulate wealth. About 11 percent of the overall population but only 4 percent of the black population are self-employed. Whites are self-employed at above-average rates of 13 percent, with Asians at 11 percent and Latinos in the middle at about 7 percent. Average earnings from self-employment are 93 percent higher for whites than for blacks. The variation in self-employment rates across metropolitan areas is also higher for all three minority groups than for whites.

Dan Black, Douglas Holtz-Eakin, and Stuart Rosenthal show that individuals' characteristics—such as age, immigrant status, education, and so on—are important determinants of whether a particular person is self-employed, but they do not vary across metropolitan areas in ways that can explain variation in self-employment rates and earnings in different cities.

The authors also examine city-level variables and show that the degree of segregation of the minority population within a given metropolitan area does not have an important impact on minority self-employment rates. What does make a difference is the purchasing power of minority groups in a city. In cities with wealthier minority populations, higher rates of minority self-employment are observed. Apparently, the economic power of the minority community is important to sustain minority entrepreneurs. There are several possible channels through which a minority group's economic clout could influence the self-employment rate, including various consumer discrimination theories and improved access of minorities to lenders. Distinguishing among these alternatives will play an important role in determining the policy implications of the authors' findings.

Conclusion

Taken together, the papers presented in this volume show that significant progress can be made in disentangling economic issues that affect and are affected by urban areas. Each provides new facts or models that will prove useful to policymakers, academics, students, and others. Their findings should prove useful in devising solutions to problems and developing ways to exploit opportunities for welfare-enhancing urban development. We believe the papers will provide a valuable foundation for future analysis and policy interventions as the problems and opportunities created by urban areas continue to evolve.

EDWARD L. GLAESER
Harvard University and Brookings Institution

MATTHEW E. KAHN
Tufts University

Decentralized Employment and the Transformation of the American City

IN 1899 ADNA WEBER began his masterpiece on urban growth in the nineteenth century by writing, "The most remarkable social phenomenon of the present century is the concentration of population in cities."[1] One hundred years later, the evolution of cities is still among the most interesting and important of social phenomena. America is in the midst of an urban transformation so profound that it is changing completely the spatial organization of economic activity. In 1900 urban America lived and worked in high-density communities that allowed most people to travel with their own feet. By the middle of the century, the typical city still had a dense urban core where people worked, but the majority of urban residents lived in suburban communities and commuted by cars. At the dawn of the twenty-first century, jobs have followed workers, and America is increasingly a nation of moderate-density edge cities.[2]

The data document a truly massive change in the American city. In 1940 only one of the ten largest cities in the United States (Los Angeles) had a population density below 10,000 people per square mile. In 1990 population density levels are below 7,500 people per square mile in seven out of the ten largest cities. Cities of the past were built at higher densities because, after all, in 1920 cars were rare.[3] Even in 1960, only 61 percent of commutes were by

The authors thank the National Science Foundation for financial support. Jesse Shapiro and Meghan McNally provided extremely helpful research assistance. The authors also thank Richard Arnott, Chris Mayer, Ken Small, and conference participants for useful comments.

1. Weber (1900).
2. Garreau (1992).
3. Gibson (1998). According to the 1995 Highway Statistics Summary, U.S. Department of Transportation, in 1920 the ratio of cars to families was .33.

1

private vehicle; by 1990 the figure had risen to 83 percent.[4] In 1940 the over-whelming number of urban jobs appear to have been close to the city center. In 1996 only 24 percent of jobs in metropolitan areas are within three miles of the central business district. The dense walking city of the nineteenth century has been replaced by the medium-density driving city of today.

This decentralization of the American city proceeded in two waves. First, people moved their residences to the suburbs. This movement of urban workers to the suburbs started in the late nineteenth century with the first commuter trains and streetcars. The introduction of the mass-produced automobile democratized the suburbs and led to a massive reshaping of the urban landscape. But as late as 1960, 63 percent of jobs were in the central city, and 51 percent of metropolitan area population lived in the suburbs.[5] People lived at low densities, but they worked at high densities.

In 2000 people both live and work in the suburbs. This paper is focused on the second wave of urban development: the decentralization of employment. First, we document basic facts about the decentralization of employment. In 1996 we find that across the United States, the average metropolitan area is remarkably decentralized.[6] The median employee works seven miles from the city center, and the median resident lives eight miles from the city center. New York City is apparently the only major metropolitan area that really has a monocentric employment structure (the median employee in New York works only 3.8 miles from the city center). Chicago, for example, is almost as decentralized as Los Angeles. Across cities, we show that the correlation between city age and decentralization is surprisingly weak, and that regional patterns are less extreme than is often thought. The Northeast and the Midwest have many areas that are just as decentralized as the South and the West.

We use cross-industry variation to try to understand what drives the suburbanization of industry.[7] We examine four reasons why firms choose

4. U.S. Department of Transportation (2001).
5. Mieszkowski and Mills (1993).
6. There is no generally accepted, rigorous definition of decentralization. We would like to compare these figures against some existing historical or international norm. However, our zip code level data are not available before 1994, and no international equivalents exist (to our knowledge). We take 100 percent centralization as a benchmark and feel quite comfortable thinking of metropolitan areas that have less than one-quarter of their employment within three miles of their central business district as being decentralized.
7. Using a county level data set, Carlino (1985) concludes that manufacturing suburbanization has led to the decentralization of people and nonmanufacturing industries. This work is complementary to our own because we believe that people follow jobs and jobs follow people. Cooke (1983) concludes that both agglomeration economies and economizing on transportation costs help explain manufacturing suburbanization in Cincinnati.

particular locations: land costs, access to ideas, access to workers, and transport cost savings for inputs and outputs. This framework emphasizes the fact that cities exist to save transport costs for goods, people, and ideas.[8] We use a number of (admittedly weak) proxies for land use to test whether industries that use more land tend to suburbanize. Industries with higher electricity usage (a possible proxy for land use) are more likely to decentralize. Manufacturing industries, which are generally more land intensive, are also more likely to decentralize.

One piece of evidence suggesting that firms suburbanize to have access to workers is that industries whose workers are more likely to suburbanize are more likely to suburbanize their employment. However, interpreting this result is difficult. This fact might occur because some firms are more likely to suburbanize for other reasons, and those firms will naturally choose to minimize labor costs and hire more suburbanized workers.

To address this concern, we use cross-city, cross-industry data. We ask whether industries whose national employment patterns suggest that they are likely to suburbanize in a given city do indeed suburbanize more than the norm of either that city or their industry. This appears to be the case. We also find, across metropolitan areas, that places that were more suburbanized in population in 1969 had faster decentralization of employment between 1969 and 1997. Jobs have followed people.

Of course, this is not to minimize that people also follow jobs. Our view is that the worker–job location relationship is two sided. We believe that both consumption and production amenities matter deeply for the location of workers and firms. One example of an urban production amenity may be the role that density can play in speeding the flow of ideas.

Our best test of the importance of idea flows in dense urban centers is to examine whether skill-intensive industries are less likely to decentralize. The essence of this test is that by observing what industry-level features predict demand for centralization, we can get at what cities do well. Thus, if we could measure which industries have a high demand for up-to-date ideas, and we notice that these industries locate in cities, then it is natural to infer that cities are good at providing up-to-date ideas. In our case, we try to measure the demand for new ideas by the skill level of the industry and by the extent to which workers in the industry use computers.

We find that the relative centralization of skilled industries appears to be a fairly robust phenomenon. Industries with more skilled workers—which we

8. Glaeser (1998).

see as a measure of the intellectual intensity of the industry—and industries in which workers use computers—also a proxy for intellectual intensity—are more likely to locate in the city center. This finding is particularly surprising since high human capital workers are more likely to suburbanize, and this would naturally induce high human capital industries to suburbanize as well.[9]

Our final goal is to investigate the role of government in the location of employment. Following the methodology of Thomas Holmes and our own prior work on cities, we look at whether there are political boundary effects on employment, holding distance from the city center constant.[10] While significant boundary effects show up in most metropolitan areas, they are sometimes positive and sometimes negative. There seem to be two patterns of government-employment relationships across U.S. metropolitan statistical areas (MSAs). In some cities, a pro–central city bias appears to come about because relatively rich suburbs fight to stop employment growth in their areas. However, some central cities tax businesses so much that they drive businesses away. We have attempted to create a categorization across metropolitan areas of these different types of cities.

This paper has two main conclusions about the decentralization of industry in America. First, workers' residential preferences appear to be extremely important. If spatial patterns in the past were dictated mainly by the productivity advantages of particular locales for firms, spatial patterns now seem to be driven as much by consumption advantages experienced by workers. Second, the primary force fighting decentralization seems to be the urban advantage in speeding the flow of ideas. Our proxies for idea intensiveness are the most reliable predictors of centralization.

Stylized Facts

Before discussing our analytical framework, we begin with a set of stylized facts about the decentralization of urban jobs. We have two sources of data. The first source is county-level data on population and employment by major industries from the Department of Commerce Regional Economic Information System (REIS) CD-ROM. These data provide us with a time series on the decentralization of employment. Our second source of data contains employ-

9. The fact that firms with workers in the suburbs tend to locate in the suburbs is driven by industries with older workers and workers with families, not industries with high human capital workers.
10. Holmes (1998); Glaeser, Kahn, and Rappaport (2000).

ment information at the zip code level for every metropolitan area zip code in the United States in 1996. Most of our empirical work will rely on this zip code level information.

Data Description

The Department of Commerce's Zip Code Business Patterns 1996 data provide total employment by zip code and firm counts by firm employment size by four-digit SIC level by zip code.[11] The Zip Code Business Patterns data are extracted from the Standard Statistical Establishments List, a file of all known single and multiestablishment companies maintained and updated by the Bureau of the Census. The data set identifies 10,556 zip codes within 335 metropolitan areas. There are 454 three-digit SIC industries identified (by the 1987 classifications). Most of the nation's economic activity is covered in this series. Data are excluded for self-employed persons, domestic service workers, railroad employees, agricultural production workers, and most government employees.

We locate each zip code to determine whether it lies within an MSA and what its distance is from the MSA's central business district (CBD). The locations of the CBDs are given by the 1982 Economic Censuses Geographic Reference Manual, which identifies the CBDs by tract number. The data source for each zip code's distance from the CBD is found in Chenghuan Chu.[12] Although zip codes are not ideal geography (owing to their unusual shapes), they do offer the opportunity to study within-MSA variation in economic activity. Our empirical work focuses on the 9,454 zip codes that are within thirty-five miles of a CBD.

Basic Facts

Figure 1 shows the cumulative distribution of population and employment by distance from the central business district across the United States as a whole. The figure illustrates that 25 percent of employees work within three

---

11. Taking the midpoint of employment within each size category and using an employment level of 1200 for firms that are top coded at 1000, we calculate a zip code's total employment by SIC code. We aggregate industry employment up to the three-digit SIC level.

12. Chu (2000). The GIS (geographic information systems) software package ArcView is used to calculate the distance from the centroid of each ZIP code to the centroid of the corresponding CBD. ZIP code centroid data are from the *ESRI Data and Maps* CD-ROM (Environmental Systems Research Institute, Inc., 1999) and the MARBLE geocorrelation engine (www.ciesin.org).

Figure 1. The Distribution of People and Jobs in Metropolitan Areas

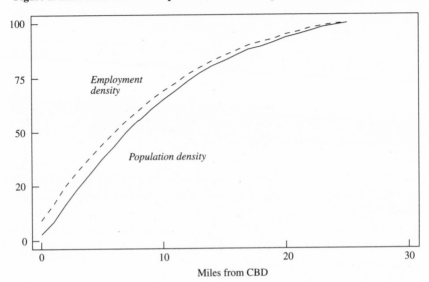

miles of their metropolitan area center, and 20 percent of people live within three miles of the city center.

Figure 1 makes two points. First, most metropolitan employees work more than five miles from the city center. On average, the monocentric model is a fairly poor approximation for the reality of American cities. Second, while employment is slightly more centralized than population, the difference is not that large. Basically, population and employment track each other well.

Figure 2 examines the employment decentralization for the three largest metropolitan areas: New York City, Los Angeles, and Chicago. New York City is one city that truly does fit the monocentric model. More than 45 percent of New York's employment works within three miles of the city center (Wall Street).[13] Several factors help to explain the centralization of New York City. First, New York's geography makes sprawl particularly difficult. The Wall Street area is surrounded on three sides by water. As such, access is difficult, and as the city grew, it could only spread in one direction without

---

13. As we do throughout the paper (except for figure 3), we are here examining primary metropolitan statistical areas. We consider the consolidated metropolitan statistical area (CMSA) just too large to use meaningfully. However, there is no question that the measured centralization of New York City would decline if we looked at CMSAs.

Figure 2. The Distribution of Jobs in Three Major Metropolitan Areas

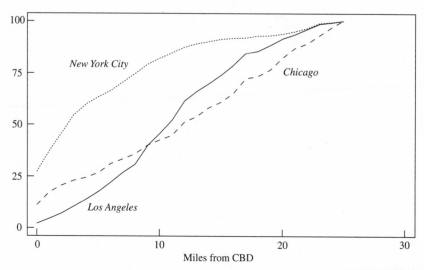

Miles from CBD

crossing water.[14] Second, New York's primary industry, financial services, is both extremely information intensive and not a large consumer of land. The older New York industries (textiles, printing) that had less need for up-to-the-minute knowledge and greater need for land have spread. Indeed, the difficult period in New York City from 1970 to 1990 reflected the disruptions caused by the exodus of those older industries. Third, New York is an older city, and its infrastructure was built for higher-density levels.

Los Angeles is often viewed as the paradigmatic sprawl city.[15] One has to go out eleven miles from the central city of Los Angeles to find as large a share of employment as New York has within three miles. Los Angeles differs in industrial mix (it is one of the few large cities that have a larger share of employment in manufacturing than does the United States as a whole). Los Angeles's port still has large, land-intensive employers. While Los Angeles does have knowledge-intensive employers, they are less in need of immediate information flows than finance. Los Angeles really came of age in the car era, so its infrastructure is aimed at lower-density living. Finally, Los Ange-

14. Though we wish we could do more work on geography throughout this paper, data limitations restrict our ability to do much on this topic. We simply acknowledge that topography is clearly important and a pressing topic for future research.

15. Giuliano and Small (1991).

Figure 3. The Concentration of Activity in Each CMSA's Major County

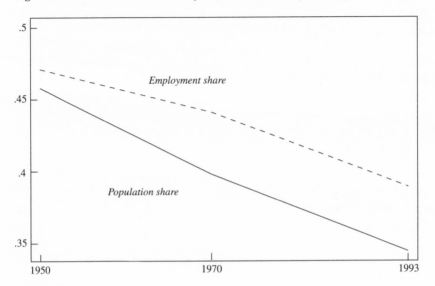

les does not have the same natural barriers as New York City that would prevent the spread of population.

The surprise for us was Chicago, which is the third line on the graph. We had expected Chicago to resemble New York City or at least to lie half way between the Los Angeles and New York models. While there is slightly more employment centralization in Chicago than in Los Angeles, Chicago looks more like Los Angeles than it looks like New York City. When we plotted similar graphs for other cities, we were consistently amazed at the extent to which the employment patterns in other American metropolitan areas resembled those of Los Angeles far more than they resembled monocentric New York.

Figure 3 shows the time series for centralization. As we do not have zip code data on employment for any time period before 1994, we are forced to use more standard county-level measures to document the trends in centralization. The data source is the Department of Commerce Regional Economic Information System (REIS) CD-ROM. We use the share of employment and population working in the largest county of consolidated metropolitan areas from 1950 to 1990.[16] This is a crude measure of centralization, but it still

16. Figure 3 is the only empirical output based on CMSA data. Since Los Angeles County is a PMSA by itself, we wanted to document suburbanization trends as such counties as Riverside and San Bernardino have grown in absolute and relative terms.

shows the basic pattern of declining centralization. In some sense, the surprise to us was not the amount of increasing decentralization. The fact that more than 50 percent of metropolitan area employment was outside of the largest county even in 1950 was startling. There are two possible interpretations of this fact. First, cities in 1950 may not have been monocentric even then. Second, consolidated metropolitan statistical areas may have contained several smaller monocentric cities in 1950.

Our Regression Approach

There are many summary measures that can capture the degree of employment centralization. However, for much of our work, we will use coefficients from the following zip code level regression:

(1) $Log\left(\dfrac{Employment}{Square\ Mile}\right) = \alpha_{MSA} + \beta * \text{Distance from CBD} + \varepsilon$

using our zip code data, where α_{MSA} is an MSA-specific fixed effect. These density regressions are fairly standard in the literature and are justified by an exponential density function (that is, *Density* = $e^{-\beta*distance}$).[17] In some cases when there are zero values for many zip codes (that is, the industry-city regressions), we work with one plus job density. The exponential density is justified in the population density literature by a power utility function. In the employment context, it can be justified by a Cobb-Douglas production function with land as an input. Generally, we run these regressions with MSA fixed effects to account for higher employment densities in some metropolitan areas. If we run this employment regression for the entire United States (including the MSA fixed effects), we find an estimate of β of –0.169 with a standard error of 0.002.[18] If we run the population gradient regression for the entire United States and include MSA fixed effects, we find an estimate of β of –0.128 with a standard error of 0.001.

Decentralization across Metropolitan Areas and Regions

We are not primarily interested in a single nationwide measure of employment decentralization. Our goal is to have measures that will enable us to

17. See DiPasquale and Wheaton (1996).
18. The MSA fixed effects allow some cities to have greater average density than others. If we did not include these fixed effects, the estimate of β would be –0.145. The lower coefficient results from the fact that cities that are lower density, on average, are also, on average, smaller geographically.

Table 1. Measures of Employment Decentralization[a]

Part A: Simple correlations, MSA[b]

	Log-level slope	Three-mile share	Ten-mile share	Median distance
Log-level slope	1			
Three-mile share	-0.275	1		
Ten-mile share	-0.695	0.506	1	
Median distance	0.652	-0.564	-0.918	1
	Part B: SIC correlations[c]			
Log-level slope	1			
Three-mile share	-0.050	1		
Ten-mile share	-0.179	0.756	1	
Median distance	0.181	-0.747	-0.909	1

a. In both panels, the log-level slope is the OLS regression coefficient of the log of zip code job density regressed on the zip code's distance from the CBD. The three-mile and ten-mile shares represent the share of metropolitan statistical area (MSA) jobs located in these respective rings. Median distance is the distance from the central business district (CBD) for the median employee. Panel A includes metropolitan areas where total employment was greater than 150,000 in 1996.

b. n = 106.

c. n = 439.

compare decentralization across metropolitan areas and industries.[19] To accomplish this aim, we estimate equation 1 separately for each MSA whose total employment is greater than 150,000. Thus, each MSA has a separate intercept (which is close to the MSA fixed effect in the nationwide regression) and an MSA slope—which will be our measure of centralization. In general, there is a strong relationship between the MSA slope and the MSA intercept—the correlation is –0.67.[20]

Our regression-based measure is not the only possible measure of employment decentralization. For example, Chu uses the share of employment within a three-mile ring of the city center.[21] Other possible measures include the share of employment within ten miles of the city center and the median distance between the city center and employees. The median distance is defined by sorting all workers by the distance between where they work and the central business district. The median distance is then the location where the median employee works; that is, exactly 50 percent of workers work closer to the CBD than this distance. While there are cases when one measure is theo-

19. A number of studies have measured employment decentralization in specific cities such as Houston (Mieszkowski and Smith, 1991), Los Angeles (Giuliano and Small, 1991), and Chicago (McMillen and McDonald, 1998). Macauley (1985) reports evidence of the flattening of population, employment, and manufacturing gradients for eighteen cities between 1940 and 1980.

20. In a standard urban model where density at the urban edge was zero, this negative relationship would be automatic if the distance to the edge of the city was constant across metropolitan areas. If this distance was not fixed, this relationship does not need to hold.

21. Chu (2000).

Figure 4. Cross-MSA Employment Gradient Distribution

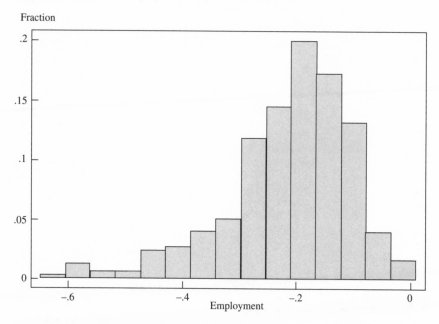

retically preferable to another, generally, there is no overwhelming case for any one measure.

We might expect that the measures would all be highly correlated, but as table 1, part a, shows, correlations are far from perfect. These relatively low correlations occur because the spatial organization of metropolitan areas is often far more complex than our models suggest. For example, Washington, D.C., has a centralized employment downtown (based on the federal government) and tremendous sprawl. Thus, it has a relatively high three-mile employment share but a relatively low ten-mile employment share and elasticity measure. As a result, we generally show results both for the three-mile ring employment share and for our basic elasticity measure.

Using either of these two measures, there is a striking degree of heterogeneity in the degree of centralization across metropolitan areas. Some cities have positive gradients, meaning that employment is generally larger away from the city center. Other MSAs are highly centralized. Figure 4 shows the histogram of our estimates. A typical standard error for one of these estimates is 0.03.

Table 2 documents the heterogeneity of employment decentralization across regions. The first four rows of each panel show the mean value of four

Table 2. Regional Differences in Employment Centralization[a]

	MSA/PMSA	Beta
East		
Average log-level slope		-0.157
Three-mile share		0.294
Ten-mile share		0.635
Median distance		7.619
Five most centralized	Springfield, Mass.	-0.312
	Buffalo-Niagara Falls, N.Y.	-0.263
	Worcester, Mass.-Conn.	-0.254
	Pawtuckett, R.I.	-0.243
	Rochester, N.Y.	-0.200
Five least centralized	Philadelphia, Pa.-N.J.	-0.121
	Jersey City, N.J.	-0.112
	Scranton--Wilkes-Barre--Hazelton, Pa.	-0.109
	New Haven-Meriden, Conn.	-0.100
	York, Pa.	-0.087
South		
Average log-level slope		-0.177
Three-mile share		0.164
Ten-mile share		0.577
Median distance		8.913
Five most centralized	El Paso, Tex.	-0.389
	Lexington, Ky.	-0.316
	Jackson, Miss.	-0.304
	Chattanooga, Tenn.-Ga.	-0.264
	Orlando, Fla.	-0.249
Five least centralized	Norfolk-Virginia Beach-Newport News, Va.-N.C.	-0.130
	Raleigh-Durham-Chapel Hill, N.C.	-0.116
	Greensboro--Winston-Salem--High Point, N.C.	-0.092
	West Palm Beach-Boca Raton, Fla.	-0.081
	Tampa-St Petersburg-Clearwater, Fla.	-0.078
Midwest		
Average log-level slope		-0.163
Three-mile share		0.176
Ten-mile share		0.542
Median distance		10.067
Five most centralized	Louisville, Ky.-Ind.	-0.278
	Madison, Wisc.	-0.267
	Des Moines, Iowa	-0.265
	Wichita, Kans.	-0.234
	Indianapolis, Ind.	-0.217
Five least centralized	Dayton-Springfield, Ohio	-0.151
	Gary, Ind.	-0.142
	Grand Rapids-Muskegon-Holland, Mich.	-0.133
	Detroit, Mich.	-0.113
	Chicago, Ill.	-0.101

Table 2. Continued

MSA/PMSA		Beta
West		
Average log-level slope		-0.155
Three-mile share		0.176
Ten-mile share		0.569
Median distance		9.267
Five most centralized	Las Vegas, Nev.-Ariz.	-0.432
	Albuquerque, N.M.	-0.396
	Tacoma, Wash.	-0.311
	Colorado Springs, Colo.	-0.281
	Denver, Colo.	-0.266
Five least centralized	Anaheim, Calif.	-0.083
	Oakland, Calif.	-0.079
	Vallejo-Fairfield-Napa, Calif.	-0.079
	San Diego, Calif.	-0.078
	Oxnard, Calif.	0.005

a. For each MSA with more than 150,000 total jobs, an OLS regression is estimated where the dependent variable is a zip code's log (job density) and the independent variable is zip code distance from the CBD. The OLS slopes are sorted by most and least centralized.

different measures of centralization by region. The rest of the table shows the five least and most centralized cities within each region. We show our basic regression measure of β (see equation 1), median distance to employee, and the share of employees within three-mile and ten-mile distances. These measures have all been weighted by MSA employment. The least centralized region is the Midwest. For three of the four measures, it has the highest degree of employment sprawl. Its largest cities, such as Detroit and Chicago, are extremely decentralized. Eastern MSAs feature the most centralized employment. The median job in the East is almost 2.5 miles closer to the CBD than the median job in the Midwest. Surprisingly, southern MSAs are more centralized than the midwestern MSAs.

Decentralization across Industries

There is also remarkable heterogeneity across industries. Substantial sprawl is ubiquitous, and there is a great deal of mass close to flat employment gradients, while some industries have remained quite concentrated. Figure 5 plots two industries that are at the extremes. Commercial banking is one of the most concentrated industries. About 50 percent of the employment in this industry lies within five miles of the city center. We suspect that this centralization may even have increased over time as deregulation of branch banking rules made it possible for large central city banks to expand elsewhere in the

Figure 5. The Distribution of Jobs for Two Industries

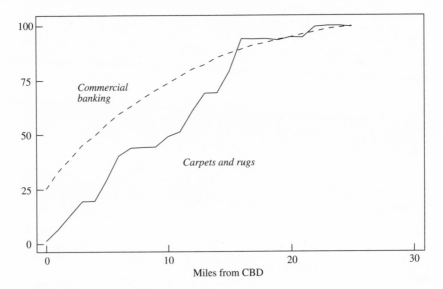

metropolitan area. Commercial banking uses little land and a great deal of information, so we are not surprised that it is one of the most centralized industries.

"Carpets and rugs" is an industry at the other extreme. This is a low human capital industry that does involve physical infrastructure. It is among the least centralized of industries. Two-thirds of the workers in the industry work more than ten miles from the city center. Much of our empirical work in the rest of the paper uses cross-industry differences in centralization to understand the important forces that explain centralization.

Our regression methodology can also be used to compare the levels of urban centralization across industries more rigorously. In this case, we estimate separate versions of equation 1 for each industry. Again, in each industry-specific regression we include separate MSA fixed effects. In this case, the MSA fixed effect captures different employment densities in each industry in each MSA. One issue with this estimation is that in a large number of zip codes, there is zero industry employment. This censoring is clearly problematic, and standard Tobit techniques will not handle it adequately (because they will still treat each zero observation identically, which will lead to estimating excessive flatness of employment densities).[22]

22. To study the robustness of our SIC estimates of equation 1, we aggregated zip code employment by .5 mile rings. Thus if the typical CBD's outer areas are thirty miles from the

Figure 6. Cross-Industry Employment Gradient Distribution

Fraction

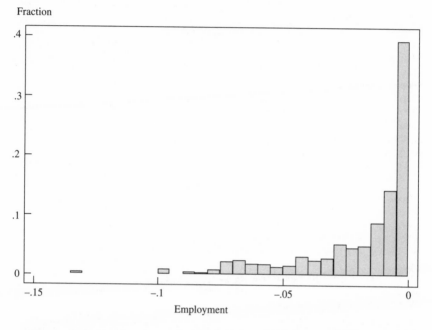

Employment

Figure 6 gives a histogram of estimated decentralization coefficients across three-digit industries. A typical standard error for these regressions is 0.001, so many of these coefficients are different statistically. The large number of basically zero coefficients is interesting and appears to be robust to many alternative specifications of the equation.

In table 1, part b, we show the correlation between three-digit SIC specific estimates of equation 1 with the share of a three-digit industry's total employment across all MSAs that is located in the inner three miles of the MSA and the share located in the inner ten miles of the MSA. These correlations are often low. Again, this low correlation supports our parallel use of both the regression-based measures and the share of employment within a three-mile ring of the city center.

Table 3 shows the ten least and most centralized industries. Business and consumer services are highly represented among the most centralized industries. This connects with the work of Jed Kolko, who documented the extent

CBD, then we construct sixty data points per industry. Estimating an employment gradient for these "aggregated data," we found the OLS gradient highly correlated with our estimates of equation 1. For a study that jointly estimates the probability that an area contains employment and the area's employment level, see McMillen and McDonald (1998).

Table 3. Centralization by Industry[a]

SIC code	Industry	Beta
	Ten most centralized	
5810	Eating and drinking places	-0.1342042
5410	Grocery stores	-0.0993439
8010	Offices and clinics of medical doctors	-0.0974595
8660	Religious organizations	-0.0972406
7380	Miscellaneous business services	-0.0964536
8320	Individual and family services	-0.0863515
7360	Personnel supply services	-0.0862626
6020	Commercial banks	-0.0847687
6510	Real estate operators and lessors	-0.0789298
7340	Services to buildings	-0.0777698
	Ten least centralized	
1030	Lead and zinc ores	-0.0000537
1400	Nonmetallic minerals, except fuels	-0.0000325
1060	Ferroalloy ores, except vanadium	-0.0000177
4600	Pipelines, except natural gas	-0.0000162
1020	Copper ores	-0.0000112
2410	Logging	-0.0000109
3760	Guided missiles, space vehicles, parts	-2.91E-06
8400	Museums, botanical, zoological gardens	4.69E-06
1420	Crushed and broken stone	0.0000205
1470	Chemical and fertilizer minerals	0.0000373

a. For each three-digit SIC industry, an OLS regression is estimated. The unit of analysis is the zip code. The dependent variable is log (1+job density), and the independent variables are MSA fixed effects and the zip code's distance from the CBD. This table reports the coefficient on zip code distance.

to which high transport costs in services appears to keep them in the highest-density areas.[23] The least centralized industries tend to be connected with natural resources. Interestingly, there is no industry with a significant positive density gradient, while there are metropolitan areas with such positive gradients.

Rethinking the Monocentric Model

Among the most important consequences of the decentralization of employment is that the traditional monocentric model is becoming an increasingly poor representation for the decentralized world.[24] Although there have been many critics of the monocentric models for decades, these criticisms have become more justified over time. We now look at three features of monocentric models and ask about the connection between these features and the decentralization of employment.

23. Kolko (1998).
24. For a detailed discussion, see Anas, Arnott and Small (1999).

The first great triumph of the monocentric model is its ability to explain why housing prices decline with distance from the city center. William Alonso's masterpiece illustrated how lower housing prices must compensate residents for the costs of commuting.[25] Therefore, a second feature of the monocentric model is that commute times should rise with distance from the CBD. But if jobs are decentralized, then commuting times may not rise with distance from the city center. Thus we expect the distance–commute time relationship to disappear in decentralized metropolitan areas.

A final element of the monocentric model is that several versions of the model predict that the poor will live in the central city. The classic version of the model argues that this situation comes about because of great demand for land among the rich. Other versions argue that this connection comes about because the poor use time-intensive public transportation.[26] We examine whether the relationship between poverty and proximity to the CBD is weaker in decentralized cities.

To examine the first implication of the monocentric model, that housing prices decline with distance from the city center, we begin by estimating a housing price gradient regression for each metropolitan area:

(2)
$$Log(\text{Median Housing Price}) =$$
$$\gamma_{MSA} + \chi_{MSA} * \text{Distance from CBD} + \Delta_{MSA} * \text{Rooms} + e.$$

We are regressing the logarithm of the zip code's median home price on distance from the CBD. The coefficient χ_{MSA} captures the extent to which housing prices rise and, therefore, poverty falls with distance from the city center. The variable rooms is the share of the zip code's housing stock that has three or fewer rooms. We then plot this estimated χ_{MSA} coefficient against the MSA level employment density gradient (from estimating equation 1) in figure 7.[27] Figure 7 shows the relationship between the slope of employment density on distance from CBD and the slope of housing price on distance from CBD. There is a strong and statistically significant positive connection between the two measures. In metropolitan areas where employment is centralized, housing prices decline with distance from the CBD. In decentralized metropolitan areas, this decline is much milder.

To test the second implication of the monocentric model, that commute times rise with distance from the city center, we begin by regressing median

25. Alonso (1964).
26. Wheaton (1977); Gin and Sonstelie (1992); or Glaeser, Kahn, and Rappaport (2000).
27. The data source for all demographic data at the zip code level is the 1990 Census of Population and Housing.

Figure 7. Cross-MSA Employment and Home Price Gradients

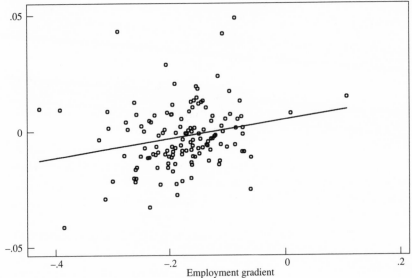

commute time (again, at the zip code level) on the distance from the city center for each metropolitan area:

(3) Log(Average Commute Time) $= \theta_{MSA} + \delta_{MSA} *$ Distance from CBD.

Average commute times come from the 1990 Census of Population and Housing's zip code residential file. For each zip code, the data set reports summary statistics for the residents who live there. The estimated coefficient δ_{MSA} reflects the extent to which commuting times rise with distance from the city center.[28]

In figure 8, we look at the relationship between these estimated commuting gradient coefficients and our estimates of the employment density–distance from the CBD. This figure shows the relationship between the slope of employment density on distance from the CBD and the slope of commute times on distance from the CBD. The graph indicates that in decentralized metropolitan areas, commute times barely rise with distance from the CBD.[29] Naturally, when the jobs are in the suburbs, people in the suburbs have shorter commutes.

28. Our key results are unchanged if we weight the regressions by zip code population.
29. As in Gordon, Kumar, and Richardson (1989).

Figure 8. Cross-MSA Employment and Commute Gradients

Commute gradient

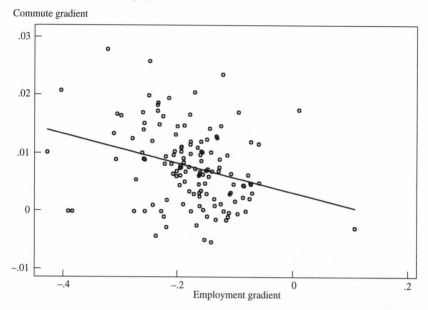

Employment gradient

To separate whether sprawl has different effects on travel speed and distance, we use the 1995 National Personal Transportation Survey (NPTS). The 1995 NPTS is a nationally representative data set of more than 20,000 households. It includes detailed information on worker commuting patterns. In table 4, we present three OLS regressions. For each commuter who lives in a metropolitan area, we construct this commuter's miles per hour, one-way travel time in minutes, and distance commuting. We regress the log of these three dependent variables on MSA fixed effects and the log of the population density at the census block where the respondent lives. Unfortunately, we do not know the distance to city center in this data set. However, we do know population density of the census block where the person lives, which serves as a rough proxy for degree of suburbanization. The three regressions in table 4 show that across the United States as a whole, people in low-density areas commute much longer distances but do so at much faster speeds. Matthew Kahn shows that vehicle mileage is much lower in denser metropolitan areas.[30] The net effect is a mild negative connection between travel time and density. This suggests that in the previous graph, the low commute time versus dis-

30. Kahn (2000).

Table 4. Travel Time, Speed, and Distance[a]

Dependent variable	Log (travel speed)	Log (travel time)	Log (travel distance)
Log (density)	-0.1100	-0.0457	-0.1557
	(0.0031)	(0.0038)	(0.0055)
R^2	0.0948	0.0441	0.0566
N	22162	22162	22162

Source: The data source is the 1995 National Personal Transportation Survey.

a. For households who live in a metropolitan area, this table reports how the population density at place of residence (based on the census block) affects travel speed, travel time, and travel distance to work. Metropolitan-area fixed effects are included in each OLS regression. Standard errors are reported in parentheses. Intercepts calculated but not shown.

tance from CBD relationship in many cities reflects the fact that in the suburbs, people are driving much farther, much faster.

The final implication of the classic monocentric model is that income will rise with distance from the city center. To see whether this fact is weaker in decentralized cities, we begin by estimating a regression (like equations 2 and 3) where we regress median household income in each zip code on distance from the city center. Median household income by zip code is reported in the 1990 Census of Population and Housing zip code file. The regression yields an estimate for each MSA of how steeply median zip code income rises with respect to distance from the CBD. We compare across metropolitan areas and ask whether the connection between income and distance from the CBD disappears in decentralized metropolitan areas. Figure 9 shows the relationship between this measure of the centralization of household income and our basic decentralization of employment measure. We find that in more decentralized cities, income is less likely to rise with distance from the city center.

A final question about the monocentric model is whether we should model edge cities as polycentric or just diffuse. Several authors, Vernon Henderson and Arindam Mitra and Kenneth Small and Shunfeng Song, have put forth a polycentric view of edge cities.[31] If these authors are right, we should appropriately model sprawled cities as just having multiple employment centers. We can then use the standard monocentric model for thinking about patterns around these cities. An alternative view is that the patterns of employment in the suburbs bear no resemblance to patterns in the city center. According to this view, suburban employment is much more decentralized, and a better model posits that employment is spread evenly throughout the suburbs. Many policy analyses that hinge on the monocentric model (for example, the loca-

31. Henderson and Mitra (1998); Small and Song (1994).

Figure 9. Cross-MSA Employment and Income Gradients

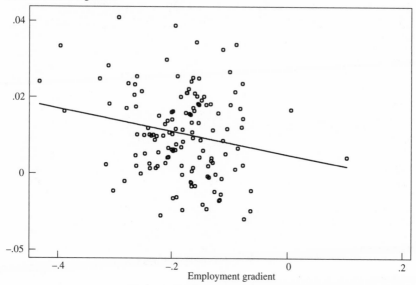

Household income gradient

tion of the poor) need to be rethought if suburban employment is really not centered at all.[32]

To examine this question, we consider the amount of employment concentration in the most dense zip codes of the inner and outer areas of the city for thirty major metropolitan areas. To be precise, we first split each metropolitan area into an inner and an outer ring, using the median distance from the CBD as the dividing line. We then sort zip codes by density and ask how much employment, in the inner and outer rings, was located in the most dense zip codes. We summed up employment (going from densest to least dense zip codes) until we had included enough zip codes to account for 5 percent of the land area of the metropolitan area as a whole. Thus, we are considering the same land area in the inner and outer rings and asking whether the densest zip codes in the outer ring are even nearly as dense as the zip codes in the inner ring.

Table 5 shows the shares of population and jobs in these densest areas of the inner and outer rings of metropolitan areas. In twenty-four metropolitan

32. For example, we might think that suburban employment may lead to pockets of poverty surrounding suburban employment centers if there are indeed such centers. However, if suburban employment is sufficiently decentralized, this seems unlikely.

Table 5. Distribution of Population and Jobs[a]

MSA	Inner ring		Outer ring	
	Employment	Population	Employment	Population
Albany, N.Y.	0.5151	0.2988	0.1234	0.1056
Atlanta, Ga.	0.4363	0.1738	0.1521	0.0943
Baltimore, Md.	0.3960	0.2926	0.1126	0.0805
Birmingham, Ala.	0.5875	0.3473	0.1251	0.0842
Boston, Mass.	0.4352	0.2792	0.0972	0.0668
Chicago, Ill.	0.2940	0.1581	0.1063	0.0290
Cincinnati, Ohio	0.4411	0.2961	0.1965	0.0935
Cleveland, Ohio	0.3252	0.1683	0.1010	0.0729
Dallas, Tex.	0.5299	0.2401	0.1609	0.1311
Denver, Colo.	0.5216	0.3599	0.2542	0.1902
Detroit, Mich.	0.2505	0.0962	0.1847	0.0563
Houston, Tex.	0.4929	0.2318	0.1596	0.1041
Kansas, Mo.	0.5017	0.3158	0.2000	0.1399
Los Angeles, Calif.	0.3145	0.1038	0.1602	0.0912
Minneapolis, Minn.	0.5395	0.2686	0.0907	0.1242
New York, N.Y.	0.5996	0.2450	0.0672	0.0695
Newark, N.J.	0.2619	0.2098	0.1282	0.0603
Oakland, Calif.	0.2695	0.2306	0.2121	0.0671
Philadelphia, Pa.	0.3433	0.3018	0.1770	0.0865
Phoenix, Ariz.	0.5582	0.3424	0.2056	0.2260
Pittsburgh, Pa.	0.4738	0.2599	0.0456	0.0368
Riverside, Calif.	0.2827	0.1118	0.2098	0.1880
Sacramento, Calif.	0.5566	0.3763	0.1234	0.1526
St. Louis, Mo.	0.4114	0.3015	0.2632	0.1086
San Antonio, Tex.	0.5454	0.2716	0.1050	0.1655
San Diego, Calif.	0.3661	0.1414	0.1886	0.0761
San Francisco, Calif.	0.5464	0.3622	0.1703	0.1230
Seattle, Wash.	0.5913	0.2893	0.1930	0.1636
Tampa, Fla.	0.2405	0.1165	0.2354	0.0838
Washington, D.C.	0.4704	0.2231	0.1469	0.0899

a. The inner ring is defined as those zip codes whose distance from the CBD is less than the MSA median. The outer ring is defined as those zip codes whose distance from the CBD is greater than the MSA median. In each ring, zip codes are sorted by job density from highest density to lowest. Zip codes are added until the total land area of the set equals 5 percent of the MSA's total area. The table reports the share of all MSA jobs and population in each of these cells.

areas, there are at least twice as many jobs in the central city centers than in the suburban centers. In many metropolitan areas, the ratio of jobs in the central city's zip codes to jobs in the suburban zip codes is more than three. The ratios for population are generally smaller. This table clearly illustrates these two facts. First, some metropolitan areas (Detroit, Riverside, Tampa) have suburban centers that really do look like their central cities. In the vast majority of metropolitan areas, however, suburban employment is much more dispersed than central city employment. On the whole, we think that suburban employment is best thought of as being decentralized, not poly-centered. This may help us to understand why suburban poverty is much less centralized.

The Basic Theory of Decentralized Employment

We think of the decentralization of employment as the result of an economic equilibrium where firms and workers balance the benefits of density against density's costs. Here, we focus on the decisions of firms, but we think of workers as simultaneously making location choices. One pervasive question is whether the decentralization of firms is primarily a response to the demand of workers for suburban life-styles or whether firms would have moved into suburbs on their own. This question is important because it helps us to understand whether cities should fight for employment by worrying about the productivity of employers or about the quality of life of employees.[33]

Arguably, the greatest theoretical achievement of urban economics is the Alonso-Muth-Mills framework for analyzing household location decisions within a metropolitan area.[34] In this model, consumers choose their proximity to the city center, trading high land prices against shorter commute times. In reality, at least two other sets of factors influence the location decision of consumers. Cities or suburbs may have amenities (attractive scenery, unsafe streets) that attract or repel. Political boundaries and public goods provision will also influence the locations of households.[35] The location of households thus comes from the interplay of commuting times, home prices, and the demand for land, nongovernment locational amenities, and government. We believe that the dominant force explaining the rise in suburbanization since 1900 is the automobile, but other authors emphasize different factors. Robert Margo attributes much importance to rising incomes that increase demand for low-density dwellings. Joe Gyourko and Richard Voith point to government policies that favor suburban living. Edwin Mills argues that big city problems drive much of modern suburbanization.[36]

33. Elsewhere, one of us has argued that the future of cities lies in their ability to become attractive havens for consumers. Glaeser, Kolko, and Saiz (2001).

34. See Brueckner's (1987) elegant synthesis.

35. Brueckner, Thisse, and Zenou (1999). Glaeser, Kahn, and Rappaport (2000) argue that the poor may disproportionately locate in central cities because suburban governments cater to the rich, and big city governments cater to the poor.

36. Margo (1992); Gyourko and Voith (1998); Mills (1992).

Although the location decisions of households have been studied extensively, the location decisions of firms have not. Several papers on decentralized employment looked at population patterns when firms were distributed in multiple locations within a city. More recent work has taken the location decision of firms more seriously and thought about the relative advantages of a central versus edge locale.[37]

Decentralization of employment is the result of firms deciding that locating in the lower density urban fringe is more profitable than locating in the city center. Profits of firms can be written as

$$(4) \qquad P(i)*A(i)*f(L, X) - W(i)*L - C(i)*X + e(j, i), \quad (4)$$

where $P(i)$ is a location-specific price net of transport costs, $A(i)$ is location-specific productivity, $f(L,X)$ is a space indifferent production function in labor and a vector of other inputs X, $W(i)$ is a location-specific wage, and $C(i)$ is a vector of location-specific other inputs. The term $e(j, i)$ refers to a firm-location specific error term to capture heterogeneity across firm-location matches, with cumulative distribution function $F(e)$.

For simplicity, we just take the levels of X and L as fixed—this means that employment per firm is fixed, and overall employment density moves only with the number of firms. Thus the overall level of employment in industry j in location i will be

$$(5) \qquad L*(1 - F(P(i)*A(i)*f(L, X) - W(i)*L - C(i)*X).$$

Employment will be a function of local prices of the final good and transport costs; local productivity differences; local labor supply; and the cost of local inputs, especially land. If we believe that local productivity differences are tied primarily to local knowledge, then this grouping comes down to which locations have advantages in transport costs for goods, people, and ideas.

The gain from writing down this model is that it suggests that the centralization of employment can help us to assess what cities provide. Essentially, this is a revealed preference argument. If we see that the industries that have the most to gain by reducing transport costs are the industries that locate in cities, then we infer that cities lower transport costs. There is a strand of literature that emphasizes estimating local production functions to determine the impact that local amenities have on production. We think that the location decisions made by industry are generally a sounder means of assessing the benefits that certain locations provide.

37. White (1976, 1988); Henderson and Mitra (1998); Ross and Yinger (1995).

What forces affecting firm profitability are likely to differ between cities and suburbs? Big cities may have some advantages in transport costs and prices of goods. They are large markets, and high density facilitates the access to customers.[38] Also, many cities were built around ports or other transport hubs that also will attract goods that have high transport costs. However, the suburbs may have better access to highways and transportation infrastructure. Many of the most famous edge cities are strongly connected to these highways, for example, the Route 128 corridor in Boston. As such, even if transport costs are an important determinant of location, we cannot say a priori whether cities or suburbs will particularly appeal to industries with high transport costs.

We have four tests of the role of transport costs. First, we look at whether industries that produce goods with a higher weight per dollar value are more likely to suburbanize. This test just looks at whether an increase in transport costs leads to suburbanization or centralization. Second, we look at services versus manufacturing with the idea that services have higher transport costs. Even though services often have weightless products (for example, haircuts), they require the provider and the consumer to be in the same physical place, and this raises transport costs. Third, we look at the extent to which, across industries, goods are shipped abroad. Fourth, we look at the extent to which industries whose customers are particularly centralized are themselves more centralized. The importance of this effect may differ across industries if some industries are likely to locate near customers and others are more likely to locate near suppliers.

A second possibility is that cities and suburbs differ in productivity, at least for some industries. One possible reason for greater urban productivity is that cities speed the flow of ideas. If firms in cities have access to more knowledge than firms in suburbs, then this will create an urban productivity advantage. Testing for the importance of intellectual spillovers is notoriously difficult. However, we expect that the demand for these spillovers will be higher in industries in which employees have higher levels of human capital and workers are more likely to use computers. We therefore test whether industries with high human capital and high computer use are more likely to locate in the urban center.

The third factor that should influence the urban centralization of firms is the location of workers and the wages that they demand in the urban core relative to the fringe. This is a difficult phenomenon to test, because the location

38. See Krugman (1991).

of workers is surely endogenous. Just as firms locate to be close to workers, workers locate to be close to firms. Indeed, one can imagine a situation with multiple equilibria. In one equilibrium, firms locate downtown, and workers crowd near them. In another equilibrium, firms decentralize, and workers locate in suburbs. One interpretation of the urban transformation is that firms and workers are just moving from one equilibrium to another. Of course, it is foolish to believe that the edge city equilibrium could have existed in a world without automobiles, but once automobiles are widespread, then both equilibria may exist simultaneously.

The mutual causality between firm and worker location makes it hard to try to isolate causal factors in employment decentralization. Despite a heroic effort by Lawrence Thurston and Anthony Yezer, who rely on the timing of decentralization to identify causality, it is still difficult to estimate whether jobs are following people or vice versa.[39] We have three approaches to this issue. First, we look at whether more suburbanization occurs in industries whose workers are predicted to suburbanize based on their demographics. Then we examine the decentralization of industries in cities where suburban location is common among the types of workers that these industries generally hire nationwide. Finally, we will look at whether employment growth has followed population suburbanization in the time series across metropolitan areas.

Explaining Decentralization across MSAs

Now we return to our empirical work and test our hypotheses about employment sprawl. First, we examine the correlates of sprawl at the MSA level. Second, we consider the correlates of decentralized employment across three-digit SIC industries.

Population and Employment

One question that will recur throughout this paper is the extent to which the suburbanization of employment is driven primarily by the suburbanization of jobs. Figure 10 graphs employment-distance density gradients on population-distance density gradients across metropolitan areas. There is a strikingly positive relationship. Cities that have decentralized populations have decentralized employment. The correlation between these two measures is .95. Of

---

39. Thurston and Yezer (1994). For another example of time series identification methods, see Greenwood and Stock (1990).

Figure 10. Cross-MSA Employment and Population Gradients

Employment gradient

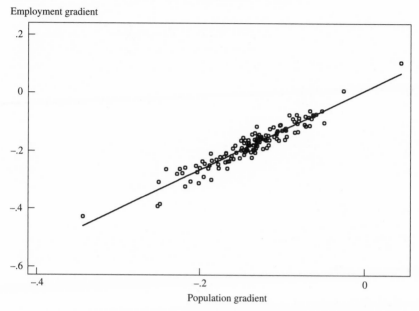

Population gradient

course, this connection does not suggest any causality, but the closeness of the two measures does suggest that it is difficult to think of the decentralization of employment without considering the decentralization of population.

Table 6 asks whether there are any cities with decentralized employment that do not have decentralized population. To answer this question, we regress the employment density–distance gradient on the population density–distance gradient (as in figure 10) and then examine the residuals. Our goal is to show cities that appear to be particularly centralized or decentralized in their employment over and above the extent predicted by the suburbanization of population in the city.

The table shows an interesting set of outliers. Madison, Wisconsin, which is fairly centralized along both dimensions, has a surprisingly high level of population centralization. The regression predicts that employment will generally be more centralized than population, but for Madison, that is not the case. The other extreme is Albuquerque, New Mexico, where employment is much more centralized than population. In most cases employment and population go together, and we are driven to believe that the connection between the two types of decentralization is extremely strong.

Table 6. Centralization of Employment Not Explained by Centralization of Population[a]

MSA/PMSA	MSA	"Unexplained" employment centralization	Employment centralization log-level slope	Population centralization log-level slope
		Top five		
Albuquerque, N.M.	200	-0.0560	-0.3957	-0.2519
Jackson, Miss.	3560	-0.0534	-0.3038	-0.1866
El Paso, Tex.	2320	-0.0529	-0.3886	-0.2490
Lexington, Ky.	4280	-0.0451	-0.3163	-0.2018
Charleston, W.V.	1480	-0.0436	-0.2265	-0.1371
		Bottom five		
Omaha, Nebr.	5920	0.0375	-0.2137	-0.1872
New York, N.Y.	5600	0.0386	-0.1588	-0.1478
Oakland, Calif.	5775	0.0413	-0.0793	-0.0916
Salem, Ore.	7080	0.0556	-0.1193	-0.1313
Madison, Wisc.	4720	0.0585	-0.2672	-0.2416

a. For each MSA, two regressions are estimated. The first regression fits log (job density) as a function of zip code distance from the CBD. The second regression fits log (population density) as a function of zip code distance from the CBD. In the second-stage regression, the OLS slope from the employment regression is regressed on the OLS slope from the population regression. This table reports the residual from this regression.

City Age and Decentralization

A second preliminary hypothesis is that heterogeneity across metropolitan areas occurs only because some cities were built earlier than others. This theory argues that decentralization of employment is inevitable and that the only reason centralized cities exist is that they were built in an era before automobiles. Figure 11 shows that there is not a statistically significant connection between the age of the city (measured as years since incorporation of the largest city) and our measure of decentralization. The pattern shown by figure 11 is that all of our oldest cities (over 200 years) are reasonably centralized, and all of our newest cities (under 60 years) are reasonably decentralized. However, in the range between 60 and 200 years old (which includes most cities), there is considerable heterogeneity. There is some connection between age and decentralization, but it does not suggest a deterministic relationship where age determines centralization.

While overall city age is not correlated with city decentralization, cities with newer suburbs are more decentralized. This is not surprising. After all, one hundred years ago, centralization was ubiquitous. The cities that have decentralized have almost by definition grown along their edges. Figure 12 shows this fact. We first regress the housing stock's "year built" on the distance from the city center for each metropolitan area. Cities with a high positive

Figure 11. Cross-MSA Employment and Age

Employment gradient

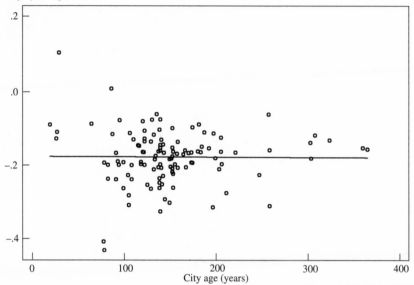

City age (years)

value for this parameter have much newer housing in the suburbs than the center city. We find that cities where this gap is largest are those that have had the most decentralization of employment. There is no question that decentralized employment required recent construction and urban change, but much of this urban change occurred in metropolitan areas with relatively old central cities. Thus, there is no guarantee that additional older cities will not decentralize further.

Cross-MSA Regressions

In table 7, we look at the determinants of MSA concentration. We use two measures. First, we use our employment density–distance gradient in regressions 1–3. In these regressions, the dependent variable is itself the estimated slope from a first-stage regression where employment density is regressed on distance from the CBD (see equation 1). Our second dependent variable (used in regressions 4–6) is the share of employment more than three miles from the CBD. Most of our results are consistent across the two measures of decentralization.

Figure 12. Cross-MSA Employment and Year Built Gradients

Employment gradient

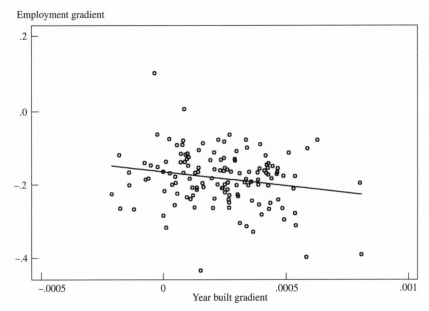

Year built gradient

Regressions 1 and 4 show our basic control variables. The first three variables are region dummies; the omitted region is the Northeast. The Midwest
and South are the most decentralized regions when there are few other controls. We interpret the coefficient of .043 in regression 1 as meaning that, on
average, employment density falls 3.9 percent more with each mile from the
CBD in the Northeast than it does in the Midwest. The coefficient of .048 in
regression 4 shows that the average metropolitan area in the Midwest has a
three-mile employment share that is 4.8 percentage points higher than the
average Northeast metropolitan area. The West and the Northeast are the most
centralized regions.

In all of our regressions, we also control for city age, metropolitan area
population, and the land area of the metropolitan area. In regressions 1–3,
older cities are more centralized, but in regressions 4–6 city age has a negative but statistically insignificant coefficient. MSA population is positively
correlated with decentralization in four of the six regressions. Metropolitan
land area is not statistically significant in regressions 1–3. Regressions 5 and
6 suggest that MSAs with more land area feature greater levels of decentralized employment, but the coefficient estimates are borderline significant.

Table 7. Explaining MSA Employment Concentration[a]

	Dependent variable log-level employment slope			Share of MSA jobs outside of the inner three-mile ring		
	(1)	*(2)*	*(3)*	*(4)*	*(5)*	*(6)*
Midwest	-0.0387	-0.0128	-0.0274	0.0480	0.0598	0.0159
	(0.0176)	(0.0205)	(0.0197)	(0.0323)	(0.0361)	(0.0352)
South	-0.0358	-0.0230	-0.0272	0.0658	0.0917	0.0790
	(0.0182)	(0.0254)	(0.0234)	(0.0311)	(0.0425)	(0.0414)
West	-0.0512	-0.0212	-0.0271	0.0009	0.0436	0.0259
	(0.0230)	(0.0231)	(0.0206)	(0.0409)	(0.0446)	(0.0401)
Log (MSA area)	-0.0128	-0.0050	-0.0067	0.0267	0.0343	0.0291
	(0.0081)	(0.0065)	(0.0061)	(0.0248)	(0.0237)	(0.0168)
Log (major city's age)	-0.0255	-0.0294	-0.0284	-0.0253	-0.0151	-0.0122
	(0.0145)	(0.0129)	(0.0130)	(0.0215)	(0.0247)	(0.0224)
Log (MSA Population)	0.0329	0.0335	0.0102	0.0587	0.0717	0.0013
	(0.0071)	(0.0097)	(0.0142)	(0.0179)	(0.0198)	(0.0276)
Percent Hispanic		0.0008	0.0007		0.0003	0.0001
		(0.0007)	(0.0006)		(0.0010)	(0.0009)
Percent with college		0.0051	0.0047		-0.0028	-0.0039
or higher degree		(0.0022)	(0.0021)		(0.0036)	(0.0035)
Percent over 65 years old		0.0072	0.0058		0.0057	0.0014
		(0.0025)	(0.0025)		(0.0044)	(0.0039)
Percent black		0.0008	0.0007		0.0006	0.0002
		(0.0011)	(0.0011)		(0.0015)	(0.0013)
Share of employment		0.4729	0.4254		0.5969	0.4533
in manufacturing		(0.2012)	(0.1954)		(0.5385)	(0.4393)
Share of employment		-0.7458	-0.7060		-0.3000	-0.1798
in service		(0.2890)	(0.2497)		(0.2420)	(0.3774)
Log (number of political			0.0239			0.0722
jurisdictions)			(0.0093)			(0.0180)
R^2	0.2123	0.4260	0.4726	0.3195	0.3840	0.5059
N	90	90	90	90	90	90

a. The unit of analysis is the metropolitan area. The dependent variables in columns 1–3 is the MSA's OLS slope from a log-level job density on zip code distance from the CBD. The dependent variable in columns 4–6 is the MSA's share of jobs outside of the inner three-mile ring. Intercepts calculated but not shown. Robust standard errors are reported in parentheses.

Regressions 2 and 5 show our demographic and industry controls. The demographics have weak effects that occasionally flip between our two specifications. Industry controls appear to be important. The share of the labor force in manufacturing predicts decentralization, and the share of the labor force in services predicts centralization. As discussed above, we interpret these results as suggesting that manufacturing is a land-intensive good with low transport costs, which is sensibly located in low-density areas. Services have higher transport costs and, therefore, locate in high-density areas that are close to consumers.

Our final regressions, 3 and 6, control for the number of political jurisdictions in each metropolitan area. We hypothesize that places with more fragmentation would see more decentralization for Tiebout-like reasons. Some firms might decentralize to be in a different political jurisdiction (and presumably receive a different bundle of public goods) in cities that are politically fragmented. In single government cities, there would be little gains from decentralization. Indeed, this seems to be the case. In both regressions, employment sprawl increases with the number of jurisdictions (but only in regression 6 is this increase significant). As the number of jurisdictions in a metropolitan area doubles, the share of people working outside of the three-mile ring rises by 7.2 percentage points. There seems to be some evidence for some political roots of decentralization, and we return to evidence on politics and decentralization later on.

Explaining Employment Decentralization across Industries

We now look at the determinants of industry decentralization. Our key dependent variable will be the employment density—distance elasticity estimated above using equation 1. In table 8, parts a and b, we look across industries at the determinants of industry-level employment decentralization. In table 8, part a, the dependent variable is an estimate of equation 1 for a specific three-digit SIC industry. We presented a histogram of the data in figure 6. There are 433 observations, one for each three-digit SIC industry in our database. Table 8, part a, shows results using our density-distance gradient, and table 8, part b, gives results using the share of industry workers outside of the three-mile ring surrounding the CBD.[40]

Regression 1 in each table shows our three basic variables. The first variable is a worker national suburbanization index. This index is created by first estimating a linear probability model using the 1990 Census of Population and Housing micro data, where we predict the probability that a household head with given demographics lives in the suburbs:

40. To test for robustness, we have estimated this regression by combining employment across metropolitan areas within .5 mile rings and then estimating density-distance gradients with this aggregate. These results are quite similar to estimates found using the unadjusted zip code data.

$$(6) \qquad I_{Suburbs,i} = \sum_j \beta_j X_{j,i} + \varepsilon_i,$$

where $I_{suburbs,\,i}$ is an indicator variable that takes on a value of one if person "i" lives in a suburb, and $X_{j,\,i}$ reflects characteristic j of worker i. Then we use the values of β_j estimated from this microregression in combination with the average values of each characteristic for each industry, k, denoted $\hat{X}_{j,\,k}$. These industry averages come from the 1990 Census as well. We then form

$$\sum_j \beta_j \hat{X}_{j,k}$$

as the predicted suburbanization index for each industry.

A second variable is meant to capture the degree to which an industry's suppliers are located in the suburbs. We use the Bureau of Economic Analysis's *Commodity by Industry Direct Requirements, 1992 Benchmark* matrix for ninety-seven two-digit SIC industries. For each industry, we calculate the share of total inputs it purchases from every other industry. Then we use the 1996 Zip Code Employment file to calculate its "national suburbanization rate." This is defined as the share of national jobs located more than ten miles from a metropolitan area's CBD. We calculate the average national suburbanization of its input suppliers for each industry. As we discuss below, we also calculate the input supplier suburbanization index by MSA/SIC. Intuitively, the input supplier index is high if an industry purchases most of its production inputs from industries that are concentrated in the suburbs. More formally we compute:

$$(7) \qquad \text{Input Suburbanization} = \sum_j \varpi_k^i s_k$$

where ϖ_k^i is the share of industry i's inputs that are bought from industry k and s_k is the share of industry k's workers that are themselves suburbanized. In practice, we are missing data on this variable for many industries. We have dealt with this by setting this value to the mean level of the index for the missing data points and including a dummy variable to indicate when their data were missing.

A third basic variable is a dummy variable that equals one if the industry is in manufacturing and zero otherwise. As reported in table 7, there seems to

Table 8. Explaining Industry Employment Concentration

Part A: Dependent variable: three-digit SIC industry log-level urbanization coefficient

Sample	Whole sample			Manufacturing only			
	1	2	3	4	5	6	7
Worker suburbanization index	0.1127	0.1466	0.1169	-0.0141	-0.0193	-0.0048	-0.0277
	(0.0786)	(0.0849)	(0.0853)	(0.0250)	(0.0234)	(0.0239)	(0.0232)
Input supplier suburbanization index	0.1272	0.1013	0.1328	-0.0506	-0.0587	-0.0489	-0.0616
	(0.0417)	(0.0421)	(0.0444)	(0.0413)	(0.0466)	(0.0374)	(0.0457)
Manufacturing	0.0168	0.0148	0.0164				
	(0.0038)	(0.0039)	(0.0038)				
Log of average firm size (workers/plants)	-0.0025	-0.0021	-0.0026	0.0028	0.0030	0.0029	0.0024
	(0.0013)	(0.0012)	(0.0013)	(0.0011)	(0.0011)	(0.0012)	(0.0009)
Percent with high school degree		-0.0156					
		(0.0230)					
Percent with college or higher degree		-0.0286					
		(0.0168)					
Percent of industry workers using computers at their job			-0.0000000937				
			(0.000000000874)				
Dollar value added per pound of output				0.00007			0.00004
				(0.00004)			(0.00003)
Share of domestic production that is exported					0.0045		0.0043
					(0.0014)		(0.0014)
Energy expenditure per dollar of output						0.0008	-0.0004
						(0.0006)	(0.0010)
R^2	0.2295	0.2419	0.2302	0.1117	0.2143	0.1572	0.1897
Number of clusters	69	69	65	20	20	20	20
Number of observations	433	433	416	123	137	137	120

Part B: Dependent variable: Share of three-digit SIC industries located outside the inner three-mile ring

Sample	Whole sample			Manufacturing only			
	1	2	3	4	5	6	7
Worker suburbanization index	1.2398	1.4203	1.3668	2.2937	2.4483	2.3566	2.3316
	(0.4496)	(0.4861)	(0.5092)	(0.5638)	(0.6560)	(0.6450)	(0.5681)
Input supplier suburbanization index	0.1375	-0.1287	-0.0514	0.1095	0.1871	0.1458	0.2315
	(0.3467)	(0.3126)	(0.2962)	(0.6421)	(0.6863)	(0.7067)	(0.6542)
Manufacturing	0.0567	0.0413	0.0563				
	(0.0308)	(0.0302)	(0.0285)				
Log of average firm size (workers/plants)	-0.0265	-0.0211	-0.0223	0.0164	0.0246	0.0245	0.0180
	(0.0121)	(0.0123)	(0.0122)	(0.0175)	(0.0198)	(0.0212)	(0.0165)
Percent with high school degree		0.0315					
		(0.1823)					
Percent with college or higher degree		-0.2781					
		(0.1289)					
Percent of industry workers using computers at their job			-0.000016				
			0.000006				
Dollar value per pound of output				-0.0019			-0.0018
				(0.0011)			(0.0011)
Share of domestic production that is exported					-0.0265		-0.0193
					(0.0248)		(0.0295)
Energy expenditure per dollar of output						-0.0021	0.0034
						(0.0092)	(0.0196)
R^2	0.0910	0.1492	0.1297	0.3554	0.3158	0.3043	0.3595
Number of clusters	69	69	65	20	20	20	20
Number of observations	433	433	416	123	137	137	120

a. Standard errors reported in parentheses. Intercepts calculated but not shown. Results reported are for regression with correction for correlation in error structure within two-digit SIC codes.

be a strong connection between manufacturing and decentralization. Our fourth basic control is average firm size. This variable comes from the 1996 Zip Code Employment file. As discussed by Benjamin Chinitz, dense cities may have a comparative advantage in providing inputs for non-vertically integrated firms.[41] Alternatively, firm size may be capturing something about the degree of entrepreneurship, and it may be that dense urban areas both help in the creation of new ideas (which would create a connection between smaller, newer firms and dense urban centers).

In table 8, parts a and b, the variables generally have the expected signs. Manufacturing industries are more likely to locate outside of the three-mile ring, and they have much flatter employment density–distance gradients. The magnitude of the manufacturing dummy is noticeably smaller here than in table 7. One possible reason for this discrepancy is that the impact of manufacturing on urban form is not just limited to the suburbanization of those firms in manufacturing. Other related industries that share inputs (including labor) or that buy or sell to manufacturers may also suburbanize in high manufacturing cities. This cross-industry effect might explain why the MSA-level coefficients on manufacturing are higher than the industry-level coefficients on manufacturing.

The worker suburbanization index has an impact on decentralization employment. Predicted worker suburbanization is a reasonable predictor of industry suburbanization across all the regressions—this is the first important fact in the table. The magnitude in table 8, part b, suggests that for each worker who is predicted to suburbanize in residence, 1.24 workers are predicted to work outside of the three-mile inner ring. Of course, the causality of this relationship is not obvious. Firms that have a comparative advantage in suburbanizing would be likely to hire workers who are also likely to suburbanize.

The effects on suburbanization of inputs are less robust. In the first regressions of table 8, part a, it appears that the input suburbanization measure is as important as the worker suburbanization measure. However, in the latter regressions of that table and in table 8, part b, the effects of input suburbanization disappear. We are left believing that there remains considerable uncertainty about the importance of input location in driving the suburbanization of industry.

Finally, we do not see the expected firm size effect. There is no significant relationship across our entire sample between firm size and central urban

41. Chinitz (1991).

Figure 13. Industry Employment by Percentage of College Graduates

Employment urbanization

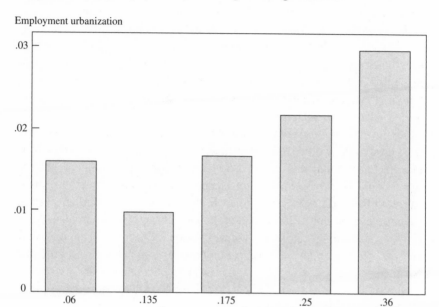

location. Furthermore, it appears (weakly) that bigger firms are slightly more likely to locate within the central city.

In regressions 2 of both tables, we examine the impact of human capital variables that are meant to get at the intellectual intensity of each industry. This addresses the possibility that firms are staying in central cities to exploit the comparative advantage that dense areas have in the transfer of ideas. Regression 2 of table 8, part a, shows that industries that employ more educated workers are more centralized. In table 8, part b, we find that there is a strong, positive effect of college education on locating inside the inner ring, but industries with more high school graduates (who do not finish college) are less likely to urbanize. This suggests a nonmonotonic relationship in which the central industries have both the most skilled and the least skilled workers.

Figure 13 shows this relationship graphically by illustrating how centralization of employment rises with the education level of the industry. In this figure, the only exception is that the industries who hire many high school dropouts are particularly likely to centralize. This may be because those workers are more likely to live in urban centers.[42]

In regression 3 we look at the share of industry employees using computers.[43] In this case, there is a weak effect that is statistically insignificant in both specifications.[44] An important fact from these tables is that variables that relate to human capital or intellectual content predict centralization. We see this and the human capital results as evidence for the view that central cities do specialize in idea-intensive industries.

Regressions 4–7 use data that are only available for manufacturing industries. As such, we are forced to use a smaller sample of three-digit manufacturing industries and to drop the manufacturing dummy from our regressions. There are three major changes in our control variables. First, based on the findings in table 8, part b, the importance of worker location becomes even stronger. It seems that manufacturing firms, more than other firms, may be strongly driven by worker location.[45] Second, as mentioned earlier, the effect of input suburbanization changes signs. Third, the firm size coefficient switches and becomes significant in both tables. Now we see the expected Chinitz effect where larger firms have less to gain from dense cities. These estimates are statistically significant in table 8, part a, but not in part b. Further work will be needed to understand why this effect appears only to work in manufacturing.

Regression 4 in each table examines our foremost measure of transport costs: dollar value per pound of output.[46] If goods weigh little (per dollar value of output), then they are easy to transport. If they weigh more, then they are harder to transport. As these goods are rarely sold directly to consumers (and rarely to consumers in the production locale), we expect the heavy products to locate away from the city center where they have better access to transportation hubs. This is what we find in table 8, part a, but not in part b. Industries with higher transport costs are more likely to suburbanize their employment. This supports the view that urban advantage in reducing transport costs has become reasonably weak.

42. See Glaeser, Kahn, and Rappaport (2000).
43. The data source is the U.S. Census web page.
44. If we include human capital in the regression, computer usage is insignificant.
45. See also Dumais, Ellison, and Glaeser (1997) for evidence.
46. The 1972 Census of Transportation provides information on the median value of output per pound of output by industry.

In regression 5, we look at whether or not the good is exported.[47] Goods that are exported presumably have little value in being close to the urban market and much value in getting easy access to the highway network. As such, they were predicted to be suburbanized, and that seems to be the case in table 8, part a.

We do not have land use at the industry level. It is possible to get expenditures on real estate. Unfortunately, these figures are often highest in industries that locate in central cities and use little actual space. Instead, we use energy expenditure as a proxy for physical space. Table 8, part a, regression 6, shows that those industries with more energy per dollar of output are more likely to suburbanize. Table 8, part b, shows an insignificant result in the opposite direction. Regression 7 puts all three variables in together. In table 8, part a, the only significant variable remaining is exported production. In table 8, part b, none of the last three variables is significant.

In table 9, we pursue two of these facts a little further by studying decentralization by MSA/SIC pairs. A unit of observation is the gradient of a certain industry in a particular metropolitan area, for example, steel in Pittsburgh. To generate the dependent variable in table 9's specifications 1 and 2, we estimated more than 14,000 regressions of the form of equation 1 for each MSA/SIC pair. The slope coefficient on distance from the CBD is used in a "second-stage" regression of the form:

$$(8) \qquad \beta_{MSA,IND} = \alpha_{MSA}^1 + \alpha_{IND}^2 + \sum_z \phi_z X_{MSA,IND}^z + \varepsilon_{MSA,IND},$$

where $\beta_{MSA,IND}$ is the slope of employment density on distance from the CBD first estimated in an MSA-specific, industry-specific version of equation 1. In all of our second-stage regressions, we include both MSA fixed effects and industry fixed effects (α_{MSA}^1 and α_{IND}^1, respectively), so that all results need to be considered relative to industry-MSA average. Our goal is to estimate the impact of MSA/industry-specific explanatory variables (denoted $X_{MSA,IND}^z$). We have omitted MSA-industry pairs when more than 90 percent of all zip codes have zero employment.

---

47. Export is constructed using data from the National Bureau of Economic Research web page. Feenstra (1997) has posted data on U.S imports and exports in 1992. Bartelesman and Gray (1996) have produced the NBER productivity data base. We use their information on industry value added. Combining the two data sets allows us to construct the share of industry output that is exported. This variable can only be constructed for manufacturing industries. Energy is the expenditure on energy inputs per dollar of value added.

Table 9. Firm Location and Desire for Suburbanization[a]

	Dependent variable:			
	MSA/SIC log-level slope specification		Share of MSA/SIC employment outside the inner three-mile ring	
	1	*2*	*3*	*4*
Worker suburbanization	-0.052	0.0050	0.1148	0.2430
index	(0.0133)	(0.012)	(0.0637)	(0.064)
Input supplier	0.0480	0.0430	0.2075	0.1960
suburbanization Index	(0.004)	(0.004)	(0.021)	(0.020)
MSA fixed effects	Yes	Yes	Yes	Yes
SIC fixed effects	Two-digit	Three-digit	Two-digit	Three-digit
R²	14,429	14,229	14,429	14,429
N	0.6945	0.789	0.537	0.595

a. The unit of analysis is the MSA/SIC pair. In specification 1 and 2 the dependent variable is the slope of a MSA/SIC-specific regression of log (employment density) on distance. The mean of this variable is -.023, and its standard deviation is 0.032. In specification 3 and 4 the dependent variable is the share of employment in a given MSA/SIC outside of the inner three-mile ring. The mean of this variable is 0.830, and its standard deviation is 0.235. The explanatory variables include MSA and SIC fixed effects and the worker suburbanization index and the input supplier suburbanization index. Both of these variables are defined in the text. Standard errors are presented in parentheses. The variable "worker suburbanization index" has a mean of 0.57 and a standard deviation of 0.154. The variable "input supplier suburbanization index " has a mean of 0.29 and a standard deviation of 0.21.

We include MSA fixed effects and some form of industry fixed effects. Thus, we will no longer be interested in general industry or general MSA characteristics. Rather, we focus on the interaction between particular industry and MSA features.

In our first two regressions of table 9, we examine the suburban population index and the suburban input supplier index in more detail. To generate this suburban index, we first estimate separate versions of the household suburbanization probability model for each MSA. For each MSA we have separate OLS coefficients that predict suburbanization. For example, in some MSAs, older workers may all suburbanize. In others, there will be more older workers still living in the central city. We then, as before, interact the coefficients from this regression with the average characteristics for the industry as a whole in the United States. Thus, for each metropolitan-area industry pair, we can estimate a separate probability of suburbanization based on the suburbanization proclivity of the MSA as a whole and the industrial characteristics of the industry outside of the MSA.[48]

48. To construct the worker suburbanization index, we use the 1990 Census of Population and Housing to calculate who is the "average" worker for each three-digit industry using the national sample. We calculate the share of each industry's workers who are black, high school graduates, college graduates, and their average age. Define industry j's worker demographic vector as $X(j)$. We use the Census data to estimate a linear probability model by MSA of household suburbanization. We use Census data to estimate a linear probability model by MSA of household suburbanization (see equation 6). The suburbanization index for demographic group j living in MSA m is then $B(m)*X(j)$.

In principle, this will address some of the endogeneity discussed above. Recall that the primary endogeneity issue is that firms that decentralize for exogenous reasons will be more likely to employ workers from the suburbs. In this case, we use industries that are more likely to hire certain types of workers at the national level and are likely to suburbanize in cities where those workers are suburbanized. Since we are controlling for industry and city fixed effects, we are only looking at the extent to which unusual suburbanization of certain types of workers in a given city raises the suburbanization of industries that are likely to hire those sort of workers. Our basic assumption is that each city is small relative to total industry employment (so that the suburbanization patterns of that city will not drive the suburbanization of the industry nationwide) and that each industry is small relative to total city employment (so that the industry's suburbanization within that city will not drive the suburbanization of citywide population).

We also estimate separate input supplier suburbanization measures for each metropolitan area. In this case, we take the nationwide input-output matrices and interact them with the extent to which other industries in that metropolitan area suburbanize. Thus, we use the extent to which industry *a*'s input suppliers (based on nationwide measures) are disproportionately suburbanized in MSA *b*.

Table 9 reports four estimates of equation 8. The regressions include different levels of SIC fixed effects. These SIC fixed effects serve to eliminate a relationship that might exist because the employment in the nation as a whole might respond to the degree to which the industry is suburbanized. In specifications 1 and 2, the worker suburbanization index is not statistically significant, but the input supplier suburbanization index is statistically significant. Its coefficient indicates that employment is more decentralized when input suppliers are more suburbanized. In regressions 3 and 4, we rerun the regressions using share of employment outside of three miles of the city center. In this case, both the worker suburbanization index and the input supplier index predict employment suburbanization, and the coefficients are statistically significant. This supports the importance of workers' suburbanization in driving the suburbanization of firms. This also suggests that input linkages may be important as well.

Table 10 presents one final piece of evidence on the relationship between job and worker location. This table attempts to exploit the timing of suburbanization to understand the nature of the jobs-workers relationship. Here we ask whether the suburbanization of employment has been faster in those areas

Table 10. Suburban Growth[a]

Dependent variable: surburban employment growth in sector (see note a for definition)

	All	Service	Manufacturing	FIRE (finance)	Government
1969 population	0.0542	0.0599	0.0881	0.0818	0.0266
share	(0.0200)	(0.0204)	(0.0260)	(0.0254)	(0.0142)
R^2	0.0772	0.0839	0.1073	0.1393	0.0246
N	322	318	322	320	322

Source: Using 1969 and 1997 data from the Bureau of Census REIS CD-ROM, we construct the share of MSA jobs in the suburban counties.

a. Suburban counties are defined as those counties that are in the MSA but do not have the largest county population in the MSA in 1969. The dependent variable in each of these regressions is the first difference of the suburban employment share between 1969 and 1997. The explanatory variable is constructed by calculating the share of the MSA's population who lived in the suburban counties in 1969. Each column reports the regression for a different employment sector. All regressions include region fixed effects and demographic controls as described in table 7. Robust standard errors are reported in parentheses. Intercepts calculated but not shown.

with more initial suburbanization of population. Has the suburbanization of employment been following the suburbanization of population? Our basic approach is to estimate the following regression:

$$(9) \quad \frac{\text{Suburban Emp}_{1997}}{\text{MSA Emp}_{1997}} - \frac{\text{Suburban Emp}_{1969}}{\text{MSA Emp}_{1969}} = B \frac{\text{Suburban Pop}_{1969}}{\text{MSA Pop}_{1969}} + \varepsilon,$$

where *Emp* represents employment in the suburbs, and *Pop* represents residential population in the suburbs. We also include an intercept, region fixed effects, and unreported demographic controls. We are particularly interested in the coefficient on the initial suburban population share. Suburbs and central city are defined just at the county level. We define the central county as the county with the largest population in 1969, and the suburbs as the residual.

In the first regression, we find that as the initial suburban population share rises by 10 percent, the growth in suburban employment is 0.5 percent higher. The other columns of the table repeat this regression for different subsectors of the economy. It seems that manufacturing, finance, insurance, and real estate are most likely to respond to the initial population share. Services are somewhat less mobile and more likely to stay in the city. Although one might think that services are especially likely to move close to people, services also have the highest transport costs and therefore might stick in the high-density area where transport costs are minimized.[49] Finally, the government sector is by far the least mobile. This final result is not surprising and suggests that government jobs have often made up for the exodus of private sector manufacturing jobs. This table provides more evidence suggesting that, increasingly, mobile firms are moving to where people want to live.

49. Kolko (1999). Services include both business and consumer services.

Politics and Decentralization

Our last and most preliminary work examines political borders. One serious issue in the decentralization of jobs is whether this decentralization has occurred because of "natural" economic forces or whether or not it is the result of various forms of government interference. Certainly, as Gyourko and Voith have argued, many national policies may have influenced the suburbanization of population, and through that, the suburbanization of industry.[50] We are not going to address this possibility. Instead, we look at whether the decentralization of industry is influenced by local governments.

There are two clear hypotheses about local governments and the suburbanization of industry. One hypothesis is that industry has suburbanized because of local governments that are bent on redistributing income using the tax base of local industry. As governments raise taxes, firms flee and industry decentralizes. It is easy to believe that the policies of mayors like John Lindsay or James M. Curley encouraged firms to flee the borders of New York City and Boston, respectively. However, many suburban communities specifically oppose negative externality-creating firms, and as a result, these firms may cluster in the more friendly central cities.

To compare these hypotheses, we use the following regression:

$$(10) \qquad Log\left(\frac{Employment}{Population}\right) = f(Distance) + I_{Central\ City} + \varepsilon,$$

where $f(Distance)$ represents a fairly flexible polynomial (including logarithms, quadratic, and third-order terms), and $I_{Central\ City}$ is a dummy variable that takes on a value of one if the zip code is within the central city's political boundaries.[51] The interpretation of $I_{Central\ City}$ is that this variable captures the extent to which employment lies disproportionately within the central city boundary, holding constant the distance from the city center. We are looking for boundary effects. In a sense, the point is to see whether there are border effects holding distance constant. We are following the methodology of Holmes and others in this procedure. In our own previous work, we have done this for poverty rates and central city boundaries and found quite significant border effects, which we interpret as meaning that central cities disproportionately attract the poor.[52]

50. Gyourko and Voith (1998); Voith (2000).
51. The MSA's center city is defined as the city within the MSA that has the largest population.
52. Holmes (1998); Glaeser, Kahn, and Rappaport (2000).

Table 11. Political Boundary Effects[a]

MSA	Center city border effect
The ten MSAs featuring the greatest negative employment effects	
Lexington, Ky.	-2.6258
San Francisco, Calif.	-2.1682
Detroit, Mich.	-1.0729
San Jose, Calif.	-1.0469
Washington, D.C.	-0.7979
Honolulu, Hawaii	-0.6865
Tacoma, Wash.	-0.6770
Norfolk-Virginia Beach-Newport News, Va.-N.C.	-0.6533
Boston, Mass.-N.H.	-0.6364
Raleigh-Durham-Chapel Hill, N.C.	-0.5471
The ten MSAs featuring the greatest positive employment effects	
Fresno, Calif.	0.8460
Greenville-Spartanburg-Anderson, S.C.	0.8523
Columbus, Ohio	0.8695
Albany-Schenectady-Troy, N.Y.	0.8739
Madison, Wisc.	0.8917
Little Rock-North Little Rock, Ark.	1.0463
Buffalo-Niagara Falls, N.Y.	1.0669
Atlanta, Ga.	1.0961
Allentown-Bethlehem-Easton, Pa.	1.1592
Grand Rapids-Muskegon-Holland, Mich.	1.2549

a. This table reports the estimate of the center city dummy based on equation 10 in the text. The dependent variable is a zip code's log (job density/population density). Center city is a dummy variable that equals one if the zip code is located in the center city.

However, in this case, there is no uniform central city effect. For some metropolitan areas, the central city is profoundly negatively associated with employment density. For others, employment shoots down when one crosses the border into the suburbs. We interpret this heterogeneity as suggesting that some center cities are relatively business friendly (relative to the suburbs) and that, in some metropolitan areas, the suburbs are quite friendly relative to business. Table 11 shows the list of the ten largest and ten smallest border effects by center city. San Francisco's and Detroit's center cities feature very large negative effects.

We looked for patterns in these border effects and found three basic facts. First, there are very clear regional effects. In the South and the Midwest, employment seems to be particularly high in the central cities. In the West, central city employment is particularly low. In the Northeast, border effects just appear to be small.

Figure 14. Center City Border Effects by MSA Size

Employment border effect

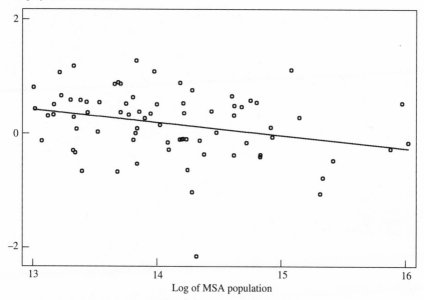

Log of MSA population

In figure 14, we document that in larger MSAs, border effects are more likely to be negative. In bigger MSAs, the central cities are more likely to repel employment, and in smaller MSAs, central cities are more likely to attract employment. Perhaps this occurs because the central cities in the largest MSAs are bigger and try to exploit firms more fully because of their greater market power. Alternatively, smaller central cities may be more desperate for firms.

Third, in figure 15, we show a connection between these center cities' effects and the urbanization of poverty. The more that poverty was centralized in the main city, the more that these border effects occur. In principle, this might reflect reverse causality where poverty is higher in the centers in these cities because the firms have left.[53] Alternatively, this might reflect the possibility that the poorest cities engage in the most redistribution, and this scares firms away.

53. Kain (1968).

Figure 15. Center City Border Effects and Urban Poverty

Employment border effect

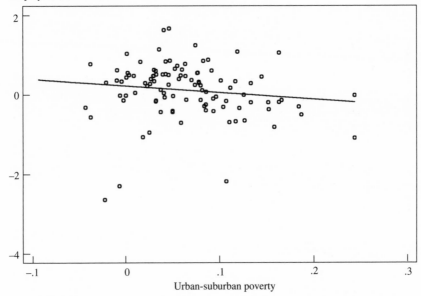

Urban-suburban poverty

Conclusion

This paper has tried to establish a set of core facts about the decentralization of employment. First, although there is considerable heterogeneity across cities and industries, it is very clear that most of America is fairly decentralized. Across regions, the share of employment within three miles of the city center is never more than 29 percent. The typical American city looks much more like Los Angeles than like New York City.

Second, in these decentralized cities, the basic Alonso-Muth-Mills framework no longer describes reality. In decentralized cities, commute times barely rise with distance. We believe that this occurs because increases in commuting distances are offset by increases in commuting speed. In decentralized cities, housing prices do not fall with distance from the city. Finally, as urban areas become more decentralized, income is less likely to rise with distance from the city center. The basic theoretical framework of urban economics really does not operate well in America's sprawling metropolises.

Third, there are few variables that predict decentralization across metropolitan areas well, but the best predictor of decentralization appears to be specialization in services. Cities that specialize in services are relatively centralized. Conversely, cities that specialize in manufacturing tend to sprawl. This connection between manufacturing and decentralization is also seen in the cross-industry data. Manufacturing is more land intensive and cheaper to transport than services, which naturally gravitate to high-density areas.

Fourth, industries that employ the highly educated have a higher degree of centralization. Industries that appear to be idea intensive are more likely to locate in the central city. This may come about because dense urban areas facilitate the speedy flow of ideas and industries that are more idea intensive want to locate in denser areas.

Fifth, the strongest determinant of whether an industry locates in the center city or the suburbs is its labor force. Using both cross-industry and industry-MSA combined variation, we find that when the work force is predicted to live in suburban areas, the firms will also locate in suburban areas. This finding suggests to us that the primary determinant of the degree of suburbanization is the demand of workers for suburban life-styles.

Finally, there is evidence that political borders matter. In many cities, there are significant effects of political boundaries on the employment-to-population ratio. However, these effects differ across metropolitan areas, and it is not yet obvious if central cities are particularly friendly or hostile to firms. However, it does seem to be true that the central cities of the East and the West are least friendly to business, and the central cities of the South and the Midwest are the most friendly to employment. These issues clearly need further research.

Comments

Richard Arnott: This is an important paper that should be widely cited and have a long half-life. The paper examines the decentralization of employment in U.S. cities during the past half century, looks at current cross-sectional differences in the degree of metropolitan employment decentralization by region, metropolitan statistical area (MSA), and three-digit industry, and explores the causes of the empirical regularities it documents.

The approach is broad brush and the methods employed rather crude, though highly intelligent. This approach is well suited to identifying robust empirical regularities —the pictures that emerge are vivid and striking and will almost surely prove to be broadly accurate—but not to discriminating between competing causal hypotheses. Thus, the paper excels in description but is less successful in explanation.

I found this a difficult paper to discuss. Because of its lack of concern with detail or theoretical or statistical refinement, it is easy to draw up a long list of technical criticisms. But since the paper does such an impressive job of giving a bird's-eye view of employment decentralization, doing so would be pedantic and not in keeping with its spirit, which is to inspire others to do more sophisticated work on the topic. Accordingly, I intend to focus on broader issues that relate to developing a research agenda for the study of employment decentralization and, more generally, urban spatial structure.

Data

I wish the authors had discussed data issues in more detail since they are experts and I am not. There has in the past been considerable uncertainty about the intrametropolitan location of jobs. The high degree of uncertainty has been evident in debates on the potential benefits of proposed light rail transit systems, since a crucial datum in estimating these benefits is the number

48

of jobs located downtown. Faced with this uncertainty, we have relied to some extent on casual observation and may as a result have systematically misperceived the extent to which employment has decentralized, almost unconsciously interpreting the dramatic changes in the downtown skyline (Boston and Los Angeles are vivid examples) to imply an increase—or at least less of a decrease than has actually occurred—in downtown employment. At this subliminal level, we have neglected to take into account that floor-area ratios of modern skyscrapers are often not much higher than those of nineteenth-century downtown buildings because of their low coverage ratios, and that downtown employment growth has been much lower than the growth in commercial floor space because floor space per worker has increased sharply. Joel Garreau's *Edge City: Life on the New Frontier* caused a stir within the urban economics community primarily because it painted such a vivid picture of the subcentering—as opposed to the dispersion—of suburban and exurban employment, but also because it forced us to evaluate our perceptions about the speed of employment decentralization.

In any event, the authors are able to document a high degree of employment decentralization through the use of the Department of Commerce's Zip Code Business Patterns 1996. This data base "provides firm counts by firm employment size by four-digit SIC level by zip code—extracted from the Standard Statistical Establishment List, a file of all known single and multiple-establishment companies maintained and updated by the Bureau of the Census." I wish the authors had discussed how these data differ from previously available data, in what ways they are superior, and especially how reliable they are. Can we be confident that they provide an accurate picture of the intrametropolitan location of employment (except for certain categories of workers excluded in the zip code data, most notably government workers and the self-employed)? Two problems in particular occurred to me as potentially serious. The first concerns multiestablishment firms that have employees working in more than one zip code. How are such firms' employees assigned to zip codes? Since head-office jobs are more centrally located than non-head-office jobs, assigning all a firm's workers to its head office would present a biased—overcentralized—picture of intrametropolitan job locations. It appears that the authors have largely avoided this problem by working with establishment rather than firm data (thus, the above quote from the paper is misleading). The second problem concerns the procedures employed, in preparing the Zip Code Business Patterns data for public distribution, to preserve the anonymity of individual firms. Are data aggregated, truncated, suppressed, and so on? This potential problem would become increasingly serious the finer the SIC classification employed. It appears that the authors circumvent these problems by working with establishment counts by establishment employment-size class.[54]

I would have more confidence in the data if the aggregate picture they portray were shown to be broadly consistent with the aggregate picture that would be obtained using alternative approaches. One such alternative approach entails the use of individual *travel diaries*, data collected by metropolitan transportation agencies on the travel patterns of sampled individuals, in order to construct the origin-destination matrices used in trip demand forecasting. If the sample of individuals whose travel diaries are collected is representative of the population, the spatial distribution of their job locations provides an unbiased measure of the actual spatial distribution.[55] An alternative approach is more exotic, making use of high-resolution, computer-generated, three-dimensional images of the metropolitan area, constructed from aerial and satellite photographs. Combining these data with geo-coded land use data would provide estimates of the floor space in various land uses by location. Then combining these estimates with estimates of the floor space per worker by location and land use would yield an estimate of employment by location. If the results of the three approaches were not broadly consistent, attempting to reconcile discrepancies would provide insight into the sources of difficulty in estimating the spatial pattern of employment.

I do not want to overstate possible problems with the zip code data. I at least am persuaded that the rapid decentralization of employment the authors document for U.S. metropolitan areas is real. I conjecture furthermore that employment decentralization has been occurring at a comparable pace in Western Europe too.

Summary Statistics

The authors present the cumulative distribution of jobs as a function of distance from the metropolitan area center for New York City, Chicago, and

54. From Bureau of the Census (1997, p. vii): "In accordance with U.S. Code, Title 13, section 9, no data are published that would disclose the operation of an individual employer. However, the number of establishments in an industry classification and the distribution of establishments by employment-size class are not considered to be disclosures, and so this information may be released even though other information is withheld from publication."

The authors apparently used the data on the distribution of establishments by employment-size class. Questions remain, however, on how the authors chose the number of employees per establishment within an employment-size class and the accuracy of their procedure.

55. In comparing the travel diary and zip code data, account would need to be taken of the job location of government employees and self-employed workers.

Los Angeles (figure 4), and for metropolitan areas in the aggregate (figure 1). But for most of the paper the pattern of employment decentralization is described by one or several summary statistics. This was generally a wise choice since the paper is chockful of information as it is. Nevertheless, this use of summary statistics is not without possible problems; one is information loss, another distortion. The authors are fully aware of these problems and, to mitigate them at several points, present results for a variety of summary statistics.

The authors employ five summary statistics: proportion of employment share in a consolidated metropolitan statistical area's (CMSA's) major county (used only once, in figure 2), share of employees within three and ten miles of the metropolitan area center, median distance of employees from the center, and the density gradient. All five suffer from the problem that they depend on the city's population. In a larger city, or as the city grows, one expects the employment share in the major county, as well as within three miles and ten miles of the center, to be lower, and the median distance of employees from the center to be higher. One also expects the absolute value of the density gradient to be smaller for larger cities. Thus, using any of these statistics, part of the measured secular increase in decentralization is attributable to the population growth that almost all CMSAs have experienced. One way around the problem is to use summary statistics of decentralization that should not be systematically related to CMSA population size. Another is to employ summary statistics of decentralization that are affected by population size but then to make an adjustment for population size.

Most of the analysis in the paper employs the density gradient as the measure of decentralization. One advantage of this statistic is that it is dimensionless, which facilitates comparison of results across studies using different units of measurement. Another is that, since the density gradient is very heavily used in studies of urban population decentralization, its use here permits easy comparison of population and employment decentralization. Its major drawback is that, if employment density is not close to being a negative exponential function of distance from the metropolitan center, it may systematically misrepresent employment decentralization and how it has changed over time. Thus, I would have found the authors' heavy use of the density gradient more compelling if they had presented some statistical evidence indicating that on average employment density does indeed fall off more or less exponentially with distance from the metropolitan center.

Diffusion versus Polycentricity

The authors attempt to measure whether suburban employment is diffuse or polycentric. They first divide each metropolitan area into an inner and outer ring using the median employment distance from the metropolitan center as the dividing line. They then sort inner-ring zip codes by employment density and ask how much employment is located in the densest zip codes, which together make up 5 percent of the entire metropolitan area. The exercise is then repeated for the outer ring, and the ratio of employment in the densest outer-ring zip codes to that in the densest inner-ring zip codes computed. A higher ratio is interpreted as indicating increased suburban centricity.

The use of ad hoc summary statistics of employment decentralization is acceptable because they are so intuitive and because there is broad agreement on what is meant by employment decentralization. The same cannot be said of ad hoc summary measures of diffusion. Consider two unit areas. In one, half the employment is in a single large subcenter, with the other half uniformly distributed. In the other, employment is evenly divided among sixteen small subcenters. In which unit area is employment more diffuse? Since the appropriate way to measure diffusion is not intuitively obvious, it is important to proceed systematically. I submit that diffusion or centricity should be measured with respect to a scale of *resolution* (analogous to pixel density).[56] At a coarse resolution, in the unit area with the sixteen identical subcenters, employment appears completely diffuse; at a fine resolution, it exhibits a high degree of centricity, perhaps a higher degree of centricity than the other unit area. One way to proceed is to measure the "degree of inequality" of employment density at different resolutions. Since the best-known index of inequality is the Gini coefficient, the centricity of employment in an area could be measured by a summary function or set of statistics giving the Gini coefficient of employment density at different resolutions. And since the spatial pattern of employment is likely to change with distance from the metropolitan center it would be useful to compute separate summary functions for different rings. From this perspective, the authors' summary measure of suburban centricity is weak in three respects: it considers only one resolution—the zip code; the resolution is not constant since zip codes vary in geographical area; and the

56. I cannot resist quoting Mandelbrot (1977, p. 19) from his book on fractals concerning a ball of thread: "At the resolution possible to an observer placed 10m. away, it appears as a point, that is, as a zero-dimensional figure. At 10 cm. it is a ball, that is, a three-dimensional figure. At 10 mm. it is a mass of threads. . . . At 0.1 mm. each thread becomes a sort of column. . . . At 0.01mm. resolution, each column is dissolved into filaform fibers."

"degree of inequality" the authors implicitly measure is analogous to the degree of inequality among the rich. To be fair, these weaknesses derive from the use of zip code data. But this suggests that zip code data alone will provide little insight into how diffuse employment is.

Endogeneity of Zip Code Areas

In his comments on the paper at the conference, Chris Mayer made the point that, since the size and boundaries of zip codes are determined to a considerable degree by the spatial pattern of employment, the analysis of employment density using zip code data generates potential problems of statistical inference. How quantitatively important these problems are remains to be investigated.

An Insightful Decomposition

A negative *population* density gradient is commonly interpreted as indicating that the structural density (floor-area ratio) of housing falls off with distance from the city center. However, Peter Mieszkowski and Barton Smith showed that for Houston the structural density of housing constructed since World War II had remained approximately constant over time, and that the observed negative density gradient was instead due to the proportion of vacant land increasing with distance from the metropolitan center.[57]

The focus of the Glaeser-Kahn paper is on *describing* the degree to which employment is decentralized. For this purpose, the point raised in the Mieszkowski-Smith paper is immaterial. But the Glaeser-Kahn paper also takes some steps toward explaining why employment has decentralized, and in this context the M-S point may be relevant.

$$\frac{\text{Workers}}{\text{Land Area}} = \frac{\text{Workers}}{\text{Commercial Land Area}} \times \frac{\text{Commercial Land Area}}{\text{Occupied Land Area}} \times \frac{\text{Occupied Land Area}}{\text{Land Area}}$$

Employment density equals the number of workers per unit area of land and does not consider the proportion of land that is vacant or in noncommercial uses. The decomposition indicates that employment density can increase because the density of workers on land in commercial use increases or because

57. Mieszkowski and Smith (1991).

a higher proportion of occupied land is in commercial use or because a larger proportion of land is occupied. A further decomposition is possible. Workers per unit area of built-on, commercial land equals workers per unit *floor* area times the floor-area ratio of commercial property. The above decompositions would be helpful in conceptualizing why employment density has increased.

Explanation

Subject to the limitations imposed by the use of the zip code data, the paper does a fine job of describing the decentralization of employment in U.S. metropolitan areas in the aggregate, over time, and by city and industry.

The steps it takes toward explanation are suggestive rather than conclusive. Many interesting simple (several of the figures) and partial correlations are presented; for example, the authors construct an industry-specific worker sub-urbanization index, which is derived from workers' propensity to suburbanize by demographic characteristics and from the demographic composition of each industry's labor force, and find that this index is strongly (partially) correlated with the degree to which industry employment is decentralized. However, the absence of an explicit conceptual framework makes interpretation of these correlations difficult. From the discussion in the paper, one might be tempted to think that each industry has a 'natural' degree of decentralization. However, since land at a particular location goes to the land use that bids the most for land there, how decentralized a particular industry is in a particular city should depend on the industrial composition of the city, as well as on the income-demographic composition of its population. Another general equilibrium determinant of a particular industry's pattern of location in a particular city is the "floor area shape" of the city—the amount of building floor area at different distances from the metropolitan center. This depends not only on the city's current economic conditions but also, since buildings and infrastructure are durable, on its history and the history of its land use controls.[58] Such considerations are partly captured by city dummies, but only partly.

Excess Commuting

Since downtowns are increasingly becoming centers for entertainment and recreation, the day may not be far off when employment is as decentralized as population.[59] Yet average commuting time in major U.S. cities will remain

58. The paper is conspicuously silent concerning the effects of land use controls on employment decentralization.
59. Glaeser, Kolko, and Saiz (2001).

between twenty and thirty minutes. This points not only to the importance of neighborhood in households' residential location choice but also to the empirical unrealism of one-dimensional representations of the locational interdependence between employment and housing.

Conclusion

The discussant's lot is an unhappy one. His primary job is to criticize. I resolved that I would comment on the paper in a manner consistent with the spirit in which it was written—to provide a vivid and stimulating bird's-eye view of employment decentralization in U.S. cities and thereby to encourage further work on the topic. I have not, however, entirely resisted the theorist's temptation to criticize empirical work, so in this conclusion would like to temper my criticism with some compliments.

I learned a lot from this paper. One of the attractions of urban economics is that it deals with phenomena that we encounter every day. It is therefore tempting to theorize on the basis of casual empiricism. I live downtown without a car, so have a central business district (CBD) view of the city. I need to be reminded from time to time that casual empiricism is dangerous and that my view of the city is distorted. This paper reminded me, as previously did Garreau, and Giuliano and Small.[60]

This paper also reminded me that technical refinement is no substitute for initiative, a strong spirit of enquiry, and a sense of what is important to the advancement of knowledge. With relatively crude tools but a lot of intelligence, the authors extracted an abundance of empirical regularities from the zip code data and developed a strong case that employment decentralization in the United States has been occurring more rapidly than I at least had perceived. The paper will no doubt stimulate numerous studies worldwide, which will probably come to similar qualitative conclusions even when considerably more sophisticated techniques are employed.

Christopher Mayer: Edward Glaeser and Matthew Kahn address one of the most important economic and social questions of our time: the transformation of the American city. Starting with the Industrial Revolution, people began to move to cities across much of the United States and elsewhere around the world. Urban residents in the nineteenth and early twentieth centuries relied on walking and public transportation rather than on the automobile to get to work every day. However, the modern city looks very different from its ear-

60. Garreau (1992); Giuliano and Small (1991).

lier counterparts. Residents live in lower densities. Jobs have moved to the suburbs. Crime and poverty are much more prevalent within center city borders. The authors document change in modern cities with an exhaustive study of employment data at the zip code level and county-level information on employment and population.

The goal of the paper is to emphasize the nature of the changes in urban form and to document possible reasons for these changes. Glaeser and Kahn suggest a number of possible factors that have changed over time: transportation costs for goods have declined in importance; workers increasingly prefer suburban locations; land costs are higher in cities; and transportation costs for ideas, which are lower in dense cities, have become more important in some industries.

This study uses a relatively new data set that has not been used before in this context. Many of these facts are not new, but the sheer weight of the evidence is overwhelming. The authors begin by showing that the most modern cities look more like Los Angeles than New York. Metro area employment has become quite decentralized, even in older cities like Chicago. This pattern is quite pervasive across most sections of the country, including the Midwest and the Northeast. Decentralization has little to do with city age, except for the very oldest—more than 200 years old—which are somewhat more decentralized than the rest of the country. In the older cities, urban employment shares have declined over time, a trend that continues today. Even poverty has become decentralized in cities that are themselves more decentralized.

Residents are also living further from city centers. Commuting time only increases slightly with distance from the central business district (CBD). In fact, suburbanization begets suburbanization. Cities that had a high share of suburban jobs in1969 have higher growth in suburban jobs over the intervening decades. Even within the suburbs, jobs do not appear highly concentrated in a small number of large job centers.

All of these facts suggest that the traditional monocentric model used for decades by urban economists is dead. The evidence might lead one to believe that cities have become more like sprawling suburbs, with a uniform distribution of people and jobs. In this context, even a polycentric model would seem inappropriate. One might even ask why cities exist at all.

Yet the picture is not quite that bleak. To begin with, residents appear to value proximity to the downtown. Most cities still exhibit a negative rent gradient; that is, house prices fall with distance from the CBD. However, the authors also document that the extent of the negative rent gradient is related to the degree of suburbanization across cities. The house price gradient in a city is positively correlated with its employment gradient. This suggests that cities may have different comparative advantages than in the past. As Americans have gotten wealthier, modern cities have increasingly specialized in producing consumer amenities: restaurants, culture, sports centers, theaters, and eclectic shopping districts. Sports franchises that once pushed to locate out in the suburbs are now staying downtown. The successful baseball stadiums in Cleveland and Baltimore are oft-cited examples of this trend.

Below, I suggest that the outlook for the cities of the future might not be as bleak as the stark facts presented by Glaeser and Kahn might initially lead one to suppose. Certainly, their face will look very different from the cities of the past. Nonetheless, the increase in the value of skills and the growth of employment in high-skill-intensive industries may actually bode well for the future development of cities.

Despite the consumer advantages of cities, the paper documents a number of reasons for the strong decentralization of the past decades. The most obvious is the transformation of manufacturing in the United States. When transportation costs were high, cities were the centers of manufacturing and shipping. Yet manufacturing has lost many jobs, and the jobs that remain are increasingly found in decentralized locations. Today, transportation costs have fallen with the use of trucks in most industries, and the prevalence of traffic congestion in most CBDs suggests that cities no longer have lower transport costs than other locations. While the authors were not as successful in documenting a direct link between transportation costs across industries and the extent of decentralization, one must surely believe that the extent of suburbanization is related to changes in the manufacturing sector.

Next the authors examine the especially tricky question of whether suburbanization is due to preferences of employers or workers—the urban economics version of the chicken and egg. They take an instrumental variables approach using cross-industry evidence. They show that industries with a greater "predicted" employee demand for the suburbs are more likely to be decentralized themselves. They also show that cities with greater suburbanization of workers in 1969 had the largest growth in suburban jobs. While this evidence is suggestive, there is always a question as to whether the factors that lead workers to desire to live in the suburbs might also lead firms to desire a suburban presence.

Consider the evidence in the paper on political boundary effects: the extent to which firms locate just outside the boundary of the city. While overall evidence on political boundary effects is mixed, the paper shows that boundary effects are biggest in the largest cities and that boundary effects are positively related to welfare boundary effects. These findings suggest that in some places firms have moved out of cities either because of high taxes to pay for social services or because of the accompanying social problems, such as crime. Yet one can easily imagine that factors such as high taxes and crime might also lead workers to desire to leave the central city. While workers might leave first, because they face lower moving costs, it is hard to measure the extent to which the preferences of either firms or workers played a larger role.

Future research might consider using other types of instruments and "natural experiments" to further address this question. A number of places have faced court-mandated changes in school funding, under which additional state resources are to be given to city schools. Kansas City is a recent example. While one would want to control for changes in taxes that fund the schools, these policy changes affect only workers, not firms, and thus could help resolve the endogeneity of worker and firm decisionmaking. School choice in Michigan, or limited vouchers in Milwaukee, are other examples of programs that sever the link between city locations and poor city schools, making it possible to isolate changes in worker demand. Future research might also use property tax limits or other statewide referendums that change relative taxes of firms versus workers to examine the relative location decisions of each group.

The paper also leaves some room for optimism for the future of cities. The authors show that cities have advantages that could become more important in modern cities. Low transportation costs for ideas induce high human capital industries to locate in a CBD. The authors show that this is true for services sector jobs as well as for jobs that require a college degree.

The downside evidence for cities is that the lowest human capital jobs are also more likely to be located in CBDs. Here again, one faces a chicken-and-egg problem, but one might again believe, as the authors suggest, that the locations of the workers drive the locations of the firms. For example, there is a large body of research suggesting that the poor have limited access to automobiles, making suburban employment quite difficult for the poorest members of society, who must rely on public transportation to get to work.

Nonetheless, some cities have taken advantage of demand by high human capital firms to encourage CBD development. A comparison of Philadelphia and Boston is instructive. Both are old northeastern cities that at the turn of the century were amongst the most prosperous in the United States. Both cities also suffered a significant decline after World Was II, with an exodus of jobs and people. More recently, since 1986, both MSAs have added jobs. Most important for the modern economy, both cities have a large presence of high-quality universities that graduate well-educated young workers.

Yet employment in the city of Philadelphia is down 12 percent, whereas employment in downtown Boston has risen slightly. Even within the same industries, much of the job growth in Philadephia has occurred in the suburbs, whereas in Boston (and the city of Cambridge), jobs have grown in a high-density environment. The most striking contrast is between two of the largest firms in the mutual fund industry, Fidelity and Vanguard. Fidelity is located in downtown Boston and has continued to add jobs and office space downtown. By contrast, Vanguard has grown exclusively in the suburbs of Philadelphia, with no downtown presence at all.

Data from the CBD office markets buttress the anecdotal observations about the relative success of the two downtown markets.[61] While Philadelphia's MSA population is nearly 60 percent larger than Boston's, its CBD office market is much smaller. In 1999 Boston had 35 million square feet of class A downtown office space, with a vacancy rate of 2.6 percent. Philadelphia had only 25 million square feet of class A office space, with a vacancy rate of 8.6 percent. Instead, Philadelphia has a much larger amount of class B office space than Boston (13 million square feet versus 4 million) and a much higher vacancy rate on class B space (17 percent versus 4 percent). In addition, there is new office construction under way in Boston. Given that class B offices are older and of poorer quality, they suggest the same pattern. Employment in high human capital firms and industries has risen in Boston, whereas in Philadelphia it has gone in the opposite direction.

What distinguishes the success of Boston relative to Philadelphia? Both have good public transportation that provides easy access to neighborhoods throughout the city and from the suburbs into the city. Both have airports that are close to the downtown, as well as city baseball stadiums, high-quality symphonies, and museums. The easiest answer is the public sector. Philadelphia has a 4-5 percent city wage tax on all residents and workers, which surely discourages highly paid workers and high human capital firms from locating downtown. It also has very high taxes on existing businesses. With a city population that is more than twice that of Boston, Philadelphia also has a reputation of being run less efficiently, although this is harder to quantify.

61. All of the data comparing Boston and Philadelphia are obtained from Grey House Publishing (2000).

Philadelphia has a much higher murder rate, although the cause and effect of crime statistics are hard to measure. Finally, Philadelphia puts far fewer resources into its public schools than does Boston.

Clearly, the comparison of Boston and Philadelphia, along with the evidence in this paper, suggests that the continued decline of cities is not inevitable. Instead, there are many things that cities can do to remain attractive places for people to live and work. Certainly, the extent to which cities impose high taxes on firms and workers has important implications for firm location. In this context, many cities may discover a premium to the efficient provision of services. Consumption benefits are also important. While imposing high taxes to keep a baseball stadium may or may not be a good investment, it is clear that encouraging restaurants, small shops, and other city amenities will encourage employees to want to remain close to the downtown. Vouchers are another way of removing the link between city living and city schools, possibly encouraging more middle-income residents to move downtown. Governments need to recognize that high human capital industries have important economic reasons to be in the CBD, but that high business taxes and regressive taxes that disproportionately hit high-wage earners will discourage the most prosperous firms and workers from locating downtown.

Nonetheless, as Glaeser and Kahn point out, there are many types of industries that will continue to exit downtowns. Manufacturing firms appear to be destined to remain in low-density locations. However, the results in this paper suggest that workers moved to the suburbs before firms. To the extent that cities become more attractive to residents, they may be able to lure people to live in cities, which often have lower housing prices than the immediately surrounding suburbs. That seems the likeliest route to encouraging firms to move back downtown and breaking the patterns of the past fifty years.

References

Anas, Alex, and Richard Arnott and Kenneth Small. 1998. "Urban Spatial Structure." *Journal of Economic Literature* 3 (September): 1426–65.

Alonso, William. 1964. *Location and Land Use*. Harvard University Press

Bartelesman, Eric, and Wayne Gray. 1996. "The NBER Manufacturing Productivity Database." Working Paper T0205. Cambridge, Mass.: National Bureau of Economic Research (October).

Brueckner, Jan K. 1987. "The Structure of Urban Equilibria: A Unified Treatment of the Muth-Mills Model." In *Handbook of Regional and Urban Economics*, vol. 2, edited by E.S. Mills, 821–45. Amsterdam: Elsevier Science Publishing Co.

Brueckner, Jan, J-F. Thisse, and Y. Zenou. 1999. "Why Is Downtown Paris So Rich and Detroit So Poor? An Amenity Based Explanation." *European Economic Review* 43 (January): 91–107.

Bureau of the Census. 1997. *County Business Patterns, 1997*. U.S. Department of Commerce.

Carlino, Gerald. 1985. "Declining City Productivity and the Growth of Rural Regions: A Test of Alternative Explanations." *Journal of Urban Economics* 18 (July): 11–27.

Chinitz, Benjamin. 1991. "Contrasts in Agglomeration: New York and Pittsburgh." In *Urban and Regional Economics*, edited by Paul C. Cheshire and Alan W. Evans, 21–31. *International Library of Critical Writings in Economics*, no. 14. Aldershot, U.K. and Brookfield, Vt.: Elgar.

Chu, Chenghuan. 2000. "Employment Suburbanization in U.S. Cities." Undergraduate thesis, Harvard University.

Cooke, Timothy. 1983. "Testing a Model of Intraurban Firm Location." *Journal of Urban Economics* 13 (May): 257–82.

DiPasquale, Denise, and William C. Wheaton. 1996. *Urban Economics and Real Estate Markets*. Prentice Hall.

Dumais, Guy, Glenn Ellison, and Ed Glaeser. 1997. "Geographic Concentration as a Dynamic Process." Working Paper 6270. Cambridge, Mass.: National Bureau of Economic Research.

Feenstra, Robert C. 1997. "NBER Trade Database, Disk 3: U.S. Exports, 1972-1994, with State Exports and Other U.S. Data." Working Paper 5990. Cambridge, Mass.: National Bureau of Economic Research (April).

Garreau, Joel. 1992. *Edge City: Life on the New Frontier*. Anchor Books.

Gibson, Campbell. 1998. "Population of the 100 Largest Cities and Other Urban Places in the United States: 1790 to 1990." Working Paper 27. Population Division of the U.S. Census. Department of Commerce (June).

Gin, Alan, and Jon Sonstelie. 1992. "The Streetcar and Residential Location in Nineteenth Century Philadelphia." *Journal of Urban Economics* 32: 92–107.

Giuliano, Genevieve, and Kenneth Small. 1991. "Subcenters in the Los Angeles Region." *Regional Science and Urban Economics* 21(July):163–82.

Glaeser, Edward. 1998. "Are Cities Dying?" *Journal of Economic Perspectives* 12 (Spring): 139–60.

Glaeser, Edward, Matthew E. Kahn, and Jordan Rappaport. 2000. "Why Do the Poor Live in Cities?" Working Paper 7636. Cambridge, Mass.: National Bureau of Economic Research.

Glaeser, Edward, Jed Kolko, and Albert Saiz. 2001. "Consumer City." *Journal of Economic Geography* 1 (January): 27–50.

Gordon, Peter, Ajay Kumar, and Harry Richardson. 1989. "The Influence of Metropolitan Spatial Structure on Commuting Time." *Journal of Urban Economics* 26 (September): 138–51.

Greenwood, Michael, and Richard Stock 1990. "Patterns of Change in the Intrametropolitan Location of Population, Jobs and Housing." *Journal of Urban Economics* 28 (September): 243–76.

Grey House Publishing. 2000. *America's Top-Rated Cities*, vol. 4, *Eastern Region.* 7th ed. Lakeville, Conn.

Gyourko, Joe, and Richard Voith. 1998. "The Tax Treatment of Housing: Its Effects on Bounded and Unbounded Communities." Working Paper 98-23. Federal Reserve Bank of Philadelphia (December).

Henderson, Vernon, and Arindam Mitra. 1998. "The New Urban Landscape: Developers and Edge Cities." *Regional Science and Urban Economics* 26 (December): 613–43.

Holmes, Thomas. 1998. "The Effect of State Policies on the Location of Manufacturing: Evidence from State Borders." *Journal of Political Economy* 106 (August): 667–705.

Kahn, Matthew. 2000. "The Environmental Impact of Suburbanization." *Journal of Policy Analysis and Management* 19 (Fall): 569–86.

Kain, John. 1968. "Housing Segregation, Negro Employment and Metropolitan Decentralization." *Quarterly Journal of Economics* 82 (May): 175–97.

Kolko, Jed. 1999. "Can I Get Some Service Here? Service Industries and Urban Density." Harvard University. Mimeo.

Krugman, Paul. 1991. *Geography and Trade*. MIT Press.

Macauley, Molly. 1985. "Estimation and Recent Behavior of Urban Population and Employment Density Gradients." *Journal of Urban Economics* 18 (September): 251–60.

Mandelbrot, B. B. 1977. *Fractals—Form, Chance, and Dimension*. Freeman.

Margo, Robert. 1992. "Explaining the Postwar Suburbanization of the Population in the United States: The Role of Income." *Journal of Urban Economics* 31 (May): 301–10.

McMillen, Daniel P., and John F. McDonald. 1998. "Suburban Subcenters and Employment Density in Metropolitan Chicago." *Journal of Urban Economics* 43: (March):157–80.

Mieszkowski, Peter, and Barton Smith. 1991. "Analyzing Urban Decentralization: The Case of Houston." *Regional Science and Urban Economics* 21(July):183–199.

Mieszkowski, Peter, and Edwin Mills. 1993. "The Causes of Metropolitan Suburbanization." *Journal of Economc Perspectives* 7 (Summer): 135–47.

Mills, Edwin. 1992. "The Measurement and Determinants of Suburbanization." *Journal of Urban Economics* 32 (November): 377–87.

Ross, Stephen, and John Yinger. 1995. "Comparative Static Analysis of Open Urban Models with a Full Labor Market and Suburban Employment." *Regional Science and Urban Economics* 25 (October): 575–605.

Small, Kenneth, and Shunfeng Song. 1994. "Population and Employment Densities: Structure and Change. " *Journal of Urban Economics* 36 (November): 292–313.

Thurston, Lawrence, and Anthony Yezer. 1994. "Causality in the Suburbanization of Population and Employment." *Journal of Urban Economics* 35 (January): 105–18.

U.S. Department of Transportation. 2001. *Journey-to-Work Trends in the United States and Its Major Metropolitan Areas, 1960-1990.* Cambridge, Mass.: John A. Volpe National Transportation Systems Center.

Voith, Richard. 2000. "Zoning and the Tax Treatment of Housing." In *Brookings-Wharton Papers on Urban Affairs*, edited by William G. Gale and Janet Rothenberg Pack, 239–65.

Weber, Adna Ferrin. 1900. *The Growth of Cities in the Nineteenth Century: A Study in Statistics.* Macmillan for Columbia University.

Wheaton, William. 1977. "Income and Urban Residence: An Analysis of Consumer Demand for Location." *American Economic Review* 67 (September): 620–34.

White, Michelle. 1976. "Firm Suburbanization and Urban Subcenters." *Journal of Urban Economics* 3 (October): 323–43.

——. 1988. "Location Choice and Commuting Behavior in Cities with Decentralized Employment." *Journal of Urban Economics* 24 (September): 129–52.

JAN K. BRUECKNER
University of Illinois at Urbana-Champaign

Urban Sprawl:
Lessons from Urban Economics

STRONG SENTIMENT AGAINST the phenomenon known as "urban sprawl" has emerged in the United States over the past few years. Critics of sprawl argue that urban expansion encroaches excessively on agricultural land, leading to a loss of amenity benefits from open space as well as the depletion of scarce farmland resources. The critics also argue that the long commutes generated by urban expansion create excessive traffic congestion and air pollution. In addition, growth at the urban fringe is thought to depress the incentive for redevelopment of land closer to city centers, leading to decay of downtown areas. Finally, some commentators claim that, by spreading people out, low-density suburban development reduces social interaction, weakening the bonds that underpin a healthy society.[1]

To make their case, sprawl critics point to a sharp imbalance between urban spatial expansion and underlying population growth in U.S. cities. For example, the critics note that the spatial size of the Chicago metropolitan area grew by 46 percent between 1970 and 1990, while the area's population grew by only 4 percent. In the Cleveland metropolitan area, spatial growth of 33 percent occurred over this period even though population *declined* by 8 percent.[2] Similar comparisons are possible for other cities.

This paper offers a technical development of arguments presented in a previous nontechnical paper (Brueckner, 2000b). I wish to thank Denise DiPasquale and the conference participants for helpful comments and suggestions.

1. For an excellent overview of the issues in the sprawl debate, see the twelve-article symposium published in the Fall 1998 issue of the *Brookings Review* (some of the articles are cited separately below).

2. See Nivola (1998, p. 18).

65

In response to concerns about sprawl, state and local governments have adopted policies designed to restrict the spatial expansion of cities. Twelve states have enacted growth management programs, with the best known being New Jersey's 1998 commitment to spend $1 billion in sales tax revenue to purchase half of the state's remaining vacant land. Under a similar program, Maryland had allocated $38 million to localities for purchase of nearly 20,000 acres of undeveloped land through 1998. Tennessee's 1998 antisprawl ordinance requires cities to impose growth boundaries or risk losing state infrastructure funds, mirroring an earlier, more stringent law in Oregon. Following the appearance of 240 antisprawl initiatives nationwide on November 1998 ballots, the November 2000 election saw many additional measures put before voters. Prominent statewide initiatives in Arizona and Colorado were defeated, but a number of local measures in California were approved.[3]

The stakes in the sprawl debate are substantial. Measures designed to attack urban sprawl would affect a key element of the American life-style: the consumption of large amounts of living space at affordable prices. Ultimately, an attack on urban sprawl would lead to denser cities containing smaller dwellings. The reason is that antisprawl policies would limit the supply of land for residential development, so that the price of housing, measured on a per-square-foot basis, would rise. In response to this price escalation, consumers would reduce their consumption of housing space, making new homes smaller than they would have been otherwise.

The goal of this paper is to assess the criticisms of urban sprawl and to identify appropriate remedies. To do so, it is important to start with a definition of sprawl. In this paper, urban sprawl will be defined as spatial growth of cities that is excessive relative to what is socially desirable. While no one doubts that spatial growth is needed to accommodate a population that is expanding and growing more affluent, the definition used here points to *excessive* growth as a problem.[4]

If the criticisms of sprawl are correct, then public policies should be altered to restrict the spatial expansion of cities. The resulting losses from lower housing consumption would be offset by gains such as improved access to open space and lower traffic congestion, and consumers on balance would be better

3. The information in this paragraph is drawn from Grant (2000); Richard Lacayo, "The Brawl over Sprawl," *Time,* March 22, 1999, pp. 45–46; Gurwitt (1999, pp. 19–20); and Rusk (1998, p. 14).

4. For an analysis of sprawl based on a much broader definition, see Downs (1999). Throughout the paper, the word "city" refers to an entire urban area. When necessary, a distinction is made between central city and suburbs.

off. But if the attack on sprawl is misguided, with few benefits arising from restricted city sizes, consumers would be worse off in the end. People would be packed into denser cities for no good reason, leading to a reduction in the American standard of living. The same conclusion would arise if some limitation of city sizes is desirable, but policymakers are overzealous. If only mild measures are needed to restrict urban growth that is slightly excessive, but draconian measures are used instead, consumers are likely to end up worse off.[5]

This paper identifies three fundamental forces that have led to the spatial expansion of cities: the growth of population; the rise in household incomes; and the decline in the cost of commuting. The paper identifies several reasons why the operation of these forces might be distorted, causing excessive spatial growth and justifying criticism of urban sprawl. These distortions arise from three particular market failures: the failure to account for the amenity value of open space around cities; the failure to account for the social costs of freeway congestion; and the failure to fully account for the infrastructure costs of new development. In each case, the market failure is analyzed, and an appropriate remedy is identified. The final pages discuss a common policy tool for dealing with sprawl, the urban growth boundary. Its pitfalls are noted, a few other issues discussed, and a conclusion offered.

The Fundamental Forces Underlying Urban Expansion

The fundamental forces underlying the spatial growth of cities are clearly delineated by the monocentric-city model.[6] This model, which portrays the city as organized around a single, central workplace, can be criticized for failing to capture the recent evolution of U.S. cities, which now often contain multiple employment subcenters. However, since the monocentric model's main lessons about the spatial expansion of cities generalize to a more realis-

---

5. The ensuing discussion does not address a different issue frequently raised in criticisms of urban sprawl, namely, the proliferation of unattractive land uses such as strip malls and fast food outlets. Because this complaint concerns the character of development rather than its spatial extent, it lies outside the present definition of urban sprawl. Although ugly development cannot be banned, a remedy for this problem lies in the use of zoning regulations and other tools of urban planning, which allow land use to be channeled toward more aesthetic outcomes. These tools can complement the policies discussed below, which are designed to limit the extent, rather than the character, of development.

6. The model was developed by Alonso (1964); Mills (1967); and Muth (1969). See Mieszkowski and Mills (1993) for a nontechnical overview.

tic, polycentric urban area, it is acceptable to use the model in an analysis of urban sprawl.

In the model, urban residents commute to the central business district (CBD), where they earn a common income y. They incur a commuting cost of t per round trip mile, so that total commuting cost from a residence x miles from the CBD equals tx. Disposable income for households living at distance x is $y - tx$, and in the simplest version of the model, this income is spent on land, which represents housing, and a nonhousing composite good. These goods are denoted q and c, respectively.

To compensate for the long commutes of suburban residents, land rent per acre, denoted r, falls as distance to the CBD increases. This decline in rent in turn causes consumers to substitute in favor of land as distance increases, leading to greater land consumption (larger houses) in the suburbs. As explained in William C. Wheaton and later in Jan K. Brueckner, land rent and land consumption depend not only on distance x but also on income y and commuting cost t. In addition, r and q depend on the common utility level enjoyed by city residents, denoted u. These variables can thus be written $r(x,y,t,u)$ and $q(x,y,t,u)$.[7]

The urban utility level is endogenous and determined by the equilibrium conditions of the model. These conditions consist of two requirements: the city must fit its population; urban residents must outbid farmers for the land they occupy. Letting $\bar{x}$ denote the distance to the edge of the city, r_a denote agricultural land rent, and n denote population, the well-known urban equilibrium conditions are

(1)
$$\int_0^{\bar{x}} \frac{2\pi x}{q(x,y,t,u)} dx = n$$

(2)
$$r(\bar{x}, y, t, u) = r_a.$$

To understand equation 1, note that since q is acres per person, $1/q$ gives people per acre, or population density. Multiplying density by the area of a ring of land ($2\pi x dx$) gives the number of people fitting in the ring, and integrating out to $\bar{x}$ then yields the number of people fitting in the city, which must equal n. Condition 2 says that urban and agricultural land rents are equal at the edge of the city. Since r falls with x, this condition ensures that urban land rent is higher than r_a at all interior locations, as seen in figure 1 (the land rent curve r_0 and the associated $\bar{x}$ value of $\bar{x}_0$ are relevant; the rest of the figure is dis-

---

7. Wheaton (1974); Brueckner (1987). See Brueckner (1987) for details.

Figure 1. Determination of City Boundary

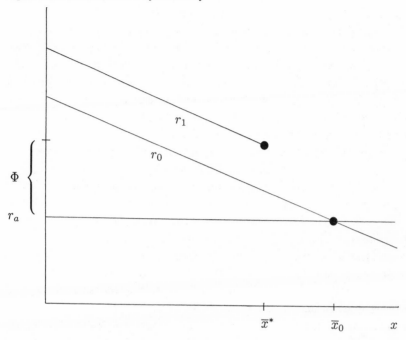

cussed below). Together, conditions (1) and (2) determine equilibrium values for u and $\bar{x}$ conditional on n, y, t, and r_a.

The influence of these parameters on the city's spatial size can be derived by comparative-static analysis of (1) and (2), which was first presented by Wheaton.[8] Wheaton established the following relationship:

(3) $$\bar{x} = g[\underset{+}{n, y}, \underset{-}{t, r_a}].$$

Thus, the spatial size of the city grows as population n or income y increases, and falls as commuting cost t or agricultural rent r_a increases.

While the effect of n on $\bar{x}$ is self-evident, the impacts of the other variables require more explanation. An increase in y affects the city's spatial size because urban residents demand more living space as they become richer. By itself, the greater demand for space causes the city to expand as housing consumption increases. But this effect is reinforced by the residents' desire to carry out their greater housing consumption in a location where housing is

8. Wheaton (1974).

cheap, namely, the suburbs. So the spatial expansion due to rising incomes is strengthened by an incentive for suburbanization.

A similar phenomenon occurs in response to investment in freeways and other transportation infrastructure. Because such investment makes travel faster and more convenient, thus reducing the cost of commuting, consumers can enjoy cheap housing in the suburbs while paying less of a commuting-cost penalty. As a result, suburban locations look increasingly attractive as commuting costs fall, which spurs suburbanization and leads to spatial growth of the city. In other words, $\bar{x}$ rises when t falls.

Finally, equation 3 shows that, as agricultural land rent rises, competition from farmers for use of the land is more intense, and the city shrinks in response. Thus, the model predicts that in regions where agricultural land is productive and hence expensive, cities will be more spatially compact than in regions where land is unproductive and cheap. Productive agricultural land is therefore more resistant to urban expansion than unproductive land, reflecting the operation of Adam Smith's "invisible hand."[9]

Brueckner and David Fansler carry out an empirical test of the comparative-static predictions in (3).[10] Using a 1970 sample of forty small to medium urbanized areas, they estimate a regression relating the city's land area to population, income, agricultural rent, and a commuting-cost proxy (the percentage of commuters using public transit). A high value for this proxy indicates a high t. Letting A denote land area, the regression results for a linear specification are as follows (absolute t statistics are in parentheses):

$$A = -41.07232 + .00041 * n - .03028 * r_a + .00620 * y - .24440 * t$$
(4)
$$\quad\quad (2.28) \quad\quad (10.03) \quad\quad (3.09) \quad\quad (3.03) \quad\quad (0.41) \quad .$$

Conforming to the predictions of the model, a city's land area rises as population and income increase, and land area falls with increases in agricultural

---

9. This effect counters a common claim among critics of urban sprawl, who sometimes argue that urban growth is an indiscriminate process, devouring agricultural land without regard to its worth. This view, however, is not consistent with the operation of a free market economy, where resources find their most productive uses. Concerns about loss of "scarce" farmland, often enunciated by critics of sprawl, are also misplaced. Because the value of farm output is fully reflected in the amount that agricultural users are willing to pay for the land, a successful bid by urban users means that society values the houses and other structures built on the land more than the farm output that is forgone. If farmland became truly scarce and in need of preservation, its selling price would be high, making the land resistant to urban encroachment.

10. Brueckner and Fansler (1983).

rent and commuting cost. The last effect is not statistically significant, however. The elasticity of A with respect to n is 1.1, indicating that a 1 percent increase in population leads to a 1.1 percent increase in land area. The elasticities for income and agricultural rent are 1.5 and -0.23, respectively.

The theory and evidence thus provide a compelling picture of how several fundamental forces (population and income growth combined with falling commuting costs) lead to urban spatial expansion. However, because the underlying model is monocentric, with all employment in the CBD, this explanation overlooks an important recent phenomenon in U.S. cities: job decentralization. It is natural to ask whether the movement of jobs out of central cities is an independent cause of spatial expansion or merely a consequence of the suburbanization of population.

Job relocation to the suburbs has been due in part to changes in the transport orientation of businesses. Rather than shipping their output through centrally located rail depots and port facilities, firms increasingly rely on truck transport and thus prefer the easy highway access (as well as the low cost) of suburban locations. However, the evidence shows that jobs also follow people.[11] In other words, job suburbanization is partly a response to the suburbanization of population, which occurs for the reasons discussed above. Thus, unlike the fundamental forces driving urban expansion, job suburbanization is partly an effect rather than a cause of this growth.

Given the confluence of an expanding national population, rising incomes, and falling commuting costs, it is not surprising that cities have expanded rapidly in recent decades. However, several market failures may distort the urban growth process, making this spatial expansion excessive relative to what is socially desirable.

These market failures, and potential remedies, are discussed in the next section.[12]

Sources of Market Failure in Urban Growth and Potential Remedies

Three market failures may lead to excessive spatial growth of cities. The first arises from a failure to take into account the social value of open space

---

11. Thurston and Yezer (1994) provide recent evidence as well as references to the prior literature on this topic.

12. It is well known that the urban equilibrium analyzed above, in which market failure is not present, is efficient. For inefficiency to arise, sources of market failure must be identified.

when land is converted to urban use. The second arises from a failure on the part of individual commuters to recognize the social costs of congestion created by their use of the road network, which leads to excessive commuting and cities that are too large. The third market failure arises from the failure of real estate developers to take into account all of the public infrastructure costs generated by their projects. This makes development appear artificially cheap from the developer's point of view, encouraging excessive urban growth.

Failure to Account for the Social Value of Open Space

To analyze the effect of this market failure, suppose that urban residents value the open space around the city. To simplify the discussion, let consumer preferences be given by the utility function $v(c,q,s)$, where s represents open space. Furthermore, let open space be measured by $s = B - \pi \bar{x}^2$, where B is the land area of the region containing the city, and $\pi \bar{x}^2$ is the land area of the city itself. Thus, s measures the amount of the region's space that is not occupied by housing. Although a more complex formulation might be more realistic, this simple framework captures the aesthetic and recreational benefits from the presence of open space near the city in an acceptable way.

With this modification of the model, the social value of the vacant land around the city includes the agricultural rent it earns and the open-space benefits it generates. In this situation, it can be shown that the condition determining the socially optimal allocation of land to urban use is

$$(5) \qquad r(\bar{x}) = r_a + \int_0^{\bar{x}} \frac{2\pi x}{q} \frac{v_s}{v_c} dx \equiv r_a + \Phi,$$

where the arguments of the land-rent function other than $\bar{x}$ have been suppressed for simplicity (compare 2). The integral in equation 5, which is denoted Φ, represents the social value of an acre of open space. This social value equals the marginal rate of substitution between s and c, which gives the open-space benefits per person in terms of the numeraire good, weighted by population at distance x ($2\pi x/q$) and summed over all x values in the city. Equation 5 thus requires that urban land rent at the edge of the city equals the social value of vacant land, which in turn equals agricultural rent plus the open-space value Φ.

Figure 1 shows the determination of the socially optimal $\bar{x}$, denoted $\bar{x}^*$. At $\bar{x}^*$, urban land rent equals $r_a + \Phi$ as required by equation 5. Note that the required differential between the urban and agricultural rents can only be achieved if $\bar{x}$ shrinks below the value $\bar{x}_0$ where the two rents are equalized. This shrinkage, by reducing the supply of urban land, leads to an escalation of land rent, as can be seen in the higher position of the rent curve r_1 relative to the original curve r_o. While this rent escalation reduces consumer purchasing power, the urban utility level nevertheless rises because of the offsetting benefits from additional open space around the city.

Figure 1 thus establishes that, in the presence of open-space benefits, the city's equilibrium spatial size, as represented by $\bar{x}_0$, is too large. The problem is that, since intangible open-space benefits do not constitute part of the income earned by the land when it is in agricultural use, the disappearance of these benefits does not show up as a dollar loss when the land is converted to urban use. The invisible hand thus ignores open-space benefits, causing too much land to be allocated to urban use and leading to excessive spatial growth of cities.

A simple form of government intervention can remedy this problem: charging a development tax on each acre of land converted from agricultural to urban use. The development tax per unit of land is set equal to Φ (evaluated at the social optimum). With such a tax, equation 5 rather than equation 2 is the equilibrium condition for decentralized conversion of land, so that the outcome is optimal.

The difficulty, of course, is that implementing such a policy requires assigning a dollar value to the open-space benefits provided by an acre of land. Although economists have tried to estimate such values, the results are not sufficiently credible to use as a reliable basis for policy.[13] This puts the policymaker in the position of having to guess the correct magnitude for a development tax. Because of the shortage of quantitative evidence on amenity

13. See Blomquist and Whitehead (1995) for an overview of contingent-valuation methods for measuring the value of environmental amenities. These methods rely on surveys that ask respondents for their willingness to pay (WTP) to preserve environmental amenities. For studies focusing specifically on the amenity value of vacant land, see Lopez, Shah, and Attolbello (1994) and Breffle, Morey, and Lodder (1998). Using previous contingent-valuation estimates, Lopez and others estimate the marginal amenity value of agricultural land for three different cases. For two cities in Massachusetts, the marginal values are $8.80 and $67.00 per acre, respectively, while the marginal value is $31.00 for a city in Alaska. These numbers are expressed on an annualized basis, with present values approximately twenty times as large. Combining these open-space values with estimates of the demand for urban land, the authors conclude that, under an optimal allocation, between 3 and 20 percent more land would be allocated to agriculture across the three cases. Although key steps in the methodology are not clear, the resulting magnitudes are plausible. Less plausible values emerge from the more recent contingent-valuation study of Breffle, Morey, and Lodder (1998). The authors surveyed residents of Boulder, Colorado, asking their WTP to keep a 5.5-acre tract of land on the urban fringe undeveloped. Total WTP for residents within a one-mile radius of the tract was $764,000, a number that exceeded the developer's $600,000 bid for the site. Such large amenity valuations, which would virtually prohibit development if used as a basis for policy, suggest that contingent-valuation methods should be applied with care.

benefits, any open-space policy is fraught with difficulties and potentially counterproductive.

A further point is that the above model may not be accurate as a picture of how open-space benefits are generated. Rather than caring in the abstract about open space outside the city, consumers may be more affected by the availability of space in their immediate neighborhoods, in the form of city parks. One might argue that if city park land is adequately provided, the amount of open space outside of cities would not be a pressing concern of most urban residents. This, in turn, would undermine the case for a development tax like the one described above.[14]

Failure to Account for the Social Costs of Freeway Congestion

The second market failure that might affect the spatial sizes of cities arises through the activity of commuting. To understand this market failure, note first that commuting costs incurred by urban residents include the out-of-pocket costs of vehicle operation as well as the "time cost" of commuting. The latter cost measures the dollar value to the commuter of the time consumed while in transit. Together, these out-of-pocket and time costs represent the "private cost" of commuting, the cost that the commuter himself bears.

When the commuter drives on congested roadways to get to work, another cost is generated by his trip, above and beyond the private cost. This cost is due to the extra congestion caused by the commuter's presence on the road. Thus, on congested roads, the true social cost of commuting for an individual includes the costs imposed on other commuters by the extra congestion that he creates. Note that while this extra congestion is slight, its impact is significant because many other commuters are affected.

Since these congestion costs are borne by others, the commuter himself has no incentive to take them into account. This missing incentive constitutes a market failure, and it means that commuting on congested roadways looks artificially cheap to individual commuters. The result is that congested roads are overused from society's point of view.

To correct this problem, reducing road usage to socially optimal levels, several steps are appropriate. Some traffic should be diverted to off-peak hours, when roads are less congested, and some car commuters should switch to public transit. In addition, because of the overlooked social costs of commuting, the average commute distance is too long from society's point of view, and it

14. Note that provision of more open space *within* cities would lead to an expansion rather than a contraction in their spatial sizes.

should be shortened. But an excessively long average commute means that cities are too spread out. Therefore, by causing people to commute too far, the market failure associated with freeway congestion can lead indirectly to urban sprawl.

Because the source of the problem is the individual's false perception of the costs of commuting, the remedy is to raise commuting costs by imposing a "congestion toll." Such a toll charges each commuter for the congestion damage he imposes on others. When a toll is levied, the out-of-pocket cost of rush hour commuting rises, and individuals have an incentive to shorten their commutes. Since this means living closer to one's job location, the ultimate effect is a spatial shrinkage of the city.

To see these arguments formally, let $T(x)$ denote the cost per mile of commuting at distance x from the CBD. This is simply the cost of crossing the narrow ring of land at x. Without congestion, $T(x)$ is simply equal to the exogenous constant t. But in the presence of congestion, $T(x)$ is given by

$$(6) \qquad T(x) = t + f(P(x), R(x)),$$

where f is a function that captures congestion costs. Its second argument, $R(x)$, gives the amount of land at distance x devoted to roads. Since greater road capacity reduces congestion, f is decreasing in R. The first argument, $P(x)$, represents the traffic flow at x. Since the city is monocentric, $P(x)$ equals the number of people *living outside* x, which is written $\int_x^{\bar{x}}(2\pi z/q)dz$ (these people must cross the ring at x to reach the CBD). Since congestion worsens as traffic rises holding capacity constant, f is increasing in P. Note that while total commuting cost for a resident living at x is tx in the absence of congestion, this cost equals $\int_0^x T(z)dz$ with congestion.

Since an added commuter at distance x raises $P(x)$ by one, the commuter imposes extra congestion costs of $f_P(P(x), R(x))$ on each of the other commuters, where the subscript denotes partial derivative. Summing across commuters, the total congestion damage done by the extra commuter at distance x equals $P(x)f_P(P(x), R(x))$. To internalize the congestion externality, a congestion toll equal to this amount should be levied on each commuter passing through the ring at x. Note that since commuters symmetrically congest one another, each commuter pays this toll. Thus, the congestion toll at distance x is given by

$$(7) \qquad \tau(x) = P(x)f_P(P(x), R(x)),$$

and for a commuter residing at x, the cumulative toll payment over his entire trip is $\int_0^x \tau(z)dz$.

Analysis of urban equilibria with congestion is difficult because commuting costs and the spatial distribution of population within the city are jointly determined as a result of the congestion phenomenon. In other words, where people live depends on commuting costs, but these costs in turn depend on where people live. Nevertheless, when the congestion externality is internalized via a toll, the effect on the spatial size of the city can be predicted intuitively. In particular, since the toll raises commuting costs, the impact on $\bar{x}$ is similar to the effect of increasing t in a model without congestion. Equation 3 shows that $\bar{x}$ falls as t rises, with higher commuting costs shrinking the city, and this same outcome occurs when congestion tolls are imposed in a model with congestion. Thus, in the absence of tolls, the city takes up too much space, as explained above.

The analysis establishing this outcome is clearest in Wheaton, although a large previous literature has investigated this type of model.[15] Wheaton's numerical examples show that imposition of congestion tolls would reduce $\bar{x}$ by 10 percent in his simulated city, from 28.9 miles to 25.9 miles. This result suggests that significant overexpansion of urban areas is caused by the failure to internalize the congestion externality.

Unlike the development tax discussed above, the proper magnitude of congestion tolls can be computed reliably, drawing on the wealth of accumulated knowledge about commuting behavior. A recent study by John Calfee and Clifford Winston, for example, computed the optimal toll as 27 cents per mile, which would generate roughly a $6 charge for a 20-mile round-trip commute.[16]

Even though economists and transportation engineers uniformly endorse congestion tolls, they are seldom levied in practice. One problem is political: even though the revenue earned from tolls would allow other taxes to be reduced, commuters view tolls as a net tax increase, which creates opposition. Another problem is the daunting logistics of collecting tolls in a manner that does not impede traffic flows. In principle, technological advances can remove this obstacle by allowing toll charges to be tallied by electronic meters carried onboard autos. Low-tech solutions such as downtown parking taxes and costly bumper stickers that permit rush-hour usage of central roadways are also fea-

15. Wheaton (1998).
16. Calfee and Winston (1998). This estimate is computed using traffic volumes and capacity conditions from the ten largest metro areas, as well as the assumption that commuting time is valued at a traditional figure of 50 percent of the wage. If this valuation falls to 20 percent, as the authors argue is more realistic, the toll falls to 11 cents per mile. In addition, see Small (1992) for an extensive treatment of the theory and realities of congestion pricing.

sible. The latter approach was implemented in Singapore, while cities in Norway have experimented with more high-tech methods of collecting tolls.

By focusing just on the out-of-pocket and time costs of commuting, the preceding discussion ignores the resource costs of the transportation infrastructure used by commuters. Because such resource costs clearly constitute part of the social cost of commuting, a failure to make commuters pay for transportation infrastructure involves the same sort of underpricing of commute trips as the failure to levy congestion tolls. Although the gasoline tax functions as a user fee for the road network, with its revenues used for construction and maintenance, the prevailing tax levels in the United States are arguably far too low to cover these costs. As a result, commuters are undercharged for the resource costs of the infrastructure they use, which again encourages excessive commuting and urban sprawl.[17]

While an increase in the gas tax would remedy this second type of underpricing, a drawback is that the tax is paid regardless of the level of congestion encountered by the road user. Thus, unlike congestion tolls, the gas tax does not have the advantage of diverting traffic away from congested roads or congested travel times. Fortunately, this apparent dilemma in the choice between a user fee like the gas tax and congestion tolls is resolved by the theory of congestion pricing. The theory shows that the revenue from congestion tolls is likely to fully cover the infrastructure costs of the road network. More precisely, if roads are built with constant returns to scale and another natural technical assumption holds, then congestion-toll revenue exactly covers the cost of an optimal-size road.[18]

This result shows that if congestion tolls are levied, there may be no need to charge a separate user fee to pay for infrastructure costs. Although the gas tax therefore could be eliminated if a universal toll system were imposed, reliance on this tax is unlikely to end. Recognizing this likelihood, an increase in the gas tax would be one approach for attacking urban sprawl. While this approach is not ideal for the reasons discussed above, a higher gas tax would represent a practical means of remedying the underpricing of commute trips that contributes to sprawl.

Failure to Fully Account for the Infrastructure Costs of New Development

A third source of market failure that affects urban growth comes from the infrastructure costs generated by new development. When a new housing

17. See Mills (1999) for a clear presentation of this argument.
18. See Small (1992).

development is built, roads and sewers must be constructed, and facilities such as schools, parks, and recreation areas are needed. Homeowners, through the property tax system, pay for this infrastructure. The market failure arises because, under typical financing arrangements, the infrastructure-related tax burden on new homeowners is typically less than the actual infrastructure costs they generate. As a result, urban development appears artificially cheap, so that too much development occurs.

A formal analysis of this effect is presented by Brueckner.[19] In his model, which is explicitly dynamic, a growing city invests in durable infrastructure in order to provide a constant level of public services to its residents. As population grows, the infrastructure stock must be enlarged to maintain the target level of services. Letting $n(T)$ denote the city's population at time T, the cost of the required infrastructure stock is $C(n(T))$.

When an additional resident is added to the city, requiring the conversion of one unit of land, the infrastructure stock must be enlarged, and the cost of doing so is given by the derivative $C_n(n(T)) > 0$. Because of the perfect durability of infrastructure, this cost of accommodating the new population is a one-time expense. With continuously growing population, however, a series of one-time costs must be incurred. Note that the annualized cost of the new infrastructure investment occurring at time T is $iC_n(n(T))$, where i is the interest rate.

From society's point of view, land is optimally converted to urban use when the net benefit from urban use of the land exceeds the agricultural rent r_a. This net benefit is equal to urban land rent minus the annualized cost of the infrastructure expansion needed to accommodate the additional population. Therefore, the condition for optimal conversion of the land is given by

(8) $$r(T, \bar{x}(T)) - iC_n = r_a.$$

To emphasize the dynamic setting, time T appears as an argument of the land-rent function, with the function rising over time in exogenous fashion. In addition, note that $\bar{x}(T)$ gives the distance to the edge of the city at time T.

To provide a tractable analysis, Brueckner imposes several simplifying assumptions.[20] As noted above, land consumption per household is fixed at one unit, and the city is linear rather than circular, with a width also equal to unity. In this case, the urban population $n(T)$ and the boundary distance $\bar{x}(T)$ are the same. Then, substituting in (8) and rearranging, the equation can be written

19. Brueckner (1997a).
20. Brueckner (1997a).

Figure 2. Determination of City Populations

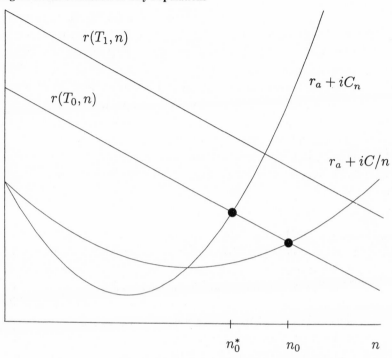

(9)
$$r(T, n(T)) = r_a + iC_n(n(T)),$$

where the argument of C_n is made explicit.

Equation 9 determines the socially optimal urban population at time T, and the solution can be seen graphically in figure 2. First note that the infrastructure cost function $C(\bullet)$ is assumed to generate U-shaped average and marginal cost curves, reflecting ranges of increasing and decreasing returns to scale in infrastructure provision. Then, the $n(T)$ that solves (9) lies where the curve corresponding to $r_a + iC_n$ (a translation of the marginal-cost curve) intersects the land-rent curve. Note that the latter curve, which gives rent at the edge of the city as a function of population, is downward sloping because rent falls with distance. The figure shows two rent curves corresponding to different times ($T_1 > T_0$) along with the optimal population size n_0^* at time T_0.

This optimal solution can be contrasted with the one emerging from current institutions. For simplicity, Brueckner focuses on a decentralized system in which each landowner in the city shares equally in paying for the existing stock of infrastructure.[21] On the assumption that infrastructure is financed by infinite-maturity bonds, the required total payment at time T can be shown to equal $iC(n(T))$, the interest on the cost of the existing infrastructure stock. Assuming that this cost is spread evenly across all the developed land in the city, each acre of land incurs a cost of $iC(n(T)/n(T)$ at time T (recall that there are $n(T)$ acres of developed land in the city at this time). Note that this equal-payment assumption does not mimic a property tax regime, where higher-valued land close to the CBD incurs a greater tax liability. However, the assumption of equal payments serves as a convenient approximation.

With the tax burden on land equal to the average-cost expression $iC(n(T))/n(T)$, the condition governing decentralized conversion of land to urban use is

$$(10) \qquad r(T, n(T)) = r_a + iC(n(T)) / n(T).$$

Note in equation 10 that the average-cost expression has replaced the marginal-cost term from equation 9. This difference yields a time T population for the city that differs from the socially optimal population, as can be seen in figure 2. The equilibrium population now lies at the intersection of the land-rent curve and the curve corresponding to $r_a + iC/n$, which is a translation of the average, rather than marginal, cost function.

Suppose the city has grown large enough to enter the range of decreasing returns to infrastructure provision, where the "average" curve $r_a + iC/n$ slopes up. Then, referring to figure 2, the equilibrium population at time T_0, denoted n_0, exceeds the socially optimal population n_0^* for that date. This relationship continues to hold as the land-rent curve shifts up over time, further enlarging the city's population. The problem is that over this range, the social cost of adding infrastructure, given by iC_n, exceeds the average cost expression iC/n, which is what landowners face under equal payments. With the equal-payment regime understating the true cost of infrastructure, development appears artificially cheap, and too much of it occurs.

The reverse relationship holds when the city is still small, as can be seen in figure 2. When the equilibrium population is below the level that minimizes C/n, the socially optimal population is larger, rather than smaller, than the equilibrium population. Thus, insufficient urban expansion occurs when population lies in the range over which infrastructure exhibits increasing returns. However, since cities have expanded greatly as the U.S. population has grown, the range of decreasing returns may be relevant today.

21. Brueckner (1997a).

The remedy for the resulting urban overexpansion is to change the financing method for infrastructure. Rather than making all owners of developed land pay for the existing infrastructure as well as additions to the stock, a system of "impact fees" can be instituted. Under such a system, landowners whose land is converted at time T are charged a one-time fee of $C_n(n(T))$ to recover the infrastructure cost associated with the conversion. No future payments are required, with the cost of subsequent infrastructure additions paid for by landowners undertaking later development. Note that unlike marginal-cost charges in a static setting, impact fees fully pay for the stock of infrastructure. This follows because the fees exactly cover the cost of each increment to the stock as it is added.

In recent years, the use of impact fees has grown in many parts of the United States.[22] Many communities in Illinois, for example, charge school impact fees, which defray the cost of new school construction. Properly computed, these fees may amount to nearly $5,000 for a three-bedroom house.[23] In addition, road impact fees are often levied to defer the cost of expanding a city's road network as population expands. Historically, impact fees have been challenged in the courts by real estate developers, who have contested the rights of communities to levy the fees or the methods used to calculate them. In some cases, the courts have ruled that impact fees do not properly reflect infrastructure costs, and they have promulgated standards to remedy such disparities.[24]

Urban Growth Boundaries as a Remedy for Urban Sprawl

Three market failures leading to urban sprawl have been identified, and in each case, a specific remedy has been prescribed. These remedies (development taxes, congestion tolls, and impact fees) each involve use of the price mechanism to correct urban sprawl. Policymakers, however, often favor a much blunter instrument. This instrument is usually called an "urban growth boundary," but other terminology is sometimes used. Rather than relying on

22. See Altshuler and Gomez-Ibanez (1993) for an overview of impact fee usage and Fischel (1990) for further discussion.
23. Calculations in Brueckner (1997b) compute school impact fees by combining data on school construction costs per square foot, space requirements per student, and the number of students generated by new houses of various sizes. For Illinois, the resulting fee for a three-bedroom house is $4,560.
24. Altshuler and Gomez-Ibanez (1993).

taxes or congestion tolls to limit sprawl, an urban growth boundary (UGB) is a zoning tool that slows urban growth by banning development in designated areas on the urban fringe. In effect, imposition of such a boundary involves drawing a circle around a city and prohibiting development outside the circle.[25]

A UGB is easy to implement, but it has great potential for misuse. The problem is similar to the one that arises in taxing development to preserve open space, namely, the need for guesswork. In particular, without a careful inquiry into the sources of market failure, policymakers cannot gauge the exact extent of urban overexpansion. As a result, there is a danger that a UGB may be much too stringent, needlessly restricting the size of the city and leading to an inappropriate escalation in housing costs and unwarranted increases in density.

For example, the failure to charge fully for the cost of infrastructure may result in a city that is 5 percent too large in area. Eager policymakers, however, may impose a growth boundary that ultimately makes the city area 15 percent smaller than in the absence of intervention. Such a draconian policy could be so harmful that society would be better off with no government intervention at all.

The way to avoid such errors is to attack urban sprawl at its source by imposing the specific remedies outlined above. Proper congestion tolls and impact fees can be computed with a high degree of reliability, ensuring that the resulting adjustments in urban spatial size are right from society's point of view. A development tax designed to preserve open space works equally well provided that a proper measure of open-space benefits can be computed.

The best known example of an urban growth boundary is from Portland, Oregon. Although some commentators claim that Portland's UGB is responsible for excessive house-price escalation in that city, as suggested by the above argument, others argue that the boundary is so loose that its price effects are negligible. This controversy illustrates an important point, namely, that there is no way to tell whether a UGB is set properly without focusing on the underlying market failures that lead to urban sprawl. Regardless of which view of the Portland case is correct, urban growth boundaries retain the potential for excessively restricting city sizes, and they should be used with great care.

A Numerical Example Showing the Effect of a Misplaced UGB

To get a sense of the effect of inappropriately restricting the spatial size of a city through an urban growth boundary, it is useful to consider a numerical

25. See Ding, Knaap and Hopkins (1999) for a recent analysis of UGBs.

example. To generate such an example, housing production is added to the simple model described earlier, following the approach of Brueckner.[26] Housing is produced with capital and land, and for purposes of the example, the production function is assumed to be of the Cobb-Douglas form with constant returns to scale. The utility function is also assumed to be Cobb-Douglas.

Parameter values for the simulated city are chosen realistically.[27] Then, two urban equilibrium conditions analogous to equations 1 and 2 are solved numerically using Mathematica. The results, which are presented in the first column of table 1, show that in equilibrium, the city has a radius of 30.8 miles and that its residents reach a utility level of 359.6. The price per unit of housing falls as distance from the CBD increases, leading to an increase in housing consumption over distance.[28] Combined with a decline in building heights over distance (not shown), this increase in dwelling size generates a dramatic decline in population density as distance increases. Finally, the table shows differential land rent in the city, which is the total land rent in excess of r_a generated between the CBD and $\bar{x}$. This differential rent constitutes the additional income that accrues to absentee landowners (over and above agricultural rent) because of the existence of the city.

To gauge the effect of an inappropriate UGB, suppose that the above equilibrium is not distorted in any way by market failure. The results of imposing a UGB in this situation can give a sense for the potential damage that can be done when an overly restrictive UGB is imposed under circumstances when market failures are present, but where only a mild restriction on $\bar{x}$ is warranted. To this end, suppose that the UGB is set at fifteen miles, leading to

26. Brueckner (1987).

27. The simulated city is assumed to have a population of 800,000 households, representing 2 million people if households realistically contain 2.5 people. Household income is set at $40,000 per year, and land rent per acre is set at $250, which corresponds to a land value of $5,000 per acre under a 5 percent discount rate (this yields rent of $160,000 per square mile). Capital's exponent in the constant-returns production function is set at 0.75, and a multiplicative factor of 0.03 is applied to the production function so that realistic population densities are generated. The utility exponent on housing consumption is set at 0.5. Finally, the commuting cost parameter is set at $500, a value that includes both money and time cost, as follows: Assuming an out-of-pocket cost of $0.30 per mile and 250 round trips per year leads to a value of $150 per year for the money cost of commuting per mile. A yearly income of $40,000 implies an hourly wage of $20, which yields a time cost per mile of $0.66 assuming a traffic speed of 30 miles per hour (commuting time is valued at the full wage). Time cost is then $330 per mile per year, yielding a total money plus time cost of $480, which is rounded up to $500.

28. Note that units of measurement for housing consumption (square feet, square meters, and so on), can be specified arbitrarily. A rescaling of consumption, however, would require an opposite rescaling of the price per unit.

Table 1. The Effects of an Urban Growth Boundary

Item	Equilibrium city	City with UGB[a]
$\bar{x}$	30.8	15.0
Utility	359.6	335.5
Population density		
At CBD	52,098	90,914
At $x = 15$	12,178	21,252
At $\bar{x}$	1,734	...
Housing price		
At CBD	3,093	3,554
At $x = 15$	2,042	2,346
At $\bar{x}$	1,170	...
Housing consumption		
At CBD	6.47	5.63
At $x = 15$	7.96	6.92
At $\bar{x}$	10.51	...
Differential land rent	2.82×10^9	3.45×10^9

a. Income increase required to offset utility loss from UGB: $2,942 (7 percent of original income).

more than a 50 percent reduction in the radius of the city. The consequences of this restriction are shown in the second column of table 1.

Utility falls from 359.6 to 335.5, so that the urban residents are worse off. To see the reasons for this loss, note that the price per unit of housing rises throughout the truncated city, yielding a decline in housing consumption. This dwelling-size reduction tends to raise population density, an effect that is strongly reinforced by an increase in building heights (not shown). As a result, the city's population density rises dramatically. Finally, differential land rent increases substantially, indicating that absentee landowners are better off under the UGB.

Thus, the results show that by packing people into a smaller city, the UGB raises the price of housing and cuts housing consumption. To get a sense of the magnitude of the resulting welfare loss, consider the following exercise. With the UGB in place, let consumer income be increased until the utility level achieved is the same as the equilibrium level from the first column of the table. The required increase in income, which gives a measure of the consumer welfare loss from the UGB, is equal to $2,942. Thus, canceling the welfare loss requires a 7 percent increase in income.

Recognizing that the UGB imposes a very dramatic 50 percent reduction in the city's radius, this compensating income increase seems modest in size. This reflects two facts. First, population density in the region beyond a distance of fifteen miles is relatively low, so that the share of the population needing reaccommodation after imposition of the UGB is not commensurate with the land area reduction. Second, the displaced population is mostly housed through increases in building heights, without a dramatic decline in housing consumption.

While urban residents are hurt, an overall efficiency verdict on the UGB must also take into account the welfare of absentee landowners. To see that this overall verdict is negative, suppose that the government were to raise the income of each household so as to cancel the loss from the UGB.[29] Could the government recover the cost of the subsidy by taxing away the resulting increment in differential land rent? Calculations show that the land-rent increment falls well short of the required transfer to households.[30] As a result, the government cannot compensate consumers for the effect of the UGB while maintaining the incomes of absentee landowners, indicating that the UGB reduces overall welfare. Thus, the lesson of the analysis is that unwarranted restrictions in the spatial sizes of cities harm urban residents while lowering overall welfare.[31]

Although the model underlying the numerical example has a single type of household, the real-world impact of a UGB will be felt by consumers from different income groups. Moreover, it is likely that low-income households will be more adversely affected than the rich by any UGB-induced escalation of housing prices. Reflecting this possibility, consumer groups concerned about adverse effects on housing affordability joined housing developers in opposing several of the antisprawl measures appearing on the November 2000 ballot.[32] Furthermore, if the environmental benefits that may result from an attack on sprawl constitute a luxury good, valued more by high- than low-income households, incidence of such policies may be skewed even more in favor of the well-off.

29. The required payment of $2,942 to each of 800,000 households would involve a total transfer of $2, 354 x 10^6. The resulting higher incomes would in turn raise urban land rents beyond the pretransfer level, with differential land rent in the city rising to $3.74 x 10^9.

30. With differential rent prior to imposition of the UGB equal to $2.82 x 10^9, the increment equals $920 x 10^6, which falls well short of the required transfer of $2,354 x 10^6.

31. While there is little empirical evidence on the effects of UGBs in the United States, a number of empirical studies show the effects of other types of land-use restrictions on U.S. housing prices, with positive impacts typically found. For a survey of such studies, see Fischel (1990). UGBs are also found elsewhere in the world, and their harmful effects on housing affordability have been most thoroughly studied in the case of Korea. See Kim (1993) and Son and Kim (1998).

32. Habitat for Humanity joined housing developers in opposing antisprawl measures in Arizona and Colorado. See Richard A. Oppel Jr., "Efforts to Restrict Sprawl Find New Resistance from Advocates for Affordable Housing," *New York Times*, December 26, 2000, p. A18.

Developing this theme, a recent theoretical literature on urban growth controls abstracts from the market failures considered above and portrays growth-control policies as a way for landowners to raise their incomes (and perhaps their quality of life) at the expense of renters. The latter group pays higher housing prices as a result of the growth control's restriction on expansion of the city.[33]

Other Factors Contributing to Sprawl

While market failures discussed earlier would appear to be prime culprits in generating excessive spatial growth of cities, additional forces contributing to this outcome can be identified. The first is another fiscal effect, which arises from the process of "voting with one's feet." This phrase refers to the tendency of high- and middle-income consumers to form separate jurisdictions for the provision of public goods such as education, public safety, and parks. Such jurisdictions tend to be created on the urban fringe, which exacerbates the tendency toward urban expansion.

As explained by Charles M. Tiebout, the goal of well-off consumers in forming such separate jurisdictions is to gain control over the level of public spending, which can then be set high enough to provide the high-quality schools and public services that such consumers demand.[34] An additional benefit comes from avoiding the need to subsidize the public consumption of poor households, who contribute little of the tax revenue required by local governments. To protect these benefits, the residents of suburban communities often impose minimum-lot-size restrictions and other fiscal zoning regulations designed to deter poor households from entering the community.

One way to diminish this tendency for Tiebout sorting (thus limiting the resulting urban expansion) is through a metropolitan taxing authority. Such an authority would divert funds from well-off suburban communities to the poor central city, limiting the gains from formation of such communities. However, political opposition from well-off households dooms most attempts to create metropolitan governments.[35]

A number of other fiscal effects may contribute to urban sprawl. One such effect arises through the federal tax subsidy to owner-occupied housing, which

33. See, for example, Brueckner (1995); Helsley and Strange (1995).
34. Tiebout (1956).
35. See Orfield (1998) for an instructive discussion of the politics of metropolitan government in Minneapolis.

arises because imputed rental income is untaxed. Harvey Rosen shows that if imputed rent were instead taxed, housing consumption for homeowners would fall by 10 to 20 percent, with the exact number depending on household income.[36] Since the resulting reduction in dwelling sizes would reduce the consumption of land, the spatial sizes of cities would ultimately fall in the absence of the housing tax subsidy.

It is interesting to note, however, that another set of federal policies, those designed to maintain farm incomes, may offset the sprawl-inducing effects of the federal tax subsidy to homeowners. By raising the income-producing potential of the land, policies such as farm price supports tend to increase agricultural land rent, which has the effect of restricting, rather than encouraging, urban spatial expansion (recall equation 3). While these two policies may thus have offsetting effects on urban expansion, the policies in any case are designed to promote social goals (homeownership, the family farm) that are separate from the issue of urban sprawl. As a result, attempts to alter the policies to address the sprawl problem would probably be unwarranted.

Finally, another fiscal force arising through the property tax may also contribute to urban sprawl. As shown by Brueckner and Hyun-A Kim, the property tax reduces the intensity of land development (that is, building heights), which lowers population densities.[37] Lower densities, in turn, cause cities to spread out, creating sprawl. However, Brueckner and Kim's analysis identifies a countervailing effect that arises through the property tax's tendency to reduce dwelling sizes, which raises population densities. While the net effect of the tax on urban spatial size is thus ambiguous, simulation results suggest that it may be positive in a realistic model, making the property tax a potential culprit in the excessive spatial expansion of cities.

Byproducts of an Attack on Sprawl

An attack on urban sprawl might produce several byproducts. These include upgrading and redevelopment in central neighborhoods, which help to reverse the process of central-city decay. In addition, the higher densities generated by an attack on sprawl may improve the quality of urban life by fostering social interaction.

36. Rosen (1985).
37. Brueckner and Kim (2000).

As noted earlier, many commentators argue that excessive urban spatial growth contributes to the decay of central cities by reducing the incentive to redevelop land near the center. Central-city decay, however, would be a problem even in the absence of the market failures leading to urban sprawl. The reason is that the suburbanization forces generated by rising incomes and falling commuting costs reduce the demand for aging central-city housing, depressing its price and diminishing the incentive for upgrading and redevelopment. By inappropriately increasing the supply of developed land, overexpansion of cities exacerbates this tendency by putting further downward pressure on housing prices. Thus, the incentive for upgrading and redevelopment of aging dwellings is further reduced.

If, however, sprawl is attacked with an instrument such as a development tax, then the city ultimately shrinks, and housing prices rise everywhere. By raising the return to real estate investment, this price escalation is likely to spur redevelopment efforts in central neighborhoods.[38] Thus, one byproduct of an attack on sprawl at the urban fringe may be upgrading and redevelopment in decaying central neighborhoods. Although there is no formal analysis of such an effect in the literature, the issue could be analyzed by adapting one of the existing models of urban growth with durable housing.[39]

Many commentators criticize the process of suburbanization, and its attendant "car culture," as weakening the nation's social bonds by spreading residences out in low-density patterns that discourage interaction.[40] Formally, such commentators appear to be arguing that the city's average population density is a kind of public good, whose level is chosen incorrectly by the decentralized development process. In other words, since the social gains from an increase in average density are not captured by atomistic housing developers, the equilibrium city is too spread out from society's point of view.

If this argument is correct, then it would appear that supernormal profits could be earned by building relatively dense, large-scale housing developments that internalize the density externality. Such developments, which would tend to limit the extent of urban expansion, are evidenced in several planned communities whose design follows the principles of the "new urbanism." If such efforts show long-term success, this may indicate that the social-interaction argument has merit. Otherwise, continued low-density

---

38. See Rosenthal and Helsley (1994) for an empirical analysis of redevelopment.
39. See Brueckner (2000a) for an overview.
40. See, for example, Schwartz (1980).

development on the urban fringe would suggest that consumers prefer the type of neighborhoods that developers have been building all along.

Relaxation of zoning requirements that limit residential density is a prerequisite for the exercise of consumer sovereignty in this area of urban design. While such regulations may simply ratify the previous low-density preferences of consumers, they may also constrain current choices, causing cities to be more spread out than people would like.

Conclusion

When crafting policies to address sprawl, policymakers must recognize that the potential market failures involved in urban expansion are of secondary importance compared with the powerful, fundamental forces that underlie this expansion. For example, while the failure to fully charge for infrastructure costs may impart a slight upward bias to urban expansion, the bulk of the substantial spatial growth that has occurred across the United States cannot be ascribed to such a cause. Instead, this growth mostly reflects fundamentals such as the nation's growing population and rising affluence. Because of the secondary role of market failure, a draconian attack on urban sprawl is probably not warranted. By greatly restricting urban expansion, such an attack might needlessly limit the consumption of housing space, depressing the standard of living of American consumers. Instead, a more cautious approach, which recognizes the damage done by unwarranted restriction of urban growth, should be adopted.

Such caution is a built-in feature of the development taxes, congestion tolls, and impact fees discussed above, which attack sprawl at its source by correcting specific market failures. Urban growth boundaries, by contrast, can easily yield undesirably draconian outcomes because they are not directly linked to the underlying market failures responsible for sprawl. However, because UGBs simply require an extension of existing zoning powers, local policymakers may find them more convenient to use than taxes or tolls. UGBs may therefore end up as the instrument of choice for attacking urban sprawl. One lesson of the discussion is that policymakers should resist the temptation to impose stringent UGBs, recognizing that a substantial restriction of urban growth is likely to do more harm than good.

Comments

Edwin Mills: My views on urban sprawl differ from Jan Brueckner's but by less than might be imagined. He discusses market failure; I discuss governments' failures to get prices right. The unifying observation is that every market failure reflects a failure of governments to get prices right. The difference is in recommended government actions. Those who emphasize market failure mostly want governments to do more. In most cases, I want government to do less; in the crucial area of road pricing, I want governments to do something different from what they have been doing. On issues related to urban sprawl, I believe that government causes of misallocations are patent and simple.

I start with three simple observations. First, "sprawl" is a pejorative term, meaning excessive suburbanization. It would be better to use the neutral term. Second, suburbanization has taken place in every urban area of the world in which it has been studied for most of the past half century; in this country and in at least a few others, for at least a century. Suburbanization has gone farther here than in most countries. We have plentiful cheap land and, until the sprawl police agitated the population, we used it pretty much in accordance with relative prices. Third, there is no intrinsic relationship between suburbanization and traffic congestion. Suburbanization includes dwellings and businesses. I can easily imagine a scenario in which business and population suburbanization occurred so as to reduce commuting distances dramatically in comparison with a monocentric business location pattern. U.S. suburbanization has not been accompanied by falling commuting distances, and I believe this is a much more important issue than excessive suburbanization.

Brueckner understands that invasion of farmland is a nonissue. Except for two world wars, excess, not deficient agricultural output, has been the U.S.

scenario during most of the twentieth century. By now, about half of farm income comes from federal subsidies, and much of the subsidization presumably gets capitalized in farm land prices.[41] No responsible forecast anticipates agricultural shortages for the foreseeable future.

Open space is a similar nonissue. Federal, state, and local governments can and do buy as much land for parks, forests, and so on as their constituents are willing to pay for at fair market prices. In addition, governments can and do buy land for future open space preferences insofar as the democratic process can represent such preferences. The problem comes because governments use the police power to confiscate ownership rights of landowners to preserve open space. The federal government has historically been the worst offender, but state and local governments are now doing the same thing with "growth boundaries" and related police power actions. Imposing the costs of open space preservation on private land owners motivates governments to preserve excessive amounts of open space.

The government action that most promotes excessive suburbanization is local government land use controls. Both central city and suburban governments impose draconian limits on business and residential density—prohibition of multifamily dwellings, minimum lot size requirements, height limitations, floor-area ration limits, and a panoply of other controls. Such controls patently force excessive decentralization of metropolitan areas. They are imposed pursuant to parochial desires of residents to exclude low-income and minority people, whose interests are not represented at the local level since they are not there. As long as local governments can impose land use controls in the interest of their residents, no actions at any government level, such as growth boundaries, can have effects that will not increase distortions. Although motivations are less clear, local governments also impose density and other controls on commercial real estate.

Undoubtedly, the most distorting action of governments in metropolitan areas is the underpricing of transportation. The optimum user fee of an uncongested urban road is the opportunity cost of the land plus the depreciation of the right-of-way plus the operating cost of the road (traffic control, snow removal, and so on) all converted to a vehicle mile basis. I have calculated that a fuel tax of about ten times the typical U.S. level, say $2.50 per U. S. gallon instead of $0.25, would be a good approximation to an optimal user fee.[42] The result would be a gasoline price of about $4.00 to $4.50 per gallon, typical of

41. U.S. Department of Agriculture.
42. Mills (1998, pp. 72–83).

prices in Europe and East Asia. Whether my calculation is accurate or not, it is patent that U.S. metropolitan road use is vastly underpriced.

Central cities are not innocent. The city of Chicago imposes severe density limits on downtown office buildings and, in the lakefront communities stretching from the Chicago River north for about five miles (where most of the city's residents of above median income live), has downsized residential densities about 50 percent in the past thirty years. Minorities are proportionately represented on the city council, but typically the councilman has almost complete control over zoning in his or her district. Residents lobby to zone out additional high-density structures. Since the reasons they give do not stand up to the simplest analysis, the central motivation, never mentioned, is presumably the most obvious one: to limit competing housing supply in order to raise the prices of their units.[43] Appropriate pricing and inexpensive improvements— traffic control, especially in central cities, and a modest amount of suburban road building—would practically eliminate urban congestion. Car owners would curtail frivolous drives, move closer to workplaces (especially by suburban house swaps that would reduce suburb-to-suburb cross-hauling) and gradually drive smaller, more fuel-efficient vehicles. Residential densities near central business districts and suburban employment subcenters would increase to the extent permitted by land use controls. Fuel tax revenues could be used to reduce distorting real estate taxes, which would also increase business and residential densities if permitted.

Fixed rail commuting is much more underpriced than auto use, but its excess capacity may justify large subsidies, in contrast with road use, which is close to capacity in many metropolitan areas.

The current antisprawl fad is "growth boundaries," a draconian police power control that Brueckner discusses thoroughly. If one wants to know the effects of growth boundaries, or of less stringent controls of land use conversion from rural to urban uses, plenty of examples are available.[44] U.S. house prices are less than three times the annual incomes of occupants. In northern Europe and East and South Asia, the ratios are three to ten in many countries. For example, in 1990 house prices were ten times occupants' incomes in Seoul, which had rigidly enforced greenbelt and other controls on land use conversion. At about that time, the government relaxed controls and house prices fell to five times incomes just before the East Asian crisis. In countries with rigid conversion controls, population densities are high, and road con-

43. See Mills (2000).
44. Angel and Mayo (1996).

gestion is at levels unheard of in this country. Even in Canada, which has nearly unlimited amounts of usable land, house prices relative to incomes in Vancouver and Toronto are 50 percent greater than they are on the U.S. side of the border, because of stringent conversion controls.

Nobody gains from pervasive artificial increases in house prices. The one-time housing capital gain is precisely offset by proportionate increases in actual or implicit rents. Elderly people who are about to downsize anyway will gain if they want to conserve part of their capital gain and do not mind leaving an inadequate legacy for housing to their heirs. Of course, if southern California has stringent controls and Phoenix does not, Californians will cash in their houses and move to Phoenix, living handsomely on modest pension or other assets and on the difference between housing costs in Phoenix and California.

Michael Kremer: This paper contains both a positive and normative analysis of urban sprawl. On the positive side, the paper concludes that urban spatial growth is mainly because of increased U.S. population, rising income, and falling commuting costs. On the normative side, it discusses three reasons why growth may be excessive: failure to account for benefits of open space, extra congestion on roads, and failure to charge for the true costs of infrastructure.

Effective measures against urban sprawl will cause cities to be more densely populated. If these measures are appropriate, then the loss in housing consumption will be offset by other gains. If not, consumers will end up worse off.

The paper suggests that road taxes and user fees for infrastructure, along with a potential new development tax, are appropriate responses to the distortions in urban expansion. It then cautions against urban growth boundaries as a blunt instrument.

I agree with most of the analysis. I have a few minor caveats and a couple of suggestions for taking the analysis a step further.

My main problem is with the analysis of the benefits of open space. As the author notes, the typical urban resident may not get huge benefits from preserving open space outside cities in general. Subsidies for agriculture are likely to outweigh any benefits of open space. Similarly, developers are already likely to have to make various payoffs and concessions in exchange for the right to build, even if these are not explicitly treated as infrastructure fees.

To the extent that people do care about preserving open space, it is probably because they drive past it and would like to see prettier views. This objective suggests a somewhat more targeted approach: instead of taxes on developing agricultural land outside urban boundaries, perhaps these taxes could be on converting land that is visible from well-traveled roads. More broadly, zoning regulations could control unsightly commercial developments along roads. For example, parking lots could be encouraged to be placed behind stores, rather than between stores and the road. I think we may currently be in an equilibrium in which the only way stores can convince customers that parking is available is by displaying the parking in front of the store. Instead, stores could use signs to direct people to parking in the back.

A case could also be made that while the first appearance of a 7-11 spoils the view, the nth appearance does not, suggesting that a nonlinear tax might be appropriate.

Of course, another option would be to follow the lead of the United Kingdom and change property rights to allow hiking through private property, at least on marked trails. Under this type of regime, the benefits of open space outside cities are much clearer.

If the city has a fixed amenity, such as a harbor, property values should increase. This may constitute an important reason for support for urban growth boundaries.

The fiscal externality associated with suburban growth is likely to be quite large, and I expect would outweigh the other effects modeled in the paper in its quantitative importance. For example, when a high-income person moves from Washington, D.C., to Virginia, he or she creates a substantial negative externality for others in Washington.

This paper examines whether incentives for urban expansion are optimal, but it does not go on to examine whether individual communities will have appropriate incentives to control urban growth. This is particularly important when there are different jurisdictions in the city and in the suburbs. If there are many different suburbs, and people drive through several different suburbs, then incentives to control road congestion and views from roads will not be adequate. Incentives to prevent flight from cities by those seeking to avoid taxes will also be inadequate.

References

Alonso, William. 1964. *Location and Land Use*. Harvard University Press.

Altshuler, Alan A., and Jose A. Gomez-Ibanez. 1993. *Regulation for Revenue: The Political Economy of Land Use Exactions*. Brookings.

Angel, Shlomo, and Stephen Mayo. 1996. "Enabling Policies and Their Effects on Housing Sector Performance: A Global Comparison." Istanbul: Habitat II.

Blomquist, Glenn C., and John C. Whitehead. 1995. "Existence Value, Contingent Valuation, and Natural Resources Damage Assessment." *Growth and Change* 26 (Fall): 573–89.

Breffle, William S., Edward R. Morey, and Tymon S. Lodder. 1998. "Using Contingent Valuation to Estimate a Neighborhood's Willingness to Pay to Preserve Undeveloped Land." *Urban Studies* 35 (April): 715–28.

Brueckner, Jan K. 1987. "The Structure of Urban Equilibria: A Unified Treatment of the Muth-Mills Model." In *Handbook of Regional and Urban Economics,* vol. 2, edited by Edwin S. Mills, 821–45. North Holland.

Brueckner, Jan K. 1995. "Strategic Control of Growth in a System of Cities." *Journal of Public Economics* 57 (July): 393–416.

——. 1997a. "Infrastructure Financing and Urban Development: The Economics of Impact Fees." *Journal of Public Economics* 66 (December): 383–407.

——. 1997b. "Calculation of School Impact Fees." Unpublished paper. University of Illinois at Urbana-Champaign.

——. 2000a. "Urban Growth Models with Durable Housing: An Overview." In *Economics of Cities*, edited by Jacques-Francois Thisse and Jean-Marie Huriot, 263–89. Cambridge University Press.

——. 2000b. "Urban Sprawl: Diagnosis and Remedies." *International Regional Science Review* 23 (April): 160–71.

Brueckner, Jan K., and Hyun-A Kim. 2000. "Urban Sprawl and the Property Tax." Unpublished paper. University of Illinois at Urbana-Champaign.

Brueckner, Jan K., and David Fansler. 1983. "The Economics of Urban Sprawl: Theory and Evidence on the Spatial Sizes of Cities." *Review of Economics and Statistics* 55 (August): 479–82.

Calfee, John, and Clifford Winston. 1998. "The Value of Automobile Travel Time: Implications for Congestion Policy." *Journal of Public Economics* 69 (July): 83–102.

Ding, Chengri, Gerrit J. Knaap, and Lewis D. Hopkins. 1999. "Managing Urban Growth with Urban Growth Boundaries: A Theoretical Analysis." *Journal of Urban Economics* 46 (July): 53–68.

Downs, Anthony. 1999. "Some Realities about Sprawl and Urban Decline." *Housing Policy Debate* 10 (4): 955–74.

Fischel, William A. 1990. "Do Growth Controls Matter? A Review of the Empirical Evidence on the Effectiveness and Efficiency of Local Government Land Use Regulation." Lincoln Institute of Land Policy, appearing in Hearing before the Subcommittee on Policy Research and Insurance of the House Committee on Banking, Finance, and Urban Affairs, 101 Cong. 2 sess. August 2, 74–137. Government Printing Office.

Grant, Peter. 2000. "The Debate over Sprawl Has Only Just Begun," *Wall Street Journal,* November 8, 2000, p. B14.

Gurwitt, Rob. 1999. "The State vs. Sprawl." *Governing* (January): 18-23.

Helsley, Robert W., and William C. Strange. 1995. "Strategic Growth Controls." *Regional Science and Urban Economics* 25 (August): 435–60.

Kim, Kyung-Hwan. 1993. "Housing Prices, Affordability, and Government Policy in Korea." *Journal of Real Estate Finance and Economics* 6 (January): 55–71.

Lopez, Rigoberto, Farhed Shah, and Marilyn Attolbello. 1994. "Amenity Benefits and the Optimal Allocation of Land." *Land Economics* 70 (February): 53–62.

Mieszkowski, Peter, and Edwin S. Mills. 1993. "The Causes of Metropolitan Suburbanization." *Journal of Economic Perspectives* 7: 135–47.

Mills, Edwin S. 1967. "An Aggregative Model of Resource Allocation in a Metropolitan Area." *American Economic Review, Papers and Proceedings* 57 (May): 197–210.

——. 1998. "Excess Commuting in U.S. Metropolitan Areas." In *Network Infrastructure and the Urban Environment,* edited by Lars Lundqvist, Lars Gevan Mattson, and Tschango Kim, 73–83. Springer-Verlag.

——. 1999. "Truly Smart 'Smart' Growth." *Illinois Real Estate Letter.* Summer: 1–7.

——. 2000. "Effects of Downzoning on Chicago's North Lakefront Commercial Areas." Northwestern University. Mimeo.

Muth, Richard F. 1969. *Cities and Housing.* University of Chicago Press.

Nivola, Pietro S. 1998. "Fat City: Understanding American Urban Form from a Transatlantic Perspective." *Brookings Review* 16 (4): 17–19.

Orfield, Myron. 1998. "Conflict or Consensus: Forty Years of Minnesota Metropolitan Politics." *Brookings Review* 16 (4): 31–34.

Rosen, Harvey S. 1985. "Housing Subsidies: Effects on Housing Decisions, Efficiency, and Equity." In *Handbook of Public Economics,* vol. 1, edited by Alan J. Auerbach and Martin Feldstein, 373–420. North Holland.

Rosenthal, Stuart S., and Robert W. Helsley. 1994. "Redevelopment and the Urban Land Price Gradient." *Journal of Urban Economics* 35 (March): 182–200.

Rusk, David. 1998. "The Exploding Metropolis: Why Growth Management Makes Sense." *Brookings Review* 16 (4): 13–15.

Schwartz, Barry. 1980. *"The Suburban Landscape: New Variations on an Old Theme." Contemporary Society* 9 (September): 640–50.

Small, Kenneth A. 1992. *Urban Transportation Economics.* Harwood Academic Publishers.

Son, Jae-Young, and Kyung-Hwan Kim. 1998. "Analysis of Urban Land Shortages: The Case of Korean Cities." *Journal of Urban Economics* 43 (May): 362–84.

Thurston, Lawrence, and Anthony M. J. Yezer. 1994. "Causality in the Suburbanization of Population and Employment." *Journal of Urban Economics* 35 (January): 105–18.

Tiebout, Charles M. 1956. "A Pure Theory of Local Expenditures." *Journal of Political Economy* 64 (October): 416–24.

U.S. Department of Agriculture. Economic Research Service. Annual issues. *Agricultural Income and Finance Situation and Outlook.*

Wheaton, William C. 1974. "A Comparative Static Analysis of Urban Spatial Structure." *Journal of Economic Theory* 9 (October): 223–37.

——. 1998. "Land Use and Density in Cities with Congestion." *Journal of Urban Economics* 43 (March): 258–72.

STEVEN RAPHAEL
University of California, Berkeley

MICHAEL A. STOLL
University of California, Los Angeles

Can Boosting Minority Car-Ownership Rates Narrow Inter-Racial Employment Gaps?

DURING THE PAST three decades, considerable effort has been devoted to assessing the importance of spatial mismatch in determining racial and ethnic differences in employment outcomes. The hypothesis posits that persistent racial housing segregation in U.S. metropolitan areas coupled with the spatial decentralization of employment have left black and, to a lesser extent, Latino workers physically isolated from ever-important suburban employment centers. Given the difficulties of reverse commuting by public transit and the high proportions of blacks and Latinos that do not own cars, this spatial disadvantage literally removes many suburban locations from the opportunity sets of inner-city minority workers.

Mismatch proponents argue that closing racial and ethnic gaps in employment and earnings requires improving the access of spatially isolated minorities to the full set of employment opportunities within regional economies. Improving accessibility can be accomplished through a combination of community development, residential mobility, and transportation programs.[1] Among the latter set of options, a potential tool for enhancing

We thank David Card, Ed Glaeser, John Quigley, Ken Small, Eugene Smolensky, and Cliff Winston for their valuable input. This research is supported by a grant from the National Science Foundation, SBR-9709197, and a Small Grant from the Joint Center for Poverty Research.

1. Examples include such federal government programs as Empowerment Zones, the experimental residential mobility program "Moving to Opportunities" (MTO), and the Department of Transportation's "Access to Jobs" program. For evaluations of MTO, see Ludwig (1998); Ludwig, Ladd, and Duncan in this volume; Katz, Liebman, and Kling (forthcoming). For a description of the Access to Jobs program, see GAO (1999). For an evaluation of the job creation effects of state enterprise zone programs, see Papke (1993).

accessibility would be to increase auto access for racial and ethnic minorities. Racial differences in car-ownership rates are large, comparable in magnitude to the black-white difference in home-ownership rates documented by Melvin L. Oliver and Thomas M. Shapiro.[2] Moreover, car-ownership rates for low-skilled workers are quite sensitive to small changes in operating costs, suggesting that moderate subsidies may significantly increase auto access for racial and ethnic minorities.[3]

In this chapter, we assess whether boosting minority car-ownership rates would narrow inter-racial employment rate differentials. We pursue two empirical strategies. First, we explore whether the effect of auto ownership on the probability of being employed is greater for more spatially isolated populations. The housing segregation literature demonstrates that blacks are highly segregated from the majority white population and in a manner that isolates blacks from new employment opportunities. Latino households are also segregated, though to a lesser degree than black households. If mismatch reduces minority employment probabilities, and if auto ownership can partially undo this effect, the employment effect of auto ownership should be greatest for the most segregated populations (that is, blacks, then Latinos, then whites).[4] We test this proposition using microdata from the Survey of Income and Program Participation (SIPP).

Next, we investigate whether the differences in the car-employment effects between blacks and whites increases with the severity of spatial mismatch. If spatial mismatch yields a car-employment effect for blacks that is larger than that for whites, then the black-white difference in the car-employment effect should be larger in metropolitan areas where blacks (relative to whites) are particularly isolated from employment opportunities. To test this proposition, we first estimate the black-white difference in the car-employment effect for 242 metropolitan areas in the United States. Next, we construct corresponding metropolitan-area measures of the relative spatial isolation of blacks from employment opportunities. We then test for a positive relationship between these two metropolitan-area level variables.

We find strong evidence that having access to a car is particularly important for African Americans and Latinos. We find a difference in employment rates between car-owners and non-car-owners that is considerably larger among blacks than among whites. Moreover, the car-employment effect for

2 . Oliver and Shapiro (1997).

3. Raphael and Rice (2000).

4. Massey and Denton (1993); Stoll and others (2000); Frey and Farley (1996); Massey and Denton (1989).

Latinos is significantly greater than the comparable effect for non-Latino whites yet significantly smaller than the effect for blacks. Finally, the black-white difference in the car-employment effect is greatest in metropolitan areas where the relative isolation of blacks is most severe. Our estimates indicate that raising minority car-ownership rates to that of whites would considerably narrow inter-racial employment rate differentials.

Auto Access, Race, and Labor Market Prospects

During the past three decades, household access to automobiles in the United States has increased considerably. Between 1969 and 1995, the average number of automobiles per household doubled from one to two. Moreover, this increase coincided with a 17 percent reduction in household size. Over the same period, the number of households with zero vehicles declined from 13 million (21 percent of the 1969 household population) to 8 million (8 percent of the 1995 household population). Hence near the end of the century, household access to automobiles in the United States is nearly universal.[5]

These aggregate figures, however, mask sharp differences in auto ownership across households of different racial and ethnic groups. Figure 1 presents 1995 distributions of the number of cars per household for white, black, and Latino households. The data are drawn from the 1995 Nationwide Personal Transportation Survey, which provides a large representative sample of the U.S. population. The differences evident in the figure are glaring. While 5.4 percent of white households have zero automobiles, 24 percent of black households and 12 percent of Latino households do not own a single car. These differences indicate that black and Latino households are disproportionately represented among households with no automobiles.[6] In addition, among households with at least one car, 51 percent of black households and 39 percent of Latino households have only one vehicle, compared with 33 percent of white households.[7]

5. These figures come from *Our Nation's Travel: 1995 Nationwide Transportation Survey Early Results Report*, Department of Transportation, 1999.

6. While black households were 12 percent of all households in 1995, they accounted for 35 percent of households with no vehicles. Latino households were 7.8 percent of all households in 1995 but 12 percent of households with no vehicles.

7. There are also large differences in auto access rates by household income. For households with incomes of less than $25,000, $25,000 to $55,000, and $55,000 plus, the percent with zero vehicles in 1995 is approximately 18, 4, and 1 percent, respectively. Hu and Young (1999).

Figure 1. Distribution of the Number of Household Automobiles by Race and Ethnicity, 1995

Percent

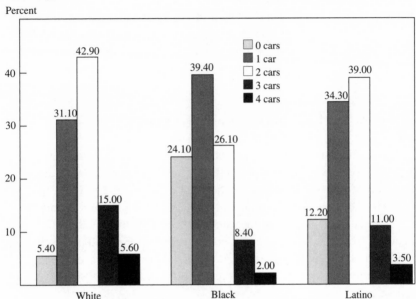

Source: Tabulated from the1995 Nationwide Personal Transportation Survey.

Several factors may contribute to these large differences in automobile ownership. Household incomes and wealth (in savings and equity in housing) are much lower among minority households.[8] This should surely limit one's ability to make large purchases and limit access to capital markets.[9] In addition, some researchers have raised the possibility that blacks face systematic price discrimination in the market for new cars. In an audit study of Chicago auto dealerships, Ian Ayres and Peter Siegelman document that car salespersons make initial and final offers that are consistently and substantially higher for black auditors than for white auditors. However, in an analysis of consumer expenditure survey data, Goldberg finds no evidence that blacks pay

8. Oliver and Shapiro (1997).

9. There is some indirect evidence that the low car-ownership rates among low-income households is the result in part of capital constraints. In a survey of Earned Income Tax Credit recipients, Smeeding, Ross Phillips, and O'Connor (forthcoming) find that recipients of the substantial lump-sum payments under the program often use the money to purchase an automobile. There are also some media reports of racial discrimination in the financing terms that black car buyers experience at car dealerships. See Diana B. Henriques, "New Front Opens in Effort to Fight Race Bias in Loans," *New York Times,* October 22, 2000, and "Hidden Charges: A Special Report; Extra Costs on Car Loans Draw Lawsuits," *New York Times,* October 27, 2000, sec. A1.

higher prices for new cars (holding car attributes constant).[10] An alternative factor may be differences in insurance costs faced by minority households. Scott E. Harrington and Greg Neihaus provide evidence for the state of Missouri that insurance premiums are much higher in predominantly minority neighborhoods.[11] While the authors find that these higher premiums are justified by higher realized loss ratios in minority neighborhoods (and hence, that the higher premiums do not reflect discriminatory behavior by insurers), the results still indicate that insuring a car costs more for residents of predominantly minority, urban communities. These cost differentials should influence those black and Latino individuals that are on the margin between owning and not owning a car.

The proposition that having access to a reliable car provides real advantages in finding and maintaining a job is not controversial. In most U.S. metropolitan areas, one can commute greater distances in shorter time periods and, holding distance constant, reach a fuller set of potential work locations using a privately owned car rather than public transit.[12] For low-skilled workers, being confined to public transit may seriously worsen employment prospects for many reasons. First, public transportation is slower than private transportation and thus substantially increases the time cost of travel. Second, suburban employer locations are less accessible by public

10. Ayres and Siegelman (1995); Goldberg (1996). The difference in the results between these two studies may be attributed to the fact that while Ayres and Siegelman study the offer distribution faced by black car buyers, Goldberg examines the price distribution conditional on a transaction occurring. Specifically, if potential black car buyers that receive very high price offers from dealers drop out of the market, the offer-price distribution and the transaction-price distribution will not be similar. Hence, measuring discrimination by the mean price differential using the latter distribution will underestimate the degree of price discrimination against blacks. Goldberg explores this possibility using standard sample-selection methods and concludes that her estimates are not affected by sample selection. The selection-correction results, however, are not explicitly presented. Hence, one cannot assess the precision of the selection models (in particular, the estimate of the covariance between the residuals from the selection equation and the price equation). Other differences between the two studies include the fact that while Goldberg analyzes a national sample, Ayres and Siegelman analyze a sample of Chicago dealers. In addition, information from the Consumer Expenditure Survey used in the Goldberg study on auto make, model, and options purchased, while detailed, is far from complete, while the auditors in the Ayres and Siegelman study bargain over the exact same models in the same dealerships. The mixed results of these two very well-done studies indicates that further research on this question is warranted.

11. Harrington and Neihaus (1998).

12. Stoll (1999) analyzing a sample of adults in Los Angeles and Holzer and others (1994) analyzing a national sample of youths show that car owners search greater geographic areas and ultimately travel greater distances to work than do searchers using public transit or alternative means of transportation.

transit. Thus, not having access to an automobile geographically constrains low-skilled workers, especially minority workers. Finally, public transit schedules tend to offer more frequent service during traditional morning and afternoon peak commute periods, while low-skilled workers are more likely to work irregular hours.[13] This incongruity in schedules may result in longer commutes, a relatively high probability of being late, or both.

Moreover, the residential location choices of low-skilled workers are likely to be geographically constrained by zoning restrictions limiting the location and quantity of low-income housing. Such constraints may limit the ability of low-skilled workers to choose residential locations within reasonable public-transit commutes of important employment centers. For minority workers, residential location choices are constrained by relatively low incomes and pervasive racial discrimination in housing rental and sales markets.[14] The existing mismatch literature clearly demonstrates that low- and semi-skilled employment opportunities are scarce in minority neighborhoods relative to the residential concentration of low-skilled and semi-skilled labor, and that these differences in accessibility affect the employment rates of minority workers.[15] In addition, several authors have demonstrated intrametropolitan patterns of employment growth that favor nonminority neighborhoods.[16] Hence, one might argue that having access to a car would be especially important in determining the employment outcomes of minority workers.

Several researchers have found large differences in employment outcomes between those with and without access to an automobile. Harry J. Holzer, Keith R. Ihlanfeldt, and David L. Sjoquist find that youths with cars experience shorter unemployment spells and earn higher wages than youths without cars. This study also finds differential effects of auto access by race, showing car effects on unemployment spells that are larger for black than for white youth. Paul Ong analyzes a sample of welfare recipients residing in Califor-

13. Stoll (1999); Holzer and others (1994); Stoll and others (2000); Holzer and others (2001); Holzer and Ihlanfeldt (1996); Ihlanfeldt and Young (1996); Hughes (1995). Hamermesh (1996) analyzes the likelihood of working irregular hours in the United States. Both education and age have strong negative effects on the probability of working shifts from 7 P.M. to 10 P.M. and 10 P.M. to 6 A.M. for both men and women. Hence the young and the less educated are more likely to work nontraditional schedules. Black men are also significantly more likely to work these irregular hours, while for women there is no effect of race.

14. Yinger (1995).

15. Stoll and others (2000); Mouw (2000); Raphael (1998a, 1998b); Weinberg (2000). Extensive reviews of the spatial mismatch literature are provided by Holzer (1991); Ihlanfeldt and Sjoquist (1998); Kain (1992); and Pugh (1998).

16 . Mouw (2000); Raphael (1998a, 1998b); Stoll and Raphael (2000); Glaeser and Kahn, this volume.

nia and finds substantial differences in employment rates and hours worked between those with and without cars. Ong fails to find effects of auto access on wages and argues that the lack of a wage effect indicates that unobserved heterogeneity is not a factor in explaining the employment results. Katherine M. O'Regan and John M. Quigley find large car-employment effects for recipients of public aid using data from the 1990 decennial census. Finally, Steven Raphael and Lorien Rice estimate car-employment effects using geographic variation in auto insurance premiums and state gasoline taxes as instruments for car ownership.[17] The authors find two-stage-least-squares (2SLS) car-employment effects that are comparable in magnitude to OLS estimates and car effects that are generally larger for workers with lower earnings potential.

To the extent that transportation barriers constrain the employment opportunities available to minority populations, relaxing these constraints may improve the employment prospects of minority workers. In this chapter we explore the potential impact of improving minority access to private transportation.

Modeling the Effects of Auto Ownership on Employment: Two Empirical Strategies

Our empirical strategy makes use of a simple linear probability model of employment determination. Assume that the categorical variable, E_i, indicating whether individual i is employed depends on individual skills, S_i, and one's spatial accessibility to employment locations, A_i. Spatial accessibility is akin to the density of one's employment opportunity set, where accessible employment opportunities are those within a reasonable commute distance of one's residence. We assume that both accessibility and skills positively affect the probability of being employed according to the linear equation

(1) $$E_i = \alpha_1 A_i + \alpha_2 S_i + \alpha_3 B_i + \varepsilon_i.$$ (1)

where ε_i is a mean-zero, randomly distributed disturbance term and B_i is an indicator for black individuals.

Car ownership (denoted by the indicator variable, C_i) affects employment status by improving accessibility—that is, car owners can have access to a greater proportion of a regional labor market than can non-car-owners. This

---

17. Holzer, Ihlanfeldt, and Sjoquist (1994); Ong (1996); O'Regan and Quigley (1999); Raphael and Rice (2000).

implies that $E(A|B, C=1) > E(A|B, C=0)$. For blacks, the expected difference in employment rates between car owners and non-car-owners is given by the expression

$$\Delta_B = E(E \mid B = 1, C = 1) - E(E \mid B = 1, C = 0)$$
$$= \alpha_1 [E(A \mid B = 1, C = 1) - E(A \mid B = 1, C = 0)]$$
$$+ \alpha_2 [E(S \mid B = 1, C = 1) - E(S \mid B = 1, C = 0)]$$

(2) $$\Delta_B = \alpha_1 \Delta_B^A + \alpha_2 \Delta_B^S,$$

where Δ_B^A is the expected accessibility difference between black car owners and non-car-owners and Δ_B^S is the comparable expected skill differential. The "true" car effect is given by the first term (the accessibility boost multiplied by the effect of accessibility) while the second term is the portion of the difference in employment rates between black car owners and non-car-owners owing to inherent productivity differences.

Identifying the true car effect requires statistically distinguishing the portion of the employment rate differential caused by improved accessibility from the portion of the differential reflecting differences in average skill endowments. One approach to tackling this issue would estimate an adjusted employment difference between car owners and non-car-owners holding constant all factors that determine employment and that differ systematically across these two groups. Unfortunately, the set of covariates included in most microdata sources is likely to be incomplete and, hence, such regression-adjusted estimates of the car-employment effect may be biased by the omission of important unobservable factors.

An additional problem that is likely to bias estimates of the car-employment effect concerns the fact that auto ownership and employment are likely to be simultaneously determined. If the probability of owning a car depends positively on the probability of being employed, it is simple to show that OLS estimates of a car-employment effect will be biased upward.[18] Moreover, this

18. Suppose that employment is determined by $E_i = \alpha_0 + \alpha_1 C_i + \varepsilon_i$, while car ownership is determined by $C_i = \beta_0 + \beta_1 E_i + \eta_i$. Assume that α_1 and β_1 are both greater than zero. The probability limit of the OLS estimate of α is equal to $\mathrm{cov}(E,C)/\mathrm{var}(C) = \mathrm{cov}(\alpha_0 + \alpha_1 C + \varepsilon, C)/\mathrm{var}(C) = \alpha_1 + \mathrm{cov}(\varepsilon, C)/\mathrm{var}(C)$. The first term in this expression is the true car-employment effect while the second is the simultaneity bias. Since an increase in the employment probability increases the likelihood of owning a car (by assumption), $\mathrm{cov}(\varepsilon, C)$ is positive and hence the OLS estimate of α_1 is positively biased. Solving for the reduced form for C and calculating the relevant covariance yields the exact expression of the bias $\mathrm{cov}(\varepsilon, C)/\mathrm{var}(C) = [\mathrm{var}(\varepsilon)/\mathrm{var}(C)] [\beta_1/(1 - \alpha_1\beta_1)]$. One estimation strategy that would correct for both simultaneity and omitted-variables bias would be to find instruments for car ownership and estimate employment effects using a two-stage-least-squares (2SLS) estimator. Below we supplement our basic OLS results with estimates of car-employment effects using 2SLS estimators.

simultaneity bias cannot be fixed by controlling for all relevant determinants of employment.

Our empirical strategy identifies lower-bound estimates of the car-employment effect for blacks by comparing the empirical boost to black employment rates associated with owning a car to the comparable boost to white employment rates. If omitted variables and reverse causality account for comparable portions of the black and white empirical car-employment effects, the observed car effect for whites can be used to net out these biases for blacks. Specifically, define Δ_W as the employment rate difference between car owners and non-car-owners for whites comparable to the difference for blacks defined above. If we assume that the effects of skills and accessibility on employment are comparable across races, then subtracting this difference for whites from that for blacks yields the expression

$$(3) \qquad \Delta_B - \Delta_W = \alpha_1(\Delta_B^A - \Delta_W^A) + \alpha_2(\Delta_B^S - \Delta_W^S),$$

where Δ_W^A and Δ_W^S are the expected differences in accessibility and skill endowments between whites with and without cars. If we assume that the skill differential between car owners and non-car-owners is comparable across races, the term involving skills drops out of the equation, eliminating the omitted-variables bias. In other words, assuming that $\Delta_B^S = \Delta_W^S$, equation 3 reduces to

$$(4) \qquad \Delta_B - \Delta_W = \alpha_1(\Delta_B^A - \Delta_W^A).$$

This final expression gives the differential effect of cars on the probability of being employed caused by racial differences in the accessibility boost of having access to a car.

Equation 4 is a lower-bound estimate of the car-employment effect for blacks since it "differences-away" the accessibility improvement realized by white car owners. If we were to assume that the entire employment rate differential between white car owners and white non-car-owners was because of unobservable heterogeneity (that is to say, $\Delta_W^A = 0$, $\Delta_W^S > 0$), then equation 4 provides an accurate estimate of the black car-employment effect. This, however, is unlikely. For reasons discussed above, even the residents of jobs-rich suburban communities are likely to benefit from access to a car. Nonetheless, using this net estimate of the car-employment effect for blacks should partially mitigate concerns about omitted-variables bias.

The quantity in equation 4 will be greater than zero if two conditions are satisfied. First, accessibility must matter (that is, $\alpha_1 > 0$). Otherwise, there would be no employment benefit to car ownership. Second, the accessibility benefits of owning a car must be greater for blacks than for whites—that is, $\Delta_B^A > \Delta_W^A$. This latter condition may fail to hold for several reasons. First, blacks may be no more spatially isolated from employment opportunities than are whites, and hence, there would be no differential benefit associated with having access to a car. Alternatively, the spatial isolation of blacks may be so extreme that even having access to a car does not neutralize the deleterious employment consequences of mismatch. If this were the case, there may still be some benefit to car access for both blacks and whites, but there would be no differential improvement in black accessibility. Hence, testing for a positive double-difference estimate as described by equation 4 provides a rather strict test of the mismatch hypothesis.

The estimate in equation 4 requires assuming that the skill differentials between car owners and non-car-owners are comparable across racial and ethnic groups. We can relax this assumption somewhat by holding constant those skill and demographic variables that are readily observable. A regression adjusted double-difference comparable to that in equation 4 comes from estimating the equation

$$(5) \qquad E_i = \beta_0 + \beta_1 B_i + \beta_2 C_i + \beta_3 C_i * B_i + \delta \mathbf{X}_i + v_i,$$

where all observable determinants are included in the vector $\mathbf{X}_i$, and the adjusted double-difference is given by the coefficient β_3 on the interaction term between the indicator variables for car owners and black workers. This coefficient measures the extent to which the car-employment effect for blacks exceeds that for whites. In equation 5, the identification assumption concerning relative skills reduces to assuming comparable differences across racial groups in unobserved skills between those with and without cars and comparable returns to observable and unobservable skills. The assumption of comparable returns to observable skills can be relaxed by interacting race with all other control variables. This model is given by the equation

$$(6) \qquad E_i = \beta_0 + \beta_1 B_i + \beta_2 C_i + \beta_3 C_i * B_i + \delta \mathbf{X}_i + \gamma B_i * \mathbf{X}_i + v_i.$$

The main argument underlying the double-difference estimates in equations 4 through 6 is that the effect of auto access on employment status should be larger for more spatially isolated populations. We employ two empirical strategies designed to assess this proposition. Our first strategy exploits the differences in the extent of segregation between blacks and whites and between Latinos and whites. The second strategy makes use of intercity variation in spatial mismatch conditions.

Interracial and Interethnic Comparisons of the Car-Employment Effects

Both blacks and Latinos are residentially segregated from the majority non-Latino white population. In addition, the intrametropolitan patterns of segregation are similar, with both Latinos and blacks more likely to reside in older inner-city and inner-ring suburban communities.[19] However, conventional segregation indexes show that blacks are much more segregated, and in turn, spatially isolated from high-growth suburban employment centers, than are Latinos.[20] Hence, if car ownership partially neutralizes the adverse employment effects of being spatially isolated, we would expect the largest employment differentials between those with and without cars for black workers, the next largest differential for Latinos, and the smallest differential for non-Latino white workers.

In this section, we estimate the double-difference car effects in equations 4 through 6 using a black-white comparison, a black-Latino comparison, and a Latino-white comparison.[21] The simplest test of the mismatch hypothesis would assess whether the black-white double-difference estimate is positive and statistically significant. The more stringent test of the mismatch hypothesis would be to test for positive significant double-difference estimates in the black-white, Latino-white, and black-Latino comparisons. Affirmative findings in all three comparisons would suggest that the ordering of the car-employment effects is statistically significant and associated with the degree of housing segregation.

We draw data from the fourth waves of the 1991, 1992, and 1993 Survey of Income and Program Participation (SIPP). These surveys provide large nationally representative samples that include standard labor force participation, demographic, and human capital variables. The fourth wave topical modules collect information on the number of cars present in a household and,

---

19. Massey and Denton (1993).

20. This can be seen by comparing values of the black-nonblack and Latino–non-Latino dissimilarity indexes for metropolitan areas with large Latino populations. The dissimilarity index measures the proportion of either of the populations being characterized that would have to move to yield a perfectly integrated metropolitan area. The black-nonblack and Latino–non-Latino dissimilarity indexes in 1990 were 86 and 66 for Chicago, 66 and 53 for Los Angeles, 74 and 56 for Miami, 71 and 54 for New York, and 61 and 45 for San Francisco. Frey and Farley (1996).

21. In all models, we define exclusive racial/ethnic categories—that is, non-Latino black, non-Latino white, and Latino.

for up to three cars per households, the person identifiers of the owners of each automobile.

We use these data to construct three measures of automobile access. The first uses the person numbers attached to the autos of each household to explicitly identify individuals that own a car. The survey provides person numbers for up to two owners. Hence in a household with two adults and one car in which both adults self-identify as being the owner, both adults are coded as owning a car. Our second measure is another binary indicator that is coded to one if anyone in the household owns a car. The final measure accounts for differences in household size. Specifically, we calculate the ratio of the number of cars present in a household to the number of working-age adults per household (18 to 65).

We restrict the sample to civilians, 18 to 65 years of age, with no work-preventing disabilities. We also restrict the sample to whites, blacks, and Latinos. For models using the indicator of individual car ownership, we further restrict the sample to individuals in households with three or fewer cars present. This restriction is needed for this variable only since the survey collects information on person numbers for up to three cars maximum. This additional restriction eliminates 6 percent of the observations.

Table 1 presents mean auto accessibility rates for whites, blacks, and Latinos calculated from the combined 1991, 1992, and 1993 SIPP samples.[22] For each of the three measures of auto access, the table presents figures for the three racial/ethnic groups overall and stratified by educational attainment and age. There are large and statistically significant differences in car access rates, regardless of how they are defined. For the indicator of individual car ownership, 76 percent of whites own cars, compared with 49 percent of blacks and 50 percent of Latinos. The household level measure of auto access indicates smaller yet significant and substantial differentials. There is an approximate 20 percentage point difference between the percent of white and black households that own at least one car and a 15 percentage point difference between white and Latino households. The largest differences are observed for the

22. Each wave of the SIPP provides longitudinal monthly labor market, demographic, and program participation information for four months. During the early 1990s, each complete panel provides monthly longitudinal data for slightly more than two years. Since we use the fourth waves of each panel, the data correspond to the year following the start date of the samples. Hence, the data from the 1991 panel correspond to 1992, the 1992 panel to 1993, and the 1993 panel to 1994. For each survey, we use labor market information as of the thirteenth month of the panel. The topical module information on auto ownership does not correspond to a given month within the wave and hence applies to the entire four-month period corresponding to the fourth wave of the survey.

Table 1. Means of the Alternative Measures of Automobile Access, by Race/Ethnicity, Educational Attainment, and Age, 1992–94[a]

	White	Black	Latino
Panel A: Indicator of individual car ownership			
All	0.756 (0.002)	0.491 (0.006)	0.504 (0.007)
Less than 12 years	0.651 (0.007)	0.342 (0.014)	0.449 (0.011)
12 years	0.742 (0.003)	0.470 (0.010)	0.480 (0.011)
13 to 15 years	0.753 (0.004)	0.520 (0.013)	0.575 (0.015)
16 years	0.798 (0.005)	0.683 (0.020)	0.639 (0.027)
More than 16 years	0.853 (0.005)	0.751 (0.023)	0.722 (0.031)
18–25	0.498 (0.005)	0.163 (0.010)	0.275 (0.012)
26–35	0.789 (0.004)	0.547 (0.012)	0.584 (0.011)
36–45	0.836 (0.003)	0.598 (0.013)	0.581 (0.014)
46–55	0.825 (0.004)	0.649 (0.016)	0.603 (0.019)
56–65	0.817 (0.005)	0.648 (0.020)	0.520 (0.025)
Panel B: Indicator of the presence of a car in the household			
All	0.951 (0.001)	0.749 (0.006)	0.803 (0.005)
Less than 12 years	0.906 (0.004)	0.563 (0.015)	0.771 (0.009)
12 years	0.956 (0.001)	0.746 (0.009)	0.793 (0.009)
13 to 15 years	0.961 (0.002)	0.808 (0.010)	0.841 (0.011)
16 years	0.953 (0.002)	0.907 (0.012)	0.823 (0.014)
More than 16 years	0.952 (0.003)	0.897 (0.016)	0.862 (0.023)
18–25	0.940 (0.002)	0.663 (0.013)	0.785 (0.011)
26–35	0.951 (0.002)	0.772 (0.010)	0.824 (0.009)
36–45	0.952 (0.002)	0.766 (0.011)	0.788 (0.011)
46–55	0.962 (0.002)	0.782 (0.014)	0.833 (0.014)
56–65	0.954 (0.003)	0.809 (0.016)	0.761 (0.021)
Panel C: Cars per adult household member			
All	1.135 (0.003)	0.671 (0.007)	0.725 (0.008)
Less than 12 years	1.052 (0.011)	0.438 (0.015)	0.620 (0.012)
12 years	1.146 (0.006)	0.648 (0.011)	0.692 (0.013)
13 to 15 years	1.153 (0.007)	0.747 (0.014)	0.867 (0.017)
16 years	1.110 (0.008)	0.880 (0.021)	0.965 (0.029)
More than 16 years	1.160 (0.010)	0.967 (0.028)	1.021 (0.047)
18–25	1.042 (0.009)	0.486 (0.014)	0.629 (0.015)
26–35	1.080 (0.006)	0.737 (0.014)	0.749 (0.012)
36–45	1.178 (0.007)	0.677 (0.013)	0.730 (0.017)
46–55	1.211 (0.009)	0.741 (0.019)	0.844 (0.024)
56–65	1.230 (0.010)	0.813 (0.026)	0.739 (0.028)

a. Standard errors are in parentheses. The sample combines the fourth waves of the 1991, 1992, and 1993 Survey of Income and Program Participation.

ratio of automobiles to adult household members. Here, there is a mean white-black difference of 0.46 and a white-Latino difference of 0.41.

The patterns within educational and age groups are comparable, although the largest differences are evident among the young and relatively less educated. For example, the black-white difference in the mean of the indicator of individual car ownership is over 0.30 for high school dropouts and 0.10 for those with more than sixteen years of school. The black-white difference in this variable for individuals 18 to 25 years of age is approximately 0.34, while the difference for those 56 to 65 is 0.17.

To the extent that owning a car has real employment effects, the large differences evident in table 1 indicate that closing these gaps may narrow inter-racial employment differentials. In the remainder of this section, we first discuss estimates of the double-difference car effects based on equations 4 through 6 above using the entire sample. Next, we assess whether the relative importance of auto access in determining minority employment rates varies by observable measures of human capital such as age and educational attainment. Finally, as a robustness check, we present estimates of the importance of automobile access using instrumental variables as an alternative identification strategy.

Double-Difference Estimates Using the Entire Sample

Table 2 presents the employment rate tabulations needed to calculate the unadjusted double-difference estimates. The table provides employment rates for whites, blacks, and Latinos overall and by car access status. Panel A presents results using the indicator of individual car ownership, panel B presents comparable results for the household car variable, while panel C makes use of the ratio of cars to adult household members. Since this latter variable is not dichotomous, for the purposes of this table we split the sample into those respondents with values of the ratio that are above and below the median value.

Starting with the overall employment rates in the first row of each panel, blacks and Latinos have considerably lower employment rates than do whites.[23] The white employment rate exceeds the black and Latino employment rates by 9.5 and 11 percentage points, respectively. For individuals with cars, these differences are nonexistent or much smaller. In panels A and C, black car owners have higher employment rates than white car owners, while for the household car variable, the comparable differential is only 3 percentage points. This pattern is striking given that black car owners are, on average,

23. The overall employment rates differ slightly between panel A and panels B and C owing to the additional restriction needed to compute this measure of auto accessibility.

Table 2. Employment Rates by Race/Ethnicity and Car-Ownership Status and the Unadjusted Double-Difference Estimates

Item	White	Black	Latino	$\Delta^2_{Black\text{-}White}$	$\Delta^2_{Black\text{-}Latino}$	$\Delta^2_{Latino\text{-}White}$
Panel A: Indicator of individual car ownership						
All	0.763 (0.002)	0.668 (0.006)	0.653 (0.006)	—	—	—
With car	0.803 (0.005)	0.827 (0.007)	0.773 (0.007)	—	—	—
Without car	0.623 (0.005)	0.493 (0.007)	0.503 (0.010)	—	—	—
Difference	0.179 (0.005)	0.334 (0.011)	0.270 (0.012)	0.155 (0.012)	0.065 (0.017)	0.091 (0.012)
Panel B: Indicator of the presence of a car in the household						
All	0.764 (0.002)	0.672 (0.006)	0.658 (0.006)	—	—	—
With car	0.771 (0.009)	0.741 (0.006)	0.698 (0.007)	—	—	—
Without car	0.641 (0.009)	0.468 (0.013)	0.476 (0.007)	—	—	—
Difference	0.130 (0.008)	0.273 (0.013)	0.222 (0.016)	0.143 (0.015)	0.051 (0.021)	0.092 (0.017)
Panel C: Cars per adult household member						
All	0.764 (0.002)	0.672 (0.002)	0.658 (0.006)	—	—	—
Above median*	0.785 (0.002)	0.807 (0.008)	0.752 (0.009)	—	—	—
Below median**	0.702 (0.004)	0.573 (0.008)	0.593 (0.008)	—	—	—
Difference	0.083 (0.004)	0.234 (0.012)	0.159 (0.012)	0.151 (0.012)	0.075 (0.017)	0.076 (0.012)

Source: The data come from combining the fourth waves of the 1991, 1992, and 1993 Survey of Income and Program Participation. Standard errors are in parentheses.
* Indicates observations with values of cars per adult household members that are above the sample median for this variable.
** Indicates observations with values of cars per adult household members that are below the sample median for this variable.

slightly less educated than white car owners (see appendix table A-1). The white-Latino employment rate differentials among car owners are also considerably narrower than the overall difference, ranging from 3 to 7 percentage points. In contrast, the employment rate differentials among workers without cars are pronounced. For this group, white employment rates exceed black employment rates by 13 to 17 percentage points and Latino employment rates by 11 to 16 percentage points.

These patterns translate into larger car-employment effects for blacks and Latinos than for whites. In the bottom row of each panel, the first three figures present unadjusted, group-specific estimates of the car-employment effect. For the individual car ownership variable, the percentage point differences in employment rates between those with and without cars are 18 for whites, 33 for blacks, and 27 for Latinos. For the household variable in panel B, the comparable figures are 13, 27, and 22, while the similar differences for the cars-per-adult ratio results in panel C are 8, 23, and 16. Recall, the spatial mismatch hypothesis predicts that the effect of car access should be largest for those workers who are most isolated from employment opportunities. If segregation from whites proxies for such spatial isolation, the patterns evident in table 2 for each of the auto access measures confirm this prediction.

To test whether the relative differences in the car-employment effects are significant, the last three columns of table 2 present calculations of three unadjusted double-difference estimates. The first subtracts the white car effect from the black car effect, the second subtracts the Latino car effect from the black car effect, while the final estimate subtracts the white car effect from the Latino car effect. All nine double-difference estimates are positive and significant at the 1 percent level. Hence, for all measures of auto access, the car-employment effect for blacks is larger and statistically distinguishable from that for Latinos and whites, while the effect for Latinos is larger and statistically distinguishable from that for whites.

To be sure, the estimates in table 2 do not adjust for differences in skills and other characteristics that affect labor market outcomes and that may differ inter-racially and between those with and without cars. Appendix table A-1 presents average values for several variables for the sample stratified by race-ethnicity and by the individual car ownership variable. The patterns in table A-1 indicate that the car owner–non-car-owner differences in observable variables such as education and age are comparable for whites, blacks, and Latinos. This pattern is reassuring and suggests that our identifying assumption is reasonable. Nonetheless, there are slight differences across groups.

Table 3. Regression-Adjusted Double-Difference Estimates of the Effects of Car Ownership on Minority Employment Prospects[a]

	$\Delta^2_{Black\text{-}White}$	$\Delta^2_{Black\text{-}Latino}$	$\Delta^2_{Latino\text{-}White}$
Panel A: Indicator of individual car ownership			
Specification 1	0.155 (0.012) ***	0.065 (0.017) ***	0.091 (0.012) ***
Specification 2	0.155 (0.012) ***	0.059 (0.016) ***	0.085 (0.012) ***
Specification 3	0.102 (0.013) ***	0.035 (0.019) *	0.067 (0.013) ***
Panel B: Indicator of the presence of a car in the household			
Specification 1	0.143 (0.015) ***	0.051 (0.021) ***	0.092 (0.016) ***
Specification 2	0.125 (0.014) ***	0.033 (0.019) *	0.081 (0.016) ***
Specification 3	0.094 (0.015) ***	0.032 (0.020)	0.044 (0.017) ***
Panel C: Cars per adult household member			
Specification 1	0.146 (0.009) ***	0.041 (0.013) ***	0.105 (0.009) ***
Specification 2	0.120 (0.008) ***	0.047 (0.012) ***	0.067 (0.008) ***
Specification 3	0.092 (0.009) ***	0.041 (0.014) ***	0.050 (0.009) ***

* Significant at the 10 percent level of confidence.
** Significant at the 5 percent level of confidence.
*** Significant at the 1 percent level of confidence.
a. Standard errors are in parentheses. Specification 1 includes a dummy variable for black (or Latino in the white/Latino comparisons), the auto access variable, and an interaction term between the access variable and the minority variable. Specification 2 adds to specification 1 controls for gender, marital status, school enrollment, whether an infant is present in the household, dummies for five educational categories, dummies for nine age categories, a complete set of interaction between the age and education dummies, and 135 state-year dummy variables. Specification 3 interacts the black (Latino) dummy variable with all of the explanatory variables including the 135 state-year dummy variables.

Moreover, the marginal effects of each of these variables on the likelihood of being employed may vary across racial and ethnic groups.

To account for these possibilities, table 3 presents adjusted double-difference estimates based on equations 4 through 6.[24] The table presents three panels of results corresponding to the three measures of auto access. The three columns of figures consecutively present the black-white, black-Latino, and Latino-white double-difference estimates using three model specifications. Specification 1 only includes a dummy variable for race (or ethnicity), car ownership, and an interaction between the two. These estimates are equal to the unadjusted double-differences presented in table 2.[25] Specification 2 adds controls for gender, marital and school enrollment status, whether an infant is present, dummy variables for the five educational attainment categories listed in appendix table A-1, a set of dummies for the nine age categories

24. Each figure in the table is a double-difference estimate from a separately estimated model. The figures are the coefficients on the interaction term between race and the car-ownership variable as illustrated in equations 5 and 6.

25. For the cars-to-adults measure, the unadjusted figures in table 3 deviate from those presented in table 2, because for these models we do not dichotomize this variable.

listed in this table, and a complete set of interactions between the educational and age dummies. The model also includes 135 dummy variables for state-years, hence adjusting for differences in state economic conditions that might affect employment probabilities.[26] Specification 3 fully interacts race (or ethnicity in the Latino-white models) with all of the explanatory variables, including the 135 state dummies. This latter specification is equivalent to estimating separate models by race and calculating the double-difference estimate from the difference in the race-specific coefficients on auto access.

For the black-white comparison, adding the variables in specification 2 does not appreciably affect the double-difference estimates. For models using the individual car ownership variable, the double-difference estimate from specification 2 is exactly equal to the unadjusted estimate. For the other two variables, adding the controls of specification 2 reduces the double-difference estimates slightly. Adding interactions between black and all of the explanatory variables (specification 3) yields larger declines in the double-difference estimates. The relative car effects decline to 0.102, 0.094, and 0.092 for the models using the individual car owner, household car, and cars-per-adult-household-member variables, respectively. Nonetheless, these effects are still two-thirds the size of the unadjusted estimates and are significant at the 1 percent level of confidence.[27]

The results for the black-Latino and Latino-white double-difference estimates are comparable. The adjusted estimates from specifications 2 and 3 are slightly less than the corresponding unadjusted double-difference estimates. For the Latino-white comparisons, all differences are statistically significant at the 1 percent level. For the black-Latino comparisons, the significance level varies across the three auto access measures, though in general these effects are statistically significant at either the 1 or 10 percent level of confidence. Hence, as with the unadjusted estimates, the regression-adjusted employment effect of autos for blacks is larger and statistically distinguishable from the comparable effects for whites and Latinos, as are the differences between Latinos and whites.

The results in table 3 combined with the figures on car-ownership rates in table 1 and the overall employment rate differences in table 2 can be used to

---

26. For each year of the SIPP, we created 45 state dummy variables, giving us 135 in all. We cannot create dummy variables for the full fifty states because the SIPP aggregates some states with small populations into larger groups.

27. Note the regressions using specification (3) include more than 300 control variables.

characterize the importance of racial and ethnic differences in auto access rates in explaining employment rate differentials. We start by making the conservative assumption that the entire base car effect (the effect for whites in each model) captures unobserved skill differentials between car owners and non-car-owners (and by extension, that there is no employment effect of car ownership for whites). Under this assumption, the differential effects for blacks and Latinos present estimates of the impact of car ownership on the probability of being employed for members of these groups. Hence, multiplying the difference in car ownership rates between blacks and whites by the differential effect of car ownership provides a lower bound estimate of the effect on black employment rates of eliminating the racial gap in car-ownership rates.

The figures in table 2 indicate a black-white employment rate differential of 9 to 9.5 percentage points and a Latino-white differential of 11 percentage points. For the most detailed specification of the models using the individual car-ownership variable, the double-difference estimate suggests that gaining access to a car increases black employment probabilities by 0.102. Multiplying this figure by the black-white mean difference in this auto access variable (which is calculated from the figures presented in table 1) indicates that raising the black auto ownership rate to the level of whites would increase the black employment rate by 0.027. This corresponds to a 28 percent reduction in the black-white employment rate differential. Similar calculations for the household auto variable (again, using the smallest estimates of the double-difference from specification 3) indicates that closing the racial gap in this variable would increase the black employment rate by 0.019. This corresponds to a 21 percent reduction in the black-white employment rate differential. The results from the cars-per-adults model yields the largest predictions. Specifically, the double-difference estimate from specification 3 of this variable suggests that closing the black-white gap in this auto access measure would increase the black employment rate by 0.043. This accounts for 43 percent of the black-white employment rate differential.

Similar calculations using the Latino-white double-difference estimates suggest that closing the gaps in auto ownership rate between Latinos and whites would have much smaller effects on the Latino-white employment rate gap. Estimates of the proportion of this employment rate gap attributable to differences in auto access range from 6 percent based on the model using the household auto variable to 19 percent based on the model using the cars-per-adults measure.

Heterogeneity in the Relative Car Effects

The results presented above indicate that, on average, having access to a car has disproportionately large effects on the employment rates of minorities, with the largest effects on African Americans. Here, we explore whether these relative car effects vary by age and educational attainment. There are several reasons to suspect that the employment effects of auto access may be heterogeneous. The employment prospects of low-skilled and young workers would be more sensitive to automobile access if such workers rely heavily on informal search methods such as looking for help wanted signs and submitting unsolicited applications. Moreover, since employment opportunities in central cities tend to be skewed toward the skilled, the car effects for low-skilled minority workers may be particularly large since these workers may be best matched to suburban job markets.[28]

To test for heterogeneity in the relative car effects, we define four educational attainment categories (high school dropout, high school graduate, some college, and college graduate) and four age categories (18 to 31, 31 to 40, 41 to 50, and 51 to 65). We then use these categories to stratify the sample into sixteen age-educational subsamples. For each subsample, we separately estimate linear employment probability models comparable to equation 5. The specification for each regression includes dummies for race, auto access, and the interaction between the two, linear age and educational attainment variables (when possible) and the interaction between these two variables and race, controls for gender, marital status, school enrollment, whether an infant is present, and the 135 state-year dummy variables. The coefficient on the interaction term between race and auto access provides the subsample estimates of the double-difference car effect.

Table 4 presents results for the black-white double differences. The table presents separate results for each auto access measure. The clearest pattern is the relationship between the double-difference estimates and age. With few exceptions, the differential impact of owning a car on black employment rates (relative to that for whites) is small and statistically insignificant for workers over 40 years of age. For individuals 40 and under, the relative car effects for blacks are generally positive and significant.

28. Kasarda (1985, 1989) documents the change in the composition of central city employment bases over the first thirty or so years of the postwar period. This research shows general declines in central city employment in industries that employ low- and semi-skilled workers and increases in employment in industries employing relatively high-skilled workers. More recent evidence on continuing decentralization of employment is presented in Glaeser and Kahn in this volume.

The patterns across education groups vary across the alternative measures of auto access. For the indicator of individual auto ownership, the relative effects are largest for high school graduates and workers with some college education. The relative ordering of these effects, however, differs across age categories. For the models using the indicator of a household automobile, only three of the estimates are significant at the 1 percent level, two for the youngest workers with some college education and the point estimate for college graduates that are 31 to 40 years of age. The results using the cars-per-adult measure indicate a more uniform relationship with education. For workers with a high school education or greater, the relative car effects roughly decline with educational attainment. For high school graduates, there are positive relative effects for all age groups that decline with age. The double-difference estimates are generally positive for high-school dropouts and significant for the two middle-age categories. In summary, the results in table 4 indicate that the black-white double-difference estimates are largest for young workers and workers with educational attainment levels that are less than a college degree.

We also estimated comparable double-difference models for the Latino-white comparisons. These results are presented in appendix table A-2. There are few consistent patterns. When positive, the double-difference estimates are generally smaller than the comparable black-white estimates.

Race-Specific Car-Employment Effects Using Instrumental Variables

The identification strategy employed thus far relies on the assumption that the unobserved skill differentials between car owners and non-car-owners are similar across racial groups. Under this assumption, the double-difference car effect for blacks is purged of the effect of omitted variables. In the discussion of the problems associated with OLS, we noted that besides omitted-variables bias, the simultaneous determination of employment and auto access is likely to bias OLS estimates upward. If this bias is comparable in magnitude across racial groups, the differencing strategy will also eliminate this problem. However, there is little reason, a priori, to believe that this is so. The simultaneity bias is a complicated function of the group-specific car-employment effect, the effect of employment on car ownership, the variance in car ownership, and the variance of the residual from the structural employment equation.[29] Since the evidence thus far suggests that several of these

29. See note 18.

Table 4. Regression-Adjusted Double-Difference Estimates of the Black-White Relative Employment Effect of Auto Access by Age-Education Categories[a]

	High school dropout	High school graduate	Some college	College graduate
Panel A: Indicator of individual car ownership				
18–30 years old	0.073 (0.079)	0.129 (0.035) ***	0.119 (0.041) ***	0.066 (0.050)
31–40 years old	0.158 (0.075) **	0.079 (0.032) ***	0.247 (0.040) ***	0.121 (0.047)***
41–50 years old	0.013 (0.074)	0.024 (0.040)	0.078 (0.056)	-0.036 (0.063)
51–65 years old	0.000 (0.064)	0.044 (0.057)	-0.125 (0.111)	0.063 (0.104)
Panel B: Indicator of the presence of a car in the household				
18–30 years old	0.047 (0.061)	0.060 (0.038)	0.125 (0.048) ***	0.014 (0.074)
31–40 years old	0.130 (0.080) *	0.035 (0.040)	0.226 (0.051) ***	0.176 (0.062)***
41–50 years old	-0.033 (0.089)	-0.023 (0.052)	-0.042 (0.071)	-0.037 (0.077)
51–65 years old	0.011 (0.078)	0.084 (0.071)	-0.135 (0.135)	0.095 (0.126)
Panel C: Cars per adult household member				
18–30 years old	0.088 (0.060)	0.182 (0.031) ***	0.108 (0.030) ***	0.159 (0.049)***
31–40 years old	0.089 (0.043) **	0.163 (0.125) ***	0.126 (0.025) ***	0.085 (0.031)***
41–50 years old	0.116 (0.061) **	0.078 (0.031) **	0.047 (0.040)	-0.029 (0.036)
51–65 years old	0.023 (0.032)	0.081 (0.033) **	0.036 (0.043)	-0.028 (0.050)

* Significant at the 10 percent level of confidence.
** Significant at the 5 percent level of confidence.
*** Significant at the 1 percent level of confidence.
a. Standard errors are in parentheses. Separate regressions are estimates for each age-education cell. Each figure is the coefficient on the interaction term between a black dummy variable and the relevant auto access variable from a regression including the auto access variable, the black indicator, the interaction between these variables, linear controls for education and age and interactions of these two variables with the black dummy variable, controls for gender, marital status, school enrollment, whether there is an infant in the household, and 135 state-year dummies.

factors differ by race and ethnicity, the differencing strategy is unlikely to adequately address simultaneity bias.

One estimation strategy that would break the simultaneity between car ownership and employment is to find instruments for auto ownership and re-estimate the race-specific car-employment effects using a 2SLS estimator. Raphael and Rice pursue this strategy using state-year level variation in state gasoline taxes and average automobile insurance premiums.[30] The results from this study indicate that the estimated effects of auto access on employment status and on weekly hours worked using 2SLS are comparable in magnitude to OLS estimates. Here, we make use of these instruments to estimate race-specific 2SLS estimates of the car employment effect in order to assess whether the relative ordering of the car-employment effects remains after accounting for potential simultaneity bias.[31]

30. Raphael and Rice (2000).
31. Raphael and Rice (2000) provide a detailed analysis of the first-stage relationship between automobile ownership, state gas taxes, and average auto insurance premiums. They

Table 5 presents race-specific OLS and two-stage-generalized least squares (2SGLS)[32] estimates of the effect of car access on employment for each of the three measures of auto access. To conserve space, the table only reports the coefficients on the car access variable, the first-stage coefficients for the two instruments, and the results from F-tests of the joint significance of the two instrumental variables in the first-stage regressions.[33] In all models, the OLS estimates of the car-employment effects are smaller than the 2SGLS estimates. However, the standard errors on the car effects in the instrumented estimates are quite large, and the OLS estimates are generally within one standard deviation of the 2SGLS point estimates. For whites, the OLS estimates are significant at the 1 percent level in all three models, while the 2SGLS estimates are significant at the 5 percent level for the indicator of individual car ownership and the car-per-adult variable. The results for whites support the contention that the double-difference estimates are likely to be lower bounds of the car access effects on black employment rates since it implicitly assumes that whites experience no accessibility advantage from owning a car.

For black workers, both the OLS and 2SGLS estimates of the car-employment effects are significant at the 1 percent level for all models. Moreover, both the OLS and instrumented results yield point estimates of the car effects that are larger than those for white workers. Similarly, the OLS and 2SGLS estimates for Latinos are all significant at the 5 percent level.[34]

---

demonstrate strong first-stage correlations between the two instruments and auto ownership rates that are not being driven by outlier states, and that are generally stronger for low-earning potential workers (that is, the negative effects of the instruments on car ownership rates are generally larger for low-skilled workers). The authors also present discussion of the determinants of these instruments and argue that state-level variation in these variables are unlikely to be related to unobservable determinants of employment probabilities.

32. Since the instruments vary between state-years but not within, any correlation within state-years of the residuals from the employment equation will lead to 2SLS estimates of the coefficient standard errors that are biased downward. See Shore-Sheppard (1998). Although this does not affect the consistency of the parameter estimates, this does affect statistical inference. To account for this problem, we estimate a 2SGLS model that allows state-year error components in the second stage. This estimator is discussed in detail in Raphael and Rice (2000) and Shore-Sheppard (1998). The 2SGLS estimates yield standard errors that are larger than the standard errors from ordinary 2SLS.

33. The model specifications are similar to those used above with one exception. Since the instruments vary at the state-year level, we cannot include the 135 state dummy variables in the specification. To account for variation in economic condition across states, we control for the state-level unemployment rate for the year corresponding to the observation. The full details of the model specifications are discussed in the notes to table 5.

34. Concerning the first-stage relationships, the gas tax and insurance costs variables exert negative and individually significant effects at the 1 percent level of confidence in each model. Moreover, the minimum F-statistic for the tests of the joint significance of the instruments in the first stage is 20.

Table 5. Ordinary Least Squares and Two-Stage Generalized Least-Squares Estimates of the Car-Employment Effect, by Race and Ethnicity[a]

	White			Black			Latino		
		2SGLS			2SGLS			2SGLS	
	OLS	Second stage	First stage	OLS	Second stage	First stage	OLS	Second stage	First stage
A. Indicator of Individual Car Ownership									
Car access	0.129 (.005)	0.203 (.109)	–	0.230 (.013)	0.372 (.154)	–	0.199 (.013)	0.392 (.101)	–
Gas taxes	–	–	-0.002 (.0006)	–	–	-0.007 (.001)	–	–	-0.008 (0.001)
Insurance	–	–	-0.0002 (.00002)	–	–	-0.0002 (.00005)	–	–	-0.0003 (.00006)
F statistic*	–	–	44.894 (.0001)	–	–	20.410 (.0001)	–	–	34.808 (.0001)
B. Indicator of the Presence of a car in the household									
Car access	0.107 (.008)	0.322 (.240)	–	0.196 (.013)	0.348 (.147)	–	0.163 (.015)	0.266 (.132)	–
Gas taxes	–	–	-0.001 (.0003)	–	–	-0.008 (.002)	–	–	-0.010 (.001)
Insurance	–	–	-.0006 (.00001)	–	–	-0.0002 (.00005)	–	–	-0.0003 (.00006)
F statistic*	–	–	26.558 (.0001)	–	–	25.920 (.0001)	–	–	32.998 (.0001)
C. Cars per adult household member									
Car access	0.012 (.002)	0.089 (.040)	–	0.105 (.008)	0.203 (.080)	–	0.073 (.010)	0.197 (.095)	–
Gas taxes	–	–	-0.003 (.001)	–	–	-0.013 (.002)	–	–	-0.011 (.003)
Insurance	–	–	-0.0005 (.00004)	–	–	-.0004 (.00007)	–	–	-0.0007 (.0001)
F statistic[b]	–	–	81.182 (.0001)	–	–	39.806 (.0001)	–	–	32.57 (.0001)

a. Standard errors are in parentheses. Both the OLS models and the two stage generalized least-squares models include controls for five education categories, nine age categories, interactions between the age and education categories, gender, marital status, school enrollment, whether there is an infant in the household, and the unemployment rate defined at the state-year level.
b. This row provides results from a test of the joint significance of the instruments in the first-stage regression.

While the 2SGLS results presented in table 5 are measured somewhat imprecisely, the estimates tend to support the results from our differencing strategy presented in tables 2 through 4. We find statistically significant car effects in nearly all of the models after instrumenting. Moreover, the point estimates of these effects indicate that cars matter more for blacks and Latinos than for whites. While the standard errors on these estimates are large, the consistency between these results and those presented in the previous section should, we hope, allay some of the concerns about simultaneity bias.

Cross-City Comparisons of the Relative Importance of Car Access

Our first empirical strategy infers differential spatial isolation by assuming that segregation from whites and being spatially isolated from employment opportunities are synonymous. Based on this indirect inference, we then test for an interaction between the car-employment effect and mismatch by comparing the car effects for groups that differ with respect to their degree of residential segregation from whites. An alternative approach would directly measure the degree of spatial isolation from employment and test for a positive relationship between empirically observed car effects and the direct measure of mismatch. Our second empirical strategy takes this form.

Specifically, for the black-white comparisons only,[35] we estimate the adjusted double-difference car effect (equation 5) separately for 242 U.S. Primary Metropolitan Statistical Areas (PMSAs) using data from the 5 percent Public Use Microdata Sample (PUMS) of the 1990 Census of Population and Housing. We restrict the PUMS sample to civilian black and white observations that are 18 to 65 years of age with no work-preventing disabilities. Unlike the detailed information about household autos in the SIPP, the census only identifies whether someone in the household owns a car. Hence, our estimates of the car effects using the PUMS are based on this measure only.

The model specification used to estimate the PMSA-level measure of the double-difference is shown in appendix table A-3. The table provides regression results using the entire census sample for two model specifications: a basic model with controls for race, auto access, and an interaction term, and a more complete model with a specification very similar to those used in the

---

35. For this strategy we focus on the black-white comparisons only because in many PMSAs, the number of Latino observations is prohibitively small.

analysis of the SIPP data.[36] The results correspond closely to the SIPP results. Access to a car has a much larger effect for blacks than for whites. Moreover, adjusting for observable covariates does not alter the size of the relative car effect. We use the latter specification to estimate separate equations for each of 242 PMSAs. The coefficients on the interaction terms between race and car access from these 242 regressions provide our dependent variable.

Next, we construct several race-specific, PMSA-level measures of spatial isolation from employment opportunities using zip code place-of-work employment data from the 1992 Economic Census and zip code population counts from the 1990 Census Summary Tape Files 3B. We construct two MSA-level indexes by race that measure the imbalance between residential distributions and employment distributions. The first index is a jobs-people dissimilarity index.[37] The dissimilarity index ranges from zero to one and gives the proportion of people (or jobs) that would have to move to yield a perfectly even distribution of persons and jobs across zip codes within the metropolitan area. Hence, higher values indicate poorer spatial accessibility to jobs. For example, our dissimilarity index value between blacks and retail jobs in Chicago is 0.74. This indicates that 74 percent of blacks would have to move (across zip codes) to be spatially distributed in perfect proportion with the spatial distribution of retail employment.[38]

The second index is a jobs-people measure of exposure to employment opportunities. The exposure index measures the number of jobs per 100 zip code residents in the zip code of the average black (or white) resident of the PMSA.[39] The index is a weighted average (multiplied by 100) of the zip code level jobs-to-population ratios using the number of blacks in each zip code (or

36. Two minor differences in the PUMS specifications are that we do not control for the presence of an infant and that we add an indicator variable for work-limiting disabilities.

37. Define *Black$_i$* as the black population residing in zip code *i*, *Employment$_i$* as the number of jobs located in zip code *i*, *Black* as the total black population in the metropolitan area, and *Employment* as the total number of jobs in the metropolitan area. The dissimilarity score between blacks and jobs is given by $D = \frac{1}{2}\Sigma|Black_i / Black - Employment_i / Employment|$, where the summation is over all zip codes in the PMSA.

38. Martin (forthcoming) constructs a similar index for thirty-nine PMSAs using county-level data. The author finds that job decentralization between 1970 and 1990 increased the dissimilarity between blacks and jobs while the residential mobility of black households decreased dissimilarity. The net effects of these offsetting employment and population changes were increases in the spatial isolation of black households from employment over the time period studied.

39. Using the variable definitions in note 37 above, the employment exposure index is calculated using the equation $E = 100*\Sigma(Black_i/Black) * (Employment_i/Population_i)$. We thank Ken Small for suggesting this alternative index.

Table 6. Means of the Spatial Mismatch Indices Measuring Segregation between Population and Employment Opportunities for Metropolitan Areas Identified in the 1990 PUMS[a]

Item	Blacks/jobs indexes	Whites/jobs indexes	Difference (black-white)
	Retail employment dissimilarity indexes		
Levels, 1992	0.59 (0.007)	0.31 (0.003)	0.28 (0.008)
Net growth, 1987–92	0.81 (0.006)	0.63 (0.006)	0.18 (0.005)
	Retail employment exposure indexes		
Levels, 1992	5.86 (0.12)	7.65 (0.06)	-1.79 (0.11)
Net Growth, 1987–92	0.50 (0.03)	0.98 (0.03)	-0.47 (0.02)

a. Standard errors are in parentheses. Each figure is the mean for the 242 PMSAs for which we were able to estimate indexes. The figures are weighted by the number of black observations observed in each PMSA. The levels indexes are calculated using zip-code level information on the number of jobs located in the zip code in 1992 and the number of people of the relevant race residing in the zip code in 1990. The net growth indexes use net job growth between 1987 and 1992, setting growth to zero for zip codes that lose employment over this time period. Information on population by zip code comes from the 1990 Census of Population and Housing Summary Tape Files 3B. Information on job counts by zip codes comes from the Economic Census for 1987 and 1992.

whites) as the weights. Here, lower values indicate poorer accessibility. Again, using Chicago as an example, the value of our retail exposure index for blacks is 4.07. Hence, in the zip code of the average black resident of Chicago there are approximately 4 retail jobs per 100 residents.

We construct these two indexes separately for blacks and whites using two alternative measures of employment opportunities: the 1992 levels of retail employment and the number of new retail jobs added between 1987 and 1992.[40] Table 6 presents weighted averages of our race-specific jobs-people mismatch indexes for 242 PMSAs.[41] All four measures indicate that blacks are more segregated from employment opportunities than are whites. Moreover, the differences in accessibility are highly significant. Comparisons of individual cities indicate that, for the most part, the jobs-people dissimilarity indexes are uniformly higher for blacks than they are for whites, while the jobs-people

40. We set net new jobs to zero in zip codes experiencing net employment losses. This tends to overstate the economic health of predominantly black zip codes, since blacks are more likely to reside in zip codes with net job loss than are whites. In results not reported here, we also constructed comparable indexes using service employment in 1992 and new service industry jobs added between 1987 and 1992. The results are qualitatively similar to those presented below. In fact, all of these measures of mismatch are highly correlated with one another.

41. We cannot calculate indexes for the full 272 PMSAs identified in the PUMS owing to differences in geography between the Economic Census and Census of Population and Housing. The thirty metropolitan areas that we are missing are generally small with relatively small black populations. The figures presented in table 6 are weighted by the black populations of the MSAs. Hence, these figures indicate the isolation from employment experienced by blacks and white in the PMSA of the average black resident in these 242 PMSAs.

exposure indexes are uniformly lower for blacks relative to whites. Appendix table A-4 presents such comparisons for the twenty metropolitan areas with the largest black populations in 1990 (accounting for roughly 60 percent of the black metropolitan population in this year). In all comparisons, blacks have poorer spatial accessibility to employment opportunities than whites.

For each of the four mismatch measures, we subtract the white-jobs index from the black-jobs index to arrive at a PMSA-level measure of the isolation of blacks *relative* to the spatial isolation of whites. *This is our key explanatory variable*. If mismatch is important, and if having a car partially undoes the consequences of mismatch, then the relative employment effect of car access for blacks should be largest in those PMSAs where blacks are most isolated (relative to whites) from employment opportunities.

Our principal empirical test entails bivariate regressions of the PMSA-level double-differences on the black-white differences in the four mismatch indexes. Figures 2 and 3 present the results from these bivariate regressions. Figures 2A and 2B present scatter plots of the double-difference car effects against the black-white differences in the retail employment level and the retail employment growth dissimilarity indexes, respectively. Figures 3A and 3B provide similar scatter plots using the black-white differences in the retail level and retail growth employment exposure indexes. In each figure we include the regression line as well as the coefficient estimates and R^2 from a weighted regression of the double-difference car effects on the differences in the isolation indexes.[42] We weight each regression by the number of black observations for the PMSA used to compute the double-difference estimate.[43] The relative weight placed on each observation is indicated by the size of the bubble in the scatter plot.

Before discussing the regression results, we should highlight a few notable aspects of the distributions of the explanatory and dependent variables that are revealed in the scatter plots. First, in figures 2A and 2B the mass of the distribution of observations lies to the right of the vertical axis, while in figures 3A and 3B the mass of the distribution of observation lies to the left of the vertical axis. Since higher values of the dissimilarity index and lower values of the exposure index indicate greater spatial isolation from employment opportunities, the patterns in the black-white differences in the indexes indicate that in nearly all metropolitan areas (with the exception of a handful) blacks

42. We also ran regressions of the double-difference car effect on the ratio of the black-to-white jobs/people indexes. This specification yields nearly identical results.

43. We also estimated the models in figures 2 and 3 without weighting. This uniformly leads to larger and more statistically significant coefficient estimates.

Figure 2. Scatter Plots of the Double-Difference Car Effects Against Black-White Differences in the Retail Dissimilarity Indexes

Part A. Using the retail employment dissimilarity index

Double-difference car effect

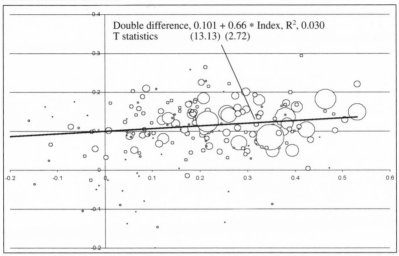

Double difference, 0.101 + 0.66 * Index, R^2, 0.030
T statistics (13.13) (2.72)

Black-white difference in retail employment dissimilarity index

Part B. Using the retail employment growth dissimilarity index

Double-difference car effect

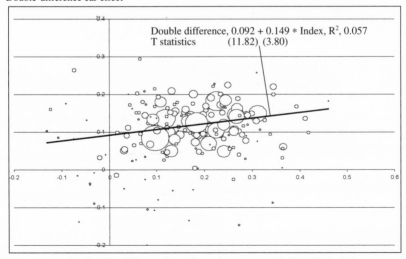

Double difference, 0.092 + 0.149 * Index, R^2, 0.057
T statistics (11.82) (3.80)

Black-white difference in retail employment growth dissimilarity index

Figure 3. Scatter Plots of the Double-Difference Car Effects Against Black-White Differences in the Retail Exposure Indexes

Part A. Using the retail employment exposure index

Double-difference car effect

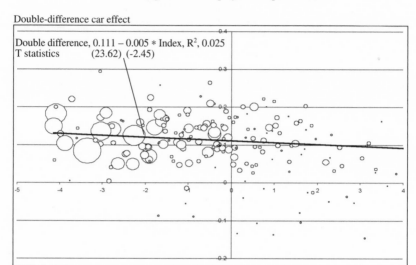

Black-white difference in retail exposure index

Part B. Using the retail employment growth exposure index

Double-difference car effect

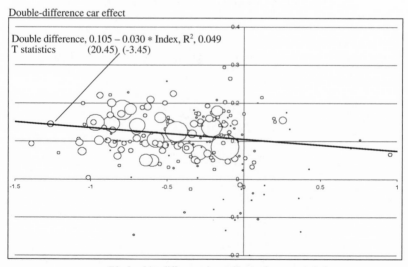

Black-white difference in retail growth exposure index

have poorer spatial accessibility to employment than do whites. Moreover, for those areas where the reverse is true (leading to negative black-white differences in the dissimilarity indexes and positive black-white differences in the exposure indexes) black populations are quite small (as is evident from the small bubbles). Hence, figures 2 and 3 demonstrate the nearly uniform inferior access of blacks to employment opportunities.

For the distribution of the dependent variable, the mass of observations lies above the horizontal axis. This indicates that in all but a few metropolitan areas, the effect of car ownership on the employment rates of blacks exceeds the comparable effects for whites. Moreover, the size of the bubble plots where the reverse is true (white car effects are larger than black car effects, yielding adjusted double differences that lie below the horizontal axis) is generally small. These results complement the findings of the SIPP analysis by showing that fully interacting the model with geography does not eliminate the relatively greater importance of auto access in determining black employment rates.

In figures 2A and 2B there are clear positive relationships between the PMSA-level relative car effects and the relative isolation of blacks from retail employment opportunities. The coefficient on the difference in dissimilarity indexes is positive and significant for both the retail levels difference (p value of 0.007) and the retail growth difference (p value of 0.000). In figures 3A and 3B we observe statistically significant negative relationships between the relative car effects and differences in the retail employment level exposure index ($p = 0.015$) and the retail employment growth index ($p = 0.001$). Hence, these bivariate relationships indicate a statistically significant relationship between the relatively large car-employment effects for blacks and the degree of relative spatial isolation from employment opportunities.

One might argue that the bivariate regressions presented in figures 2 and 3 do not control for possible selection across metropolitan areas along personal and human capital characteristics that may be driving these significant relationships. However, the double-differences used as the dependent variable are already purged of the effect of educational attainment, age, and the other covariates listed in appendix table A-3. Moreover, since our dependent variable measures the *differential* car effect for blacks after eliminating the base car effect for whites, any inter-PMSA sorting that is also occurring among white workers is netted out of the inter-PMSA variation in our dependent variable. Furthermore, since the regressions used to generate the dependent variable are estimated separately for each metropolitan area, the relative car effect estimates have also been purged of any cross-PMSA variation in the returns (in terms of the marginal effects on employment probabilities) to observable covariates.

Nonetheless, there still may be omitted metropolitan area characteristics that coincide with racial differences in spatial isolation from employment. For example, the quality of public transit may vary from area to area, or the total area covered by the PMSA may vary. Although we do not have extensive controls for PMSA characteristics, we do have a few measures that we add to the specifications of the models in figures 2 and 3. Table 7 presents weighted regression results in which the dependent variable is the PMSA-level adjusted double difference. For each segregation index we estimate two specifications: the first controlling for the racial difference in segregation scores only, and the second adding the proportion of PMSA workers that commute by private auto (calculated from our 5 percent PUMS sample), the total land area, a variable measuring the average population density,[44] and dummies for PMSA population quartiles. The first eight models present separate regressions for the four segregation indexes, while the final two models control for all of the differences in segregation scores in the same specification.

For the two indexes based on retail employment levels, adding these additional variables increases the point estimates and statistical significance of the effect of relative black spatial isolation. For the models using differences in segregation scores based on retail employment growth, adding these variables causes slight reductions, though the effects are still statistically significant and have the proper sign. Hence, the bivariate results survive adding additional covariates to the models. Controlling for all four dissimilarity scores at the same time yields rather imprecise point estimates. Nonetheless, F-tests of the joint significance of all four measures fail to reject the hypothesis that all of the coefficients are zero.

In summary, the results in figures 2 and 3 and table 7 strongly confirm the proposition that the relative importance of auto access on the employment prospects of blacks is more important in metropolitan areas where blacks are more spatially isolated from employment opportunities than are whites. Moreover, the positive effect of relative isolation on the relative car-employment effect survives additional controls for metropolitan area characteristics.

---

44. The variable measuring average population density was downloaded from the web page created by Cutler, Glaeser, and Vigdor (www. nber.org/data/segregation.html), which contains the data analyzed in Cutler, Glaeser, and Vigdor (1999).

Table 7. Regression of the Adjusted Double-Difference Car Effect on the Black-White Differences in the Dissimilarity and Exposure Indexes Measuring Segregation between Population and Employment Opportunities[a]

	1	2	3	4	5	6	7	8	9	10
Retail dissimilarity indexes										
Black-white difference in 1992 levels	0.066 (0.024)	0.079 (0.027)	–	–	–	–	–	–	0.016 (0.040)	0.016 (0.042)
Black-white difference in 1987–92 net growth	–	–	0.149 (0.039)	0.092 (0.042)	–	–	–	–	0.087 (0.054)	0.015 (0.057)
Retail exposure indexes										
Black-white difference in 1992 levels	–	–	–	–	-0.005 (0.002)	-0.008 (0.002)	–	–	-0.002 (0.003)	-0.005 (0.003)
Black-white difference in 1987–92 net growth	–	–	–	–	–	–	-0.030 (0.009)	-0.019 (0.009)	-0.014 (0.011)	-0.004 (0.011)
Proportion commuting to work by private auto	–	-0.049 (0.089)	–	-0.045 (0.089)	–	-0.023 (0.087)	–	-0.024 (0.089)	–	-0.031 (0.089)
Land area[b]	–	0.003 (0.013)	–	-0.002 (0.013)	–	-0.002 (0.013)	–	-0.002 (0.013)	–	-0.001 (0.013)
Population density[c]	–	-0.004 (0.002)	–	-0.003 (0.002)	–	-0.004 (0.002)	–	-0.002 (0.002)	–	-0.003 (0.002)
R^2	0.030	0.119	0.057	0.106	0.025	0.133	0.049	0.106	0.071	0.135
F statistic[d]	–	–	–	–	–	–	–	–	4.555	3.115
(P value)	–	–	–	–	–	–	–	–	(0.002)	(0.016)
N	242	242	242	242	242	242	242	242	242	242

a. Standard errors are in parentheses. All regressions include a constant and a set of dummy variables for MSA population quartiles. The regressions are weighted by the number of black observations used to calculate the double difference.

b. Land area is measured in tens of thousands of acres.

c. This variable gives the number of people per square kilometer in thousands.

d. This row presents the test-statistics and p-values from a test of the joint significance of the four segregation indexes.

Conclusion

The results of this paper show that having access to a car has disproportionately large effects on the employment rates of workers that are spatially
isolated from employment opportunities. We find the largest car-employment
effects for the most segregated minority populations. Moreover, we find strong
evidence that the difference between the black and white car-employment
effect is greatest in metropolitan areas where the relative isolation of blacks
from employment opportunities is most severe. Given the large differences in
car-ownership rates that we document, these results indicate that lack of access
to transportation plays a large role in explaining black-white, and to a lesser
degree Latino-white, differences in employment rates. By extension, these
results also suggest that increasing car access may be an effective policy tool
for narrowing these employment gaps.

To be sure, employment policies that increase auto-ownership rates will
also increase the externalities associated with increased private auto work
commutes and nonwork trips. Nearly all metropolitan areas in the United
States suffer from traffic congestion that exceeds the social optimum, given
the challenges associated with optimally pricing road usage. Increasing auto
ownership through a subsidy to operating costs would surely increase traffic congestion. In addition, more autos will certainly translate into more air
pollution.

There are reasons, however, to suspect that increasing auto access for
blacks and Latinos would not add appreciably to congestion and pollution.
Since black and Latino residential distribution is centralized and concentrated,
those who commute to jobs in city centers are unlikely to increase congestion
on inbound freeway routes. Moreover, those who locate employment in the
suburbs will have commutes that are in the reverse direction of the largest
peak-period flows. Katherine M. O'Regan and John M. Quigley have made
a similar point quite decisively in their discussion of the possible congestion
consequences of increasing car-ownership rates among welfare recipients.[45]
Another factor limiting the addition to congestion costs concerns the fact that
many of these individuals work nonstandard schedules and, hence, would be
making private auto commutes at times of the day when the external costs of
an additional trip are low. Finally, even an extreme policy that raises minority car-ownership rates to the level of whites would purchase new autos for a
minority of a minority of the U.S. working-age population. Hence, both the

45. O'Regan and Quigley (1999).

congestion and pollution externalities caused by such policies are likely to be small.

Finally, the results presented here do not provide enough information to compare the relative efficacy (in terms of alleviating inner-city employment problems) of community development initiatives, residential mobility programs, training programs, and policies designed to increase automobile accessibility. Of course, to the extent that all such policies alleviate the spatial imbalance between labor supply and demand, these policy tools may be thought of as complements rather than substitutes, with the effects of one initiative increasing the probability of success of alternatives. Nonetheless, a careful comparative analysis of the marginal benefits per dollar spent may indicate that certain policy options dominate. The strong results presented indicate that transportation policies geared toward fostering greater auto access should most definitely be considered in any comparative benefit-cost analysis of policy initiatives designed to alleviate the spatial concentration of joblessness.

Appendix

Table A-1. Means of Demographic and Human Capital Variables, by Race/Ethnicity and by the Indicator of Individual Car Ownership

	White			Black			Latino		
	Without car	With car	Difference	Without car	With car	Difference	Without car	With car	Difference
Years of schooling									
Less than 12	0.151	0.080	-0.071	0.236	0.140	-0.096	0.411	0.324	-0.086
12	0.383	0.364	-0.019	0.443	0.387	-0.056	0.379	0.347	-0.032
13 to 15	0.270	0.258	-0.012	0.240	0.266	0.026	0.157	0.204	0.047
16	0.122	0.160	0.038	0.053	0.118	0.065	0.035	0.073	0.038
16 +	0.073	0.138	0.064	0.028	0.089	0.061	0.018	0.052	0.033
Mean years of schooling	12.875	13.676	0.801	12.207	13.095	0.889	10.655	11.392	0.738
Age									
18 to 25	0.354	0.113	-0.241	0.302	0.073	-0.228	0.332	0.124	-0.208
26 to 30	0.136	0.139	0.004	0.138	0.132	-0.007	0.162	0.188	0.026
31 to 35	0.111	0.159	0.048	0.148	0.170	0.023	0.118	0.177	0.059
36 to 40	0.083	0.149	0.066	0.110	0.165	0.055	0.097	0.159	0.062
41 to 45	0.070	0.124	0.054	0.075	0.146	0.071	0.068	0.126	0.058
46 to 50	0.051	0.099	0.048	0.058	0.110	0.052	0.056	0.076	0.020
51 to 55	0.040	0.081	0.041	0.036	0.077	0.040	0.040	0.065	0.026
56 to 60	0.036	0.065	0.030	0.032	0.070	0.039	0.029	0.046	0.017
61 to 65	0.040	0.065	0.025	0.027	0.053	0.026	0.032	0.035	0.004
Mean age	31.863	39.741	7.877	32.212	40.372	8.159	31.853	37.409	5.555
Female	0.580	0.523	-0.057	0.625	0.565	-0.060	0.616	0.490	-0.125
Married	0.335	0.709	0.373	0.194	0.588	0.394	0.367	0.725	0.358
In school	0.252	0.074	-0.178	0.192	0.057	-0.135	0.157	0.071	-0.085
Infant	0.076	0.095	0.019	0.132	0.104	-0.027	0.187	0.171	0.016

Source: The sample combines the fourth waves of the 1991, 1992, and 1993 Surveys of Income and Program Participation.

Table A-2. Regression-Adjusted Double-Difference Estimates of the Latino-White Relative Employment Effect of Auto Access by Age-Education Categories[a]

	High school dropout	High school graduate	Some college	College graduate
Panel A: Indicator of individual car ownership				
18–30 years old	0.097 (0.045)**	0.065 (0.032)**	-0.035 (0.043)	0.044 (0.058)
31–40 years old	-0.145 (0.050) ***	0.004 (0.038)	0.190 (0.053)***	0.168 (0.066) ***
41–50 years old	0.074 (0.067)	0.033 (0.050)	0.293 (0.069)***	-0.003 (0.075)
51–65 years old	0.026 (0.062)	0.126 (0.066) ***	-0.164 (0.137)	-0.023 (0.139)
Panel B: Indicator of the presence of a car in the household				
18–30 years old	0.071 (0.051)	0.011 (0.041)	0.044 (0.059)	0.128 (0.078)
31–40 years old	0.001 (0.068)	-0.087 (0.050) *	0.209 (0.070)***	0.193 (0.101)*
41–50 years old	0.024 (0.084)	-0.056 (0.067)	0.277 (0.088)***	-0.142 (0.151)
51–65 years old	0.057 (0.081)	0.039 (0.084)	-0.292 (0.173)	-0.033 (0.199)
Panel C: Cars per adult household member				
18–30 years old	0.056 (0.042)	0.050 (0.027)*	0.041 (0.032)	0.056 (0.051)
31–40 years old	0.053 (0.039)	0.017 (0.023)	0.056 (0.025)**	0.078 (0.044)*
41–50 years old	0.074 (0.050)	0.117 (0.034)***	0.069 (0.043)*	-0.073 (0.029)***
51–65 years old	0.072 (0.051)	0.141 (0.049)***	-0.025 (0.070)	0.018 (0.061)

* Significant at the 10 percent level of confidence.
** Significant at the 5 percent level of confidence.
*** Significant at the 1 percent level of confidence.

a. Standard errors are in parentheses. Separate regressions are estimates for each age-education cell. Each figure is the coefficient on the interaction term between a Latino dummy variable and the relevant auto access variable from a regression including the auto access variable, the Latino indicator, the interaction between these variables, linear controls for education and age and interactions of these two variables with the Latino dummy variable, controls for gender, marital status, school enrollment, whether there is an infant in the household, and 135 state-year dummies.

**Table A-3. Linear Probability Employment Models Using the 1990
5 Percent PUMS and the Household Level Car-Ownership Variable**

Item	1	2
Black	0.134 (0.001)	0.098 (0.001)
Car	−0.148 (0.002)	−0.124 (0.002)
Black*car	0.116 (0.002)	0.107 (0.002)
Female	−	−0.158 (0.000)
Married	−	0.011 (0.000)
In school	−	−0.112 (0.001)
Disabled	−	−0.048 (0.001)
Age	−	
18–25	−	0.139 (0.002)
26–30	−	0.228 (0.002)
31–35	−	0.272 (0.002)
36–40	−	0.299 (0.002)
41–45	−	0.325 (0.002)
46–50	−	0.326 (0.002)
51–55	−	0.304 (0.002)
56–60	−	0.244 (0.002
Education		
High school	−	0.024 (0.002)
Some college	−	0.088 (0.002)
College graduates	−	0.110 (0.003)
College +	−	0.217 (0.003)
High school*18–25	−	0.151 (0.002)
High school*26–30	−	0.111 (0.003)
High school*31–35	−	0.082 (0.003)
High school*36–40	−	0.085 (0.003)
High school*41–45	−	0.074 (0.003)
High school*46–50	−	0.064 (0.003)
High school*51–55	−	0.041 (0.003)
High school*56–60	−	−0.003 (0.003)
Some college*18–25	−	0.132 (0.002)
Some college*26–30	−	0.121 (0.003)
Some college*31–35	−	0.076 (0.002)
Some college*36–40	−	0.066 (0.003)
Some college*41–45	−	0.055 (0.003)
Some college*46–50	−	0.045 (0.003)
Some college*51–55	−	0.031 (0.003)
Some college*56–60	−	−0.012 (0.003)
College graduate*18–25	−	0.195 (0.003)
College graduate*26–30	−	0.144 (0.003)
College graduate*31–35	−	0.070 (0.003)
College graduate*36–40	−	0.047 (0.003)
College graduate*41–45	−	0.034 (0.004)
College graduate*46–50	−	0.030 (0.003)
College graduate*51–55	−	0.017 (0.003)
College graduate*56–60	−	−0.022 (0.004)
College +*18–25	−	0.054 (0.006)
College +*26–30	−	0.043 (0.004)
College +*31–35	−	0.004 (0.004)
College +*36–40	−	−0.016 (0.004)
College +*41–45	−	−0.031 (0.004)
College +*46–50	−	−0.031 (0.004)
College +*51–55	−	−0.030 (0.004)
College +*56–60	−	−0.051 (0.004)
R^2	0.017	0.138
N	4,272,520	4,272,520

Standard errors are in parentheses. Both regressions include a constant term.

Table A-4. Dissimilarity Scores and Exposure Indexes Measuring Segregation between Population and Employment for the 20 Metropolitan Areas with the Largest Black Population in 1990

	Retail employment dissimilarity indexes				Retail employment exposure indexes			
	Levels, 1992		Net growth, 1987–92		Levels, 1992		Net growth, 1987–92	
	Black	White	Black	White	Black	White	Black	White
Atlanta	0.59	0.33	0.80	0.53	7.25	9.03	0.63	1.49
Baltimore	0.57	0.29	0.88	0.67	5.90	7.81	0.10	0.40
Birmingham	0.60	0.42	0.73	0.56	6.36	7.34	0.52	1.00
Charlotte	0.47	0.35	0.85	0.75	7.37	7.77	0.70	1.41
Chicago	0.74	0.28	0.89	0.67	4.07	8.16	0.53	1.32
Cleveland	0.67	0.26	0.84	0.57	6.13	7.76	0.37	0.91
Dallas	0.53	0.31	0.85	0.68	7.35	7.74	0.57	0.99
Detroit	0.79	0.26	0.94	0.63	4.07	8.21	0.17	1.14
Houston	0.57	0.31	0.76	0.49	5.48	8.24	0.59	1.28
Los Angeles	0.66	0.28	0.88	0.76	4.03	7.06	0.20	0.41
Memphis	0.54	0.33	0.80	0.55	5.72	8.63	0.34	1.08
Miami	0.60	0.25	0.82	0.58	5.75	8.04	0.45	1.05
New Orleans	0.49	0.35	0.69	0.60	7.81	8.20	0.87	1.33
New York	0.71	0.36	0.87	0.77	2.50	5.86	0.07	0.20
Newark	0.69	0.30	0.89	0.76	3.72	6.36	0.34	0.98
Norfolk	0.43	0.31	0.69	0.55	6.91	7.45	0.58	0.94
Oakland	0.61	0.28	0.79	0.68	5.47	7.13	0.33	0.50
Philadelphia	0.72	0.29	0.91	0.68	3.61	7.49	0.18	0.75
St. Louis	0.67	0.29	0.83	0.59	5.93	8.18	0.48	0.93
Washington, D.C.	0.56	0.35	0.82	0.64	5.82	8.09	0.28	0.72

The levels indexes are calculated using zip code level information on the number of jobs located in the zip code in 1992 and the number of people of the relevant race residing in the zip code in 1990. The net growth indexes use net job growth between 1987 and 1992, setting growth to zero for zip codes that lose employment over this time period. Information on population by zip code comes from the 1990 Census of Population and Housing Summary Tape Files 3B. Information on job counts by zip codes comes from the Economic Census for 1987 and 1992. Approximately 60 percent of the 1990 black population living in metropolitan areas resided in one of the twenty PMSAs listed above.

Comments

Kenneth A. Small: Spatial mismatch has long posed a challenge to researchers on urban affairs. Empirical evidence from many angles suggests that it is important in the United States for explaining racial differences in employment outcomes and for suggesting potent policy interventions. At the same time, so many of the decisions involved are simultaneous that, as pointed out by Richard Arnott , it is difficult to sort out which factors are truly the causal ones.[46]

Steven Raphael and Michael A. Stoll make a convincing case that even without fully sorting out the theoretical chain of causation, one can isolate a particular facet of the problem empirically. This facet is the role of automobile ownership in ameliorating problems caused by spatial mismatch. The work reported provides direct evidence on how the transportation system affects the employment experience of spatially isolated groups. It thereby addresses nicely one of the policy tools often considered for dealing with spatial mismatch, offering strong evidence that policy intervention could make a significant difference. At the same time, the demonstration is made in such a way that it provides additional indirect evidence that spatial mismatch operates more or less according to conventional views.

The authors accomplish these advances through an insight that is clever and well targeted. The consensus view of spatial mismatch (and of the efficacy of policies involving improved transportation) implies that automobile ownership affects different groups differently in terms of employment. If spatial mismatch affects blacks more than other groups, and if it is partly responsible for blacks' higher unemployment rates, then we should see differences in the marginal impact of personal or household ownership of automobiles on employment rates.

46. Arnott (1998).

138

Such differences are found, and the authors strengthen their case by check-ing for robustness to specification along many different dimensions. It is encouraging that after all this checking, the basic result given by the simplest computation holds up well. That computation in table 2 in the paper states simply that the effects of automobile ownership on employment are greatest for blacks, intermediate for Latinos, and least for whites. Nor are these effects trivial: even after accounting for some covariates that reduce them substan-tially, they imply that between 21 and 43 percent of the black-white employment rate differential is explained by the difference in automobile ownership. If true, this is a remarkable finding: a problem often thought intractable can perhaps be addressed through measures that are rather mun-dane and well within the nation's fiscal capabilities.

The second line of empirical evidence presented looks at these car-ownership effects across metropolitan areas. This is a useful and again clever approach. Ultimately, though, I find it less convincing, partly because as the sample sizes diminish for measuring the car-ownership effects, they are estimated less precisely, and partly because I am not fully satisfied with the measures of spa-tial isolation used. I think the "dissimilarity index" has little to do with accessibility to jobs, being rather a measure of how segregated the minority group is; it could measure great dissimilarity even if the effects of segregation were to put blacks within closer reach of jobs than whites. The exposure index is better but hampered by the limited employment sectors available in the Economic Census. Still, most likely the effects described by the authors are indeed due to job accessibility, just as they claim.

The authors rightly worry that car ownership is endogenous. They correct for this possibility appropriately, but the instruments apparently are weak ones and using them greatly reduces the statistical confidence in the results. That the results do not disappear (indeed, they grow stronger in magnitude) leaves their case intact, though a more stringent test would be desirable. A good topic for further research would be to more fully specify the joint deci-sion processes involved and find data to estimate them.

A type of simultaneity not addressed is that of car ownership and location. Edward L. Glaeser, Matthew E. Kahn, and Jordan Rappaport argue that a chief cause of poor people living disproportionately in city centers is that the better transit service there allows them to choose a commuting mode that is cheaper than owning a car.[47] The spatial mismatch argument used by Raphael and Stoll relies on a different mechanism—racial discrimination—causing a higher pro-

47. Glaeser, Kahn, and Rappaport (1999).

portion of poor people to live in city centers. It is not obvious, to me at least, what kind of confounding of effects might occur when both factors are operating. Still, the reliance on black-white differentials in the effects is likely to alleviate whatever confounding influence this mechanism might have on their results.

So in the end, I am left agreeing that increasing car ownership among spatially segregated minorities would improve their employment prospects. What then can we conclude about policy intervention? As the authors point out, one cannot simply recommend a policy because it would make a difference in an important social problem—costs, administrative feasibility, and incentives must be be worked out, to name just a few concerns. Still, there are other grounds to be optimistic about automobile ownership subsidies. Studies in other contexts have found automobile transportation a relatively cheap way to provide accessibility to urban residents.[48] Improving reverse-commute transit is an alternative, but it tends to be very expensive per rider, partly because of its very success—those riders who use it to land a suburban job tend to quickly abandon it in favor of buying a car as soon as accumulated earnings permit. Other types of targeted special-purpose transit, such as dial-a-ride, often cost more than providing single-occupant automobile service, even with a paid driver. So within the realm of transportation policy, encouraging car ownership seems often to be a cost-effective and flexible way of addressing social problems arising from barriers to accessibility. Given Raphael and Stoll's results, car ownership is a prime candidate for addressing minority unemployment in metropolitan areas.

Much work remains before spatial mismatch is fully understood as a general-equilibrium phenomenon. But enough is known to make it clear that minority groups, especially blacks, are hurt by it. Raphael and Stoll now give us strong evidence that the damage can be notably lessened if we can bring minorities up to the levels of car ownership typical of whites. This objective may not be simple to accomplish, but it is a lot easier than dealing with the multiple problems of poor schooling, drug addiction, crime, family disintegration, and alienation that infect many minority communities. So it is nice to know that aside from providing desperately needed attention to those more underlying problems, there is something more routine that can be done.

Clifford Winston: Steven Raphael and Michael A. Stoll conclude that transportation policies fostering greater access to automobiles should be considered

---

48. Examples include Summer Myers, "New Volks for Poor Folks," proposal and cost comparisons between demand-responsive transit and taxi service in Kain (1970, p. 85).

in an effort to alleviate the spatial concentration of joblessness. In my view, before it can be concluded that any transportation policy will be helpful, a number of steps should be taken.

To begin with, the policy objective has to be clarified: should the government strive to improve the lives of the poor by increasing their access to jobs or raising their retention of jobs? While the authors confine their analysis to the first approach, it is not clear why such a narrow focus is appropriate. Indeed, the conclusion from experiments that seek to increase employment by improving transport is that it is much more important for inner-city residents to be able to retain jobs than to have greater accessibility to them.[49]

Moreover, several current policies, including poverty programs, job training, and tax credits, already attempt to spur people to join and maintain a place in the work force. What additional benefits would a new transportation policy provide? The issue at hand does not involve a market failure but a social goal—reducing unemployment at acceptable social cost. One must therefore compare the costs and benefits of all potential policies, determine which one or combination is the most cost effective, and then assess whether the optimal policy package offers sufficient economic and political returns to merit policymakers' support.

Assuming that improved transportation is found to be the appropriate instrument for increasing employment, several policies besides subsidizing automobile ownership are worth considering: providing additional subsidies to public transit; allowing private transit operators the opportunity to serve low-income and suburban areas; subsidizing employers who offer transport for their employees; subsidizing housing near suburban job centers; strengthening antidiscrimination policy in housing and credit markets, and so on. The authors only provide a basis for estimating the benefits from subsidizing auto ownership; the costs of this policy are not estimated, and the potential costs and benefits of other policies are not even acknowledged. Thus it is premature to conclude that subsidizing automobile ownership merits serious consideration.

Automobile ownership, labor force participation, and residential location are endogenous decisions. People who choose not to own a car, not to work, and reside where they cannot walk or take public transit to get to a job are in the tail of any urban population distribution. Such behavior is idiosyncratic and undoubtedly explained by many subtle influences. Structural *disaggregate* models of labor force participation, mode choice (including automobile own-

49. Winston and Shirley (1998).

ership), and residential location were developed to capture these influences. (James Heckman and Daniel McFadden were recently awarded the Nobel Prize in economics for their work in this area.) The attractiveness of individual choice models stems from the recognition that ad hoc aggregate models obscure and ignore many key influences on consumer and household behavior in product and labor markets. Choice models are also attractive because they allow one to apply standard welfare metrics, such as the compensating variation, to estimate benefits from a policy that affects consumers' utility. These models could provide a rich specification of minorities' decision to enter the labor force by accounting for the role of AFDC (now TANF) benefits, prior employment, contacts with potential employers and wages in suburban areas, available transport alternatives (public transit, carpool, van pool), and so on. An automobile ownership and mode choice model could illuminate whether minorities are financially constrained from owning a car or simply choose not to own one, and how auto ownership relates to their labor force participation. A residential location model could shed light on why low-income groups tend to live where they have difficulty finding work close to home. Even this obstacle is not always an insurmountable barrier to employment because evidence suggests that the working poor are willing to hold down jobs that require very long commutes involving multiple transfers on public transport or car pooling.[50]

The authors do not even hint at these models and simply present a reduced form aggregate model of employment differentials. Their finding that increasing auto ownership can substantially reduce minority unemployment invites disbelief and assertions that it reflects deficiencies in their modeling and econometrics. To be sure, it is difficult to predict how the authors' findings would have been affected had they used disaggregate choice models. The essential point is that estimates of the benefits from transport policies that seek to raise employment will be viewed as more credible if they are based on models that have widespread professional acceptance.

I have little doubt that a research program following these guidelines will conclude that subsidizing automobile ownership ranks at the bottom of policies that seek to increase employment in a cost-effective manner. Whether *any* transport-related policy has the potential to produce significant reductions in joblessness at socially acceptable costs is a more open question.

---

50. Winston and Shirley (1998).

References

Arnott, Richard. 1998. "Economic Theory and the Spatial Mismatch Hypothesis." *Urban Studies* 35 (June): 1171–85.

Ayres, Ian, and Peter Siegelman. 1995. "Race and Gender Discrimination in Bargaining for a New Car." *American Economic Review* 85 (June): 304–21.

Cutler, David, Edward Glaeser, and Jacob Vigdor. 1999. "The Rise and Decline of the American Ghetto." *Journal of Political Economy* 107 (June): 455–506.

Frey, William H., and Reynolds Farley. 1996. "Latino, Asian, and Black Segregation in U.S. Metropolitan Areas: Are Multiethnic Metros Different?" *Demography* 33 (February): 35–50.

Glaeser, Edward L., Matthew E. Kahn, and Jordan Rappaport. 1999. "Why Do the Poor Live in Cities?" Working Paper. Harvard University, Department of Economics.

Goldberg, Pinelopi Koujianou. 1996. "Dealer Price Discrimination in New Car Purchases: Evidence from the Consumer Expenditure Survey." *Journal of Political Economy* 104 (June): 622–54.

Government Accounting Office. 1999. *Welfare Reform: Implementing DOT's Access to Jobs Program in Its First Year.* GAO/RCED-00-14. Washington (November).

Hamermesh, Daniel S. 1996. *Workdays, Work Hours, and Work Schedules: Evidence for the United States and Germany.* Kalamazoo, Mich.: W.E. Upjohn Institute for Employment Research.

Harrington, Scott E., and Greg Niehaus. 1998. "Race, Redlining, and Automobile Insurance Prices." *Journal of Business* 71(July): 439–69.

Holzer, Harry J. 1991. "The Spatial Mismatch Hypothesis: What Has the Evidence Shown?" *Urban Studies* 28 (February): 105–22.

Holzer, Harry J., and Keith R. Ihlanfeldt. 1996. "Spatial Factors and the Employment of Blacks at the Firm Level." *New England Economic Review: Federal Reserve Bank of Boston*, special issue (May-June): 65–86.

Holzer, Harry J., Keith R. Ihlanfeldt, and David L. Sjoquist. 1994. "Work, Search, and Travel among White and Black Youth." *Journal of Urban Economics* 35 (May): 320–45.

Holzer, Harry J., John Quigley, and Steven Raphael. 2001. "Public Transit and the Spatial Distribution of Minority Employment: Evidence from a Natural Experiment." Unpublished manuscript. University of California, Berkeley.

Hu, Patricia S., and Jennifer R. Young. 1999. "Summary of Travel Trends: 1995 Nationwide Personal Transportation Survey." Department of Transportation.

Hughes, Mark. 1995. "A Mobility Strategy for Improving Opportunity." *Housing Policy Debate* 6 (1): 271–97.

Ihlanfeldt, Keith R., and David L. Sjoquist. 1998. "The Spatial Mismatch Hypothesis: A Review of Recent Studies and Their Implications for Welfare Reform." *Housing Policy Debate* 9 (4): 849–92.

Ihlanfeldt, Keith R., and Madelyn V. Young. 1996. "The Spatial Distribution of Black Employment between the Central City and the Suburbs." *Economic Inquiry* 34 (October): 693–707.

Kain, John F. 1970. "Transportation and Poverty." *Public Interest* 18 (Winter): 75–87.

——. 1992. "The Spatial Mismatch Hypothesis: Three Decades Later." *Housing Policy Debate* 3 (2): 371–460.

Kasarda, John. 1985. "Urban Change and Minority Opportunity." In *The New Urban Reality*, edited by Paul E. Peterson, 33–67. Brookings.

——. 1989. "Urban Industrial Transition and the Underclass." *The Annals of the American Academy of Political and Social Science* 501 (January): 26–47.

Katz, Lawrence, Jeffrey Liebman, and Jeffrey Kling. Forthcoming. "Moving the Opportunities in Boston: Early Results from a Randomized Mobility Experiment." *Quarterly Journal of Economics.*

Ludwig, Jens. 1998. "The Effects of Concentrated Poverty on Labor Market Outcomes: Evidence from a Randomized Experiment." Paper presented at a meeting of the Population Association of America. Chicago (April).

Martin, Richard W. Forthcoming. "The Adjustment of Black Residents to Metropolitan Employment Shifts: How Persistent Is Spatial Mismatch?" *Journal of Urban Economics.*

Massey, Douglas S. and Nancy A. Denton. 1989. "Hypersegregation in U.S. Metropolitan Areas: Black and Hispanic Segregation Along Five Dimensions." *Demography* 26 (August): 373–91.

——. 1993. *American Apartheid: Segregation and the Making of the Underclass.* Harvard University Press.

Mouw, Ted. 2000. "Job Relocation and the Racial Gap in Unemployment in Detroit and Chicago 1980-1990: A Fixed-Effects Estimate of the Spatial Mismatch Hypothesis." *American Sociological Review* 65 (October): 730–53.

Oliver, Melvin L. and Thomas M. Shapiro. 1997. *Black Wealth/White Wealth: A New Perspective on Racial Inequality.* New York and London: Routledge.

Ong, Paul. 1996. "Work and Automobile Ownership among Welfare Recipients." *Social Work Research* 20 (December): 255–62.

O'Regan, Katherine M., and John M. Quigley. 1999. "Spatial Isolation of Welfare Recipients: What Do We Know?" Program on Housing and Urban Policy Working Paper W99-003. University of California, Berkeley.

Papke, Leslie E. 1993. "What Do We Know about Enterprise Zones?" *Tax Policy and the Economy*, vol. 7, edited by James Poterba, 37–72. MIT Press.

Pugh, Margaret. 1998. "Barriers to Work: The Spatial Divide between Jobs and Welfare Recipients in Metropolitan Areas." Brookings Institution Center on Urban and Metropolitan Policy Discussion Paper.

Raphael, Steven. 1998a. "The Spatial Mismatch Hypothesis of Black Youth Joblessness: Evidence from the San Francisco Bay Area." *Journal of Urban Economics* 43 (January): 79–111.

——.1998b. "Inter and Intra-Ethnic Comparisons of the Central City-Suburban Youth Employment Differential: Evidence from the Oakland Metropolitan Area." *Industrial and Labor Relations Review* 51 (April): 505–24.

Raphael, Steven, and Lorien Rice. 2000. "Car Ownership, Employment, and Earnings." Unpublished manuscript.

Shore-Sheppard, Lara. 1998. "The Precision of Instrumental Variables with Grouped Data." Unpublished manuscript.

Smeeding, Timothy M., Katherin Ross Phillips, and M. O'Connor. Forthcoming. "The EITC: Expectation, Knowledge, Use and Economic and Social Mobility." *National Tax Journal.*

Stoll, Michael A. 1999. "Spatial Job Search, Spatial Mismatch, and the Employment and Wages of Racial and Ethnic Groups in Los Angeles." *Journal of Urban Economics* 46 (July): 129–55.

Stoll, Michael A., and Steven Raphael. 2000. "Racial Differences in Spatial Job Search Patterns: Exploring the Causes and Consequences." *Economic Geography* 76 (July): 201–23.

Stoll, Michael A., Harry J. Holzer, and Keith R. Ihlanfeldt. 2000. "Within Cities and Suburbs: Racial Residential Concentration and the Spatial Distribution of Employment Opportunities Across Sub-Metropolitan Areas." *Journal of Policy Analysis and Management* 19 (Spring): 207–32.

U.S. Department of Transportation. 1999. *Our Nation's Travel: 1995 Nationwide Transportation Survey Early Results Report*, accessed at http://www-cta.ornl.gov/npts/1995/Doc/EarlyResults.shtml.

Weinberg, Bruce A. 2000. "Black Residential Centralization and the Spatial Mismatch Hypothesis." *Journal of Urban Economics* 48 (July): 110–34.

Winston, Clifford, and Chad Shirley. 1998. *Alternate Route: Toward Efficient Urban Transport.* Brookings.

Yinger, John. 1995. *Closed Doors, Opportunities Lost: The Continuing Costs of Housing Discrimination.* New York: Russell Sage Foundation.

JENS LUDWIG
Georgetown University

HELEN F. LADD
Duke University

GREG J. DUNCAN
Northwestern University

Urban Poverty and Educational Outcomes

BETWEEN 1970 AND 1990, the number of people in the United States living in high-poverty census tracts (with poverty rates of 40 percent or more) nearly doubled, from 4.1 to 8.0 million. Children who live in poor urban neighborhoods are disproportionately likely to be members of racial and ethnic minority groups and are also at greater risk for school failure. For example, only 11 percent of fourth graders attending high-poverty schools in Washington, D.C., scored at or above basic level on the government's National Assessment of Educational Progress (NAEP) math test, far lower than the national average of 62 percent. Dropout rates in Washington remain on the order of 30 to 40 percent, many times higher than the national average.[1]

Why do high-poverty urban areas have such problems with schooling outcomes? Sociologists, psychologists, and a growing number of economists believe that the prevalence within a neighborhood of social problems such as poverty and joblessness affect the life chances of area residents. If so, policies

This paper was supported by the U.S. Department of Housing and Urban Development and the Spencer, Smith Richardson, and William T. Grant foundations, as well as the Georgetown University Graduate School of Arts and Sciences. We are grateful to Christina Clark, Josh Pinkston, and Justin Treloar for their expert assistance with the data analysis, and to Gary Brager, Carter Nicely, Jacob Schuchman, Janice Gentry, Jaki Young, Larry Rogers, Karla Brassant, Carol Wilson, and Jerry Cunningham for their assistance in compiling and interpreting the school data. Helpful comments were provided by Ruth Crystal, Janet Currie, Judie Feins, Edward Glaeser, John Goering, Jeffrey Grogger, Paul Jargowsky, Jeffrey Kling, Christopher Mayer, Edgar Olsen, Katherine O'Regan, Mark Shroder, and participants in the Brookings-Wharton Conference on Urban Affairs and the annual meetings of the Association for Public Policy Analysis and Management and the American Economic Association.

1. Jargowsky (1997); U.S. Department of Education (1999, 2000); Valerie Strauss, "One-Third of District Students Drop Out; Rate Far Higher Than U.S. Average," *Washington Post*, September 23, 1999, p. B1.

that reduce the degree of economic residential segregation may also improve the educational outcomes of poor children. Given the persistent correlation between race and social class in America, policies that help reduce the degree of neighborhood racial segregation could potentially have the same effect.[2] Unfortunately, relatively little is currently known about the effects of neighborhood conditions on children's educational outcomes. The central challenge to measuring neighborhood effects stems from the fact that most families have at least some degree of choice over where they live. As a result, correlations between neighborhood characteristics and child outcomes may reflect either the causal effects of neighborhood environments or the effects of unmeasured family attributes that influence both residential choices and children's outcomes.

Ambiguity about even the direction of this "self-selection" or "endogenous-membership" bias makes interpretation of the nonexperimental literature difficult.[3] On the one hand, those parents who are most concerned about their children's outcomes may take the initiative to relocate to a lower-poverty area. On the other hand, families whose children are predisposed toward trouble and more likely to succumb to the temptations of the street may be more likely to relocate to more affluent areas to shield their children from negative peer influences.

The best available evidence on the effects of neighborhoods on children's educational outcomes comes from the Gautreaux program in Chicago, which relocated African American public housing residents into different parts of the metropolitan area. Gautreaux families typically accepted the first apartment made available to them by the nonprofit group that administered the program, which suggests that participants had little choice over whether they ended up in a city or a suburban location. Evaluations have found that compared with those who moved to other parts of the city, suburban movers had lower dropout rates (5 versus 20 percent) and higher rates of college attendance (54 versus 21 percent).[4] But because Gautreaux was not a true experiment, there necessarily remains some question about the randomness of neighborhood assignments.

---

2. Wilson (1987, 1996); Jencks and Mayer (1990); Brooks-Gunn, Duncan and Aber (1997a,b); Jaynes and Williams (1989, pp. 319–22); Yinger (1998).

3. Findings from the nonexperimental literature are generally mixed on whether neighborhood characteristics affect children's outcomes; for excellent summaries, see Jencks and Mayer (1990); Ellen and Turner (1997); and Brooks-Gunn, Duncan and Aber (1997a,b).

4. Rosenbaum (1995); Rubinowitz and Rosenbaum (2000).

In this paper we estimate the effects of neighborhood conditions on children's educational outcomes using data from the U.S. Department of Housing and Urban Development's (HUD) Moving to Opportunity (MTO) residential-mobility program. In contrast to Gautreaux, the MTO program is a true randomized experiment. MTO has been operating since 1994 in five cities (Baltimore, Boston, Chicago, Los Angeles, and New York). This paper uses data from the Baltimore site and is the first evaluation of the program's impacts on the educational outcomes of participating children.

Eligibility for the MTO program was restricted to low-income families with children living in public housing or Section 8 project-based housing located in selected high-poverty census tracts. Families who volunteered for MTO were randomly assigned into one of three treatment groups. Members of the *experimental group* were offered Section 8 rental subsidies that could be used only for private-market housing in census tracts with very low-poverty rates (defined as 1990 poverty rates below 10 percent). These families also received counseling services and assistance in their housing search from a local nonprofit agency. Members of the *Section 8–only comparison group* were also offered rental subsidies but were not required to move to a low-poverty census tract and were not provided any additional services. Members of the *control group* received no rental subsidies. The presumption was that they would continue to live within high-poverty areas.[5] The randomized experimental design of MTO thus breaks the link between family preferences and neighborhood conditions and helps overcome the self-selection problem that plagues previous studies of neighborhood effects.

Our study measures children's educational outcomes using data obtained from administrative school records in Maryland. Specific outcome measures include student performance on standardized academic achievement tests, school absences, disciplinary actions, special education placements, grade retentions, and dropout rates. We find that elementary school children assigned to the experimental group achieved scores in both reading and math that exceeded those of the control group children by about one-quarter of a standard deviation. Younger children in the Section 8–only comparison group experience higher scores than controls in reading but not math. For adolescents, only limited data are available on academic achievement. While we find

---

5. School-level data on student exit and entry often suggest high rates of residential mobility by poor families, which raises the possibility that even the families within the control group may experience high rates of mobility out of the high-poverty baseline communities. But most of the residential mobility experienced by poor families appears to occur between or within high-poverty areas. Gramlich, Laren and Sealand (1992)

that teens in the experimental and Section 8–only groups experience a higher incidence of grade retention than controls, and may experience more disciplinary actions and school dropout as well, these differences appear to be due at least in part to differences in academic and behavioral standards between schools in high- and low-poverty areas. We hasten to add that since MTO participants are a self-selected group of public housing residents, the treatment effects estimated here may not generalize to more representative populations of low-income families.

The Moving to Opportunity Demonstration

Eligibility for the Baltimore MTO demonstration was restricted to very low-income families with children who lived in public housing or Section 8 project-based housing in one of the five poorest census tracts in Baltimore City. These tracts had an average poverty rate in 1990 of 67 percent and a crime rate that was nearly three times the state average. The baseline neighborhoods are also notable for a paucity of affluent neighbors, which previous research suggests has a distinct effect on youth outcomes from neighborhood poverty. Less than 5 percent of households in these tracts had annual incomes of $50,000 or more (in 1990 dollars), and less than 7 percent of adults in these areas had a college degree.[6]

The program was publicized in the baseline tracts by the Housing Authority of Baltimore (HAB) and a local nonprofit, the Community Assistance Network (CAN). Although we are unable to determine exactly what fraction of eligible families volunteered for MTO in the Baltimore site, data pooled together from four of the five MTO sites (Boston, Baltimore, Los Angeles and New York) suggest that around one-quarter of eligible families applied to participate.[7] Table 1 compares the sociodemographic characteristics of eligible families who lived in public housing in these four cities and volunteered for MTO with their apparently eligible neighbors who decided not to apply.

6. Goering, Carnevale and Teodoro (1996); Ludwig, Duncan and Hirschfield (2001); Brooks-Gunn, Duncan and Aber (1997a,b).

7. Goering and others (1999). This figure represents the estimated proportion of families with children living in public housing developments in the census tracts targeted by MTO program administrators. Because the proportion of families living in Section 8 project-based housing within the targeted census tracts who volunteer for MTO may be somewhat different from the rate among public housing families, this estimate may slightly over- or understate the actual proportion of all eligible families who volunteered for the program.

Table 1. Comparison of Move-to-Opportunity and Non-MTO Households in Same Public Housing Developments for Baltimore, Boston, Los Angeles, and New York Sites

Item	MTO households	Non-MTO households
N	2,414	6,813
African American (%)	54	51
Hispanic (%)	39	45
Female-headed household (%)	93	78
Household head age (years)		
Mean	35	41
Median	33	39
Number of children under 18 in household		
Mean	2.5	2.3
Median	2.0	2.0
Household head receives AFDC (%)	75	51
Household head employed (%)	22	30
Household income ($)		
Mean	9,365	10,769
Median	8,252	8,645

Source: Goering and others (1999)

Household heads who volunteered for MTO are somewhat more likely than their neighbors to be female, young, and on AFDC. If these households have the most to gain from moving to more affluent areas, then the estimated effects of residential relocation for MTO participants may overstate the effects of involuntarily relocating a more representative population of public housing residents.

Volunteers for the MTO demonstration were added to the program's waiting list. Families were drawn off the MTO waiting list over time on the basis of a random lottery beginning in October 1994 and then randomized by Abt Associates into one of the three MTO treatment groups. The final group to be drawn off the waiting list was randomly assigned into a treatment group in October 1996.

Those families assigned to the experimental group were offered Section 8 housing vouchers or certificates, which provide subsidies to lease private-market housing. As part of the program's design, these subsidies could only be redeemed for housing in census tracts with 1990 poverty rates of less than 10 percent. Families had up to 180 days from the time at which they began the housing search to identify a suitable rental unit and sign a lease. Before the housing search was initiated, CAN required experimental families to complete four workshops on topics such as budgeting, how to conduct a housing or job search, and conflict resolution. During the housing search itself CAN helped families locate suitable rental housing and negotiate leases with private-market landlords.

Of the experimental group families, 58 percent "complied" with their treatment assignment (that is, relocated through the MTO program). Of the experimental group "noncompliers," half ran up against the Section 8 rent-subsidy time limit. One-quarter of the experimental noncompliers did not successfully complete the mandatory CAN counseling program, and the remaining quarter never contacted CAN to begin the counseling program and search process after being assigned to the experimental group.

Families assigned to the Section 8–only comparison group were also given the chance to relocate with Section 8 housing subsidies. The services offered to the Section 8–only group differed from those of the experimental treatment in ways that could in principle either increase or decrease compliance rates. As with the experimental group, Section 8–only families had 180 days to identify a private-market apartment and were required to sign a one-year lease. Yet unlike with the experimental group, the relocation decisions of Section 8–only families were not constrained by the MTO program, which may contribute to higher relocation rates among Section 8–only families. On the other hand, families in the Section 8–only group received no housing search or counseling assistance beyond what was provided to all participants in HUD's Section 8 subsidy program (which in Baltimore included a brief orientation about the program rules, as well as access to information about private-market landlords who have accepted or are likely to accept housing vouchers). As it turns out, the relocation rate among the Section 8–only group in Baltimore was significantly higher than that observed among experimental families (73 versus 58 percent), a pattern that holds across MTO sites.[8] Of the Section 8–only families who did not relocate through MTO, almost all contacted the Baltimore housing office and requested a Section 8 subsidy but were then unable or unwilling to commit to a lease before the subsidy offer expired.

Conceptual Framework

A neighborhood's social composition may influence children's educational outcomes through a variety of mechanisms. Most social science theories sug-

---

8. Goering and others (1999).

gest that moving low-income children from high- to low-poverty neighborhoods will improve these children's schooling performance, although some theories suggest that such a move may be unhelpful or even harmful.

There are a number of reasons to believe that living in affluent neighborhoods filled with high-achieving students will have positive effects on the educational outcomes of poor children. Sociologists emphasize the role that neighbors and peers play in establishing local social norms regarding schooling and work, while economists emphasize the role that working- and middle-class neighbors play in demonstrating the returns to staying in school.[9] It is also possible that the average achievement level of students within an area may affect an individual child's academic outcomes by raising the level of teacher expectations or classroom instruction, or through additional "human capital spillovers" that arise when children help one another with schoolwork. A very different type of neighborhood effect may arise from variation across areas in the quality of neighborhood schools and other local institutions. However, the negative correlation in the Baltimore area between the prevalence of affordable rental housing within a neighborhood and local school quality suggests that the effects of MTO on children's school quality may be only modest.[10]

Some sociologists believe that "neighborhoods matter" but do not agree that moving school-age children from high poverty to more affluent areas will substantially change their educational outcomes. According to this view, children who grow up in areas of high joblessness are instilled with a "culture of poverty" characterized by hopelessness and a critical attitude toward mainstream institutions, attitudes that, once developed, are not readily changed. As Oscar Lewis writes, "By the time slum children are age six or seven, they have usually absorbed the basic values and attitudes of their subculture and are not psychologically geared to take full advantage of the changing conditions or increased opportunities that may occur in their lifetime."[11] It is also possible that moves from high- to low-poverty neighborhoods might have negative consequences for children's school performance. For example, low-income children in affluent neighborhoods or schools may suffer in the heightened competition for grades and other rewards in the new environment, or they may revise their opinions of their own abilities downward in response to a higher-achieving peer group.[12]

9. Wilson (1987, 1996); Manski (1993); Ludwig (1999).
10. Ladd and Ludwig (1997).
11. Lewis (1968, p.188).
12. Jencks and Mayer (1990).

The random assignment of MTO families into different mobility treatment groups enables us to overcome the self-selection problem and examine whether neighborhood conditions are related to educational outcomes. But because MTO changes every neighborhood characteristic simultaneously for participating families, we are unable to identify the specific mechanisms through which neighborhoods influence children's schooling performance. The empirical analysis reported below thus uses the MTO data to estimate the combined net effect of changing all of a family's neighborhood characteristics at once.

Our empirical strategy focuses on comparing the average outcomes of families according to the MTO treatment group to which they were assigned, regardless of whether families took advantage of the program's offer to relocate. Since the background characteristics of families in each group should on average be quite similar by virtue of the program's random-assignment design, differences across groups in postprogram outcomes can be attributed to the effects of the MTO program. These "intent-to-treat" (ITT) estimates will understate the actual effects of relocating through MTO because the compliance rates of families assigned to the experimental and Section 8–only groups are less than 100 percent.[13] The ITT effect, obtained from estimating regression equation 1, identifies the effects of offering families the opportunity to relocate through the MTO program, which are of interest to policymakers since many residential-mobility programs are likely to involve voluntary participation by families.

(1) $$Y_{int} = \alpha_1 + \alpha_2 Z_{in0} + \alpha_3' X_{in0} + \alpha_4' \delta_t + \alpha_5' \lambda_{t'} + \upsilon_{int}.$$

Regression equation 1 is estimated using a panel of person-year observations for MTO children where (t) indexes academic years since random assignment $(t > 0)$, and the educational outcome for child (i) living in neighborhood (n) in year (t) is given by Y_{int}. The key explanatory variable in the analysis, Z_{in0}, indicates whether families are assigned to the experimental $(Z_{in0} = 1)$ or control group $(Z_{in0} = 0)$. (The analysis is identical for the effects of the

---

13. Note that comparing the average outcomes of experimental or Section 8-only *movers* with the average outcomes of the control group as a whole will produce biased estimates for the effects of MTO relocation, because those who choose to move within the experimental and Section 8-only groups are a self-selected sub-group of families assigned into that group. Since the average background characteristics of movers within the experimental and Section 8-only groups will not equal those of the control group as a whole, this type of comparison will produce an estimate for the causal effects of MTO relocation that will be biased either upward or downward, depending on which types of families are more likely to relocate when assigned to the experimental and Section 8-only groups.

Section 8–only treatment.) The use of panel data allows us to control for common trends in academic outcomes over time by including a set of indicators for years since randomization (δ_t) as well as the actual academic calendar year ($\lambda_{t'}$), thus improving the precision of our estimates. The model also controls for a set of preprogram child and family characteristics from the baseline surveys and preprogram educational outcomes from the school records (X_{in0}) to account for chance differences in these variables across groups.[14] We calculate robust Huber-White standard errors that account for the panel structure of the data and the presence of multiple children from the same family.

Also of policy interest are the effects of the MTO program on those families who actually move. The effect of "treatment on the treated" (TOT) can be identified if several assumptions are met. First, the postprogram outcomes of experimental and Section 8–only group noncompliers must be identical to the outcomes these families would have experienced had they instead been assigned to the control group. This assumption seems uncontroversial for the Section 8–only noncompliers, who receive no real services from the MTO program. Whether this assumption is met for experimental noncompliers is less obvious since some of these families received the CAN counseling, although previous research suggests that even intensive youth counseling programs appear to have little impact on youth behavior.[15] A second assumption is that 58 percent of families assigned to the control group would have relocated through MTO had they been assigned to the experimental group (which equals the observed compliance rate among those families actually assigned to the experimental group), while 73 percent of control families would have moved through MTO had they instead been assigned to the Section 8–only group. This assumption will be met if the MTO random assignment was carried out properly, which appears to be the case as shown below.[16]

---

14. Our pre-program controls include a series of indicator variables for the child's age at random assignment, the child's gender and number of siblings, as well as household-head baseline characteristics such as age at randomization, employment status (full time, part time, or not working), marital status (married, not married), welfare receipt, and educational attainment (high school diploma or more, GED, high school dropout), all taken from the baseline surveys that are available for all MTO households. We also use school administrative data to control for pre-program educational outcomes for the two years prior to randomization. These include controls for pre-program grade of enrollment, school absences, CTBS reading and math scores, special education status, and grade retention for the first and second academic years prior to random assignment. For missing data we set values to zero and include a missing-data indicator in order to avoid losing observations from the analytic sample.

15. Donohue and Siegelman (1998).

16. The TOT estimate also assumes that none of the families in the control group receive either the experimental or Section 8-only treatments. This assumption is met under our defi-

The *TOT* estimate for the experimental treatment (equation 2) essentially compares the outcomes of experimental and control group families who *would* comply with the experimental treatment ($C = 1$), with a similar *TOT* effect defined for the Section 8–only treatment. In practice we can identify the *TOT* effect with the assumptions outlined above, although we cannot identify the specific families within the control group who are "potential compliers":

(2) $TOT = E[Y \mid Z = 1, C = 1] - E[Y \mid Z = 0, C = 1]$

(3) $Y_{int} = \gamma_1 + \gamma_2 D_{in0} + \gamma_3' X_{in0} + \gamma_4' \delta_t + \gamma_5' \lambda_{t'} + \eta_{int}.$

We derive the *TOT* estimates by applying two-stage least squares to equation 3, using each family's MTO assignment (Z) as an instrument for a variable indicating whether the family actually relocated through the MTO program ($D = 1$ if so, and equal to 0 otherwise). In large samples this two-stage least squares estimate converges to the ITT effect divided by the probability of compliance with the assigned treatment.[17]

We can assess the magnitude of the *TOT* effect by comparing it with the average outcome of those children in the control group whose families would have moved had they been assigned to the experimental group, known as the "control complier mean" (*CCM*). Since we do not know which control families would have complied with the experimental treatment, we estimate the *CCM* as the average outcome of those who relocate through MTO in the experimental group minus the estimated *TOT* effect, as described in equation 4:[18]

(4) $CCM = E[Y \mid Z = 0, C = 1] = E[Y \mid Z = 1, C = 1] - TOT.$

---

nition of the experimental and Section 8-only treatments as "relocation to subsidized private-market housing through the MTO program." Control families who relocate on their own into private-market housing are different from those who receive the Section 8-only and experimental treatments because their private-market housing is not subsidized. Some control families may have received something close to the Section 8-only group's treatment through HUD's Hope VI program, which funded the demolition of two of the baseline public housing buildings, although the timing of the Hope VI and MTO moves were different. Moreover, none of the control families moved through Hope VI received the additional life-skills counseling and search assistance or the relocation restrictions imposed on experimental-treatment families.

17. Bloom (1984).
18. Katz, Kling and Liebman (2001).

Data

Our study draws on three sources of data: baseline survey responses; follow-up addresses; and educational outcome measures for MTO children taken from school administrative records.

Baseline Survey Data

When MTO families enrolled in the program, household heads were required to complete a survey that asked detailed questions about the condition of the family's baseline apartment and neighborhood, the reasons for enrolling in the program, and sociodemographic characteristics of the householder such as educational attainment and employment and welfare experiences. The baseline surveys also ask householders to report basic demographic information for their children, as well as information on each child's educational history such as grade, special education placement, and general academic, mental, and physical status. The response rate to these baseline surveys equals 100 percent by construction.

Follow-up Addresses

Tracking of MTO families was conducted by Abt Associates and provides information for families at two points in time: during the immediate postprogram period, which reflects the initial postprogram moves of families; and follow-up addresses that were current as of the second half of 1997. These postprogram addresses were obtained through the use of administrative data from local housing authorities (which administer the Section 8 rental subsidies to movers in the experimental and Section 8–only groups, as well as the public housing units of nonmovers), together with change-of-address registries, credit bureaus, and a brief follow-up survey of MTO families. Surveys were conducted on the telephone for as many families as possible; those who could not be reached by phone were interviewed in person. The response rate to Abt's survey was 91 percent.

School Records

Our key outcome measures come from school administrative records on children in MTO households. Since the Maryland State Department of Education does not maintain student-level data, we obtained student records for the 1993–94 through 1998–99 academic years from the six school districts that contained the 1,243 MTO children who were of school age during the sample period (born between 1977 and 1993): Baltimore City, Baltimore County, Anne Arundel County, Howard County, Montgomery County, and Harford County. Fully 98 percent of these school-age children live in three counties during the postprogram period (Baltimore City, Baltimore County, and Howard County), with Baltimore City accounting for the vast majority (85 percent).[19]

The school districts merged information on MTO participants with school administrative records using information on the child's name, date of birth, and Social Security number. The match rates were typically fairly high. For example, for the 1998–99 academic year the Baltimore City public school system identified school records for 92 percent of the 1,061 MTO children who lived in the city during the postprogram period. The match rate for the 109 children who lived in Baltimore County at some point was 86 percent and equaled 72 percent for the 47 MTO children whose families moved to Howard County. One reason for the nonmatches may be that some MTO children attend private schools, which in Maryland are not required to report student outcomes to either county or state education agencies. Yet the baseline surveys showed that only 1.5 percent of school-age MTO children attended private schools at that time. While the proportion of children attending private schools may increase somewhat if the experimental or Section 8–only treatments have an income effect on households,[20] our best guess is that private schools are on the whole probably a small source of attrition from our data.

Our primary outcome measures come from student performance on two sets of standardized achievement test scores, the Comprehensive Test of Basic Skills (CTBS) for elementary and middle-school students, and the Maryland Functional Tests (MFT) for middle- and high-school students. Other outcome measures include the number of school absences, an indicator for disciplinary actions (equal to one if the student has been suspended or expelled from school during the year), and indicators for whether the student received spe-

19. Of the 1,243 school-age children in our sample, follow-up address data suggested that 109 lived in Baltimore County at some point during the postprogram period, while 47 lived in Howard County at some time, 21 lived in Anne Arundel County, 3 lived in Harford County, and 2 lived in Montgomery County.

20. Ludwig, Duncan and Pinkston (2000) find that the rate of welfare receipt among experimental-group household heads in Baltimore was 15 percent lower than among the control group, although there are no differences in quarterly earnings or employment rates as measured by state unemployment insurance (UI) records. Similar null findings for UI employment are reported for the Boston MTO site by Katz, Kling and Liebman (2001). For evidence of the effects of family income on private school attendance see Figlio and Ludwig (2000).

cial education services, dropped out of school, or was retained in grade.[21] While most of these outcomes are straightforward, the dropout, CTBS, and MFT measures require some additional explanation.

Our construction of a dropout measure is complicated by the fact that the Maryland education records do not directly indicate whether students have dropped out of school. We instead construct a proxy measure that is equal to one if the student is missing school data for a given academic year, had school data available for the two preceding academic years, and was at least 15 years of age on September 1 of the academic year in which the data are missing.[22] (Maryland requires students to attend school up until their sixteenth birthday.) Since some schools may retain dropouts on their active roster for financial or other strategic reasons, we also count as dropouts those teens who are at least 15 years old on September 1 of the given academic year and record 120 absences or more. Our measure is thus more accurately described as a "public school exit" measure; in principle some of these exits could reflect moves to the private school system, although we assume that most exits are due to dropout. For simplicity we refer to this as "dropping out," although readers should be aware of the limitations of this measure.

The CTBS is a commercial multiple choice standardized achievement test for math and reading skills and is designed in part to reflect what students learn in school based on surveys of local standards and curricula. The CTBS test results are reported as the student's percentile score relative to the national distribution, which facilitates comparisons of student performance across grades and academic years. The use of percentile ranks is not useful for determining how much a given student has learned over time, since a student's percentile rank could decline over time even if her achievement in an absolute sense has increased. Yet for our purposes of comparing differences across treatment groups the use of percentile rankings is fine, especially since our regressions control for age (measured through a series of years-of-age dummies).

---

21. Our grade retention variable is equal to 1 if the student is enrolled in the same grade again during the following academic year and equal to 0 otherwise. While it may seem more natural to some readers to construct a measure indicating whether the student was enrolled in the same grade the *previous* year, note that it is this year's performance level that determines the grade in which the student is enrolled the subsequent academic year.

22. We do not classify as dropouts those students whose last reported grade was 12, since missing data in the subsequent year could reflect either grade retention and dropout or successful completion of high school.

Data on CTBS test results are available only for some students in some years because of the idiosyncracies of the testing schedules of local school systems in Maryland. The Maryland Department of Education requires school districts to administer the CTBS to at least a random sample of students in grades 2, 4, and 6 sometime in February or March of each year.[23] Some school districts choose to voluntarily test the full census of students in these grades in some academic years, or voluntarily test students enrolled in other grades as well. For example, Baltimore City administered the CTBS tests to the census of students enrolled in grades K through 5 during the spring terms of the 1993–94 and 1994–95 academic years. In the spring of 1995–96 the Baltimore City school system tested only a 10 to 15 percent random sample of students enrolled in grades 3, 5, and 8, while in the spring of 1996–97 the system tested a random sample of students in grades 2, 4, and 6.[24] In 1997–98 the system again tested a census of students in grades 1 through 5, and in 1998–99 it tested all students in grades 1 through 6. In the fall of each of these academic years the Baltimore City schools administered the CTBS to the full census of eighth grade students.

Other students may be missing CTBS test score results in some years because they were absent from school during the test dates or have been classified as having a significant learning disability. While Maryland schools offer a number of make-up dates for the CTBS tests for students who are absent on the main testing days, it is possible that students who are chronically absent may miss all of the possible testing periods. Students with significant learning disabilities are exempt from the CTBS tests if their Individual Education Plan (IEP) takes them off the regular academic track (that is, if they are no longer officially working toward a regular Maryland academic diploma). Students can in some cases be taken off the regular academic track through the IEP process quite early in their schooling careers.

The MFT program requires public school students in Maryland to pass tests in reading, mathematics, and (until recently) citizenship in order to graduate from high school. Students are allowed to begin taking these tests as early as the seventh grade, although some counties also allow students to take the

23. Maryland also requires students in grades 3, 5, and 8 to take standardized tests for the Maryland State Performance Assessment Program (MSPAP). Because the MSPAP is designed to generate performance measures at the school rather than student level, these test results are not useful for our efforts to examine the effects of the MTO demonstration on the performance of participating children.

24. The random sample was drawn by a subcontractor to the Baltimore City public school system using data tapes for student enrollment in the system.

reading MFT for practice in the sixth grade. Those who fail one or more of the tests are required to take the test again the next year, until they have passed each of the tests. Most counties report MFT results for each of the different subject tests as a raw numerical score. However, some county offices record only whether the student has passed or failed the test. As a result, we measure MFT performance through a series of dichotomous pass/fail indicators. We also restrict our attention to the MFT reading test because of missing-data problems with the MFT math results.[25] As with the CTBS tests, some students may be missing MFT results either because of absences during the primary and make-up testing periods or because their IEP exempts them from the MFT requirements.

The administrative data are thus missing information for some students and years for a variety of reasons. Our estimates for the MTO program's impacts on educational outcomes may be biased if the proportion of observations for which data are missing is unequal across MTO treatment groups in some way that is systematically related to student achievement or behavior. For example, if a larger proportion of experimental than control group students are placed in special education and exempt from standardized testing, our estimates may overstate the gains in achievement scores caused by the experimental treatment. On the other hand, data points that are missing for reasons that are uncorrelated with student characteristics (for example, because of nonmatches between the MTO records and county-level administrative data, or because of limitations with the county databases themselves)[26] or for reasons that are correlated with measurable variables (such as student age and academic year) may pose less of a threat to the validity of our estimates.

25. In Baltimore City, the school district from which most of our student-years are drawn, many schools began to phase in a computerized version of the MFT math test during our sample period. We only have results from the paper-and-pencil MFT results, which will thus capture the full set of MFT reading tests but only a subset of MFT math results. Since we might expect the more effective Baltimore City schools to be the first to volunteer for the computer-assisted math testing technology, MFT math results are likely to be missing for a nonrandom sample of MTO students.

26. Many school data-management systems are better at identifying current-year information than historical student data. For example, the Baltimore City public schools were able to provide us with information on each of the outcome variables of interest for each academic year from 1992–93 through 1998–99 with the exception of disciplinary information, which was available only for 1997–98 and 1998–99. Data on disciplinary actions were also missing for the 1995–96 academic year for Howard County. Baltimore County provided us with information on school identifiers, CTBS scores, and MFT results for students in 1996–97, 1997–98, and 1998–99, but school-absence, special education, and disciplinary-action data were only available for the 1997–98 and 1998–99 academic years. The other school districts contain only a small number of children, but similar data limitations arose with their data systems as well.

We examine the sensitivity of our estimates to problems of missing data in the following section.

Finally, working with data that are reported by academic year requires some decision about which data point should represent the child's first "postprogram" year. The goal is to count only those academic years in which the child has spent a significant amount of time in her new environment as "postprogram," while at the same time not be overly conservative and discard useful postprogram information. Our solution is to initially define the first postprogram observation as beginning with the first fall term following the family's random assignment into an MTO treatment group. For example, any student who was randomly assigned into a treatment group between January 1, 1997, and December 31, 1997, would be assigned 1997–98 as the first postprogram year. All of our regression results include as a control variable the number of days between January 1 and the date on which the family is randomly assigned. Using this definition, we have 4.2 academic years of postprogram data available for the average MTO student. In the next section we show that our main findings are not sensitive to alternative definitions.

Results

In this section we provide information about the characteristics of Baltimore MTO children and their families at baseline, followed by a discussion of their relocation outcomes. We then present our estimates for the impacts of the MTO program on children's educational outcomes, including a discussion of the sensitivity of our results to problems of missing data and other estimation issues.

Background Characteristics

Table 2 presents descriptive statistics for Baltimore MTO household heads in each of the three residential-mobility groups taken from the baseline surveys. As expected, the characteristics of household heads are quite similar across treatment groups. Almost all of the household heads in the Baltimore MTO demonstration are unmarried African American women. Only about half have either a high school diploma or GED, and the large majority received AFDC benefits at baseline. Although the majority of householders report that

Table 2. Baseline Characteristics of Baltimore MTO Households

Item	Total	Experimental	Section8–only	Control
Household characteristics				
Families (N)	638	252	188	198
African American (%)	97.3	96.9	96.8	98.4
Female householder (%)	97.9	98.4	96.2*	99.0
Householder age	33.6	33.9	33.4	33.2
Number of children	2.72	2.67	2.98	2.55
Householder w/ high school or GED (%)	57.9	59.4	60.8	53.3
AFDC at baseline (%)	81.3	80.3	83.5	80.4
During last six months, someone in HH had been victim of crime (%)	50.4	54.4*	49.9	45.7
Primary reasons for enrolling in MTO (%)				
Better schools, job access	14.4	13.1	17.9	13.3
Avoid gangs, drugs	53.6	53.9	50.7	55.8
Better apartment	26.4	26.8	27.5	25.0
Other	5.4	6.4	3.8	5.8
Second most important reason (%)				
Better schools, job access	36.1	38.3	36.3	36.7
Avoid gangs, drugs	27.9	27.5	26.8	29.3
Better apartment	29.6	26.4	33.2	30.3
Other	6.5	7.8	3.7	7.4

Source: Authors' calculations from MTO baseline survey, with weighting adjustments to account for the change in the randomization algorithm during the implementation of the Baltimore demonstration (see text).
* Difference with control group is statistically significant at 10 percent.
** Difference with control group is statistically significant at 5 percent.

they have held a job for pay at some point in their lives, only one-quarter were working at baseline.[27]

Despite the very low average earnings and employment rates reported in table 2, most families did *not* enroll in MTO to gain access to better job opportunities. This finding is not necessarily inconsistent with the "spatial mismatch hypothesis," which argues that the distance between inner-city neighborhoods and suburban job opportunities helps explain low rates of inner-city employment.[28] For example it is possible that central-city residence really does affect

27. The number of families differs across the three treatment groups because the Abt randomization algorithm attached a higher probability of assignment to the experimental group. In the Baltimore MTO site, the weighting proportions for the experimental, Section 8-only, and control groups changed on February 1, 1996, from 8:3:5 to 3:8:5. This change could in principle affect our results if average economic outcomes are different across MTO cohorts. To address this possibility, we weight all of our estimates by the sampling proportions, so that the weighted fraction of families from each cohort is equal across the three MTO treatment groups.

28. Kain (1968); Holzer (1991); Raphael (1998).

Table 3. Baseline Characteristics of MTO Children Age Six or Older at Randomization

Item[a]	Total	Experimental	Section 8–only	Control
Baseline survey data				
Age at randomization	11.19 (.23)	11.50 (.40)	11.14 (.30)	10.81 (.40)
Male	.478 (.024)	.403 (.044)**,+	.502 (.037)	.558 (.035)
Last grade	5.63 (.19)	5.85 (.34)	5.53 (.26)	5.43 (.34)
Special education status	.167 (.032)	.167 (.068)	.163 (.036)	.169 (.037)
School administrative data				
Retained in grade	.053 (.010)	.036 (.014)**	.042 (.013)*	.087 (.020)
Special education status	.155 (.020)	.102 (.028)++	.236 (.039)*	.151 (.033)
Absences	15.66 (1.11)	13.83 (1.53)*	14.82 (1.58)	18.85 (2.48)
CTBS scores, national percentile				
Reading	37.59 (1.82)	36.40 (3.27)	36.77 (2.62)	39.78 (3.28)
Math	39.48 (2.96)	41.60 (5.62)	40.22 (4.14)	35.91 (4.32)
MFT pass rate, percentage				
Reading	.151 (.058)	.210 (.108)	.104 (.073)	.087 (.062)
Dropout	.008 (.004)	.008 (.006)	.009 (.007)	.008 (.006)

* Pairwise difference with the control group statistically significant at 10 percent.
** Pairwise difference with the control group statistically significant at 5 percent.
+ Pairwise difference between experimental and Section 8-only comparison groups statistically significant at 10 percent.
++ Pairwise difference between experimental and Section 8-only comparison groups statistically significant at 5 percent.
a. Standard errors in parentheses, which are adjusted to account for presence of multiple children from the same MTO family within the sample. Information on disciplinary actions only available for students starting in first year following random assignment.

employment outcomes, but MTO household heads nonetheless rank employment as a low priority in their decision about whether to move.

About 80 percent of MTO applicants report that escaping gangs and drugs is the first or second most important reason for joining the program. This motivation is not surprising given that more than half of the MTO applicants report that at least one household member had been victimized by a crime during the past six months. While this victimization rate may be somewhat over- or understated owing to telescoping, strategic behavior, or other reporting problems,[29] this figure is nevertheless substantially higher than the six-month victimization rate of 6 percent reported by residents of public housing in the nation's largest public housing authorities. Data from MTO participants in the other program sites reveal similarly high baseline victimization rates.

Table 3 presents descriptive statistics for MTO children in Baltimore during the preprogram period, taken from both the baseline surveys and administrative school records. Both the baseline surveys and the school administrative data suggest that about one in six children were receiving spe-

29. Skogan (1981); Goering, Carnevale, and Teodoro (1999).

cial education services at the time families signed up for the program. On average MTO children missed about three weeks of school per year because of absences and had scores on the CTBS reading and math tests equal to around the fortieth percentile in the national distribution. About one of every 20 MTO school-age children were required to repeat a grade in a typical preprogram year.

Table 3 also shows that the preprogram characteristics for children are generally similar across treatment groups. Although there are a few differences across treatment groups in preprogram characteristics like gender and special education status (at least as measured by school records), an *F*-test confirms that the set of preprogram variables taken as a whole is not significantly different across treatment groups. The chance differences in some preprogram characteristics shown in table 3 highlight the importance of controlling for baseline characteristics in calculating program impacts, which we do for all of the impact estimates shown below. Preprogram characteristics could in principle also interact with the effects of the MTO program, a possibility that we explore below by re-estimating program effects for subgroups defined on the basis of baseline characteristics.

Relocation Outcomes

Of those families assigned to the MTO experimental and Section 8–only groups in the Baltimore site, the proportions who relocate through the program equal 58 and 73 percent, respectively. As noted above, most of the Section 8–only noncompliers and half of the noncompliers in the experimental group did not relocate because they did not sign a lease within the Section 8 program's 180-day time limit on housing searches. Why were some families willing and able to lease private-market apartments within this time limit while others were not?

Table 4 suggests that additional children make it more difficult to find suitable housing for families in the experimental group, consistent with evidence that three- and four-bedroom apartments are difficult to find in the private rental market.[30] We also find that households headed by younger women who are on welfare are more likely to relocate through the program, perhaps because these women feel that they have more to gain from moving. Similarly, families with more to lose appear less likely to relocate. For example, experimental families who report that they have "many" friends and family in the baseline neighborhoods are significantly less likely to relocate through the

30. Popkin and Cunningham (1999); Popkin and others (2000).

Table 4. Baseline Characteristics of Baltimore MTO Movers and Nonmovers

	Experimental		Section 8–only	
Item	*Movers*	*Nonmovers*	*Movers*	*Nonmovers*
Household characteristics				
Families (N)		146	106	137.51
African American (%)	95.5	98.6	96.3	98.5
Female householder (%)	98.8	97.9	98.1**	89.3
Householder age	32.02**	36.06	32.62**	36.20
Number of children	2.44**	2.95	2.98	2.95
Householder w/ HS or GED (%)	59.7	59.0	57.9	71.9
AFDC at baseline (%)	87.5**	71.5	86.6**	72.6
During last six months, someone in HH was victim of crime (%)	54.2	54.5	47.1	59.6
Primary reasons for enrolling in MTO (%)				
Better schools, job access	10.2	16.2	18.0	17.6
Avoid gangs, drugs	57.3	49.8	50.4	51.9
Better apartment	24.4	29.7	28.0	25.8
Other	8.1	4.2	3.5	4.7
Second most important reason (%)				
Better schools, job access	34.3	43.1	37.1	33.3
Avoid gangs, drugs	30.2	24.3	26.9	26.4
Better apartment	27.7	24.8	31.6	38.7
Other	7.9	7.7	4.3	1.6
Prevalence of family in baseline neighborhood ("none" is omitted)				
Few	46.6	46.1	46.0	52.7
Many	5.7**	14.7	7.3	6.8
Prevalence of friends in baseline neighborhood ("none" is omitted)				
Few	19.5	24.9	22.9	20.2
Many	1.2**	6.9	4.5	11.6

Source: Authors' calculations from MTO baseline survey, with weighting adjustments to account for the change in the randomization algorithm during the implementation of the Baltimore demonstration (see text).
* Difference between movers and nonmovers within MTO treatment group is statistically significant at 10 percent.
** Difference between movers and nonmovers within MTO treatment group is statistically significant at 5 percent.

MTO program. The prospect of losing access to friends and family appears to be less of a constraint for households assigned to the Section 8–only group, consistent with the fact that Section 8–only movers tend to stay close to the baseline neighborhoods (figure 1).

More detailed information about the postprogram neighborhoods of MTO families is presented in table 5. These figures show that (nearly) all of the experimental compliers moved to low-poverty census tracts with 1990 poverty

Figure 1. Relocation Outcomes of Moving to Opportunity Families, 1997

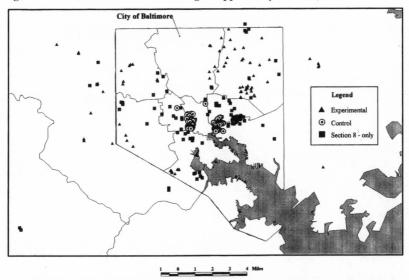

rates below 10 percent, as required by the MTO program's design.[31] Although the Section 8–only comparison group winds up in lower-poverty areas compared with control group families, only around one of every eight Section 8-only compliers voluntarily move to the lowest-poverty neighborhoods.

Table 5 also shows that the differences across MTO treatment groups in postprogram neighborhood characteristics persist even through December 1997, by which time all of the experimental families have completed their initial one-year leases and are free to relocate to higher- or lower-poverty neighborhoods as they wish. Although some control group families moved to lower-poverty neighborhoods on their own, the 1997 addresses show that only 5 percent had moved to very-low-poverty tracts (<10 percent) by this time.[32] In contrast, most of the experimental and Section 8–only compliers

31. A small proportion of experimental relocators in Baltimore moved to census tracts with 1990 poverty rates slightly higher than 10 percent. HUD and Abt Associates quickly detected the pattern and worked with CAN to ensure that all experimental relocators chose neighborhoods that met the program poverty-level requirement.

32. While the families in the control group received no mobility assistance under the MTO program, a HUD-funded Hope VI project demolished four public housing sites during our sample period, including two located in the baseline census tracts (Lafayette Courts and Lexington Terrace.) Hence all families in these buildings, including around one-fifth of the families in the MTO control group, were forced to relocate either to other public housing buildings or to private housing with Section 8 subsidies.

Table 5. Relocation Outcomes for MTO Families

Item	Baseline (all families) 1994–96	Experimental Initial postprogram	Experimental As of December 1997	Section 8–only Initial postprogram	Section 8–only As of December 1997	Control Initial postprogram	Control As of December 1997
Distribution of MTO households[a]							
Jurisdiction :							
Baltimore City	100.0	77.1	79.4	89.9	86.7	99.5	98.0
Anne Arundel County	0.0	0.8	2.0	0.0	0.5	0.0	0.0
Baltimore County	0.0	13.0	10.7	5.3	8.0	0.0	1.0
Harford County	0.0	0.4	0.4	0.0	0.0	0.0	0.0
Howard County	0.0	7.1	5.9	2.7	2.7	0.0	0.5
Montgomery County	0.0	0.4	0.4	0.0	0.0	0.0	0.0
Other	0.0	1.2	1.2	2.1	2.1	0.5	0.5
% Census tract poor:							
0–9.9	0.0	49.4	43.0	8.7	12.5	0.0	4.5
10–19.9	0.0	4.8	8.4	14.7	21.2	0.0	7.6
20–29.9	0.2	0.0	7.6	10.3	15.8	0.0	3.0
30–39.9	0.3	0.4	4.0	12.5	13.0	0.0	6.6
40–49.9	2.0	1.6	6.4	9.8	7.1	2.0	6.6
50–59.9	4.4	1.2	4.0	6.5	4.9	5.6	4.5
60–69.9	52.5	22.7	18.7	26.6	19.6	49.0	43.4
70–79.9	20.4	9.6	4.0	7.1	3.8	23.2	14.6
80 plus	20.1	10.4	4.0	3.8	2.2	20.2	9.1

a. Neighborhood characteristics are calculated using 1990 Census data.

remain in neighborhoods that are quite similar to those into which they originally moved through MTO.

MTO Program Impacts

The advantage of using administrative school records rather than surveys to measure children's educational outcomes is that multiple years of data are available for each child, information that would be difficult and expensive to obtain through a prospective longitudinal survey design. Administrative records are also less susceptible to the self-reporting problems that may arise with respect to sensitive behaviors such as academic achievement or problem behaviors. One disadvantage is that the administrative school records in Maryland are missing data elements for the variety of reasons discussed above.

Table 6 provides a first look at the missing-data issue by reporting the proportion of school-age MTO children for whom we have at least one observation for our various outcome measures during the postprogram period. In the table and throughout the remainder of the paper we focus separately on children who were at least 5 but less than 12 years of age at the time of random assignment (hereafter "young children") and children who were 12 and older at randomization (hereafter "adolescents" or "teens") for two reasons. First, the availability of achievement data varies considerably by age: while we often have results from both the CTBS and MFT testing programs for younger children, we only have results from the MFT for teens. Second, interventions such as MTO may have greater effects on achievement for younger children because the annual rate of change in children's test scores appears to decrease with age, or because young children from high-poverty areas may be more receptive to changes in social environments or are not yet as far behind in school as older children.[33] Whatever the reason, our analysis does in fact reveal differential program impacts for younger versus older children.

As seen in table 6, for elementary-school children we have at least one CTBS reading and math score for 53 and 46 percent of the sample, respectively. These proportions are roughly equal for the experimental and control groups, although the figures are somewhat lower for the Section 8–only group. We have at least one MFT result for only about one-quarter of the sample of young children but nearly two-thirds of the sample of students ages 12 and older at random assignment. For the large majority of both the younger and older samples we have at least one postprogram observation for disciplinary records, school absences, special education status, and grade retention. As a

33 . Entwistle, Alexander, and Olson (1997).

Table 6. Percent of MTO Children with Postprogram School-Records Data

Item[a]	Total	Experimental	Section 8–only	Control
Full sample born 1970–1993 (N = 1,237)				
≥ CTBS reading score (%)	33.33	36.70	28.12	33.87
≥ CTBS math score	29.35	31.96	24.40	30.83
≥ MFT reading result	33.14	36.70	28.12	33.60
≥ Disciplinary-problem observation	94.18	93.20	93.10	96.53
≥ School-absence observation	86.18	85.77	84.08	88.80
≥ Special-education status obs.	86.26	85.77	84.35	88.80
≥ Grade-retention observation	80.27	78.66	78.25	84.53
Students ≥ and <12 at				
random assignment (N = 669)				
≥ CTBS reading score (%)	52.62	60.66	41.31	54.64
≥ CTBS math score	46.19	52.59	35.74	50.24
≥ MFT reading result	26.16	29.48	20.66	27.80
≥ Disciplinary-problem observation	94.92	94.12	93.90	97.17
≥ School-absence observation	90.73	90.84	88.73	92.68
≥ Special-education status obs.	90.88	90.84	89.20	92.68
≥ Grade-retention observation	88.64	87.65	86.85	91.71
Students ≥2 at				
random assignment				
≥ MFT reading result (%)	62.17	63.41	59.62	62.73
≥ Disciplinary-problem observation	96.03	95.12	95.19	98.18
≥ School-absence observation	87.25	75.61	75.00	81.82
≥ Special-education status obs.	77.51	76.22	75.00	81.82
≥ Grade-retention observation	66.14	63.41	63.46	72.73

a. Authors' calculations from administrative school records and baseline household information for Baltimore MTO demonstration.

first cut we will assume that outcome data are missing at random (MAR) for MTO children in the Maryland administrative records, although in the next section we explore the sensitivity of our findings to this assumption.

SCHOOLING PATTERNS AMONG CONTROL GROUP CHILDREN. What are the effects of the MTO program on children's educational outcomes? To provide some context for the answer to this question, in table 7 we provide descriptive information about the developmental trajectory of children in the control group. Using data from both the pre- and postprogram periods, we calculate average educational outcomes for control group children by age. To reduce the effects of year-to-year sampling variability, the table presents three-year moving averages (for example, the results for age 11 actually represent the average outcomes for children ages 10 through 12).

Table 7 shows that in general as children in the control group age, their educational outcomes deteriorate either absolutely or relative to the national

Table 7. Developmental Patterns for MTO Control Group Children

Children's age[b]	Retained in grade	Dropout	Absences	CTBS[a] reading	CTBS[a] math	Pass MFT[a] reading	Suspended/ expelled	Special education
6	.043		10.38	38.73	38.52		.051	.090
7	.078		9.17	32.74	35.67		.041	.107
8	.080		8.58	32.48	33.60		.030	.128
9	.082		9.05	27.59	30.23		.069	.173
10	.059		11.51	22.66	27.77		.140	.208
11	.066		15.55	16.89	25.17	.169	.212	.221
12	.066		19.74	18.96	21.55	.181	.264	.215
13	.109		25.62	18.60	20.19	.212	.240	.203
14	.140		30.95			.241	.167	.184
15	.165	.125	37.51			.287	.074	.165
16	.111	.208	37.26			.316	.014	.176
17	.064	.284	34.69			.394	.039	.234
18	.071	.356	24.64				.080	.300

a. Comprehensive Test of Basic Skills; Maryland Functional Tests

b. In order to reduce sampling variability from year-to-year changes in educational outcomes, the results for each age represent three-year moving averages (so that, for example, the results for age 10 represent the average outcomes for children ages 9–11).

average. For example, while control group children on average score near the fortieth percentile in the national distribution on the CTBS reading and math tests at age six, by age 13 the average score is only at about the twentieth percentile. We also see that the proportion of students who receive special education services increases steadily over time. Grade retentions, school absences, and disciplinary problems all peak in the early or mid-teen years. The subsequent decline is presumably due to the increase in dropout rates at older ages.

The MTO experimental and Section 8–only comparison treatments seem to slow the rate of relative decline in children's test scores as they age, at least for younger children, but MTO also appears to increase the rate of grade retention among adolescents. These findings come from estimating the program's intent-to-treat impacts from equation (2), controlling for baseline child and family characteristics, preprogram educational outcomes for the first and second years prior to randomization, and a series of dummy variables indicating years since random assignment and academic calendar year.

MTO EFFECTS ON YOUNG CHILDREN. Table 8 shows the intent-to-treat effects of the MTO program on each of our educational outcomes for young children. Compared with young children in the control group, those assigned to the experimental group experience substantial gains in academic achievement as measured by standardized test scores. Experimental children are nearly 18 percentage points more likely than controls to pass the MFT reading test, which means that the experimental pass rate on this test is nearly double that of the control group. The CTBS reading and math scores of experimental children are about 7 percentile points higher than those of the control group, equal to around 29 and 26 percent of the control group means on these tests. Another way to judge the magnitude of the CTBS impacts is by comparison to the standard deviation of the test score distribution. The experimental treatment effect on the CTBS reading and math scores equal 27 and 25 percent of the standard deviation in percentile scores observed among the MTO samples, or 25 and 26 percent of a standard deviation in the national CTBS reading and math distributions.[34] In contrast to the test score results, we find no statistically significant differences between experimental and control

---

34. We calculate the standard deviation for the national percentile scores by noting that percentile rankings have by construction a uniform distribution over the integers from one through 100, and then applying the formula for a standard deviation of a continuous uniform distribution over a defined interval. See, for example, McClave and Benson (1985, p. 223).

Table 8. Intent-to-Treat Effects of MTO Program on Young Children

Item[a]	N	Control mean	Experimental versus control	Section 8–only comparison versus control
MFT, reading (fraction pass)	347	.192 (.059)	.178 (.083)**	.059 (.093)
CTBS, reading (percentile score)	458	25.13 (2.47)	7.34 (2.75)**	6.39 (3.23)**
CTBS, math (percentile score)	404	28.77 (2.69)	7.48 (3.67)**	1.48 (3.83)
Absences (days)	2,200	12.54 (1.02)	0.57 (1.16)	1.10 (1.31)
Grade retention (fraction retained)	1,711	.075 (.010)	-.013 (.013)	.002 (.015)
Disciplinary actions (fraction suspended/ expelled during year)	1,123	.150 (.026)	-.015 (.031)	.001 (.039)
Special education (fraction)	2,206	.162 (.024)	.043 (.032)	.052 (.037)

* Statistically significant at 10 percent.
** Statistically significant at 5 percent.
a. Sample restricted to MTO children ages ≥ and <12 at random assignment. Robust standard errors shown in parentheses, which are adjusted to account for panel structure of dataset and presence of multiple children from the same family within our analytic sample. Estimates are calculated controlling for preprogram educational outcomes, as well as baseline family characteristics (see text).

children with respect to special education placements, absences, grade retention, or disciplinary problems.[35]

Assignment to the Section 8–only comparison treatment appears to improve young children's CTBS reading scores by about 6 percentile points relative to controls, although the difference across groups in CTBS math scores is relatively small and is not statistically significant. The Section 8–only group also appears to pass the MFT reading test at a rate that is around 6 percentage points higher than that of controls, but the difference is again not statistically significant.

Since a child's educational performance at a point in time is a product of her current and past educational "inputs," we may expect the MTO program's impacts on educational outcomes to increase over time. Unfortunately, the data reveal no clear patterns in the program impacts over time, because of both the reasonably modest number of data points available for each academic

35. We also examine the probability of being enrolled in the same grade in year 0 and year 1, as would occur if schools in low-poverty areas have higher standards than baseline schools and thus move experimental relocators to a more appropriate grade level. However, we find no differences across treatment groups using this measure.

year and the limited number of postprogram academic years in our data. Revisiting the temporal patterns of program effects using a longer postprogram observation period is an obvious priority for future research.

We might expect some differences in the MTO program's impacts by gender because of differences in how boys and girls socialize with others, or because boys tend to spend more time outside in their neighborhoods than girls.[36] But we find that the effects of the MTO demonstration on educational outcomes in general seem to be at least as large for girls as for boys. We are unable to examine the program's effects on separate racial or ethnic groups since (as seen in table 2) almost all of the MTO participants in Baltimore are African American.

It is also possible that low-income children may be more likely to take advantage of whatever new opportunities are afforded by more affluent areas when they are actively encouraged and assisted by their parents. We test this hypothesis by reestimating the MTO program's impacts on those young children whose mothers are most likely to be engaged with school-related matters, as suggested by their mother's educational attainment or reason for volunteering for the MTO demonstration.

The results of estimating separate program impacts by parent education or motivation for program participation are somewhat mixed. Young children in households headed by someone who had a high school degree or equivalent or signed up for MTO for access to better schools seemed to experience above-average gains in CTBS math and reading scores from assignment to the experimental or Section 8–only groups. These children, however, may have experienced below-average benefits in terms of MFT reading pass rates, school absences, and other outcome measures.

MTO EFFECTS ON ADOLESCENTS. For adolescents (those 12 years old and over at random assignment) the only available measure of academic achievement is the MFT reading test, for which there are no statistically significant differences across MTO treatment groups (table 9). However, we do observe a substantial and statistically significant increase in grade retentions for experimental and Section 8–only teens relative to controls. Table 9 also reveals relatively large increases in the proportion of experimental and Section 8–only teens who are suspended or expelled from school relative to control teens, although only the experimental ITT effect is statistically significant (and only

36. Heyns (1978); Furstenberg and Hughes (1997).

Table 9. Intent-to-Treat Effects of MTO Program on Adolescents

Item[a]	N	Control mean	Experimental versus control	Section 8–only comparison versus control
MFT, reading (fraction pass)	679	.268 (.063)	.073 (.072)	-.009 (.071)
Absences (days)	825	29.85 (2.20)	2.06 (2.92)	1.78 (3.45)
Grade retention (fraction retained)	564	.092 (.021)	.065 (.032)**	.109 (.052)**
Disciplinary actions (fraction suspended/ expelled during year)	328	.126 (.033)	.086 (.050)*	.088 (.069)
Special education (fraction)	826	.202 (.049)	-.017 (.050)	.013 (.059)
Dropout	1384	.187 (.030)	.062 (.036)*	.019 (.043)

a. Sample restricted to MTO children ages ≥12 at random assignment. Robust standard errors shown in parentheses, which are adjusted to account for panel structure of dataset and presence of multiple children from the same family within our analytic sample. Estimates are calculated controlling for preprogram educational outcomes, as well as baseline family characteristics (see text).
* Statistically significant at 10 percent.
** Statistically significant at 5 percent.

at the 10 percent level). As with our study of young children's outcomes, we are unable to draw any firm conclusions about whether the program effects on these teen outcomes grow or diminish over time because of the relatively short postprogram observation period and the modest number of data points per academic year.

Among teens we observe no systematic differences in MTO effects by parental educational attainment at baseline or by the reasons that parents signed up for the program. However, since boys account for nearly three-quarters of all arrests of people under age 18 in the United States, we might expect that any increase in problem behaviors among experimental and Section 8–only teens will be concentrated among boys.[37] But in fact the point estimates for the effects of the experimental and Section 8–only treatment on disciplinary problems in school are positive and sizable for both boys and girls. One possible explanation is that teen problem behaviors in school are actually fairly similar across MTO groups, but schools serving more affluent communities have higher academic and behavioral standards than schools in poor areas. We return to this possibility in the discussion below.

EFFECTS OF TREATMENT ON THE TREATED. Finally, the results in tables 10 and 11 show our estimates for the other policy-relevant measure of MTO's

37. Maguire and Pastore (1999, p. 341).

Table 10. MTO Effects of Treatment on the Treated for Young Children

Item[a]	Experimental treatment					Section 8–only comparison treatment				
	Movers	Nonmovers	CCM[b]	Comply rate[c]	TOT	Movers	Nonmovers	CCM[b]	Comply rate[c]	TOT
MFT, reading (fraction pass)	.518	.181	.210	.52	.308 (.166)*	.203	.039	.152	.86	.051 (.105)
CTBS, reading (percentile score)	32.50	27.78	21.27	.68	11.23 (4.39)**	33.79	17.25	27.29	.85	6.50 (3.84)*
CTBS, math (percentile score)	32.15	31.47	22.41	.68	9.74 (6.11)	31.38	18.82	27.10	.85	4.28 (4.54)
Absences (days)	11.56	16.28	9.80	.55	1.76 (2.10)	13.60	16.38	12.41	.82	1.19 (1.57)
Grade retention (fraction retained)	.048	.073	.069	.58	-.021 (.023)	.072	.072	.070	.83	.002 (.018)
Disciplinary actions (fraction suspended / expelled during year)	.130	.149	.151	.57	-.021 (.056)	.150	.055	.170	.82	-.020 (.052)
Special education (fraction)	.189	.198	.102	.55	.087 (.058)	.192	.304	.146	.82	.046 (.045)

* Statistically significant at 10 percent.
** Statistically significant at the 5 percent level.
a. Sample restricted to MTO children ages ≥ 2 and <12 at random assignment. Robust standard errors shown in parentheses, which are adjusted to account for panel structure of dataset and presence of multiple children from the same family within our analytic sample. TOT estimates are calculated via two-stage least squares using each family's MTO random assignment outcome as an instrumental variable for an indicator for relocation through the MTO program. The two-stage least squares model controls for preprogram educational outcomes, as well as baseline family characteristics (see text).
b. Control complier mean equals the estimated average outcome of those families who are assigned to the control group but would have relocated through the MTO program had they been assigned instead to a treatment group.
c. The "comply rate" is calculated as the proportion of experimental or Section 8-only student-years in our panel dataset that correspond to a student whose family relocated through the MTO program.

Table 11. MTO Effects of Treatment on the Treated, Adolescents

Item[a]	Experimental treatment					Section 8–only comparison treatment				
	Movers	Nonmovers	CCM[b]	Comply rate[c]	TOT	Movers	Nonmovers	CCM[b]	Comply rate[c]	TOT
MFT, reading (fraction pass)	.348	.318	.190	.47	.158 (.142)	.202	.312	.179	.67	.023 (.102)
Absences (days)	32.32	31.05	30.54	.47	1.78 (5.56)	38.88	29.71	37.39	.67	1.49 (4.88)
Grade retention (fraction retained)	.157	.115	.048	.48	.109 (.060)*	.264	.124	.064	.67	.200 (.077)**
Disciplinary actions (fraction suspended / expelled during year)	.172	.156	.024	.47	.148 (.107)	.213	.167	.163	.66	.050 (.108)
Special education (fraction)	.185	.125	.060	.47	-.015 (.094)	.326	.234	.318	.67	.008 (.081)
Dropout	.213	.177	.100	.47	.113 (.076)	.214	.173	.203	.72	.011 (.060)

* Statistically significant at 10 percent.
** Statistically significant at the 5 percent level.
a. Sample restricted to MTO children ages ≥ and <12 at random assignment. Robust standard errors shown in parentheses, which are adjusted to account for panel structure of dataset and presence of multiple children from the same family within our analytic sample. TOT estimates are calculated via two-stage least squares using each family's MTO random assignment outcome as an instrumental variable for an indicator for relocation through the MTO program. The two-stage least squares model controls for preprogram educational outcomes, as well as baseline family characteristics (see text).
b. Control complier mean equals the estimated average outcome of those families who are assigned to the control group but would have relocated through the MTO program had they been assigned instead to a treatment group.
c. The "comply rate" is calculated as the proportion of experimental or Section 8–only student-years in our panel dataset that correspond to a student whose family relocated through the MTO program.

impacts: the effects of treatment on the treated. As noted above, in large samples the TOT effect for the experimental and Section 8–only group will equal the ITT effects shown in tables 8 and 9 divided by the proportion of families in the experimental and Section 8–only groups who relocate through the MTO program (58 and 73 percent). The TOT estimates shown in tables 10 and 11 differ somewhat from this ratio, in part because the compliance rate among those children for whom we have valid postprogram observations differs somewhat from that observed among all MTO families.

The TOT estimates for young children shown in table 10 show that the gains in CTBS reading and math scores by young children whose families move as part of the experimental group are about twice as large as the gains experienced by Section 8–only movers. Since the average change in neighborhood poverty rates was around twice as large for experimental compared with Section 8–only compliers,[38] the TOT estimates provide at least suggestive evidence that changes in children's test scores may be proportional to changes in neighborhood poverty rates. While the improvement in MFT pass rates is six times as large for the experimental than Section 8–only compliers, this is not inconsistent with a linear neighborhood effect since a pass/fail indicator is itself a nonlinear outcome measure indicating whether some underlying continuous variable (in this case reading achievement) crosses a given threshold.[39] Because most of the outcome measures available for adolescents (table 11) are also nonlinear indicators, we have little to say about whether neighborhood effects on this group are proportional to changes in neighborhood characteristics.

It is important to recognize that these comparisons of TOT effects for the experimental and Section 8–only groups provide only a rough indication of whether neighborhood effects are nonlinear. While the TOT effects may be

38. Among the Baltimore MTO sample of all school-age children (ages 5 and older at baseline), the average postprogram census tract poverty rate equaled 8.4 and 35.2 percent for the neighborhoods into which experimental and Section 8–only comparison compliers initially moved through the MTO program. In contrast, the average postprogram poverty rate for the census tracts in which the control group resided was around 70 percent. Thus the average experimental-group complier experiences a change in neighborhood poverty rates that is about 1.8 times as large as that of the average Section 8–only complier.

39. For example, suppose that all experimental and Section 8–only children have raw MFT reading scores equal to 205 at baseline, that the pass rate on the MFT reading test is 220, and that all Section 8-only compliers gain 10 points on the raw MFT scale, while experimental compliers all gain 18 points. In this case the actual gain in underlying MFT raw scores is perfectly linear with respect to changes in neighborhood poverty rates, yet there is now a 100 percentage point improvement in MFT pass rates for experimental movers and no improvement at all in pass rates for Section 8–only movers.

proportional to changes in census-tract poverty rates, they may be nonlinear for other neighborhood characteristics that could be responsible for the observed MTO effects. Moreover, the comparison of experimental and Section 8–only TOT effects may confound nonlinearities in neighborhood effects with heterogeneity in how families respond to mobility programs, since the two subgroups that chose to comply with the experimental and Section 8–only treatments could in principle have different average responses to the exact same intervention.

With these caveats in mind, as best we can judge the MTO data provide no compelling evidence to suggest that the relationship between children's outcomes and neighborhood poverty is very nonlinear. At the same time, the evidence also suggests that the program's effects are due at least in part to moving to different types of neighborhoods rather than moving *per se*, since in table 10 we find some evidence of a "dose-response" relationship in which more substantial changes in neighborhood poverty induce larger changes in young children's test scores.

Lastly, the TOT results can also be used to determine which types of families are most likely to relocate through the MTO program. If the control-complier mean for positive outcomes exceeds the mean for the control group as a whole, families whose children are disposed toward more academic and pro-social outcomes are more likely to move through MTO to more affluent areas ("positive selection"). Table 10 provides some indication of *negative selection* with respect to young children's educational outcomes, particularly with respect to children's academic achievement and special education status. While the evidence on selection with respect to adolescent schooling outcomes is more mixed (table 11), data from both the Baltimore and Boston MTO sites provide more consistent evidence of negative selection with respect to teen out-of-school problem behaviors.[40]

Sensitivity Analyses

The estimates presented in the previous section assume that postprogram school records are missing at random (MAR) for MTO children. In this section we test this assumption in four ways and conclude that as far as we can tell the results are not very sensitive to problems of missing data. We also examine the sensitivity of our findings to other estimation issues.

MISSING DATA. One way to test the MAR assumption directly is to regress a dichotomous indicator equal to one if a given outcome measure is missing

40. Katz, Kling and Liebman, (2001); Ludwig, Duncan, and Hirschfield (2001).

for a given student in a given year against a set of preprogram characteristics such as the child's baseline special education status and number of siblings, as well as the mother's marital status, age, educational attainment, and employment and welfare status, and indicators for the academic year and the child's age in each year. We find that variables indicating the academic year and the child's age in each year are strong predictors for missing data for each of these outcome variables, which is consistent with the idiosyncracies described above in the availability of school records for certain years and grades. We also find that conditional on year and age, formal F-tests suggest that the other baseline child and family characteristics are almost never significant predictors of data availability (the one exception being for our measure of disciplinary actions).[41] Conditional on age, year, and baseline characteristics, experimental and Section 8–only students are more likely than controls to be missing data on grade of attendance, absences, and special education status, but no more likely to be missing data on disciplinary actions or, perhaps more important, CTBS or MFT test results.

A related way to test the MAR assumption is to examine whether our estimates are sensitive to the inclusion of baseline control variables, since systematic patterns of missing data may cause the samples of children for whom we have valid outcome data to be unbalanced across treatment groups with respect to observable preprogram characteristics. Yet we find that our estimates for the program's impacts are generally not very sensitive to whether we control for preprogram child and family characteristics. The one exception is for CTBS math scores among young children, where the experimental ITT effect is equal to 3.7 percentile points with no preprogram controls, an effect that increases to 4.2 points after controlling for age and increases again to 7.5 points (and becomes statistically significant) when we include controls for age and other preprogram student and family characteristics.

A third way to examine the sensitivity of our estimates to the problem of missing data is to replace missing values with the most recent observation available on that variable for the student in question as in Krueger.[42] Table 12 shows that experimental children are still more likely than controls to pass the

41. Regressing these missing-data indicators against preprogram school outcomes taken from the official school records is complicated because the preprogram school outcomes are strongly correlated with the child's age for two reasons. First, older children are more likely to have valid preprogram outcome measures recorded on their school records. Second, given the gradual deterioration in average educational outcomes as children age documented above, older children will have systematically worse preprogram outcomes compared with younger children.

42. Krueger (1999).

Table 12. Intent-to-Treat Effects of MTO Program on Young Children with Interpolation of Missing Data

Item[a]	N	Experimental versus control	Section 8–only comparison versus control
MFT, reading (fraction pass)	356	.157 (.081)*	.044 (.092)
CTBS, reading (percentile score)	955	2.963 (1.552)*	2.144 (1.743)
CTBS, math (percentile score)	840	3.790 (1.893)**	.398 (1.922)
Absences (days)	2345	.002 (1.062)	.426 (1.220)
Grade retention (fraction retained)	1711	-.013 (.013)	.002 (.015)
Disciplinary actions (fraction suspended / expelled during year)	1174	-.013 (.030)	-.006 (.037)
Special education (fraction)	2346	.034 (.031)	.039 (.035)
Dropout	2674	.001 (.003)	.001 (.003)

* Statistically significant at 10 percent.
** Statistically significant at 5 percent.
a. Sample restricted to MTO children ages ≥ and <12 at random assignment. Robust standard errors shown in parentheses, which are adjusted to account for panel structure of dataset and presence of multiple children from the same family within our analytic sample. Estimates are calculated controlling for preprogram educational outcomes, as well as baseline family characteristics (see text).

MFT reading test and have higher CTBS reading and math scores when we interpolate missing values, although the magnitudes of the CTBS test score gains are about half as large as those shown in table 8. Similarly, older children in the experimental and Section 8–only group still appear to be more likely than controls to be retained in grade when we interpolate missing values in this way (table 13).[43]

One final check on the missing-data problem is suggested by the fact that test score data are more likely to be missing for special education students or those with large numbers of absences. In table 8 we showed that for younger children, special education placements may be somewhat higher among experimental and Section 8–only students than among controls. It is thus possible that the test score differences reported in table 8 could be due to the exclusion of a higher proportion of students from the bottom of the achievement distribution in the experimental and Section 8–only groups relative to controls. We examine the sensitivity of our estimates to this problem by re-

43. Yet another approach for examining the sensitivity of our analysis to missing values is to use the bounding strategy outlined by Manski (1995), although this approach is unfortunately not very informative in our application given the proportion of observations that are missing.

Table 13. Intent-to-Treat Effects of MTO Program on Adolescents with Interpolation of Missing Data

Item[a]	N	Experimental versus control	Section 8–only comparison versus control
MFT, reading (fraction pass)	811	.035 (.060)	-.024 (.061)
Absences (days)	1023	-.318 (2.199)	1.088 (2.690)
Grade retention (fraction retained)	564	.065 (.032)**	.109 (.052)**
Disciplinary actions (fraction suspended / expelled during year)	428	.062 (.039)	.056 (.047)
Special education (fraction)	1026	-.032 (.042)	.005 (.048)
Dropout	1258	.035 (.019)*	.005 (.024)

* Statistically significant at 10 percent.
** Statistically significant at 5 percent.

a. Sample restricted to MTO children ages ≥ and <12 at random assignment. Robust standard errors shown in parentheses, which are adjusted to account for panel structure of dataset and presence of multiple children from the same family within our analytic sample. Estimates are calculated controlling for preprogram educational outcomes, as well as baseline family characteristics (see text).

estimating the MTO effects after excluding students who are in special education during the preprogram period (who presumably represent most of the students whose IEP's would be upgraded in low-poverty schools to exempt them from postprogram testing) and students who have more than 20 absences during the preprogram year (and thus are presumably at above-average risk for high absences during the postprogram period). We find that the general pattern of MTO impacts is qualitatively similar to those shown above when we drop students who are in special education or often absent during the preprogram period.

OTHER ESTIMATION ISSUES. Our findings for the MTO program's impact do not appear to be sensitive to the particular estimation method used to statistically adjust for chance differences in preprogram characteristics. We use ordinary least squares for the estimates presented above because of the simplicity of calculating TOT effects with linear models. Yet in principle a probit or logit model might yield different estimates for the effects of MTO assignments on dichotomous outcomes such as suspensions, grade retention, or dropout. A log-linear model may provide a better fit for the pattern of CTBS reading and math scores across the MTO sample. And even though ordinary least squares is unbiased for count data such as school absences, Poisson or negative-binomial models may be more efficient. But these alternative estimation methods all yield qualitatively similar findings to those presented above.[44]

Similarly, the results are robust to alternative methods for defining which academic year is counted as each student's first "postprogram" observation. Our benchmark estimates presented above define each child's first postprogram academic year as the first fall following (or including) the family's random assignment. We re-estimated all of our results defining the first post-program observation as the first full academic year following the student's random assignment to an MTO treatment group (so a student who was randomly assigned some time between September 1, 1996, and August 31, 1997, would be assigned 1997–98 as her first postprogram academic year). Using this definition, the pattern of findings is qualitatively similar to those shown in tables 8 and 9.[45]

Discussion

The Baltimore MTO experiment provides a unique opportunity to overcome the self-selection problems that plague nonexperimental studies of neighborhood effects on children's schooling. In the following pages we review our main findings and discuss the implications for future research and public policy.

Findings

The offer to move families from very high- to very low-poverty neighborhoods (the MTO experimental treatment) appears to substantially improve the

44. Cameron and Trivedi (1998). Our regression adjustment focuses on controlling for pre-program characteristics, the only exceptions being indicator variables for the academic year and year since random assignment. Some might argue for also controlling for the grade in which the student is enrolled during each of the postprogram years, since students who are retained in grade during the postprogram period wind up taking easier standardized tests than they would if they had been promoted on schedule (and thus may look better with respect to the national distribution). Yet differences in grade retention are unlikely to explain our findings for standardized tests for younger children (table 8) since we observe differences in grade retentions across treatment groups for older but not younger children. More generally, when we re-estimate the MTO treatment effects controlling for the grade in which the student is enrolled each postprogram year we obtain similar findings to those shown above.

45. We find that the positive differential in special education placements for young children in the experimental group compared to controls is now statistically significant at the 5 percent level. For adolescents we find a larger effect of the experimental treatment on dropout rates compared with table 9 but a smaller effect on grade retention and disciplinary actions.

reading and math test scores of young children, defined as those between the ages of 5 and 12 at the time of random assignment. Assignment to the experimental group nearly doubles the proportion of young children who pass the Maryland Functional Testing program's reading test and increases standardized CTBS reading and math scores by around one-quarter of a standard deviation. In contrast, assigning families to the Section 8–only group, which produces less dramatic changes in neighborhood poverty rates compared with the experimental treatment, improves young children's performance on the CTBS reading test but not on other achievement measures.

For adolescents in the experimental and Section 8–only groups we find slightly higher rates of grade retention than controls and perhaps more disciplinary actions and school dropout rates as well. These findings should be qualified by the observation that our dropout measure is far from perfect, and our finding for disciplinary actions is somewhat sensitive to how we define the student's first postprogram data point. But more important, unlike with standardized achievement tests that are designed to provide consistent measures of students in different schools, the behaviors that lead to grade retention and disciplinary actions are defined by local teachers and principals and may thus vary across schools. Talking back to a teacher may be a minor offense in a high-poverty school in which guns, drugs, and gangs are common but may earn a suspension or even expulsion in a low-poverty school where behavioral problems are rare. This raises the possibility that experimental and Section 8–only teens may be subject to school sanctions more often than control teens even if there are no differences across groups in school-based problem behaviors. And in fact our data provide some support for this hypothesis.

If the additional grade retention or suspensions observed within the experimental and Section 8–only groups are caused by an increase in teen problem behavior, we would expect the experimental and Section 8-only groups to also experience more school absences and lower MFT pass rates. Absences and MFT test results are correlated with grade retention and disciplinary actions but are presumably not very sensitive to variation across schools in behavioral or academic standards.[46] We find that conditioning on each teen's absences and MFT reading status in a given postprogram period (t) hardly affects the magnitudes of the experimental and Section 8–only ITT effects on adolescent

---

46. The correlations between grade retention and absences and MFT status equal 0.40 and - 0.17, respectively; the F statistic in a regression of grade retention against these explanatory variables equals 66.3 ($p < .001$). The correlations between disciplinary actions and absences and MFT status equal 0.22 and -0.06, while the F-test of the joint explanatory power of these variables in a regression for disciplinary problems yields a statistic of 3.7 ($p < .05$).

grade retention and disciplinary actions in the same period. MTO's effects on grade retention and disciplinary problems are thus due either to changes in underlying problem behaviors that are uncorrelated with absences and test scores or, perhaps more likely, to higher behavioral and academic standards in the schools serving low-poverty census tracts.

In sum, the evidence presented here seems to suggest that the offer to relocate families in public housing from high- to low-poverty neighborhoods improves standardized achievement test scores among young children. While we have subjected our findings to a variety of sensitivity tests, there nevertheless remains the possibility that the estimated program effects may be due in part to problems of missing data. The effects of the program on teens are more difficult to determine because our measures of in-school problem behavior confound changes in the behaviors of teens with differences across schools in standards and because the measures of academic achievement available for teens are quite limited in our Maryland education data.

Policy Implications

What do these results imply for urban policy? The answer depends in part on why the MTO program improves the academic achievement of young children. For example, suppose that MTO improves young children's test scores by exposing them to schools with smaller class sizes. In this case policymakers could improve the academic outcomes of poor children in high-poverty urban neighborhoods without relocating them to lower-poverty areas, although of course policymakers may wish to relocate poor families for other reasons beyond the desire to improve children's educational outcomes. Policies that change the way that poor or minority students are sorted across schools (without moving their families) might improve the achievement of these children if changes in school quality or school-based peer interactions are important explanations for the MTO program impacts. If the MTO program impacts are because families move rather than because of any specific changes in neighborhood characteristics, then housing voucher programs may improve the educational outcomes of children in public housing even if their families do not move to lower-poverty areas.

The sensitivity of young children's outcomes to the magnitude of the change in neighborhood poverty rates that they experience suggests that MTO does not improve test scores solely through a generic moving effect. Some actual differences between high- and low-poverty neighborhoods appear to be responsible for the reported MTO program impacts, although disentangling the specific neighborhood attributes that are responsible for these effects is complicated by the fact that the program changes children's schools and all of their neighborhood attributes simultaneously.

The pattern of program impacts on test scores in reading versus math provides some limited information about the relative importance of the effects of changing schools versus changing neighborhoods. Previous studies often find that school characteristics or school-based interventions have more pronounced effects on math than reading scores, while the out-of-school environment has stronger effects on reading.[47] Thus if MTO's effects on children's test scores were due exclusively to changes in school quality, we would expect the program's impacts to be much larger for math than reading. Because the reading gains for young children in the experimental and Section 8–only groups are at least as large as their math gains, changes in neighborhood characteristics may be responsible for at least part of MTO's impact on academic achievement.[48] However, without more reliable information about the relative importance of different neighborhood and school attributes for children's outcomes, policymakers will be unable to replicate MTO's effects by targeting interventions at specific neighborhood characteristics within high-poverty urban areas.

On the other hand, policies that enable poor families to move from high-poverty areas to more economically mixed neighborhoods may improve children's educational outcomes even if we do not understand the specific mechanisms through which residential mobility operates. One way to help poor families conduct such moves is through HUD's existing Section 8 housing programs, although the degree of additional economic desegregation that will result from such policies remains somewhat unclear. Previous evaluations

47. See, for example, Ferguson and Ladd (1996); Grissmer, Flanagan and Williamson (1998); Rouse (1998).

48. In principle another way to disentangle school from neighborhood effects is to focus on the difference in neighborhood effects on test score changes during the school year (when children are exposed to family, neighborhood, and school factors) and during the summer term (when children are primarily exposed to family and neighborhood factors, setting aside the possibility of summer school). This disaggregation requires test scores measured at the beginning and end of each academic year, while the school records in Maryland typically only provide a spring test score for children. Previous research by Entwisle, Alexander, and Olson (1997) attempts to distinguish between the effects of school and out-of-school factors by focusing on patterns of summer "fall back" across neighborhoods. The authors find that children attending elementary school in high-poverty neighborhoods have smaller test-score gains than children from low-poverty areas during the summer but not during the school year, suggesting that differences in home and neighborhood environments may be responsible for much of the variation in achievement across neighborhoods. This pattern is presumably not explained by differences across areas in summer school attendance, since children from high-poverty areas are presumably more likely to attend summer school than those from low-poverty areas.

of a 1970s housing experiment suggest that providing rental subsidies to families who already live in private-market housing seems to generate little change in neighborhood quality. In contrast, MTO families relocate to lower-poverty areas compared with controls, even those families who are assigned to the Section 8–only comparison group. One reason for the difference in mobility outcomes may be the relatively brief eligibility period associated with the 1970s program. Another explanation is that MTO participants are a self-selected group of families who have expressed a desire to move.[49]

In any case, the data from MTO suggest that offering housing vouchers to public housing residents may help at least some families who wish to move to lower-poverty neighborhoods to do so. Previous research suggests that the average unit cost is no higher with housing vouchers than with public housing or Section 8 project-based housing.[50] Thus if the government is committed to providing housing assistance to poor families in some form, the additional budgetary cost of shifting families from public housing to vouchers may be minimal.

While the cost differences between project-based housing and housing vouchers may be small, the differences in the benefits to society may be substantial, particularly if voucher recipients are provided with assistance and incentives to move to lower-poverty areas. Our Baltimore MTO data suggest that even young children assigned to the Section 8–only comparison group (whose families are not constrained to move to very low-poverty areas) experience an improvement in reading test scores of one-quarter of a standard deviation relative to control children, which may increase lifetime earnings by as much as $9,600 for boys and $7,900 for girls. MTO also appears to reduce violent criminal behavior by teens (which may be offset somewhat by an increase in property thefts), improve the health of children and their parents, and reduce welfare receipt.[51]

49. Struyk and Bendick (1981); Mills and Lubuele (1997). Other possible explanations for the difference across programs in residential mobility include potential differences in housing market conditions between the 1970s and the 1990s or differences in the responsiveness of residents of public versus private market housing to rental subsidies. Some support for the importance of family preferences for mobility rather than these other explanations comes from Jacob's (2000) study of Chicago families who have been involuntarily displaced from public housing buildings that are scheduled for demolition. Jacob finds that these families experience only modest changes in neighborhood conditions, which in turn do not translate into detectable changes in their children's educational outcomes.

50. Weinberg (1982); Olsen and Barton (1983); Mayo (1986); Shroder and Reiger (2000).

51. Krueger (1999); Katz, Kling and Liebman (2001); Ludwig, Duncan and Pinkston (2000); Ludwig, Duncan and Hirschfield (2001).

Economic desegregation may also be achieved through more indirect means. For example, historically many suburban townships have tried to limit the availability of low-cost housing through zoning restrictions. State-level judicial decisions that force municipalities to zone more affordable housing may help open up the suburbs to low-income families. Policies to reduce residential segregation by race and ethnic group may also achieve some degree of economic desegregation since African Americans and Hispanics are more likely than whites to live in high-poverty areas, even after accounting for differences across racial and ethnic groups in poverty rates. Interventions that may help reduce racial segregation in housing markets include stepped-up enforcement of fair housing laws.[52] More research is needed to determine whether the impacts of such policies on children's educational outcomes would be similar to those reported here for MTO participants.

More generally, a systematic assessment of the benefits and costs of large-scale programs to move poor families from high- to low-poverty neighborhoods requires information about program effects on families who remain behind in central city areas, as well as on those who live in host neighborhoods. If neighborhood effects are proportional to changes in neighborhood attributes, a possibility that we cannot reject in the MTO data, any improvements in outcomes experienced by poor children who move will be offset by negative effects on children in host neighborhoods. Put differently, if neighborhood effects are linear, then reducing the degree of economic segregation will not affect the overall volume of social problems.[53] Society may still wish to expand residential-mobility programs in this case if gains to poor families are given more weight than are losses by affluent families, although more evidence is necessary for understanding the magnitude of any such trade-offs. Despite (or perhaps because of) these uncertainties, the estimated effects of the MTO program on children's educational and other outcomes are large enough to motivate increased research and policy attention to new housing-mobility efforts.

---

52. Kirp, Dwyer and Rosenthal (1995); Mills and Lubuele (1997); Jargowsky (1997); Yinger (1998).
53. Jencks and Mayer (1990).

Comments

Jeffrey Kling: Most social scientists believe that the social environment influences children's educational achievement. The importance of residential location in affecting children's education, however, is a subject on which there is conflicting evidence.[54] Given the increase in the spatial concentration of poverty, however, this question has taken on increasing urgency. Study of this issue has been hampered for at least two main reasons. First, the range of variation in residential location is often limited among otherwise similar children. Second, the fact that observably similar children (for example, same age and demographics) are living in different locations may reflect choices made by their families that are indicative of factors unobserved by an analyst. It is difficult to credibly identify the importance of residential location as distinct from those unobserved factors.

The research design in this paper uses a randomized demonstration program known as Moving to Opportunity (MTO) to address both of these issues. Section 8 rental vouchers from the Department of Housing and Urban Development (HUD) were provided by lottery to public housing residents. Some vouchers were valid only in low-poverty neighborhoods and were bundled with counseling services (the experimental group), while others could be used to move to any location (the Section 8 comparison group). Those who did not receive a voucher (the control group) retained their eligibility to continue to live in their original public housing project unit. The consequences of this design for research are that similar groups of families are living in vastly different neighborhoods, and that the randomization implies that, on average, the groups offered and not offered the vouchers through the lottery will be similar in observable and unobservable characteristics. This is a tremendous

54. Jencks and Mayer (1990).

advantage for these authors in having potentially convincing results that could identify the impact of residential location on educational outcomes.

Other results using MTO data, collectively summarized in a volume edited by John Goering and Judie Feins, indicate that the impact of residential location on children may be particularly important. Research from the New York site indicates reductions in child behavior problems, in addition to the research cited by the authors on reductions in teen criminal behavior and children's physical health and behavior.[55] None of the other existing studies using the MTO demonstration effectively studies educational outcomes. This novel and innovative paper addresses a critical gap in our knowledge.

Besides the randomization of the housing voucher offers, the other principal element of this research design is the linkage of MTO participants to administrative data on educational outcomes, such as test scores, grade retention, absences, and disciplinary actions. When Jens Ludwig first discussed the idea for this project with me in 1995, I was frankly skeptical that these data could be produced, mainly because of the multitude of government agencies involved. So I am pleased to be able to congratulate this team of researchers for truly creating new knowledge through their combination of data entrepreneurship and analytical skill.

Use of administrative records in this research does have some fundamental limitations, however. For example, the data indicate increased grade retention and suspensions among teens in families offered vouchers through the MTO program. This may accurately describe the experiences of these teens. Yet the schools attended by those who have moved through the MTO program have changed at the same time as their residential location. It is not clear whether administrative records are indicative of different behavior by the youth or of different standards being applied to the same behavior in different schools. My prior intuition was that the role of different standards could be important, and the authors provide some evidence in support of this idea. Thus, I agree with the authors' conclusion that the results on grade retention and suspensions for teens are difficult to interpret.

Another limitation is that many children do not have records of test scores. The authors are very clear about the reasons for missing data, including problems linked to test records using individual identifiers, schools testing children with differing frequency, and students missing tests because of absence or special education classification. Among children ages 5–12, the

55 . Goering and Feins (2001); Leventhal and Brooks-Gunn (2001); Ludwig, Duncan, and Hirschfield (2001); Katz, Kling, and Liebman (2001).

result is that there is substantial missing data for the sample in the post-randomization time period. Depending on the measures, test scores are available for 46 percent (Comprehensive Test of Basic Skills, math), 53 percent (CTSB, reading), and 26 percent (Maryland Functional Test, reading) of the sample. Although data missing at random would not affect the results of these analyses, these reasons are not random and may well be related to residential location itself.

A number of sensitivity analyses have been provided by the authors to assess the potential impact of missing data on the results. There is substantially more missing data for the Section 8 comparison group than in the other two groups, for example, which could be a source of bias. It is reassuring, therefore, to find that these differences, at least for test scores, appear to be largely driven by differences in the ages and the pre-program characteristics of children—which can occur by chance in any lottery with a small sample.

The results, however, do display some instability. In some cases, the results depend on the control variables used or the estimation method.[56] Even though the data are generated from a randomized experiment, nonexperimental methods must be used to address the missing data issues, and these methods are subject to standard criticisms about the potential importance of functional form and omitted variables.

To give a concrete example of how missing data could lead to bias, consider families in the experimental group, whose probability of using an offered MTO voucher to move is about 20 percentage points higher for those with valid CTSB scores than for those with missing scores. This clearly indicates that the test score data are not missing at random but missing in a manner directly related to residential location choice. Now consider the counterfactual counterparts of these families in the control group (the "control compliers" who would have moved though MTO if offered a voucher). For unbiased

56. Specifically, the sensitivity analysis of the CTSB math score for the Experimental group indicates that adding statistical controls for pre-program student and family characteristics in addition to age increased the estimated intent-to-treat (ITT) effect from statistically insignificant 4.2 percentile points to a statistically significant difference of 7.5. However, the treatment-on-treated (TOT) effect estimated with covariates is not statistically significant, indicating sensitivity to the estimation method.

For the Section 8 Comparison group CTSB reading score, there is almost no difference between the estimated ITT and TOT effects. Since about 15 percent of this group did not move through the MTO program, we would expect the TOT estimate to be larger. As noted by the authors, the TOT will simply be the ITT divided by the compliance rate when covariates are used that are uncorrelated with treatment group assignment. The fact that this does not hold indicates that the choices of covariates matter and that the results are at least somewhat sensitive to the estimation approach.

estimation, given the authors' evidence that there is selection in mobility and that the compliers do differ from noncompliers, experimental and control compliers would need to be equally over-represented among those with valid test score data. This would not be true if the over-representation of experimental program movers was because of more extensive testing in schools outside the center city (not attended by the control compliers). Although further evidence would be needed to ascertain whether this potential source of bias is important, the authors have not refuted that it could be.

I believe it should be clearly acknowledged that a wide range of biases is possible given the large extent of missing data—which may be missing for systematically different reasons across the MTO groups. The direction of most biases from the missing data is difficult to assess and could be positive or negative. Given the extent of the missing test scores, the small sample sizes, and the focus on outcomes in one city, I also believe we should be cautious in our interpretation of these results.

I do find the results in this paper highly suggestive and a very valuable contribution to our understanding of the impact of residential location on educational outcomes, although far from conclusive. These results should undoubtedly encourage HUD to make the study of children's educational achievement a top priority in their planned interim evaluation of MTO next year. To provide more conclusive evidence, I recommend that consistent data from all five cities in which the MTO demonstration took place be collected on children's educational achievement and the learning environment in their schools.

Katherine M. O'Regan: This is an extremely well-done piece of research on an incredibly important topic. It provides strong evidence for the impact of mobility and improving neighborhoods on families in public housing. The paper addresses one avenue of impact, through educational outcomes of the children, for a specific type of policy option: public housing residents who wish to move to private-market housing and do so through subsidies that must be used in neighborhoods with low poverty rates (at least for one year).

Before the collection of Move-to-Opportunity (MTO) studies currently under way, we have operated with very imperfect assessments of the likely effect of such policies (because of limited data and methodological issues). I believe the benefits of this paper go beyond the much improved evidence for this program option, informing a broader array of policies in somewhat different contexts. In forming policy we are almost always dealing with imperfect information on likely impact, on whom, and how. Besides the strong evidence on the narrow program gained in this work, there are less strong, but suggestive, findings that can be gleaned from the work. The authors have included some extensions in their work. My comments focus on perhaps a wider range of polices, or on helping current policymakers tailor these results to their specific urban circumstances.

General structure. The basic structure of the research is an experimental design in which the authors have two comparison groups. The experimental group receives the treatment of a voucher, with some limits on the geography and the timing of its use, and with some additional services to aid in the search process. The first comparison group also receives a treatment, but the treatment differs in two critical ways: households are not limited to low-poverty neighborhoods, and these households do not receive additional services. Finally, the control group receives no treatment at all.

Most of the empirical work then focuses on two classic forms of impact. First, the intent-to-treat effect (ITT), which contrasts outcomes for the entire group that is offered treatment to the entire comparison group(s). And second, the treatment-on-treated effect (TOT), which looks solely at changes in outcomes for those who have accepted treatment compared with the appropriate comparison group(s). Each of these effects is important as each one addresses somewhat different policy questions.

Although the authors are discussing the impact of improving neighborhoods, technically the treatment assessed under the TOT is one of changing residence, period. It is not quite one of improving neighborhoods, since enforcement of the neighborhood restrictions may not be complete, and it is not necessarily one of improving schools. Movers include people who have moved out of public housing but not to improved neighborhoods (very few for this sample), people who have moved from the neighborhood but potentially not the school (this may also be quite small for this sample), and those who have improved both neighborhood and school. Although the current experiment may primarily include only the final group, it is worth thinking about what could be learned by distinguishing among these alternative treatments.

Alternative treatments. The authors note in their conclusion that one cannot directly test whether the observed outcomes are because of changes in the schools attended by the children, changes in their environments, or some combination. The nature of the effects (reading scores in particular) are suggestive of more than just school changes.

It might be informative to try to push the assessment further to consider alternative views of the "treatment" and compare the TOT for children who experience at least two possibilities: treatment 1, changing neighborhoods only (same school); treatment 2, changing neighborhoods and schools.

If it is the schools themselves that matter, and only the schools, treatment 1 should have no effect on recipients' educational outcomes. And treatment 2 is somewhat closer to how people may be interpreting the current TOT numbers in the paper. It would be informative to have estimates of these impacts. This exercise is similar to the one already conducted by the authors, distinguishing the academic outcomes of students by the household's motivation for moving. These subset analyses are not quite as "clean" as focusing on the ITT effects, but they help push the data as far as possible.

Generalizing beyond Baltimore. The authors are careful to place their results within the context of Baltimore, or when possible, the collection of MTO cities. Here I consider ways to improve our ability to generalize from these results. At least three general categories of characteristics affect the size of the program's impact and the likelihood that someone will participate in the program. Those issues affect how applicable these results are to another environment. The categories are the characteristics of the people in the program; the characteristics of the neighborhoods and schools they go to; and the characteristics of the neighborhoods and schools they leave.

The first category is explicitly discussed in looking at the take-up rates (likelihood of accepting treatment). The authors find that the pre-program academic performance does not affect the take-up rate. They also provide information in table 4 on a variety of characteristics that could potentially affect take-up (and size of impact) that could vary across cities. The related discussion helps policymakers outside of Baltimore assess what proportion of their target population is likely to participate in such a program.

However, it is likely that more than the household's characteristics will affect take-up and impact. The authors note that households that seem to have more to gain or less to lose are more likely to participate in the treatment program. Along these lines, the quality of the baseline neighborhood (and the potential new neighborhoods) should also affect participation. Although table 5 presents evidence on the differential improvement in neighborhoods attained for each group, it does so in aggregate. Disaggregating by mover status would help other jurisdictions predict participation rates (and impacts) for their areas and possibly explain some of the variation in participation across MTO sites.

For example, one might think that characteristics of neighborhoods around public housing would greatly affect whether people choose to participate in the program. Nationally, about 20 percent of public housing units with families are located in neighborhoods with jointly above-average rates of various negative characteristics, classified as underclass by Ann Schnare and Sandara Newman.[57] Sixty-eight percent of Baltimore's family public housing units are in such neighborhoods (second highest in the country in cities with populations of 500,000 or more). This may create a much greater incentive to move in Baltimore than in other cities, but we can not quite tell that from the data in their current form.

Control group and HOPE IV. It would also be helpful to break out those control group families affected by the HOPE VI redevelopment project. While little can be done to have a truly unaffected control group, we can learn a little more by looking at this group specifically.

If one looks at the net change in neighborhood distributions, and assumes they capture most gross flows, approximately forty-nine families moved from those neighborhoods with the highest poverty rates (60 percent or more). If all HOPE VI families made this move, then almost all of the improvement in neighborhoods observed in the control group is related to the HOPE VI program. It is worth identifying this group for several reasons.

First, not all areas have Hope VI relocation as their counterfactual. Such areas might then expect much less mobility among their public housing recipients. Second, some of this neighborhood improvement is transitory. Some fraction of this group will be relocating back to the two HOPE VI sites, Lafayette Courts and Lexington Terrace. In fact, 152 families did return to Lafayette after its redevelopment.[58]

Return rates appear to differ dramatically by HOPE VI development, depending in part on the mobility programs established during relocation, the availability of Section 8 and public housing alternatives, the number of redeveloped units (now that one-to-one replacement on site is not required), and whether any selection criteria are used for returning families. Again, this would differ by locality.

Furthermore, the HOPE VI redevelopment did provide the area with a wide range of additional neighborhood services, from a new police substation in the Lafayette Courts neighborhood, to a Boys and Girls club program, parenting programs, and mentoring programs. Pre- and postsurveys of perceived

57. Schnare and Newman (1997).
58. HUD (2000).

safety find a marked decline in the fear of crime. (It also resides in portions of Baltimore's Empowerment Zone.) There was also an increase in employment and a decrease in welfare use among residents of the housing project over this time.

So, while many stayed in this neighborhood, the quality of the neighborhood appears to have changed, perhaps dramatically. This is not much of an issue for the research at hand at this point, since the time periods barely overlap. It does matter for additional follow-up and for policy options. The programs considered in the experiment are moving with a voucher from public housing, and moving with extra counseling but restrictions on where one goes. This second program leads to bigger neighborhood changes and perhaps bigger impacts on education and more. But an alternative scenario is HUD's redevelopment of the public housing neighborhoods, changing neighborhoods but not necessarily schools.

Program modification. If at all possible, it would be nice to have some additional information on the loss of participants during the early stages of the counseling and search process. The program implemented is but one version of such a voucher program with mobility restrictions, and it would help to get a sense of which program characteristics really matter and which really cost in participation. The contrast with the voucher program is not quite the control one would like, as there are several differences between the programs: restrictions on use of the voucher, requirements for workshops, and the provision of counseling and support services. The authors do provide some summary information that suggests important differences. While half of those not participating in the experiment never started the voucher and workshop process, almost all of the Section 8 comparisons at least applied for the voucher. Of those remaining experimentals who did not find housing, about a quarter dropped out before completing their required workshops. This does suggest that each portion of the program may have its own "cost," and eventually we would hope to assess these components separately.

To push this point, all of the residents affected by HOPE VI were offered the same support for searching as other HUD certificate recipients. In Baltimore and the surrounding counties, this includes no restriction on the location of housing, but it turns out that Baltimore is part of a regional mobility program that *potentially* provides counseling and support services, geared in part to get households out of the poorest neighborhoods. The availability of such services may be most relevant to the HOPE VI voucher recipients, as they would be involved with HUD relocation staff as part of the HOPE VI project.

Some of the approaches taken by this regional mobility program appear similar to those services received by the experimental group, without the geographic requirements. The program reports that 68 percent of the families served moved to low poverty areas. It is possible that a primary avenue of impact in the MTO program is the counseling and support, rather than the limits on the re-location areas. In that case, perhaps a somewhat different version of this program could increase take-up rates with not much loss of impact per treated household.

One way to gain some insight into this issue (whether some modification in program design could improve the impacts) is by examining information on the participants in the MTO experiment group early on. The authors' breakout of when participants dropped out is helpful; additional information on who dropped out—and why—would be extremely useful. If it is not possible to interview some of these participants, perhaps interviews with the counselors with whom these participants interacted would be suggestive.

Conclusion. The entire body of work on the MTO experiments is providing the type of research greatly needed in the literature on neighborhood effects and mobility. This particular piece has focused on the academic impacts but has also attempted to push beyond the narrow (though quite strong) results of this one program option. Both activities provide a serious contribution to our knowledge.

References

Bloom, Howard S. 1984. "Accounting for No-Shows in Experimental Evaluation Designs." *Evaluation Review* 8 (April): 225–46.

Brooks-Gunn, Jeanne, Greg J. Duncan, and J. Lawrence Aber. 1997a. *Neighborhood Poverty, Volume I: Context and Consequences for Children*. Russell Sage Foundation.

——.1997b. *Neighborhood Poverty, Volume II: Policy Implications in Studying Neighborhoods*. Russell Sage Foundation.

Cameron, A. Colin, and Pravin K. Trivedi. 1998. *Regression Analysis of Count Data*. Cambridge University Press.

Card, David, and Alan B. Krueger. 1996. "School Resources and Student Outcomes: An Overview of the Literature and New Evidence from North and South Carolina." *Journal of Economic Perspectives* 10 (Fall): 31–50.

Donohue, John J., and Peter Siegelman. 1998. "Allocating Resources Among Prisons and Social Programs in the Battle Against Crime." *Journal of Legal Studies* 27 (January):1–43.

Ellen, Ingrid Gould, and Margery Austin Turner. 1997. "Does Neighborhood Matter? Assessing Recent Evidence." *Housing Policy Debate* 8 (4): 833–66.

Entwistle, Doris R., Karl L. Alexander, and Linda Steffel Olson. 1997. *Children, Schools, and Inequality*. Westview Press.

Ferguson, Ronald F., and Helen F. Ladd. 1996. "How and Why Money Matters: An Analysis of Alabama Schools." In *Holding Schools Accountable: Performance-Based Reform in Education*, edited by Helen F. Ladd, 265–98. Brookings.

Figlio, David, and Jens Ludwig. 2000. "Sex, Drugs and Catholic Schools: Private Schooling and Non-Market Adolescent Behaviors." Working Paper 7990. Cambridge, Mass.: National Bureau of Economic Research.

Furstenberg, Frank F., and Mary Elizabeth Hughes. 1997. "The Influence of Neighborhoods on Children's Development: A Theoretical Perspective and a Research Agenda." In *Neighborhood Poverty: Policy Implications in Studying Neighborhoods*, vol. 2, 23–47. Russell Sage Foundation.

Goering, John, Katherine Carnevale, and Manual Teodoro. 1996. *Expanding Housing Choices for HUD-Assisted Families*. Department of Housing and Urban Development.

Goering, John, and Judie Feins, eds. 2001. "Choosing a Better Life: A Social Experiment in Leaving Poverty Behind." Unpublished manuscript. City University of New York (February).

Goering, John, and others. 1999. *Moving to Opportunity for Fair Housing Demonstration Program: Current Status and Initial Findings*. Department of Housing and Urban Development, Office for Policy Development and Research.

Gramlich, Edward, Deborah Laren, and Naomi Sealand. 1992. "Moving into and out of Poor Urban Areas." *Journal of Policy Analysis and Management* 11 (Spring): 273–87.

Grissmer, David, Ann Flanagan, and Stephanie Williamson. 1998. "Why Did the Black-White Score Gap Narrow in the 1970's and 1980's?" In *The Black-White Test Score Gap*, edited by Christopher Jencks and Meredith Phillips, 182–228. Brookings.

Heyns, Barbara. 1978. *Summer Learning and the Effects of Schooling*. Academic Press.

Holzer, Harry J. 1991. "The Spatial Mismatch Hypothesis: What Has the Evidence Shown?" *Urban Studies* 28 (February): 105–22.

Jacob, Brian. 2000. "The Impact of Public Housing Demolitions on Student Achievement in Chicago." Working Paper. University of Chicago, Harris School of Public Policy.

Jargowsky, Paul A. 1997. *Poverty and Place: Ghettos, Barrios, and the American City*. Russell Sage Foundation.

Jaynes, Gerald David, and Robin M. Williams. 1989. *A Common Destiny: Blacks and American Society*. Washington: National Academy Press.

Jencks, Christopher, and Susan E. Mayer. 1990. "The Social Consequences of Growing Up in a Poor Neighborhood." In *Inner-City Poverty in the United States*, edited by Laurence Lynn and Michael McGeary, 111–86. Washington: National Academy Press.

Kain, John F. 1968. "Housing Segregation, Negro Employment, and Metropolitan Decentralization." *Quarterly Journal of Economics* 82 (May): 175–97.

Katz, Lawrence F., Jeffrey R. Kling, and Jeffrey B. Liebman. 2001. "Moving to Opportunity in Boston: Early Results of a Randomized Mobility Experiment." *Quarterly Journal of Economics* 116 (May): 607–54.

Kirp, David L., John P. Dwyer, and Larry A. Rosenthal. 1995. *Our Town: Race, Housing, and the Soul of Suburbia*. Rutgers University Press.

Krueger, Alan B. 1999. "Experimental Estimates of Education Production Functions." *Quarterly Journal of Economics* 114 (May): 497–532.

Ladd, Helen F., and Jens Ludwig. 1997. "Federal Housing Assistance, Residential Relocation, and Educational Opportunities: Evidence from Baltimore." *American Economic Review* 87 (May): 272–77.

Leventhal, Tama, and Jeanne Brooks-Gunn. 2001. "Moving to Opportunity: What About the Kids?" Unpublished manuscript. Columbia University (February).

Lewis, Oscar. 1968. "The Culture of Poverty." In *On Understanding Poverty: Perspectives from the Social Sciences*, edited by Daniel P. Moynihan, 187–200. Basic Books.

Ludwig, Jens. 1999. "Information and Inner City Educational Attainment." *Economics of Education Review* 18 (1): 17–30.

Ludwig, Jens, Greg J. Duncan, and Paul Hirschfield. 2001. "Urban Poverty and Juvenile Crime: Evidence from a Randomized Housing-Mobility Experiment." *Quarterly Journal of Economics* 116 (May): 655–80.

Ludwig, Jens, Greg J. Duncan, and Joshua C. Pinkston. 2000. "Neighborhood Effects on Self-Sufficiency: Evidence from a Randomized Housing-Mobility Experiment." Working Paper 159. Northwestern University-University of Chicago Joint Center for Poverty Research.

Maguire, Kathleen, and Ann L. Pastore, eds. 1999. *Sourcebook of Criminal Justice Statistics, 1998.* Government Printing Office.

Manski, Charles F. 1993. "Adolescent Econometricians: How Do Youth Infer the Returns to Schooling?" In *Studies of Supply and Demand in Higher Education*, edited by Charles T. Clotfelter and Michael Rothschild, 43–57. University of Chicago Press.

——. 1995. *Identification Problems in the Social Sciences.* Harvard University Press.

Mayo, Stephen. 1986. "Sources of Inefficiency in Subsidized Housing Programs: A Comparison of U.S. and German Experience." *Journal of Urban Economics* 20 (September): 229–49.

McClave, James T., and P. George Benson. 1985. *Statistics for Business and Economics*, 3d ed. Dellen Publishing.

Mills, Edwin S., and Luan Sende Lubuele. 1997. "Inner Cities." *Journal of Economic Literature* 35 (June): 727–56.

Olsen, Edgar O., and David M. Barton. 1983. "The Benefits and Costs of Public Housing in New York City." *Journal of Public Economics* 20 (April): 299–332.

Popkin, Susan J., and Mary K. Cunningham. 1999. *Searching for Housing in the Chicago Region.* Washington: Urban Institute.

Popkin, Susan J., and others. 2000. *The Hidden War: Crime and the Tragedy of Public Housing in Chicago.* Rutgers University Press.

Raphael, Steven. 1998. "The Spatial Mismatch Hypothesis of Black Youth Joblessness: Evidence from the San Francisco Bay Area." *Journal of Urban Economics* 43 (January): 79–111.

Rosenbaum, James E. 1995. "Changing the Geography of Opportunity by Expanding Residential Choice: Lessons from the Gautreaux Program." *Housing Policy Debate* 6 (1): 231–70.

Rouse, Cecilia E. 1998. "Private School Vouchers and Student Achievement: An Evaluation of the Milwaukee Parental Choice Program." *Quarterly Journal of Economics* 113 (May): 553–602.

Rubinowitz, Leonard S., and James E. Rosenbaum. 2000. *Crossing the Class and Color Lines: From Public Housing to White Suburbia.* University of Chicago Press.

Schnare, Ann, and Sandra Newman. 1997. "The Failure of Housing Programs to Deliver on Neighborhood Quality." *Housing Policy Debate* 8 (4): 703–41.

Shroder, Mark, and Arthur Reiger. 2000. "Vouchers versus Production Revisited." *Journal of Housing Research* 11 (1): 91–108.

Skogan, Wesley G. 1981. *Issues in the Measurement of Victimization.* U.S. Department of Justice, Bureau of Justice Statistics.

Struyk, R. J., and M. Bendick, eds. 1981. *Housing Vouchers for the Poor: Lessons from a National Experiment*. Washington: Urban Institute.

U.S. Department of Education. 1999. *Promising Results, Continuing Challenges: The Final Report of the National Assessment of Title I*. Office of the Under Secretary, Planning and Evaluation Service.

——. 2000. *The Condition of Education* (http://nces.ed.gov/pubs2000/coe2000 [August 1, 2000]).

U.S. Department of Housing and Urban Development. 2000. "HOPE VI: Community Building Makes a Difference."

Weinberg, Daniel. 1982. "Housing Benefits from the Section 8 Housing Programs." *Evaluation Review* 6 (February): 5–24.

Wilson, William J. 1987. *The Truly Disadvantaged*. University of Chicago Press.

——.1996. *When Work Disappears: The World of the New Urban Poor*. Alfred A. Knopf.

Yinger, John. 1998. "Housing Discrimination Is Still Worth Worrying About." *Housing Policy Debate* 9 (4): 893–927.

JANET CURRIE
University of California, Los Angeles

JEFFREY GROGGER
University of California, Los Angeles

Explaining Recent Declines in Food Stamp Program Participation

THE FOOD STAMP PROGRAM (FSP) is one of the largest transfer programs in the United States, having provided nearly $24 billion in benefits to 27.5 million families in 1994.[1] Participation in the FSP hovered around 20 million persons per year during the 1980s but rose sharply in the early 1990s to a peak of approximately 27.5 million persons in 1994. Participation then began to fall dramatically, declining back to 20 million participants by 1998. About three-fourths of this decline occurred between 1996 and 1998.[2]

Previous research has shown that most of the fall in the caseload has stemmed from falling numbers of single-parent families that receive food stamps.[3] The caseload has also fallen dramatically for two other groups: able-bodied adults without dependents (ABAWDs) and most legal immigrants. However, since they constitute a relatively small share of the FSP caseload, they account for only 22 percent of the overall caseload decline. Finally, Sheena McConnell and James Ohls show that the decline in the caseload has been much more dramatic in urban than in rural areas.[4]

Declines in the food stamp caseload may be either good or bad news, depending on the reasons for the decline. A number of hypotheses have been offered. The first is that welfare reform has caused the decline. The Personal Responsibility and Work Opportunity Restoration Act of 1996 (PRWORA)

The authors thank Gary Burtless, Edward Glaeser, John Karl Scholz, and Robert Schoeni for helpful comments, and the National Institutes of Health for financial support. Robert Schoeni also generously provided the aggregate caseload data used in the paper. Ming Li and especially Matthew Neidell provided excellent research assistance.

1. U.S. Committee on Ways and Means (1998).
2. Castner and Cody (1999).
3. U.S. Department of Agriculture (1999).
4. U.S. Department of Agriculture (1999); McConnell and Ohls (2000).

made it more difficult for single mothers to receive cash welfare and may have had the largely unintended consequence of making it more difficult for them to have access to food stamps. PRWORA also included provisions limiting the use of food stamps by ABAWDs and legal immigrants. Hence, PRWORA seems to have affected precisely those groups that have shown the greatest decline in the food stamp caseload.

A second, closely related hypothesis is that the climate surrounding welfare reform has increased the stigma and also the transaction costs associated with participating in food stamps. Little direct evidence is available about the importance of stigma and transaction costs, so one contribution of our study is to analyze direct proxies for these concepts.

A third hypothesis is that the decline in the caseload is because of the recent economic boom. If families are leaving the rolls because they are better off, then this is presumably a good thing. However, if needy families are leaving because it has become more difficult for them to gain access to food stamps, then most observers would feel that this was a negative consequence of welfare reform, and one that merited some remedial action. Our paper provides some new evidence on these competing hypotheses, using both aggregate administrative and household-level data.

We find that among households with incomes less than 300 percent of poverty, 20 percent of the decline in FSP utilization can be attributed to lower unemployment, while 30 percent is due to the implementation of the new Temporary Assistance for Needy Families program. The later effect is concentrated among single heads and in central cities. We also show that single heads are more sensitive than other households to increases in the transaction costs associated with applying for food stamps. Together, these results suggest that efforts to restore FSP benefits to needy households should focus on reducing application costs for single heads in central cities.

Background

The FSP began as a small pilot program in 1961 but had become a national program by 1974.[5] In contrast to the rules for cash welfare receipt under the old AFDC (Aid to Families with Dependent Children) program and the new TANF (Temporary Aid for Needy Families) program, most rules for the FSP

5. Much of the information in this section comes from U.S. Committee on Ways and Means (1999) or from Castner and Anderson (1999).

are set at the federal level. This is because the FSP is designed to offset state variation in welfare programs to at least some extent.[6] Moreover, unlike AFDC/TANF, the FSP is available regardless of family structure, which makes it a particularly important part of the social safety net for low-income households. While PRWORA gave even more control over cash welfare to states, Congress deliberately retained the centralized nature of the FSP. This decision underlines the importance many policymakers attach to providing a minimum federal safety net through the FSP.

Although most FSP rules are set at a federal level, the program is usually operated through the same state welfare agencies and staff that run the AFDC/TANF and Medicaid programs. States do have a say about some administrative features such as the length of eligibility certification periods, the design of outreach programs (which may receive 50 percent federal cost-sharing), and about any "workfare" requirements for participation in the program, but we are not aware of any research that has tied variations in these features of the program to participation rates.

Currently, the Food Stamp Program operates as follows: the FSP household is defined as either a person living alone or a group of people who live together and customarily purchase food and prepare meals together. Households made up entirely of AFDC/TANF recipients are automatically eligible for food stamps. For other households, it is necessary to go through an eligibility determination, and monthly cash income is the main determinant of eligibility.

The FSP uses both the household's "gross" monthly income and its counted (or "net") monthly income. Gross income includes all of the household's cash income from most sources, including income from welfare programs.[7] Net income is derived by subtracting out a standard deduction, 20 percent of earned income, and deductions for shelter and child care. Households must have a gross income that does not exceed 130 percent of the federal poverty guidelines, and net monthly income that does not exceed the federal poverty line. Finally, household assets must be less than $2,000. Benefits are calculated by taking the maximum benefit level for a household of a certain size and subtracting 30 percent of the net income. In 1998 the maxi-

6. For example, food stamp benefits amount to less than a third of the combined AFDC/TANF and food stamp benefits in states, such as California, that have high cash welfare benefit levels, while in low-welfare-benefit-level states, such as Texas, FSP income constitutes more than half of the household's combined benefits. U.S. Committee on Ways and Means (1999). There is much more uniformity in the combined benefit levels than in AFDC/TANF benefits alone.

7. Income from sources such as federal energy assistance and income tax refunds is excluded.

mum food stamp benefit for a family of three was $321 a month. The rules regarding deductions and assets are somewhat more liberal for households with elderly or disabled members, so that such households generally receive higher benefits than otherwise similar households without these members.

Program benefits have traditionally been provided in the form of coupons that can be exchanged for food at participating stores. These coupons may be used to purchase a wide range of foods, the most significant exception being hot foods that are for immediate consumption. Food stamp benefits are usually issued monthly by welfare agencies. In the past this was generally done either by mailing recipients an authorization-to-participate card, which could be redeemed for coupons at specified places (such as a post office), or by directly mailing food stamp coupons to recipients.

The recent introduction of electronic benefit transfer (EBT) systems represents the first major shift in the way the program has been administered since 1977.[8] Most EBT systems work much like bank debit cards. Recipients are given EBT cards with a magnetic stripe. At the check-out, the recipient enters a personal identification number in a terminal to authorize EBT payment of the food stamp purchase. The terminal connects to the EBT system's central computer, which maintains an account for the recipient. If the personal identification number (PIN) is verified, and the recipient has enough funds to cover the transaction, then the purchase is authorized, and the amount is deducted from the recipient's balance. Since Maryland pioneered EBT in 1993, twenty other states have adopted EBT statewide, and 75 percent of FSP benefits are now in the form of EBT rather than coupons. The PRWORA mandated that all states switch to EBT by October 2002.[9]

Economic Conditions, Welfare Reform, and the FSP

Cash welfare programs have been the main focus of welfare reform in the 1990s. PRWORA replaced the old AFDC program with a new program called TANF, which differed from AFDC in several important ways. First, under AFDC, states had the power to set benefit levels and thus to influence caseloads. However, given benefit levels, they had little discretion over who was eligible to receive benefits. Under TANF, states have much more power to

8. The Food Stamp Act of 1977 made significant changes to program regulations, tightening eligibility requirements and administration and removing the requirement that food stamps be purchased by participants. See "Food Stamp and Commodity Distribution Programs," Title XII, P.L. 95-113.

9. "Frequently Asked Questions" (http://fnsl.usdc.gov/fsp/menu/admin/ebt/ebt.htm [March 6, 2001]).

design their own welfare programs. TANF also sets time limits and stiffer work requirements for welfare recipients.

In order to understand the ways that welfare reform and economic conditions may have affected FSP caseloads, it is useful to think of the probability of food stamp participation as the product of three quantities: $P = I * E * T$, where I indicates the probability that a person is income eligible, E is the probability that the person is eligible conditional on having a low income (that is, that they meet other program rules), and T is the take-up rate.

By improving economic conditions, boom times will reduce I and thereby reduce participation in the FSP. Similarly, if women leave poverty for high-income jobs as a result of welfare reform, then P will fall because I falls. However, welfare reform may also have reduced P directly by changing the probability that a person with a given income is eligible for the FSP. PRWORA granted states flexibility in specifying sanctions for failure to comply with FSP work requirements and allows states to sanction the food stamp benefits of welfare families who fail to satisfy requirements of the state's TANF program.

Both types of sanctions may reduce or eliminate the family's FSP benefits for a period of up to several months. Several analysts have suggested that these sanction policies could have important effects on the FSP caseload. However, other evidence suggests that enforcement of these types of sanctions has been relatively lax—in 1996, 40 percent of the 5.5 million people technically subject to work and training requirements were exempted.[10]

PRWORA also required ABAWDs to meet stiff work requirements and limited their participation in the FSP to only three to six months in any thirty-six-month period, unless the person is enrolled in a work or training activity. However, again, most states have waived these requirements for at least some fraction of their ABAWD caseloads.[11] And as discussed above, PRWORA disqualified legal immigrants from participation in the FSP, although many states have taken measures to cover these people using state-only funds.

Finally, even in the absence of changes in income or eligibility rules, welfare reform could affect the take-up of FSP benefits by eligibles. As discussed above, families who leave the cash welfare rolls as a result of welfare reform are no longer automatically eligible for food stamps and must go through certification (and periodic recertification) of their eligibility.

10. Gabor and Botsko (1998); General Accounting Office (2000); Dion and Pavetti (2000); U.S. Committee on Ways and Means (1998).
11. Gabor and Botsko (1998).

This process is likely to greatly increase the transaction costs associated with participation for many families. The average FSP application takes nearly five hours of time to complete, including approximately 2.3 trips to an FSP office. Recertification for benefits takes 2.8 hours and at least one trip. Out-of-pocket application costs average about $10.31, or 6 percent of the average monthly benefit.[12] States generally require families with earnings to be recertified more often than families without earnings because their benefits may change more often. Higher transaction costs are likely to be associated with lower take-up by eligibles and thus with lower participation, other things being equal.

Welfare diversion policies may also increase the transaction costs associated with applying for food stamps. Many states have established procedures intended to divert would-be welfare recipients from applying for cash welfare. For example, applicants may be told that they must first satisfy job search requirements, or they may be offered lump sum financial assistance on the condition that they do not apply for cash aid within a certain period. While federal law continues to require that food stamp applications be accepted upon an applicant's first visit to the welfare office, these diversion policies may also deter people from applying for food stamps.[13]

Finally, the publicity and discussions surrounding welfare reform may have increased the stigma associated with using food stamps, as well as the stigma associated with using cash welfare. If such stigma is important, then it could result in declines in welfare utilization even among groups who are not directly affected by welfare reform, such as the elderly.

Previous Evidence about the Decline in FSP Caseloads

The literature on trends in the FSP caseload is somewhat underdeveloped relative to the large and growing literature discussing trends in the use of cash welfare.[14] However, since one of the leading hypotheses about trends in the FSP caseload is that they are driven by changes in the welfare caseload, the literature on welfare caseloads is clearly germane.

The key question addressed in this literature is whether recent declines in the welfare caseload have been driven primarily by welfare reform or by

12. Ponza and others (1999).
13. Dion and Pavetti (2000).
14. See Blank (1997); Council of Economic Advisers (1997, 1999); Ziliak and others (2000); Figlio and Ziliak, (1999); Wallace and Blank (1999); Grogger and Michalopoulos (1999); Grogger (2000); Moffitt (1999); Schoeni and Blank (2000); Haider and Klerman (2000).

improvements in the economy. Unfortunately, no consensus has emerged. The estimates vary with factors such as the length of the sample used and the data source. Estimates in the literature suggest that declines in unemployment could have accounted for between a quarter and two-thirds of the recent decline in welfare caseloads.

The chief source of variation in measures of welfare reform is that various state waivers from federal AFDC rules were granted between 1992 and the passage of PRWORA in 1996. By the time PRWORA became law, thirty-seven states had obtained such waivers allowing them to implement some form of state-level welfare reform.[15] After PRWORA, states implemented their new TANF programs between October 1996 and January 1998, so that there was less variation in the timing of these changes.

Although this lack of variation may present a problem for our study, the fact that the FSP caseload is more heterogeneous than the TANF caseload (which consists overwhelmingly of single mothers) offers some additional sources of variation. For example, we might not expect the elderly FSP caseload to be strongly affected by welfare reform or by the economic boom, although it is possible that increases in welfare-reform-related stigma could reduce caseloads among the elderly. These arguments suggest that it is important to examine the behavior of different segments of the caseload, rather than only looking at aggregate caseloads.

About evidence on changes in the FSP caseload itself, it is useful to keep our disaggregation of the changes into changes in *I, E,* or *T,* in mind. First, it is clear from the available evidence that decreases in the fraction of people who are income-eligible for the program cannot explain the whole decline in the caseload. If one examines the FSP caseload as a percentage of the population that is income-eligible, one sees an increase followed by a decline. In 1990, 1995, and 1998, respectively, 40.9, 48.6, and 38.9 percent of the population with incomes less than 130 percent of poverty participated in the FSP.[16] Using data from the Current Population Survey (CPS), Parke Wilde and others perform decompositions of the change in the caseload between 1994 and 1998 and find that 28 percent of the decline can be explained by a falloff in the share of households with low income, while 55 percent was due to a decline in participation among the income-eligible.[17]

Econometric estimates based on aggregate caseload data find that between 12 and 56 percent of the decline in FSP caseloads can be attributed to declines

15. U.S. Department of Health and Human Services (1997).
16. Currie (forthcoming).
17. Wilde and others (2000).

in unemployment, suggesting that the remainder may be due to welfare reform or to other factors.[18]

Although some of this decline could be because of sanctions, or rules limiting the eligibility of ABAWDs and legal immigrants (that is to declines in E), the evidence suggests that there has also been a decline in T (take-up among eligibles), particularly among single mothers. For example, Pamela Loprest found that two years after leaving AFDC/TANF, only 31 percent of former welfare recipients were receiving food stamps, even though most of those who exit welfare for work remain income-eligible for food stamps. This study was based on a national survey of former recipients, but similar findings have been reported using state-level administrative data.[19]

Sheila Zedlewski and Sarah Brauner examine data on households with children who had participated in the FSP between January 1995 and the survey date. When surveyed between February and October 1997, one-third of these families had left the program. Zedlewski and Brauner find that families who had been on welfare were more likely than other families to have exited, and that the difference was greatest at the lowest levels of income.[20] If families were choosing not to participate because of improvements in their financial positions, then one might expect differences in participation to be greatest at the highest levels of income.

The General Accounting Office reports that between 1994 and 1997, the number of lunches served to children by the National School Lunch Program rose by 6 percent. During 1998, demand for emergency food assistance provided by Catholic Charities grew by 38 percent.[21] These figures suggest that declines in FSP usage may have contributed to real hardship for some families.

This decline in take-up among eligibles appears to be an entirely urban phenomenon. McConnell and Ohls show that FSP caseloads declined much more

18. Estimates surveyed by Dion and Pavetti (2000) lie between 28 and 44 percent. The 12 percent and 55 percent estimates are from Wilde and others (2000). The lower estimate is based on a specification that includes contemporaneous unemployment, while the upper estimate is from a specification that includes a single lag of the caseload. Including four lags of the caseload and four lags of unemployment yields an estimate of 35 percent. In our view, much of the controversy over whether to include lagged caseloads reflects confusion about whether the short- or longer-run effects are being estimated. We have chosen to present models without lagged caseloads, so our estimates correspond to longer-run effects. Also, as we show, it is difficult to separate out the effects of unemployment and TANF in short time series, which suggests that one should view estimates based on short-time periods with some suspicion.

19. Loprest (1999); Dion and Pavetti (2000).

20. Zedlewski and Brauner (1999).

21. General Accounting Office (1999).

slowly in rural areas and, in sharp contrast to the evidence for urban areas, the decline that did occur in rural areas can be entirely accounted for by a reduction in the number of income-eligible households. McConnell and Ohls also show that rural households have higher take-up conditional on eligibility than urban households, and that their level of satisfaction with the program is higher. For example, they are more likely to feel that they are treated respectfully by their caseworkers. Because of this difference in perceptions about treatment, McConnell and Ohls speculate that the differences between rural and urban areas may be largely due to higher transaction costs and stigma in urban areas.[22] We investigate this issue further below.

A somewhat older literature also points to stigma and transaction costs as two key determinants of FSP participation. Robert A. Moffitt was one of the first to suggest that stigma might deter eligible families from participating in the FSP. However, a recent USDA study of FSP eligibles found that only 7 percent of eligible nonparticipating households gave stigma as their main reason for nonparticipation, although half answered affirmatively to at least one of the survey questions about stigma.[23] These survey results also suggest that transaction costs may be considerable but do not establish a direct link between such costs and participation. Rebecca Blank and Patricia Ruggles found that participation in the FSP increased with the size of the benefit, suggesting that households trade off the costs and benefits when deciding whether or not to participate.[24]

Beth Osborne Daponte, Seth Sanders, and Lowell Taylor investigate these issues further, using a sample of 405 households in Allegheny County, Pennsylvania.[25] The authors conducted a randomized experiment in which the treatment group was informed about their eligibility status and about the size of any benefits they were eligible for. The control group was not. Consistent with Blank and Ruggles, those entitled to the largest benefits were most likely to apply for food stamps when given this information: the take-up rate was over 90 percent for those eligible for over $202 in benefits, compared with only 40 percent among those eligible for less than $41. This finding also suggests that transaction costs or stigma are significant barriers to take up.

22. McConnell and Ohls (2000).
23. Moffitt (1983); Ponza and others (1999).
24. Blank and Ruggles (1996).
25. Daponte, Sanders, and Taylor (1999).

Empirical Methods

As discussed above, most previous studies of welfare caseloads and all of the existing econometric studies of food stamp caseloads rely on administrative data on aggregate caseloads. These models generally take the following form:

(1) $\ln(FDST_{st}) = a_0 + a_1 UNEMP_{st} + a_2 \mathbf{W}_{st} + a_3 \mathbf{STATE}_s + a_4 \mathbf{YEAR}_t + e_{st}$,

where $FDST_{st}$ is the participation rate (that is, number of households that participate divided by the total number of households) for state s in year t; $UNEMP$ is the state unemployment rate; $\mathbf{W}$ is a vector of time-varying attributes of the state's welfare program; $\mathbf{STATE}$ is a vector of state indicators or state-specific time trends; $\mathbf{YEAR}$ is a vector of year dummies, and e_{st} is an idiosyncratic error term. State-year trends may or may not be included in the model.

We follow this tradition by first estimating model 1 using data on the aggregate caseload.[26] In our base specification, the vector $\mathbf{W}$ includes several variables that have appeared in previous studies of the effects of welfare reform on welfare use.[27] These include the (logarithm of the) maximum welfare benefit payable to a family of three; a dummy variable that is equal to one in all years between the implementation of a state-wide welfare reform and the implementation of TANF in state s; and a second dummy equal to one in all years after the implementation of the state's TANF program. These two dummy variables are modified so that if, for example, the waiver or TANF program was implemented mid-year, the value of the dummy variable would be 0.5 in that year and one in subsequent years.

In our base specification, state and year dummies are included in order to capture unobserved characteristics of states or years that are related to both FSP caseloads and welfare reform. This specification implicitly assumes that the only unobservable determinants of welfare reform that influence food stamp use are either time-invariant characteristics of states or characteristics of years that affect all states in the same way. If time-varying unobservable state-specific characteristics influence the timing of welfare reform, however, then the state-fixed effects approach may yield inconsistent estimates. Hence,

26. We are grateful to Robert Schoeni for this suggestion and also generously providing us with the aggregate caseload data.

27. See Blank (1997); Council of Economic Advisers (1997, 1999); Ziliak and others (2000); Figlio and Ziliak (1999); Wallace and Blank (1999); Grogger and Michalopoulos (1999); Grogger (2000); Moffitt (1999); Schoeni and Blank (2000).

we also estimate models including state-specific time trends. These models control for any unobserved characteristics of states that trend smoothly over the sample period.

One contribution of our study is to explicitly compare results obtained using aggregate caseload data with those obtained using data from the Current Population Survey. It has been suggested that the aggregate caseload data may provide a better estimate of participation rates than self-reported CPS data. CPS respondents may not recall some spells of FSP use, or may not wish to report them. A particular concern is that increasing stigma associated with welfare programs could be associated with increases in the under-reporting of participation, so that the decline in welfare caseloads calculated using CPS data would be exaggerated.

However, administrative data also suffer from inaccuracies. For example, the same household may be counted more than once if it goes on and off the program in the course of a year, and policies associated with welfare reform may increase the amount of this type of caseload "churning." In order to make the comparison between the two data sets, we will take the microlevel CPS data, aggregate it up to the state-year level, and estimate model 1.

A further important drawback of administrative data is that it is not possible to control for household characteristics that may be important determinants of food stamp utilization. Nor is it possible to disaggregate the caseload, which is necessary to allow the effects of policy changes to affect different segments of the caseload differently. Hence, the next step in our analysis will involve estimating models using the household-level CPS data of the following form:

$$(2) FDST_{ist} = b_0 + b_1 \mathbf{X}_{ist} + b_2 UNEMP_{st} + b_3 \mathbf{W}_{st} + b_4 \mathbf{STATE}_s + b_5 \mathbf{YEAR}_t + e_{ist},$$

where $FDST_{ist}$ is an indicator equal to one if family i participated in the food stamp program in state s at time t; and $\mathbf{X}_{ist}$ is a vector of family attributes that may affect food stamp use, including maternal education, age, and race, the number of children in the family, the age of the youngest child (in models for families with children), the sex of the respondent, and whether the family lives in a central city, the rest of a metropolitan statistical area (MSA), or in a rural area.[28] These variables are highly significant determinants of food stamp

28. Specifically, we include mother's age; mother's age squared; indicators for whether she is a high school dropout, has some college, or has at least a college degree; indicators for whether she is married; dummy variables for one child, two children, and so on, up to six or more; indicators for black or other race, for the age of the youngest child, and for the sex of the respondent (usually the household head); and an indicator for residence in central city, in

participation. Because the policy variables vary only at the state-year level, we correct all of our household-level model standard errors for possible correlations in the e_{ist} within state-year clusters. Model 2 was first estimated for all households, so that the estimates could be compared with those obtained using aggregate data. We then narrowed the scope to households with income less than 300 percent of the federal poverty line, since these households are likely to be more strongly affected by welfare reform and also by unemployment. Within this group, we first isolated households with elderly members, since these households are subject to somewhat different rules, as described above, and we estimate models separately for households with elderly members but without children.

In the remaining caseload, we estimated separate models for the following demographic groups: single-headed households, married couples with children, married couples without children, and adults living alone. Single heads are most likely to be affected by welfare reform, since many of them receive welfare. Married couples (with or without children) and households with elderly members but without children make an interesting "control group" since they should not be directly affected by welfare reform (except to the extent that they are headed by immigrants). Finally, most ABAWDs will fall in the adults living alone category. We also estimated separate models for urban, central city, and rural households.

Finally, our review of the literature highlighted that factors affecting the participation of eligibles may be of primary importance. Hence, we estimate models that include two factors that are likely to have a direct influence on stigma and transaction costs: the adoption of the EBT program and the recertification interval for working families. Although EBT systems were introduced to reduce administrative costs and deter fraud, it seems likely that recipients using an inconspicuous debit card would perceive less stigma than those who continue to use the more visible brown coupons. Some smaller stores, however, are not equipped to take EBT, so that it is possible that the conversion to EBT could limit access to some food stores. We make use of the fact that there is considerable variation across states in recertification rates and in the adoption of EBT in order to estimate the effect of these policies on FSP utilization. These models take the form:

---

the balance of MSA, or undetermined whether central city or balance of MSA. When we examine subgroups, some of these variables are omitted. For example, models for single heads do not include "married," and models for all households do not include age of youngest child.

(3) $FDST_{ist} = c_0 + c_1 X_{ist} + c_2 UNEMP_{st} + c_3 W_{st} + c_4 EBT_{st} + c_5 RECERT_{st} + c_6 STATE_s + c_7 \mathbf{YEAR}_t + e_{ist}.$

Data

Our CPS data are taken from the 1981 to 1999 waves of the March survey. Since the questions about food stamp participation refer to participation during the last year, these files yield a data set covering the period 1980 to 1998. The unit of observation is the household.

Annual state-level information about welfare policy and unemployment is matched to each household's record. Information on unemployment rates, TANF implementation dates, waiver dates, and maximum welfare benefits comes from the Council of Economic Advisers. Data on the EBT program are from the U.S. Department of Agriculture.[29] Information about recertification intervals comes from the FSP quality control (QC) files and is unfortunately only available to us from 1989 on, so that regression models including this variable can be estimated only over the 1989 to 1998 period.[30] The QC data consist of representative samples of administrative data provided by the states to the U.S. Department of Agriculture. The USDA uses the data for audit purposes, comparing actual payments with the payments prescribed by the program rules. One of the data items included on the files is the household's certification interval. We use these data to compute the average recertification interval for working families with children by state and year.

Recall that working families are generally subject to shorter recertification intervals than those who receive welfare only. Thus, mean recertification intervals are likely to be affected by the fraction of welfare families in the caseload and by the way that working families are treated. By focusing only on working families, we avoid picking up changes in the composition of the FSP caseload (which could itself be affected by welfare reform), and focus only on changes in the treatment of working families.[31]

Table 1 provides an overview of some of our key data series. On aggregate, U.S. participation in the FSP during the 1990s went up and down smoothly, although there was considerable variation across states in the timing of these changes. Table 1 also shows that participation rates calculated from the CPS

29. Council of Economic Advisers (1999); U.S. Department of Agriculture (2000).
30. U.S. Department of Agriculture (various years).
31. U.S. Department of Agriculture (various years).

Table 1. Summary Statistics by Year

Year	1980	1982	1984	1986	1988	1990	1992	1994	1996	1998
A. Food stamp participation by group										
Administrative data	0.084	0.088	0.088	0.080	0.076	0.080	0.100	0.105	0.096	0.082
All CPS	0.082	0.086	0.081	0.074	0.071	0.076	0.089	0.091	0.082	0.062
Household income <300% poverty	0.142	0.146	0.145	0.137	0.136	0.146	0.163	0.165	0.153	0.122
Single parents	0.417	0.430	0.402	0.407	0.400	0.416	0.442	0.447	0.386	0.326
Married parents	0.124	0.127	0.124	0.111	0.108	0.128	0.152	0.152	0.139	0.103
Married, no children	0.049	0.065	0.067	0.056	0.056	0.055	0.073	0.069	0.067	0.044
Elderly members, no children	0.085	0.082	0.081	0.072	0.072	0.070	0.076	0.075	0.069	0.059
Adults living alone	0.107	0.117	0.122	0.107	0.110	0.120	0.115	0.130	0.120	0.103
Immigrants	-	-	-	-	-	-	-	0.204	0.172	0.132
All urban	0.142	0.145	0.143	0.134	0.140	0.144	0.166	0.171	0.151	0.123
Central city	0.185	0.189	0.191	0.174	0.190	0.192	0.210	0.231	0.198	0.165
Rural	0.147	0.156	0.155	0.150	0.141	0.157	0.157	0.159	0.158	0.117
B. Means of key policy variables (standard deviations in parentheses)										
Maximum welfare Benefits ($1,000s)	5.910	5.220	5.050	5.190	5.090	4.810	4.580	4.370	4.130	3.970
	(2.160)	(1.920)	(1.950)	(1.920)	(1.920)	(1.890)	(1.820)	(1.720)	(1.610)	(1.510)
Unemployment	6.850	9.250	7.290	6.970	5.480	5.470	6.890	5.680	5.210	4.430
	(1.600)	(2.280)	(2.180)	(2.230)	(1.890)	(1.140)	(1.610)	(1.320)	(1.240)	(1.190)
Recertification Intervals for working families with children	-	-	-	-	8.800	8.800	9.050	8.700	8.110	7.720
					(2.530)	(2.530)	(2.480)	(2.950)	(3.100)	(3.350)
C. Number of states with policy in place										
TANF	0	0	0	0	0	0	0	0	24	51
State-wide welfare waiver	0	0	0	0	0	0	3	11	28	0
State-wide EBT system	0	0	0	0	0	0	0	1	5	28

are systematically lower than those calculated using administrative data, with the gap emerging in about 1984 and persisting (and perhaps growing further) during the 1990s. This trend in under-reporting offers an additional rationale for the inclusion of year effects and state-year trends in our models, and for the comparison of estimates obtained using aggregate administrative data and CPS data.

Table 1 also confirms that the timing and magnitude of recent declines in the food stamp caseload vary considerably between demographic groups and between urban and rural areas. For example, while the participation rate among single-headed households fell from 46.2 to 32.6 percent between 1993 and 1998, a decline of 29 percent, the participation of married households with children and without children fell by 37 percent and 39 percent, respectively, during the same interval. It is most unlikely that the decline in these two groups is directly related to welfare reform, since married households with children are not usually eligible for cash assistance.

Some of the decline among married households could be due to the PRWORA restrictions on participation of immigrants in the FSP, although immigrants do not make up a large enough share of low-income households with married heads to have accounted for declines of these magnitudes. Households with elderly members and no children under 18 years old also show declines in FSP participation of 20 percent, and many of the comments about households with married heads apply equally well to them. Finally, adults living alone, the group that was most directly affected by PRWORA restrictions on ABAWDs, show a relatively small decline in FSP participation of only 15 percent between 1993 and 1998. These figures strongly suggest that while welfare reform may have been important to some groups, there were other factors driving the decline in FSP caseloads.

The second panel of table 1 shows that the aggregate food stamp caseload follows trends in the unemployment rate. In fact, food stamp participation appears to follow the unemployment rate with a one-period lag. We have estimated models using lagged unemployment rather than the contemporaneous unemployment rate in order to account for this pattern. The effects of unemployment are slightly stronger in these models, but the other coefficients are essentially unchanged, so in what follows, we show the estimates obtained using contemporaneous unemployment for the sake of comparability with other studies. The recertification intervals for the period 1989 to 1998 are also shown. These intervals were fairly constant until 1993 and then declined.

For measures of welfare reform, the last panel of table 1 shows the rapid rise in the number of states with waivers from the AFDC program after 1991. Table 1 also indicates that most states implemented TANF in 1996 or 1997, as discussed above. In contrast, there is a good deal of variation in the timing of the adoption of EBT technology.

Results

Estimates of model 1 are shown in columns 1 and 2 of table 2. The first column shows results estimated using administrative data on aggregate caseloads. These regression models use state-year population counts as weights. The second column shows results estimated using CPS data aggregated to the state-year level. These estimates are weighted using state-year cell sizes. The coefficients in both columns 1 and 2 are scaled for comparability to the estimates using household-level CPS data, which are shown in columns 3 and 4.[32] Column 3 shows estimates that do not include the X vector of household characteristics, while column 4 shows what happens when these control variables are included.

The first panel of the table shows estimates without state-year trends, while the second panel shows the effects of including them. A comparison of the estimates in the two panels shows that the differences between the columns are reduced when state-year trends are included in the models. Hence, we focus on these estimates in much of the discussion below.

A comparison of the administrative data and the aggregated CPS data (columns 1 and 2) shows the following: welfare waivers are not estimated to have a statistically significant effect in either data set; TANF implementation has a significant negative effect on FSP participation, which is of similar magnitude in both data sets; the estimated effect of maximum welfare benefits is negative in both data sets but larger in the regressions using administrative data; and unemployment has a positive and significant effect on FSP participation, which is of similar magnitude in both data sets. Thus, any inferences one could draw about the relative importance of unemployment rates, TANF, and waivers are the same, whether one uses administrative data or data created by aggregating the CPS.

32. Specifically, they are multiplied by 0.079, which is the mean participation rate in the CPS data.

Table 2. Comparison of Estimates from Aggregate Caseload and CPS Data, 1980–98[a]

Variable[b]	1 Aggregate caseload	2 CPS aggregated	3 CPS no controls	4 CPS controls
	A. No state-year trend			
Welfare waiver	-3.5	-4.6	-7.6	-7.7
	(1.6)	(2.5)	(2.5)	(2.0)
TANF	-3.1	-8.1	-10.7	-9.0
	(4.3)	(5.7)	(4.7)	(3.7)
Unemployment	4.1	4.9	4.8	3.9
	(0.4)	(0.4)	(0.4)	(0.3)
Ln maximum	-30.0	-13.0	-20.3	-16.3
welfare benefits	(6.7)	(6.9)	(7.5)	(5.9)
Observations	969	969	1079076	1079076
R^2	0.885	0.774	0.008	0.164
	B. Including state-year trend			
Welfare waiver	-2.5	-2.6	-6.2	-4.4
	(1.6)	(2.3)	(2.3)	(2.0)
TANF	-6.1	-7.6	-8.4	-9.5
	(2.9)	(4.1)	(3.4)	(3.1)
Unemployment	3.1	4.3	3.3	3.2
	(0.3)	(0.5)	(0.5)	(0.4)
Ln maximum	-44.5	-21.7	-28.2	-24.3
welfare benefits	(6.4)	(7.9)	(8.0)	(7.1)
Observations	969	969	1079076	1079076
R^2	0.922	0.813	0.008	0.165

a. Standard errors adjusted for state-year clustering in parentheses.

b. The dependent variable in column 1 is the log of the ratio of the number of households receiving food stamps to the total population in a given state and year. The column 1 regression is weighted by the total population. The dependent variable in column 2 is the log of the ratio of the weighted number of households receiving food stamps to the weighted number of households in a given state and year (where the weight is the March CPS household weight). The column 2 regression is weighted by the number of households in a given state and year. The coefficients and standard errors in columns 1 and 2 are multiplied by .0789 (the average weighted fraction of households receiving food stamps in the CPS) to adjust them to a comparable measurement as the estimates in columns 3 and 4. The dependent variable in columns 3 and 4 is a dummy variable for whether any member of the household received food stamps. Regressions in columns 3 and 4 are weighted by the March CPS household weight. All regressions include year dummies and state dummies. Additional regressors in column 4 include age and age squared of household respondent, gender of respondent, dummies for respondent's education (dropout, some college, college or more), dummies for respondent's race (black, other non-white), dummies for MSA central city, MSA balance, and MSA nonidentifiable, a dummy if respondent is married, and dummies for the number of children in household (1, 2, 3, 4, 5, 6 or more). All reported coefficients and standard errors are multiplied by 1,000.

The negative effect of the maximum welfare benefit rate is perhaps surprising but persists in all of our models (except those for adults living alone, as shown below). Higher welfare benefits should lead to higher welfare caseloads, with corresponding increases in FSP caseloads, other things being equal. A possible explanation for a negative relationship between welfare benefits and FSP caseloads is that in states with lower welfare benefits, a higher fraction of the FSP caseload is food stamps–only and the relative importance of the food stamp benefit is higher. The stigma associated with food stamp participation may also be lower in states in which the FSP is less closely associated with welfare.

A comparison of the estimates in columns 2 and 3 shows the effects of aggregation. Note that the estimated effects of TANF and the unemployment rate are similar whether we use the aggregated CPS or the household level data. The biggest change when we move to household-level data is that the effect of waivers becomes more negative and is now statistically significant, although the difference between the column 2 and column 3 estimates is not statistically significant.

Finally, a comparison of columns 3 and 4 shows the effects of controlling for the 'X' variables that are available in household-level data. The inclusion of these variables tends to slightly increase the estimated effect of TANF and to decrease the estimated effect of waivers, bringing it back into line with the column 1 and 2 estimates.

Thus, we conclude that the estimated effects of TANF, welfare waivers, and unemployment are very similar whether one uses administrative or CPS data and whether one uses aggregate or household-level data. Moreover, the household-level data offer the possibility of controlling for relevant **X** variables and also for disaggregating the caseload in interesting ways.

Estimates Using CPS Household-Level Data

Estimates from model 2 are shown in table 3 for different demographic groups. Once again, the top panel shows estimates without state-year trends, while the second panel shows estimates including these trends. In the models without trends, the coefficient on the unemployment rate is significant for every group. The estimated effects of the unemployment rate are robust to the inclusion of state-year trends except for the elderly, where unemployment becomes statistically insignificant. The panel 2 estimates imply that among families with incomes less than 300 percent of poverty, a 1 percentage point increase in unemployment is associated with a .5 point decline in FSP participation.

Since the overall 1993 to 1998 decline in participation for this group was 5 percentage points, this estimate implies that the 2 percentage point decline in unemployment that occurred over the same interval was responsible for about 20 percent of the 5 percentage point decline in the food stamp caseload among those with incomes less than 300 percent of poverty. Note that in this

Table 3. Effects of Policy Variables on Food Stamp Usage by Different Groups, 1980–98[a]

Variable[b]	1 <300 percent poverty	2 Single heads	3 Married parents	4 Married no kids	5 Elderly no kids	6 Lone adults
A. No state-year trend						
Welfare waiver	-14.5	-20.4	-7.4	-18.7	-12.8	-22.0
	(3.5)	(9.0)	(6.7)	(6.7)	(4.9)	(6.7)
TANF	-17.1	-38.4	8.3	-4.9	-32.2	-21.3
	(6.9)	(30.8)	(11.0)	(11.0)	(16.9)	(14.0)
Unemployment	6.5	13.6	8.5	4.1	2.7	4.3
	(0.6)	(1.8)	(1.0)	(1.1)	(0.8)	(1.2)
Ln maximum welfare benefits	-24.8	-4.3	-38.7	-41.5	-32.6	37.7
	(9.7)	(30.3)	(18.9)	(18.3)	(16.1)	(17.5)
MSA central city	-1.3	-4.1	-9.4	-2.9	-3.7	-0.4
	(2.6)	(6.9)	(3.7)	(3.8)	(3.4)	(4.3)
MSA balance	-38.2	-70.6	-39.5	-14.5	-22.5	-32.9
	(1.8)	(5.8)	(3.0)	(3.2)	(2.4)	(4.0)
Observations	592849	85891	157762	50842	158761	81571
R^2	0.161	0.211	0.087	0.028	0.072	0.085
B. Including state-year trend						
Welfare waiver	-7.8	-7.3	-0.4	-13.9	-12.8	-15.4
	(3.5)	(8.9)	(7.5)	(8.0)	(4.6)	(6.8)
TANF	-16.2	-54.0	-3.8	-4.1	-17.6	-21.0
	(5.9)	(18.6)	(10.6)	(12.8)	(11.7)	(14.2)
Unemployment	5.2	10.9	7.7	5.9	1.5	4.1
	(0.7)	(2.1)	(1.2)	(1.4)	(1.0)	(1.3)
Ln maximum welfare benefits	-38.6	-100.1	-58.5	-34.5	-29.7	54.7
	(12.2)	(35.5)	(21.1)	(23.3)	(16.2)	(22.1)
MSA central city	-1.1	-4.7	-9.2	-2.7	-3.0	0.2
	(2.6)	(7.0)	(3.7)	(3.8)	(3.3)	(4.4)
MSA Balance	-37.9	-71.3	-39.7	-14.0	-22.1	-32.1
	(1.9)	(5.8)	(3.0)	(3.3)	(2.4)	(4.0)
Observations	592849	85891	157762	50842	158761	81571
R^2	0.161	0.213	0.088	0.029	0.075	0.087

a. Standard errors adjusted for state-year clustering in parentheses.
b. All regressions are weighted by March CPS household weight. Additional regressors include age and age squared of household respondent, gender of respondent, dummies for respondent's education (dropout, some college, college or more), dummies for respondent's race (black, other non-white), dummy if MSA nonidentifiable, year dummies, and state dummies. Columns 1 and 5 include a dummy if respondent is married. Columns 1–3 include dummies for the number of children in household (2, 3, 4, 5, 6 or more). Column 2 includes the age of the youngest child in the household. All reported coefficients and standard errors are multiplied by 1,000.

low-income sample, the effects of both TANF and unemployment are greater than in the full sample shown in table 1.

For single mothers the estimated effect of unemployment is even greater, but so are the declines in the FSP caseload. Our estimates imply that 16 percent of the 13.6 percentage point decline in participation can be explained by reductions in unemployment. The comparable figures for married heads with children, married heads without children, households with elderly members but without children, and adults living alone are 26 percent, 43 percent, 13 percent, and 44 percent, respectively. Thus, economic conditions have the least explanatory power for the decline in the FSP caseload among single mothers and the most explanatory power for married households without children and single adults, as one might expect.

Column 1 shows that in the low-income sample, both welfare waivers and TANF had significant negative effects on FSP participation (though the estimated size of the waiver effect is somewhat sensitive to the inclusion of state-year trends). The panel 2 estimates imply that implementation of a waiver was associated with about a .8 percentage point decline in FSP participation rates, while TANF implementation reduced participation by 1.6 percentage points. Thus, TANF may have been responsible for 30 percent of the decline in FSP caseloads in this group. The preferred panel 2 estimates suggest that this TANF effect was entirely concentrated among single mothers. For this group, the panel 2 estimates imply that 40 percent of the decline in FSP participation is because of TANF.

Both panels suggest (unexpectedly) that much of the effect of welfare waivers was felt by households with elderly members (and no children) and by adults living alone, and that waivers can explain much of the overall decline in FSP participation among these groups. It is possible that states that implemented welfare waivers took other measures that made food stamps less attractive to these households, or that the increasing stigma associated with welfare in those states discouraged participation.

Finally, the estimated effects of central city and balance-of-MSA residence suggest that FSP use is highly concentrated among central city residents and among rural residents. That is, suburban households are much less likely to participate than other households. This pattern is particularly pronounced among single parents.

Table 4 examines the urban/rural dichotomy further by estimating separate models for all urban, central city, and rural residents. This table suggests that welfare reform had no impact on FSP caseloads in rural areas. Moreover, a comparison of columns 1 and 2 suggests that all of the impact of welfare reform in urban areas was felt in central cities. Among central city residents, declines in unemployment can account for 18 percent of the decline in FSP participation, while TANF accounts for 38 percent.

Table 4. Effects of Policy Variables on Food Stamp Usage by Urban/Rural, 1980–98[a]

	A. No state-year trend			B. Including state-year trend		
Variable[b]	1	2	3	4	5	6
	Urban	Central city	Rural	Urban	Central city	Rural
Welfare waiver	-14.6	-19.8	-20.1	-6.5	-9.2	-12.0
	(3.9)	(6.0)	(8.1)	(4.3)	(7.5)	(8.0)
TANF	-24.9	-31.2	-8.3	-23.4	-24.5	-5.2
	(7.8)	(12.3)	(23.7)	(7.3)	(12.4)	(22.4)
Unemployment	5.9	7.9	5.3	5.0	6.3	4.0
	(0.7)	(1.1)	(1.1)	(1.0)	(1.4)	(1.3)
Ln maximum	-51.0	-50.5	-17.3	-77.5	-67.2	-21.7
welfare benefits	(12.1)	(17.4)	(16.8)	(14.9)	(24.5)	(22.0)
MSA central city	40.5	-	-	40.5	-	-
	(2.4)	-	-	(2.4)	-	-
Observations	312437	158685	176840	312437	158685	176840
R^2	0.176	0.202	0.143	0.176	0.202	0.144

a. Standard errors adjusted for state-year clustering in parentheses.

b. All regressions are weighted by March CPS household weight. Additional regressors include age and age squared of household respondent, gender of respondent, dummies for respondent's education (dropout, some college, college or more), dummies for respondent's race (black, other non-white), dummy respondent married, dummies for the number of children in household (1, 2, 3, 4, 5, 6 or more), year dummies, and state dummies. All reported coefficients and standard errors are multiplied by 1000.

Direct Measures of Transaction Costs and Stigma

The first panel of table 5 presents estimates of model 3, which include our direct measures of transaction costs and stigma: recertification intervals for working families and an indicator for whether the state had adopted EBT. Because we were able to obtain the QC data only from 1989, these models are estimated over the 1989 to 1998 period.

For the sake of comparison, the second panel of table 5 shows estimates similar to those presented in tables 3 and 4 above, except that the models are estimated over the shorter time period. Note that it is difficult to obtain precise estimates of the effects of unemployment over this period. The estimated effects of TANF and waivers are qualitatively similar to those estimated above: TANF is significant only for single-parent households and households in rural areas, while waivers have significant negative effects on participation for adults living alone.

The estimates in the first column of the first panel suggest that longer recertification intervals increase participation in the FSP among single parents. The coefficient suggests that each one-month increase in the recertification interval would lead to a 0.5 percentage point increase in the FSP participation rate. Rural households also respond significantly to recertification intervals,

Table 5. Effects of Recertification Intervals and EBT, 1989–98 (including state-year effects)[a]

Variable[b]	1 Single heads	2 Married parents	3 Married no kids	4 Elderly no kids	5 Lone adults	6 Urban	7 Central city	8 Rural
	A. Estimates including recertification intervals and EBT							
Recertification interval	5.4	2.8	-0.7	1.1	0.5	1.1	1.4	3.1
	(1.9)	(1.7)	(1.6)	(0.9)	(1.9)	(1.0)	(1.5)	(1.4)
EBT system	-13.0	14.7	19.3	6.4	-16.2	-6.4	-10.9	15.9
	(12.9)	(12.0)	(11.2)	(8.5)	(12.6)	(9.4)	(12.0)	(9.2)
Welfare waiver	-6.2	2.7	-14.7	-7.5	-13.3	-3.6	-4.0	-8.2
	(8.8)	(7.0)	(8.0)	(4.8)	(7.1)	(4.2)	(6.3)	(7.9)
TANF	-34.5	4.1	-3.8	-15.2	-14.2	-17.2	-10.0	-5.2
	(15.6)	(12.1)	(12.8)	(11.2)	(14.2)	(6.3)	(9.6)	(20.9)
Unemployment	0.6	4.1	0.6	1.4	2.0	0.0	-3.4	5.4
	(3.7)	(2.8)	(3.0)	(1.9)	(3.1)	(1.8)	(2.4)	(3.3)
Ln maximum welfare benefits	16.0	-5.9	-89.6	66.9	-60.8	4.6	48.3	86.0
	(105.6)	(67.2)	(77.6)	(45.8)	(62.7)	(44.4)	(59.3)	(53.3)
Observations	46198	70937	23396	80896	41816	160775	79393	83967
R²	0.201	0.089	0.031	0.067	0.088	0.175	0.202	0.144
	B. Comparison estimates for 1989–98 excluding recertification intervals and EBT							
Welfare waiver	-8.2	2.2	-13.6	-7.8	-14.1	-4.1	-4.6	-8.1
	(9.0)	(7.0)	(8.1)	(4.7)	(7.0)	(4.2)	(6.4)	(8.1)
TANF	-39.0	2.5	-2.3	-16.0	-15.4	-18.0	-11.2	-5.5
	(16.1)	(11.9)	(12.9)	(11.0)	(13.8)	(6.5)	(10.1)	(21.0)
Unemployment	-0.5	4.4	1.2	1.5	1.5	-0.4	-4.1	6.4
	(3.7)	(2.7)	(3.0)	(1.9)	(3.0)	(1.8)	(2.4)	(3.3)
Ln Maximum Welfare Benefits	10.8	-22.9	-102.9	58.5	-48.6	6.3	49.7	60.8
	(106.3)	(67.3)	(79.1)	(44.2)	(62.6)	(44.1)	(59.6)	(52.8)
Observations	46198	70937	23396	80896	41816	160775	79393	83967
R²	0.201	0.089	0.031	0.067	0.088	0.175	0.202	0.144

a. Standard errors adjusted for state-year clustering in parentheses.
b. All regressions are weighted by March CPS household weight. Additional regressors include age and age squared of household respondent, dummies for respondent's education (dropout, some college, college or more), dummies for respondent's race (black, other non-white), year dummies, and state dummies. Columns 1–5 include dummies for respondent's education dummies for MSA central city, MSA balance, and MSA nonidentifiable. Columns 4 and 6–8 include a dummy if respondent is married. Columns 1, 2, 6–8 include dummies for the number of children in household (2, 3, 4, 5, 6 or more). Columns 6–8 also include dummy if 1 child in household. Column 1 includes the age of the youngest child in the household. All reported coefficients and standard errors are multiplied by 1,000.

though the size of the effect is somewhat smaller. Of our demographic groups, single heads might be expected to have the most difficulty going through the recertification process, since they need to find child care. Similarly, households in rural areas are likely to face larger costs of attending recertification interviews than those in urban areas. Thus the two groups that one might expect to have the most difficulty going through the recertification process seem to be most affected by recertification intervals.

The adoption of EBT (which was hypothesized to reduce stigma) has marginally significant positive effects on married households without children and in rural areas. It is possible that married households without children are particularly sensitive to the stigma of using food stamps.

In summary, the estimates in table 5 provide direct evidence on the importance of transaction costs and stigma and suggest that some groups may be particularly sensitive to these factors. It is worth noting that the recertification interval measures only one dimension of transaction costs.[33] Unfortunately, we are not aware of any state-level panel data about additional dimensions of transaction costs such as the length and complexity of application forms, fines on states as a result of food stamp quality control audits (which may result in greater vigilance in enforcing rules), or the vigor with which employment and training requirements for FSP recipients are enforced. Our results using the recertification interval suggest that collecting data of this kind may be a fruitful area for future inquiry.

Extensions

Welfare waivers and later TANF gave states considerable latitude in designing their welfare programs. It is of potential interest to try to account for the variation in specific policies across states. That is, if TANF reduced partici-

---

33. A recent report documents many other factors that can be thought of as increasing transactions costs. O'Brien and others (2000, pp. 4–5). These authors find that the mean length of a food stamp application is twelve pages, and that ten states have applications of nineteen pages or more. Much of this length and complexity is due to questions about income or resources that "would not ordinarily count against a food stamp applicant's benefits or eligibility." For example, applications ask about children's income and bank accounts, gifts from churches and synagogues, income from plasma donations, and receipts for garage sales. Forty-three states also ask about assets that cannot legally be considered in determining food stamp eligibility, including burial plots, the value of a home, personal belongings, and life insurance policies.

pation in the FSP, which specific TANF policies were responsible for this result?

Two policies that may be especially important are food stamp sanctions and diversion programs, as discussed above. We attempted to measure these policy changes by estimating models similar to those shown in table 5, except that they included two additional variables. The first is an indicator equal to one if the state had "severe" food stamp sanctions. This indicator is taken from Vivian Gabor and Christopher Botsko, who classify states as having stringent sanctions if they: reduced or eliminated a family's food stamp benefit for failing to comply with TANF work requirements; sanctioned the entire household or imposed lengthy sanction periods for failing to comply with FSP work requirements; and had few if any waivers exempting able-bodied adults without dependent children from the food stamp time limits imposed by PRWORA. This indicator variable is set to equal zero before 1997 and is set to one in 1997 and afterward in the seven affected states.[34]

The second variable is an indicator equal to one if the state used lump sum diversion programs. By this we mean a program in which potential welfare applicants are offered cash assistance in return for a pledge to refrain from applying for welfare benefits for a specified period. Information about whether the state used lump-sum diversion comes from Dion and Pavetti.[35] Lump sum diversion programs were generally adopted between 1996 and 1997, though a few states adopted them as early as 1993.

The lump sum diversion variable was not statistically significant in any of our models. The sanctions variable was insignificant in models without state-year trends and often positive and significant in models with state-year trends. Given the construction of this variable, the most sensible explanation of this result is that it is difficult to distinguish between our sanctions variable and a state-year trend.

Models Controlling for Immigration Status

PRWORA explicitly limited FSP benefits for legal immigrants, and FSP participation has fallen substantially among this group. Unfortunately, questions about immigration status were only added to the CPS in 1994. George Borjas has analyzed the 1993 to 1997 CPS data and finds that participation differentials between immigrants and natives can be explained entirely by differences in socioeconomic characteristics, particularly educational attain-

34. Gabor and Botsko (1998).
35. Dion and Pavetti (2000).

ment.[36] Moreover, although FSP use fell faster among immigrants than natives overall, the trends outside of California were similar. In other words, a faster decline among immigrants in California is what drives the diverging national trends for the two groups. These findings cast some doubt on whether welfare reform can be responsible for the decline in FSP participation among immigrants, except perhaps in California.

In our view, the estimates shown in table 5 cast considerable doubt on the wisdom of attempting to sort out the effects of TANF and unemployment in short time series. Nevertheless, we did attempt to use the 1993 to 1998 data to estimate separate models for immigrant households (that is, households in which the respondent was an immigrant). We did not find statistically significant effects of either TANF or unemployment in these models.

Models Controlling for Increases in the Generosity of Medicaid

Aaron Yelowitz suggests that the initial rise in FSP caseloads in the late 1980s and early 1990s may be related to increases in income cutoffs for the Medicaid program over this period.[37] Newly eligible families who applied for Medicaid may have learned of their eligibility for the FSP at the same time, since both programs are generally administered out of welfare offices. Alternatively, families who did not find it worthwhile to incur the transaction costs associated with applying for food stamps may have found it worthwhile to apply for both Medicaid and food stamps. In any case, Yelowitz finds that for every ten newly eligible families who took up Medicaid benefits, four also took up food stamps. Thus, his estimates suggest that changes in Medicaid eligibility may have accounted for as much as half of the run-up in the FSP caseload in the early 1990s, and that it may be important to control for increases in the generosity of the Medicaid program in our regression models.

Yelowitz suggests including an indicator equal to one if the youngest child in the household is eligible for Medicaid. This specification is awkward in our context, since we examine households with and without children. Hence, as an alternative, we experimented with including the Medicaid income cutoffs for children of various ages in regression models similar to those shown in table 5. This change in specification had little impact on our results.

36. Borjas (1999, 2000).
37. Yelowitz (2000).

The Earned Income Tax Credit

Since we infer that TANF and changes in unemployment together account for roughly half of the decline in FSP caseloads, it is worth asking whether we can explain the rest of the decline in caseloads using other important policy changes that took place over the 1990s. The Earned Income Tax Credit may be a particularly important policy among families with children, since the generosity of the credit expanded greatly after 1993. To the extent that the EITC "made work pay," it may have raised families far enough out of poverty to take them off the FSP. Bruce Meyer and Dan Rosenbaum estimate that the EITC can account for 37 percent of the increase in the employment rate of single mothers between 1992 and 1996. Overall increases in the generosity of the program are captured by the year effects in our models. However, after 1993 the credit expanded more rapidly for families with two children than families with one child, as Joseph V. Hotz, John Karl Scholz, and Charles Mullin point out.[38]

We estimated an additional version of our models for single and married heads with children that included the EITC phase-in subsidy rate as a regressor. These estimates suggested that the EITC had a statistically significant effect among single heads, though not among married heads. Indeed, among the single heads, our estimate suggests that expansion in the generosity of the EITC available to families with more than one child could explain about one-fourth of the decline in the FSP participation of this group. Despite the importance of the EITC for explaining the FSP caseload, however, adding it to our models had essentially no effect on the estimates of the other coefficients.

Conclusions

We find that both decreases in the unemployment rate and TANF have contributed to the recent declines in FSP caseloads. Our estimates are remarkably similar whether we use administrative data or data from the CPS, and whether we use aggregate or household-level data. They suggest that among households with incomes less than 300 percent of poverty, changes in unemployment accounted for 20 percent of the decrease in FSP participation between 1993 and 1998, while TANF accounted for 30 percent.

---

38. Meyer and Rosenbaum (1999); Hotz, Mullin, and Scholz (2000).

This TANF effect was concentrated among single heads—in this group, declines in unemployment account for only 16 percent of the decline in the FSP caseload, while TANF accounted for 40 percent. We also find that the TANF effect is significant only in central cities. In these locations, changes in unemployment explain 18 percent of the decline in FSP participation, whereas TANF explains 40 percent. Thus, TANF was associated with large declines in FSP participation among single heads and in central cities, a finding which suggests that efforts to restore food stamp benefits to households in need should focus on this group.

Our analysis of recertification intervals suggests that single heads have also been affected disproportionately by recent decreases in certification intervals. It is possible that other types of transaction costs associated with the food stamp application process may weigh heavily on this group. Since TANF increases the transaction costs that former welfare recipients face in obtaining food stamps, this result suggests that efforts to reduce these costs could reverse some of the effects of TANF on the FSP caseload.

Comments

Gary Burtless: The Food Stamp Program (FSP) is essentially a negative income tax (NIT) along the lines suggested by Milton Friedman and James Tobin. Like an NIT, the FSP has an income guarantee. The guarantee is scaled to provide a family that does not have any other income with enough resources to buy a minimal diet. As the family's own resources increase above zero, the FSP benefit is phased out using a modest tax rate—roughly 30 percent (a 24 percent rate is applied on earned income). When 30 percent of a family's countable income is higher than the basic allotment level or when its gross income is above 130 percent of the federal poverty threshold, the family is no longer eligible for the FSP.

To be sure, the benefit is not paid out in the form favored by Friedman and Tobin—as cash. Instead, it is given as coupons that are redeemable in grocery stores as food. Since the monthly allotment only pays for a basic diet, and because people need food to survive, most economists believe the welfare value of one dollar in food coupons is approximately the same as one dollar in cash.

This paper describes what has happened to participation in the FSP during the past decade. Briefly, participation in the FSP rose through about 1993, and then it declined. This cycle in program participation will not come as a shock to anyone who understands just two facts: the FSP is structured like an NIT; and the United States had a business cycle in the 1990s in which the unemployment rate peaked in 1992 and then fell to a thirty-year low. Because a higher unemployment rate is likely to increase the percentage of families that have low incomes, it is also likely to boost the percentage that qualifies for an NIT-type transfer, such as food stamps.

230

Nearly everyone likely to read the paper is aware of the two facts just mentioned. The authors therefore also examine the underlying causes of change in participation in the FSP (besides the rise and fall in the unemployment rate). One question the authors pose is particularly interesting to students of welfare reform: did changes in programs other than food stamps affect participation in the FSP? The nation's cash welfare system was overhauled during the 1990s. The federal law on public assistance was drastically changed in 1996. Even before 1996, Congress granted to states the option of introducing major changes in the way they determined eligibility for cash benefits and calculated monthly payments. The intended effect of these reforms was to make it harder for families headed by a working-age adult to obtain cash benefits. The reforms also made it much harder for families to remain continuously on the cash assistance rolls, even assuming they gained eligibility for benefits in the first place.

In the 1970s and 1980s, before these reforms took place, families applying for and obtaining cash public assistance were automatically entitled to FSP benefits. With only a little extra effort, they could get a monthly allotment of food coupons on top of their cash assistance check. In fact, families receiving cash assistance benefits are eligible for food stamps, even if they do not meet the usual income test for FSP benefits. Because the FSP is an NIT-type program, people other than cash-assistance recipients may also draw benefits, assuming their resources fall below the income and asset limits of the program. One important consequence of welfare reform is that fewer families will become or remain eligible to receive cash assistance payments as a result of participating in cash assistance programs. This is not solely because the FSP rules have been changed (although the FSP eligibility rules were also modified by the 1996 welfare reform law). It is because changes in eligibility rules for cash public assistance will affect the number of families who are indirectly entitled to FSP benefits.

This description of FSP eligibility suggests that in the 1980s and early 1990s many families probably received FSP benefits solely because they also received other cash assistance payments. If a family received cash assistance payments, its cost of obtaining food coupons was low. If a family did not receive cash aid, applying for FSP benefits required a special trip to the welfare office. An extra trip was also needed every time the family sought to reestablish its eligibility. By making cash benefits harder to obtain, welfare reform increased the transaction cost of obtaining FSP benefits for an important class of potential recipients.

Figure 1. Number of AFDC Cases, 1960–2000

Millions

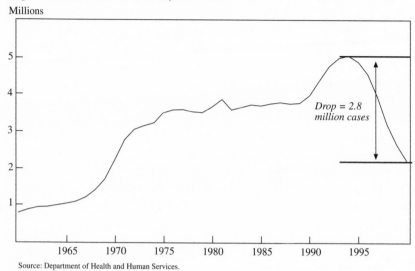

Source: Department of Health and Human Services.

Figure 1 shows the impact of welfare reform and a healthier economy on the welfare rolls during the past decade. The figure displays the number of Aid to Families with Dependent Children (AFDC) or Temporary Aid for Needy Families (TANF) cases since 1960. The figure shows plainly that the recent drop in cash assistance caseloads is unprecedented. From 1960 through 1993, the unemployment rate went up and down without a noticeable impact on the trend in the AFDC caseload. (The effect of unemployment on the caseload would be more noticeable if the chart tracked the percentage of single-mother families drawing benefits.) The cash assistance rolls have sometimes increased when the unemployment rate was falling, as in the late 1960s, in 1971–73, and in the late 1980s. And the caseload once fell when the unemployment rate was increasing, in 1981–83. My guess is that most of the steep decline in the AFDC-TANF rolls since 1994 has been driven by tighter eligibility rules (produced by welfare reform) and more generous earnings supplements for low-income breadwinners with dependents (caused by liberalization of the Earned Income Tax Credit program).

Figure 2 shows that these policy changes have produced the intended effect. They have pushed up the employment rate of mothers who were most likely to collect cash assistance benefits, namely mothers not currently married who live with their dependent children under age 18. For purposes of comparison, the figure also shows the trend in the employment-population ratio of married mothers who currently live with their spouses and their dependent

Figure 2. Employment Population Ratio of Mothers Who Live with Their Own Minor Children, 1978–99

Percent of civilian population

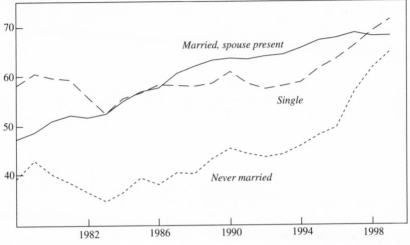

Source: Bureau of Labor Statistics.

children under age 18. Employment among married mothers, who are only rarely eligible to receive cash public assistance, has clearly grown much more slowly since 1994 than it has among single mothers. The "single" mothers in the chart include divorced, separated, and never-married mothers but do not include widows (who are likely to qualify for Social Security survivors' benefits rather than cash assistance).

Since 1994 single mothers' employment-population ratio has jumped 12 percentage points, after remaining almost constant for sixteen years. The increase in employment is even more spectacular among mothers with the greatest involvement in cash assistance programs, namely, never-married mothers. The employment-population ratio of never-married mothers jumped almost twenty points (or more than 40 percent) after 1994.

Part of the jump is traceable to a healthier job market, but most is probably because of policy changes in the cash public assistance programs or the earned income credit. Both single and married mothers should have benefited from the drop in unemployment after 1994. The stark difference in employment trends between single and married mothers offers powerful evidence that some change in the environment besides the low unemployment rate has affected the fortunes of single mothers.

The authors analyze changing FSP participation rates using the Current Population Survey (CPS) as well as administrative data. These data are used to help the authors sort out the relative contributions of the unemployment rate and other factors on the trend in FSP participation. Their results clearly show that the unemployment rate is significant in affecting FSP participation. Another consistent finding is that introduction of welfare waivers and TANF eligibility rules are associated with reduced rates of FSP participation.

Analysts could extend this work in a way that sheds more light on FSP participation. "Transaction cost" and "welfare stigma" are useful additions to modern thinking about public transfer programs. Analysts could learn more about the importance of these effects (separately or in combination) if they focused on narrower populations than the ones that are the focus of this paper.

Consider transaction costs. A rational economic agent who does not care what other people think about her will obtain any government transfer she knows about if she believes the size of the benefit justifies the expense and time associated with obtaining it. A potential applicant for FSP benefits must weigh two crucial questions. Is she eligible for benefits? Is the benefit large enough to justify the cost of applying?

To analyze the participation decision with precision, the analyst should focus on the decisions of people who have incomes and wealth holdings that are low enough to make them eligible for FSP benefits. Janet Currie and Jeffrey Grogger focus on populations that have incomes below 300 percent of the official poverty line. The eligibility guidelines for the FSP require that families have gross incomes below 130 percent of the poverty line and net incomes below 100 percent of the poverty line. Thus a large percentage of people in the samples analyzed in this paper would be ineligible to draw FSP benefits, regardless of the rate of unemployment or the state of the economy.

The eligible population can be usefully divided into narrower subpopulations. The lower a family's income, the more likely it is that the family will be eligible for benefits and the larger the family's benefit entitlement will be. The bigger the benefit, the more likely it is that the payment will exceed the transaction cost of obtaining it. It is interesting to know how FSP participation rates change when the transaction cost of participating changes But to make this comparison interesting, the analyst must hold constant the approximate value of the FSP benefit in the examined population. To accomplish this, researchers could analyze a variety of groups of low-income families, with each group defined by countable income or potential benefit level. The analysis should then focus on obtaining consistent time-series estimates of the proportion of families in each group that participates in the FSP.

This analytical approach has been used by a few researchers in the past. Sheila R. Zedlewski and Sarah Brauner divide their sample into three different groups of families that are potentially eligible to receive FSP benefits.[39] Families in the lowest income group have incomes below one-half of the poverty line. Families in the next group receive incomes between one-half and one times the poverty line. And families in the highest income group receive incomes between 1.0 and 1.3 times the poverty line. Not surprisingly, Zedlewski and Brauner find that the participation rate is highest in the group with lowest income. In comparison with families in the highest income group, families receiving incomes below one-half of the poverty line were two and one-half times more likely to participate in the FSP. [40]

We can divide the eligible population into narrower income classes or into groups of families that receive different forms of cash public assistance or that receive no cash assistance payments at all. For families collecting cash aid, the transaction cost of obtaining food stamps is much lower than it is for families that do not receive cash assistance. When Zedlewski and Brauner divide their sample into families who receive cash public assistance and those who do not, they find that families exiting the cash assistance rolls are approximately as likely to collect FSP benefits as families with similar incomes who never collected cash assistance. Holding family income constant, families who do not collect cash assistance are much less likely to receive food stamps than families collecting cash aid. It therefore follows that the sharp drop in the cash assistance rolls has directly contributed to the fall in FSP participation among families with incomes below the FSP eligibility limits.

By focusing on the trends in FS participation among income-eligible families collecting cash assistance and among income-eligible families who do not collect assistance, analysts might be able to answer three questions critical to understanding recent participation trends:

—How has the changing U.S. income distribution affected the percentage of families who are income-eligible for FSP benefits? (Presumably, the lower unemployment rate after 1993 boosted earnings and thus reduced the percentage of American families with incomes below 130 percent of the poverty threshold.)

—How has welfare reform affected the proportion of low-income families who collect cash assistance? That is, how has reform affected the percentage of families who face higher transaction costs in obtaining food stamps? Assuming that the program rules did not change at all, how big would that effect have been? This effect of reform could in principle be estimated based

39. Zedlewski and Brauner (1999).
40. Zedlewski and Brauner (1999, fig. 3).

on observed FSP participation rates in cash assistance and non-cash-assistance families in the period before reform.

—How have the changes in the FSP itself affected participation rates— above and beyond the effect of reform in the cash assistance programs?

It may not be possible for regression analysis to produce reliable estimates of each of these effects. But laying out the issues clearly and making rough-and-ready estimates of the size of the individual effects (perhaps using estimates from previous empirical studies) would help researchers and policymakers understand the full effects of welfare reform on participation in the FSP.

Even if the results of this kind of analysis only provide informed guesses about the relative impact of unemployment and policy reform on food stamp participation, the guesses would shed light on the coefficient estimates obtained in this study.

Robert F. Schoeni: The food stamp caseload, like participation in the old Aid to Families with Dependent Children (AFDC), now Temporary Aid for Needy Families (TANF), has declined at record rates during the past six years. The decline itself has been heralded by some as the ultimate indicator of the success of welfare reform. The objective of the paper by Janet Currie and Jeff Grogger is to determine why the food stamp caseload has fallen so dramatically. Addressing this question is important, and I have only a few additional comments that they have not already incorporated.

However, I do have some general observations that fall into three categories. First, I argue that the most salient policy question stimulated by the decline in food stamp participation is one that has not yet been addressed. Second, one of the objectives of caseload studies like Currie and Grogger's is to determine the share of the change in participation that is due to policy and the share due to local labor market conditions. However, I argue that the study design that has been used leads to an underestimate of the role of labor market conditions. I spend most of my time on the third and final issue. Arguably the most important welfare research question at stake right now is estimating the causal effects of the 1996 reforms. Several recent studies, including Currie and Grogger, have adopted different approaches, and I describe the strengths and weaknesses of these designs. I have a strong hunch that we will see an explosion of research in the coming months that use these approaches, and it is especially important to understand their strengths and weaknesses now as the debate over the reauthorization of welfare reform begins to intensify.

What would we really like to know about food stamp participation? The dramatic decline in the food stamp caseload has been interpreted in two ways.

Advocates of reform believe that the policy changes have helped families move off of aid, become self-sufficient, and enhance their well-being. Others have argued that the decline in food stamp participation has been too large to be explained by successful exit from aid generated by either welfare reform or the expanding economy. Instead, it is argued that the historically strong connections between the AFDC and food stamp programs meant that when AFDC/TANF families were sanctioned or hit time limits, caseworkers were not telling families that they could retain their food stamp eligibility even though they were ineligible for TANF. The implication of this argument is that there is a growing number of families who need food stamps, and they are eligible for assistance but are not receiving it. Determining which story is accurate is arguably the most important task for research on the food stamp program today.

In theory, this question can be answered quite easily. One simply would like to estimate program "take-up"—that is, the share of families eligible for food stamps who actually participate in the program—over time. If take-up has declined, then there is reason to believe that the reform of welfare may have had an effect on the food stamp program above and beyond the direct changes in food stamp policy. If not, then there is reason to be optimistic about the consequences and causes of the steep decline.

The Department of Agriculture (by way of a research contractor) estimates take-up of the Food Stamp Program using the March Current Population Survey.[41] However, not all of the information needed to determine eligibility is collected in the CPS, making it difficult to accurately estimate take-up. This exercise became even more difficult after the Personal Responsibility and Work Opportunity Restoration Act of 1996 (PRWORA) was enacted because the variation in food stamp policy across states increased. It is now very difficult to accurately determine which families are eligible for food stamps in each state using existing national survey data. Moreover, there is evidence that AFDC/TANF is under-reported in the March CPS, and that under-reporting began to increase around 1993.[42] Under-reporting probably affects food stamp participation as well. So besides not accurately estimating the denominator— the number of families eligible for food stamps—we cannot even accurately estimate the numerator—the number of families actually on aid—using survey data.

Perhaps someone will devise a way to accurately estimate take-up of food stamps (and TANF) using existing survey. But I am not optimistic. Instead, I

41. Castner (2000).
42. Bavier (1999).

argue that we need a concerted effort to collect the information that will allow us to determine which families are in fact eligible, combined with an effort to better understand the reporting of program participation in national surveys. We cannot really understand the effectiveness of our social safety net if we cannot even accurately identify families who are either eligible for or receiving assistance.

The role of the economy is underestimated. Many studies identify the effects of welfare reform and economic conditions by using time-series of cross sections. Like Currie and Grogger, the unit of observation within each cross section is the state, and the unit of time is a year. The models typically include state and year effects (and sometimes state-specific time trends and lagged values of the dependent variable), thereby identifying the effects of policy and state labor market conditions by variation in the implementation of reform and labor market conditions within states over time. The unemployment rate or employment growth rate is typically used to represent economic conditions. Most all of these studies then use the point estimates to calculate the "percent explained" by labor market conditions. The studies typically estimate this quantity as the change in the unemployment rate multiplied by the coefficient estimate on the unemployment rate divided by the total change in program participation over the period.[43]

This is a reasonable approach for obtaining an unbiased estimate of the effects of policy. However, it is highly unlikely that the full effects of economic conditions can be captured by the unemployment rate, employment growth rate, and even a longer set of indicators. Instead, the year effects included in the model are most likely capturing a large share of the effects of economic conditions. And it turns out that the year effects are typically quite big in these models, suggesting a large, unexplained change over time in welfare participation. Therefore, I have a strong hunch that this "percent explained by" exercise is leading us to put much too little emphasis on economic conditions.

Identifying the effects of welfare reform. Research that has tried to determine whether welfare reform has been effective has generally used one of four different study designs: leavers studies, simple trends in the outcomes of interest, "residual" analysis, comparison of changes in outcomes with control groups, and changes in policy within state over time. Currie and Grogger use the last, which in theory has the most promise.

1. Leavers studies: Probably all fifty states have commissioned a "leavers study," and many groups are using this approach to analyze national data.

43. Blank (2001); Council of Economic Advisers (1997, 1999); Figlio and Ziliak (1999); Levine and Whitmore (1998); Wallace and Blank (1999); Ziliak and others (2000).

The simplest design of these studies is to estimate the circumstances of families that have left aid. Some studies have compared the situation of families after they left aid with their situation while they were on welfare. With few exceptions, these studies only analyze families who left aid either before or after TANF, but not both. The typical finding is that 60 to 70 percent of leavers are working, and their income is not all that much different from when they were on aid.[44]

The problem with this study design is that it does not help determine the causal effects of reform. In the worst—but most common—case, we do not know whether families who left under TANF were any worse than families who left under AFDC. And even if there were differences in leavers in these two policy regimes, it is nearly impossible to associate the differences in outcomes to PRWORA itself because of unobserved changes over time that are not accounted for. Moreover, policies can affect whether families enter welfare, which is not captured by studies that only analyze leavers.

2. Simple trends and residual analysis: The simple change in poverty, welfare participation, teen fertility, and other outcomes of interest before versus after reform obviously cannot be interpreted as the effects of reform per se. There were many other changes during this period that could account for these improvements, most notably the record-setting economic expansion.

A common approach to dealing with confounding factors is what I call the "residual" approach. For example, a model is estimated—using time-series of cross-sections—with welfare participation as the dependent variable, and local labor market conditions as the key righthand side variable. The model also includes year effects, or more simply an indicator of "reform," that takes the value of 1 during the period after reform, 0 otherwise. The coefficient estimate on this indicator of "reform," after adjusting for observable labor market conditions and perhaps other factors, is interpreted as the effect of reform itself. This approach has been and will continue to be widely used. However, the inability to sufficiently control for all unobserved factors that are correlated with reform clearly make this approach problematic.

3. Residual analysis with comparison groups: An alternative to the simple before-after comparison is to consider a control group and then compare the change for the group expected to be affected by the policy change with the change for the group not expected to be affected by the policy. This approach has been used widely. The underlying assumption is that the comparison group would experience the same pattern of outcomes as the "treatment" group had the treatment group not been treated. It is very hard to think of a

44. Levine and Whitmore (1998); Wallace and Blank (1999); Ziliak and others (2000).

group of comparison families that are similar enough to families actually affected by policies that would conform to this requirement, but yet at the same time they themselves are not potentially affected by the policy change.

4. Changes in policy within states over time: The final approach is to identify the effects of welfare reform through variation in policies within states over time. Specifically, consider a model that is very similar to Currie and Grogger's:

$$(1) \ P_{st} = Waiver_{st} * \beta_{Waiver} + TANF_{st} * \beta_{TANF} + Economy_{st} * \beta_{Econ} + \gamma_s + \gamma_t + \varepsilon_{st}.$$

In this model, P stands for employment of single mothers (or any of the outcomes targeted by welfare reform) in state s in year t. *Waiver* and *TANF* are the two key policy variables, both entered as dummy variables. Both indicators are equal to the fraction of the year for which a state has a waiver or a TANF plan in place. Labor market factors—*Economy*—are controlled for with variables such as the unemployment rate and employment growth rate. Year effects (γ_t) and state effects (γ_s) are also included in the model. This approach, which I have used myself, has the most potential, and it will most likely continue to be used widely.[45] However, this design has several limitations.

One set of limitations concerns the timing of policy effects: Policies can affect outcomes at several points in their life cycles. Perhaps the debate surrounding the policy change or the approval of a policy change—even before it is implemented—can affect behavior. More typically it is assumed that policies affect outcomes when the policy is implemented. Moreover, model 1 assumes that the policy affects the outcomes immediately upon implementation, and that the effect is the same over time. However, one alternative hypothesis is that families can rely on their friends and relatives or their savings for some period of time; only after they have exhausted these resources will families enter the labor market, change their family structure, or adopt other coping strategies. Or perhaps policies that are legally in place on a given date are not fully and effectively implemented until a later date because government institutions are slow to change. For whatever reason, it takes time for the reforms to have an effect, and ideally this dynamic process should be represented in the model. But in reality, it is nearly impossible to address these issues with annual data and only a few years of postreform observations.

Other, unobserved, factors may affect the outcomes, including the availability of child care, transportation, Medicaid coverage, and other programs that are difficult to quantify. Although models like 1 may not directly examine these factors, state, year, and state-specific time trends are included in an

45. Council of Economic Advisers (1999); Schoeni and Blank (2000).

attempt to capture the unobserved factors that may be correlated with the observed variables. However, states often change related policies simultaneously, making this assumption problematic.

Another limitation is that there is insufficient variation in explanatory factors. The model requires state variation to identify the effect of the policy variables. The variable *TANF* varies among states, but all states implemented their TANF policies within a sixteen-month time period. Therefore, identification is tenuous, especially using annual data.

Two maintained assumptions of model 1 are that state welfare policies do not induce migration across state lines, and welfare policies are exogenous to the dependent variables (conditional on the control factors). The empirical evidence finds a small effect of welfare generosity on migration across state lines, suggesting that any induced bias would also be small.[46] However, the available evidence is from AFDC, not TANF. Exogenous policy setting is the maintained assumption in almost all studies of this nature. Understanding why different states adopted the exact set of policies they did at the time they did should be an important part of this research agenda.

Finally, there are many different policies and practices. Model 1 represents TANF with a single dummy variable. However, many policies were changed, and the variation across states is substantial. This last characteristic holds out some promise for researchers to identify the effects. But the number of different policies is so large, it will be difficult to fully and accurately represent them all. In addition, even if one can characterize the policies that are on the books, the way in which the policies are implemented, including the zeal and culture of the caseworkers, undoubtedly plays an important role in determining how policies translate into good outcomes. And this quality of implementation may be correlated with the nature of the policy. Accounting for this important dimension of the process is virtually impossible with national data.

In sum, my comment has been quite pessimistic about our ability to determine the causal effects of welfare reform. With that said, I think the approaches described above—and others—must be explored. The policy question that these studies attempt to answer is of first-order importance. That the nature of the change makes it very difficult to cleanly identify the causal effects of welfare reform should not deter us from pressing ahead, but we do so with a clear understanding of the limitations of the various approaches.

46. Gresenz (1999).

References

Bavier, Richard. 1999. "An Early Look at the Effects of Welfare Reform." Draft. Office of Management and Budget.

Blank, Rebecca. 1997. "What Causes Public Assistance Caseloads to Grow?" Working Paper 6343. Cambridge, Mass.: National Bureau of Economic Research (December).

——. 2001. "What Causes Public Assistance Caseloads to Grow?" *Journal of Human Resources* 36 (Winter): 85–118.

Blank, Rebecca, and Patricia Ruggles. 1996. "When Do Women Use AFDC and Food Stamps? The Dynamics of Eligibility vs. Participation." *Journal of Human Resources* 31 (Winter): 57–89.

Borjas, George. 1999. "Immigration and the Food Stamp Program." Harvard University, Department of Economics (September). Mimeo.

——. 2000. "Welfare Reform and Immigration." Harvard University, Department of Economics (July). Mimeo.

Castner, Laura. 2000. "Trends in FSP Participation Rates: Focus on 1994 to 1998." Washington: Mathematica Policy Research for the U.S. Department of Agriculture (November).

Castner, Laura, and Randy Anderson. 1999. *Characteristics of Food Stamp Households: Fiscal Year 1998*. Advance Report. U.S. Department of Agriculture, Food and Nutrition Service (July).

Castner, Laura, and Scott Cody. 1999. *Trends in FSP Participation Rates: Focus on September 1997*. U.S. Department of Agriculture (November).

Council of Economic Advisers. 1997. "Technical Report: Explaining the Decline in Welfare Receipt, 1993–1996." Washington (May).

——. 1999. "Technical Report: The Effects of Welfare Policy and the Economic Expansion on Welfare Caseloads: An Update." Washington (August).

Currie, Janet. Forthcoming. "U.S. Food and Nutrition Programs." In *Means-Tested Transfer Programs in the United States*, edited by Robert Moffitt. University of Chicago Press for NBER.

Daponte, Beth Osborne, Seth Sanders, and Lowell Taylor. 1999. "Why Do Low Income Households Not Use Food Stamps? Evidence from an Experiment." *Journal of Human Resources* 34 (Summer) 612–28.

Dion, Robin, and LaDonna Pavetti. 2000. *Access to and Participation in Medicaid and the Food Stamp Program: A Review of the Recent Literature*. U.S. Department of Health and Human Services (March).

Figlio, David N., and James P. Ziliak.1999. "Welfare Reform, the Business Cycle, and the Decline in AFDC Caseloads." In *Welfare Reform and the Economy: What Will Happen When a Recession Comes?*, edited by Sheldon Danziger, 17–48. Kalamazoo, Mich.: W. E. Upjohn Institute for Employment Research.

Gabor, Vivian, and Christopher Botsko. 1998. *State Food Stamp Policy Choices under Welfare Reform: Findings of a Fifty-State Survey.* U.S. Department of Agriculture (May).

General Accounting Office. 1999. "Food Stamp Program: Various Factors Have Led to Declining Participation. RCED-99-185" (July.)

——. 2000. "Welfare Dynamics: State Sanction Policies and Number of Families Affected." HEHS-00-44 (March).

Gresenz, Carol. 1997. "An Empirical Investigation of the Role of AFDC Benefits in Location Choice." Working Paper DRU-1611-RC. Santa Monica, Calif.: Rand Corporation.

Grogger, Jeffrey. 2000. "Time Limits and Welfare Use." Working Paper 7709. Cambridge, Mass.: National Bureau of Economic Research (May).

Grogger, Jeff, and Charles Michalopoulos. 1999. "Welfare Dynamics under Time Limits." Working Paper 7353. Cambridge, Mass.: National Bureau of Economic Research (September).

Haider, Stephen, and Jacob Klerman. 2000. "A Stock-Flow Analysis of the Welfare Caseload: Insights from California Economic Conditions." Santa Monica, Calif.: Rand (September).

Hotz, V. Joseph, Charles Mullin, and John Karl Scholz. 2000. "The Earned Income Tax Credit and Labor Market Participation of Families on Welfare." University of California, Los Angeles, Department of Economics (December). Mimeo.

Levine, Phillip B., and Diane M. Whitmore. 1998. "The Impact of Welfare Reform on the AFDC Caseload." In *National Tax Association Proceedings, 1997,* 24–33. Washington: National Tax Association.

Loprest, Pamela. 1999. "Families Who Left Welfare: Who Are They and How Are They Doing?" Discussion Paper 99-02. Washington: Urban Institute.

McConnell, Sheena, and James Ohls. 2000. "Food Stamps in Rural America: Special Issues and Common Themes." Washington: Mathematica Policy Research (May).

Meyer, Bruce, and Dan Rosenbaum. 1999. "Welfare, the Earned Income Tax Credit, and the Labor Supply of Single Mothers." Working Paper 7363. Cambridge, Mass.: National Bureau of Economic Research.

Moffitt, Robert A. 1983. "An Economic Model of Welfare Stigma." *American Economic Review* 73 (December): 1023–35.

——. 1999. "The Effect of Pre-PRWORA Waivers on AFDC Caseloads and Female Earnings, Income, and Labor Force Behavior." Northwestern University and University of Chicago, Joint Center for Poverty Research.

O'Brien, Doug, and others. 2000. *The Red Tape Divide: State-by-State Review of Food Stamp Applications.* Washington: America's Second Harvest.

Ponza, Michael, and others. 1999. *Customer Service in the Food Stamp Program.* Contract 53-3198-40-025. U.S. Department of Agriculture, Food and Nutrition Service (July).

Schoeni, Robert, and Rebecca Blank. 2000. "What Has Welfare Reform Accomplished? Impacts on Welfare Participation, Employment, Income, Poverty, and Family Structure." Working Paper 7627. Cambridge, Mass.: National Bureau of Economic Research (March).

U.S. Committee on Ways and Means. 1998. *Green Book, 1997.* Government Prining Office.

——. 1999. *Green Book, 1998.* GPO.

U.S. Department of Agriculture. 1999. *Who Is Leaving the Food Stamp Program? An Analysis of Caseload Changes from 1994 to 1997.* Office of Analysis, Nutrition, and Evaluation, Food and Nutrition Service (March).

——. 2000. *Food Stamp Program Electronic Benefits Transfer (EBT) Project Status.* (February).

——. Various years. *Technical Documentation for the Fiscal Year [various years] FSP QC Database and QC Minimodel.* Food and Nutrition Service.

U.S. Department of Health and Human Services. 1997. *Setting the Baseline: A Report on State Welfare Waivers* (http://aspe.os.dhhs.gov/hsp/isp/waiver2/title.htm).

Wallace, Geoffrey, and Rebecca M. Blank. 1999. "What Goes Up Must Come Down? Explaining Recent Changes in Public Assistance Caseloads." In *Economic Conditions and Welfare Reform,* edited by Sheldon H. Danziger, 44–90. Kalamazoo, Mich.: W. E. Upjohn Institute for Employment Research.

Wilde, Parke, and others. 2000. "The Decline in Food Stamp Participation in the 1990's." U.S. Department of Agriculture, Food and Nutrition Service (June).

Yelowitz, Aaron. 2000. "Did Recent Medicaid Reforms Cause the Caseload Explosion in the Food Stamps Program?" University of California, Los Angeles, Department of Economics.

Zedlewski, Sheila R., and Sarah Brauner. 1999. "Are the Steep Declines in Food Stamp Participation Linked to Falling Welfare Caseloads?" Working Paper on the New Federalism. Washington: Urban Institute (November).

Ziliak, James P., and others. 2000. "Accounting for the Decline in AFDC Caseloads: Welfare Reform or Economic Growth?" *Journal of Human Resources* 35 (Summer): 570–86.

DAN BLACK
Syracuse University

DOUGLAS HOLTZ-EAKIN
Syracuse University

STUART ROSENTHAL
Syracuse University

Racial Minorities, Economic Scale, and the Geography of Self-Employment

SELF-EMPLOYMENT IS receiving substantial attention in the United States and elsewhere. The notion that self-employment is beneficial for both individuals and for society as a whole has a long history in the United States; witness Horatio Alger's stories and references to them in modern culture.[1] Among the recent echoes is the notion that encouraging entrepreneurship would be a good strategy for improving the economic status of blacks. According to *Washington Post* journalist William Raspberry, Paul Pryde, president of Capital Access Group LLC, has argued that there "is a need to shift the black focus from jobs to ownership, from income to wealth, from political office to using politics to improve the climate for black business development."[2] This paper sheds light on the striking racial differences in the frequency of self-employment by examining how the characteristics of local populations affect the decision of minorities to enter self-employment.

Our research bridges several recent areas of interest. First, there is now an extensive econometric literature on self-employment. Much of the focus has been on two related questions: at a given point in time, what factors determine who is self-employed and who is not. Or, alternatively, over the course of, say,

We thank Robert Fairlie, Bruce Fallick, and Edward Glaeser for useful comments. We also thank the Center for Policy Research for financial support, Peter Howe and Chada Phuengphinij for research assistance, and Esther Gray for her assistance in preparing the manuscript.

1. See Holtz-Eakin, Rosen, and Weathers (2000) for an examination of self-employment and income mobility in the United States.

2. William Raspberry, "Shifting the Focus from Jobs to Ownership," *Washington Post*, May 4, 1991, p. A23. See Green and Pryde (1990). Pryde is coauthor of *Black Entreneurship in America*.

245

a year, who makes a transition from or into self-employment.[3] A central point of this literature has been the degree to which access to capital limits the ability of individuals to enter self-employment, especially the role of such constraints in explaining racial differences in self-employment rates. Our research also draws on the literature in discrimination. In particular, Stephen G. Bronars and George J. Borjas (hereafter referred to as BB) and Dan Black construct simple equilibrium models of the decision to enter self-employment when consumers or employers may be prejudiced. Using data from the 1980 census, BB found that the likelihood of minority self-employment in a given area increased with the fraction of the minority population in that area. Black also shows that spatial concentration of minorities into enclaves serves to reduce the incidence of discrimination by employers.[4]

Finally, our analysis is also indirectly related to the literature on spatial mismatch. In that literature the suburbanization of jobs coupled with suburban housing (and labor) market discrimination against minorities reduces the employment opportunities of inner-city minorities.[5] Although the implications of spatial mismatch for employment and compensation outcomes have been extensively studied, implications for minority self-employment rates have been largely overlooked. A possible response of minority groups to spatial mismatch, however, would be to seek out self-employment opportunities. Because racial segregation (and discrimination) is closely associated with concerns of spatial mismatch, this suggests that increased segregation could be associated with greater minority self-employment, other things being equal.

The starting point for our investigation is the considerable spatial variation in self-employment rates, in general, and race-specific self-employment rates, in particular. In all that follows, individuals are defined as self-employed if they report self-employment as their principal job on their 1990 census form. Based on that definition, table 1 shows regional rates of self-employment for men, 25 to 64 years old, living in urban areas; these individuals are the focus of our analysis. As shown, the overall U.S. self-employment rate of 11.4 percent embodies a range from 9.9 percent in the Northeast to 12.7 percent in the Pacific region; a difference of nearly 30 percent.

For race-specific rates of self-employment, two facts stand out. First, the overall rate of self-employment differs greatly across races, ranging from a

3. On one or both of these questions, see Evans and Jovanovic (1989); Fairlie and Meyer (1996); Holtz-Eakin, Joulfaian, and Rosen (1994); Bruce (1999); and Holtz-Eakin and Dunn (2000).
4. Meyer (1990); Borjas and Bronars (1989); Black (1995).
5. For example, Gabriel and Rosenthal (1996); Kain (1992, 1968); Zax (1990).

Table 1. Regional Self-Employment Rates, Males, 25 to 64 Years Old

Region	All	White	Black	Hispanic	Asian
Northeast	0.0985	0.107	0.0387	0.0421	0.0662
Middle Atlantic	0.112	0.119	0.0384	0.0609	0.122
East-North Central	0.105	0.111	0.0320	0.0551	0.101
West-North Central	0.117	0.121	0.0390	0.0620	0.0798
South Atlantic	0.117	0.131	0.0492	0.0887	0.137
East-South Central	0.105	0.119	0.0397	0.112	0.122
West-South Central	0.122	0.146	0.0470	0.0758	0.114
Mountain	0.125	0.141	0.0429	0.0655	0.107
Pacific	0.127	0.145	0.0546	0.0685	0.112
United States	0.114	0.127	0.0427	0.0682	0.111

Source: Authors' calculation, Public Use Micro Sample of the 1990 Census.

low of 4.3 percent among blacks to 12.7 among whites. Second, within individual minority populations, the spatial variation in self-employment rates across census regions is considerable. For blacks, the lowest rate is 3.2 percent, while the highest rate (5.5 percent) is nearly 70 percent greater. Among Hispanics, the difference is an even more striking 166 percent (11.2 percent versus 4.2 percent), while among Asians, the highest rate of 13.7 percent is roughly double the lowest rate (6.6 percent). In contrast, among whites, the difference between highest and lowest is 36 percent (14.6 percent versus 10.7 percent).

In analogous fashion, table 2 documents the regional disparity in the returns to self-employment.[6] The table shows that earnings among the self-employed averaged nearly $37,000, but that this is composed of earnings that range from $33,000 to $41,000—a difference of 25 percent. As with table 1, table 2 makes clear that there is tremendous variation among national averages for different racial groups (ranging from $20,000 to $48,000) and across regions within each racial group. Taken as a whole, tables 1 and 2 demonstrate clearly the tremendous spatial variation in the incidence and remuneration of the self-employed, and this variation is even more pronounced among minority groups.

Why? As noted earlier, there has been considerable previous research on the economics of self-employment. We focus on three strands. In the first, pri-

---

6. Our data are the "labor earnings" of those who report themselves as self-employed. In general, it is not clear if the self-employed distinguish between the return to capital invested in their businesses and the return to their labor effort. See Yuengert (1996). Hence, the "return to self-employment" is a concept fraught with ambiguity. However, we have no reason to believe that these reporting issues differ systematically across races or regions.

Table 2. Regional Self-Employment Earnings

Dollars

Region	All	White	Black	Hispanic	Asian
Northeast	40,974	41,782	25,930	25,188	43,155
Middle Atlantic	37,930	38,567	24,448	30,396	57,902
East-North Central	36,716	36,787	21,570	41,901	68,727
West-North Central	34,652	34,807	18,184	31,315	48,005
South Atlantic	36,261	38,147	17,844	36,038	40,069
East-South Central	35,698	37,658	17,061	33,964	62,687
West-South Central	33,679	36,820	14,564	22,377	37,921
Mountain	32,808	34,361	11,988	20,753	37,962
Pacific	38,562	40,436	21,140	28,019	37,599
United States	36,566	37,903	19,627	30,264	47,770

Source: Authors' calculation, Public Use Micro Sample of the 1990 Census.

mary attention is paid to demographic factors that influence the decision to be self-employed—age, education, family history of self-employment, and so on. In this view, spatial variation in self-employment rates and earnings derives from differences in the characteristics of individuals that make up regional populations. We return to this below.

The second focuses on capital market constraints that force the self-employed to finance their business start-up from own wealth holdings.[7] In this view, racial disparity in the distribution of wealth translates directly into racial disparity in the rate of self-employment. Such concerns have led, in part, to the establishment and enforcement of the Community Reinvestment Act (CRA), one goal of which is to make capital more accessible to minority households living in neighborhoods that historically have been underserved by the lending community. This line of reasoning undoubtedly helps to explain the overall white-minority self-employment gap. However, in the absence of region-specific capital market failures, capital market constraints are unlikely to explain the substantial regional variation in self-employment among individual minority groups as described in tables 1 and 2.

The final class of explanations focuses on demand- and supply-side effects of racial discrimination and segregation that restrict the size of local markets to which minorities have access. In what follows, we refer to differential demand on the basis of the race of the ownership as "discrimination," while recognizing that this often carries a negative connotation. In practice, our data do not allow us to tell this apart from a strong preference for the products of a specific racial group (for example, ethnic food products). We will continue

7. See, for example, Meyer (1990).

with the terminology below but emphasize that it need not carry a negative significance.

One prominent version is a demand-side argument due to BB. In effect, BB argue that consumer discrimination lowers the size of the local sales market and the return to self-employment. The result is lower self-employment earnings and rates among those racial groups subject to this form of discrimination. Alternatively, to the extent that racial segregation is associated with spatial mismatch, as noted earlier, a supply-side response of minorities may be to seek out self-employment opportunities to offset diminished earnings opportunities in the wage sector.[8] While this idea has not previously been examined, it suggests that segregation could be associated with an enhanced propensity for self-employment among minority groups. We will return to the BB approach and the roles of minority population scale and segregation in greater detail. Notice, however, that these ideas share the notion that location-specific features have the potential to explain the regional variation displayed in self-employment rates and earnings.[9]

To anticipate the outcome, our principal finding is that racial variation in self-employment and earnings is positively linked to the purchasing power of minorities in the metropolitan-area market. In contrast, self-employment outcomes are largely not related to the degree of racial segregation. Thus, whereas we find little support for higher minority self-employment in response to increased racial segregation, we do find support for the idea that the economic scale of the minority market affects the ability of an area to sustain minority entrepreneurs. This latter finding is consistent with the BB argument that consumer-based discrimination restricts minority self-employment opportunities when local minority communities are not of sufficient scale to offset such effects.

In the following pages, we provide a simple analytical framework of the determinants of self-employment and self-employment earnings. We describe our data and undertake some preliminary analyses. We discuss our econo-

---

8. Kain (1968, 1992).

9. There is a related literature that focuses on cross-national differences in rates of entrepreneurship and self-employment. See, for example, Cowling and Mitchell (1997); Robson (1997) and Taylor (1996) on the United Kingdom; Carrasco (1997) on Spain; Johansson (2000) on Finland; Blanchflower (2000) on the Organization for Economic Cooperation and Development as a whole; and Harhoff, Stahl, and Waywood (1998), Pfeiffer and Pohlmeier (1992), and Georgellis and Wall (1999) on Germany. A key issue in many of these studies is whether lack of access to capital inhibits the transition to self-employment. An important difference in our work is that regions share a common capital market and institutional framework.

metric approach and its results. Finally, we offer a summary with suggestions for future research.

Analytical Framework

We develop a framework for understanding the link between consumer discrimination and equilibrium self-employment rates and earnings (by race) relying on a simplified version of the model of Borjas and Bronars (BB).[10] The formal derivation is relegated to appendix A to this chapter; here we highlight only the key features of the setup and the major implications.

Suppose there are only two racial groups, whites (W) and blacks (B). Whites "discriminate" (in the sense discussed above) in that they prefer to buy from white entrepreneurs, other things equal. Specifically, if both a white entrepreneur and a minority entrepreneur charge P for the same product, whites treat the price from the minority to be αP, where $\alpha > 1$. Thus, they will prefer to buy from the white entrepreneur, and α is an index of the severity of discrimination. For simplicity, we assume that minorities do not discriminate.

An individual chooses between being a self-employed entrepreneur or working at a wage and salary job on the basis of the earnings in each opportunity.[11] Each worker in the wage-salary sector earns the same amount. In contrast, the productivity of each self-employed individual depends on the individual's ability, with the result that in equilibrium the relatively high-ability individuals choose entrepreneurship.[12] Ability is exogenously distributed, and the distributions may be different for blacks and whites.

Discrimination and the racial composition of the population affect the equilibrium from both supply and demand perspectives. From the supply side, the key effect is the difference in the skills of whites and minorities. If the skill distributions are identical, then an increase in the share of minorities has no effect. However, if there are more high-skilled whites, a shift

10. Borjas and Bronars (1989).

11. For convenience our model assumes full employment—everyone is self-employed or working in a wage/salary job.

12. Taken at face value, the model has the counterfactual prediction that self-employment earnings are uniformly higher than wage and salary earnings. If individuals choose on the basis of utility—not simply earnings—this will be relaxed, but the additional generality brings substantive complication and little insight. Also, the assumption that earnings are dictated solely by ability stems from our assumption that there are no capital market constraints, uncertainty, or learning issues that affect the decision to be self-employed.

toward more minorities will place downward pressure on earnings in the wage-salary sector.

On the demand side, discrimination reduces purchases by whites. In the other direction, increases in the "economic clout" of minorities—as measured by the incomes per capita of blacks—raises the demand for the goods of self-employed minorities.

Drawing together these effects yields three key insights. First, an increase in discrimination—which has purely demand-side origins—lowers self-employment among blacks, reduces the price of minority entrepreneurs' output, and, by extension, lowers their earnings. Testing this idea is difficult, however, because discrimination is not observed. As a result, there is no observable empirical analogue to an "increase in discrimination."

Alternatively, the second insight is that we are able to examine the relationship between self-employment (and earnings) and the racial composition of the population. Unfortunately, the theory delivers no strong prediction about this relationship. Intuitively, changing the mix of whites and minorities affects both the mix of skills in population—a supply-side effect—and the mix of demand for self-employed products. There is no clear prediction regarding which shift will dominate. To clarify, suppose that the distributions of skills are identical for whites and blacks. In this case, an increase in the minority share of the population has no direct impact on the supply side. It will raise self-employment *if* blacks buy more per capita from the self-employed than do whites. If they buy less, then self-employment falls. Moreover, the ambiguous effect carries directly over to earnings.

The final important insight is that an increase in the per capita income of the minority community increases the self-employment rate, and self-employment earnings, of minorities. Thus, a more stringent test of whether discrimination limits the scope of minority self-employment is to test whether the economic scale of the minority community affects the self-employment rate of minorities, rather than relying on the relative size of the minority community alone. We turn now to our strategy for pursuing such a test.

Data

Our data are drawn from the Public Use Micro Sample (PUMS) of the 1990 census. We focus on men, 25 to 64 years old. In addition, we restrict our sample to those living in metropolitan areas identified in the 1990 PUMS, all of which have populations in excess of 100,000.[13] These data contain infor-

13. A complete list of the metropolitan areas is contained in appendix B to this paper.

Table 3. Metropolitan-Area Variation in Self-Employment Rates

Item	All	White	Black	Hispanic	Asian
Average	0.114	0.127	0.0427	0.0682	0.111
Median	0.109	0.120	0.0413	0.0600	0.110
Minimum	0.069	0.079	0	0	0
Maximum	0.243	0.244	0.111	0.270	0.321
Standard deviation	0.027	0.0313	0.0201	0.0407	0.0561
Coefficient of variation	0.235	0.246	0.472	0.597	0.505

Source: Authors' calculation, Public Use Micro Sample of the 1990 Census.

mation on more than 1.6 million individuals. Finally, when necessary, we augment our data on individuals with data on the characteristics of metropolitan areas. In some instances these data are calculated directly from the Census while in other cases they are drawn from the Census web site.

To gain a feel for the data, in tables 3 and 4 we begin by revisiting the spatial variation in self-employment rates and earnings, this time focusing on variation across metropolitan areas. Consider the first column of table 3, which shows summary statistics for the 273 metropolitan areas in our sample. As shown, the average self-employment rate is 11.4 percent, while the median rate is a bit lower—10.9 percent. Across cities, however, the variation is substantial. The minimum rate is 6.9 percent (in Fayetteville, North Carolina), while the maximum (in St.Cloud, Minnesota) is 24.3 percent. Measuring the degree of variation differently, the standard deviation of the self-employment rate (across metropolitan areas) is 2.7 percentage points, or about 24 percent of the mean (see the last line of the table). The remaining columns of the table provide the same statistics for various racial groups in the sample. Blacks, Hispanics, and Asians, compared with whites, display a common pattern—each has a lower average rate of self-employment but (especially relative to the mean) displays more variation across metropolitan areas. In short, the metropolitan-level variation is substantial.

Table 4 repeats this analysis, focusing instead on earnings from self-employment. Again, one finds considerable geographical variation in the return to self-employment. And again, on earnings, racial minorities differ from whites in both the mean—lower, with the exception of Asians—and the variation—higher, with the exception of blacks.

One possibility is that some locations are "good" for self-employment, while others are not as favorable. If so, then the variation in tables 3 and 4 might be driven largely by factors common to all racial minorities. To gauge the degree to which this is the case, table 5 examines the cross-city correla-

Table 4. Metropolitan-Area Variation in Mean Self-Employment Earnings

Item	All	White	Black	Hispanic	Asian
Average	36,566	37,903	19,627	30,264	47,770
Median	36,011	37,320	18,333	27,032	44,631
Minimum	18,095	17,965	0	0	0
Maximum	70,777	71,845	67,000	122,923	135,481
Standard deviation	7,716	8,264	11,975	18,207	25,264
Coefficient of variation	0.211	0.218	0.101	0.602	0.529

Source: Authors' calculation, Public Use Micro Sample of the 1990 Census.

tion in rates of self-employment and in earnings from self-employment. The largest correlation in self-employment rates is between whites and blacks (0.41); the remainder are quite low or even negative (Hispanics and Asians). Similarly, cross-city correlations in earnings are relatively low or negative. Here the largest is again between whites and blacks, while there is a negative correlation between whites and Asians.

In short, there appears to be little support for a simplistic notion that the variation is strictly because of location. This finding raises several possibilities. First, self-employment decisions could depend strictly on individual characteristics, and these attributes vary across populations in different cities. Alternatively, self-employment could also depend on the individual *plus* the characteristics of the population of the individual's city; this is precisely the prediction of the BB discrimination model. To investigate these avenues, however, requires imposing more structure on our data.

Econometric Issues

Our objective is to estimate the effect of city-by-city variation in the racial mix and the racial distribution of income on the race-specific rates of self-employment. One method for doing so would be to specify a model of the form

(1) $$y_{ij}^* = \mathbf{X}_{ij}\beta + \mathbf{Z}_j\gamma + u_{ij},$$

where the dependent variable is the latent desire for self-employment of the *i*th person in the *j*th city, $\mathbf{X}_{ij}$ is a vector of characteristics for the person, $\mathbf{Z}_j$ is a vector of characteristics of the *j*th city, (β, γ) are the parameters to be estimated, and u_{ij} is the error term. The parameters of equation (1) could be estimated, for example, using a probit or logit technique, a strategy followed by BB.

An alternative, which we pursue, is to follow David Card and Alan Krueger and estimate linear probability models of the form

(2) $$y_{ij} = \mathbf{X}_{ij}\,\beta + \alpha_j + u_{ij},$$

where α_j is a city-specific effect.[14] Card and Krueger use this approach in their analysis of school quality in the South. As they note, the fixed effects capture all the local variation that is not explained by individual characteristics of respondents but do not identify the source of that variation. To learn about the source, we use the estimated fixed effects, $\hat{\alpha}_j$, as dependent variables in models of the form

(3) $$\hat{\alpha}_j = \mathbf{Z}_j\,\gamma + e_j.$$

As the $\hat{\alpha}_j$ are estimated simultaneously with the individual characteristics, they may be thought of as the citywide variation in self-employment rates that are orthogonal to variations in the individual characteristics.[15]

We estimate equation 2 using OLS separately by four mutually exclusive race/ethnicity categories: white, black, Hispanic, and Asian. Our $\mathbf{X}$ vector includes a quartic in the respondent's age, a vector of dummy variables indicating the respondent's education (less than high school, a high school drop out, some college, associate's degree, bachelor's degree, and a graduate degree—high school graduates are the excluded category), a vector of dummy variables for the respondent's marital status (divorce, separated, widowed, and never married; married is the excluded category), dummy variables indicating that the respondent is disabled, or a veteran, a set of dummy variables indicating when immigrants immigrated to the United States, and a fixed effect for the city in which the respondent lives. We recover the estimated city fixed effect $\hat{\alpha}_j$, which becomes data for our subsequent analysis.

14. Card and Krueger (1992).
15. What are the relative merits of our approach versus direct estimation of equation 1? First, direct estimation of this equation has the effect of weighting the estimates by the size of the city, which strikes us undesirable. That is, the characteristics of each metropolitan area get "counted" for each individual in the metropolitan area—thus giving a relative large impact from populous locations. The basic theory due to Borjas and Bronars predicts that *cities* should differ in their self-employment rates based on the racial composition of their populations. That is, each city should be the unit of observation with the implication that variation induced by Abilene and New York City should be treated equally. Our approach does just exactly that. Of course, we could reweight the data and estimate (1), but our approach is more direct. Second, our approach avoids the distributional assumptions embodied in a traditional logit or probit analysis of equation 1. Finally, our approach is computationally much less costly.

Results

We begin with the parameter estimates from the individual-level first-stage regressions. (We report the results in their entirety in appendix A and in tables B-1 through B-7 in appendix B to this paper.) Although not the focus of our attention, it is useful to check the degree to which our estimates reinforce the findings of previous studies of self-employment. Not surprisingly, they are quite similar to the estimates based on cross-sectional evidence. To highlight a few results, we find that immigrants, married couples, and more highly educated individuals have higher self-employment rates.

Having documented that our approach is similar to that of others' in the literature on the determinants of self-employment, we turn to the main focus of our attention: the role of metropolitan-area characteristics. To begin, we display in table 6a the correlations in the estimated city-specific effects (by racial group) for self-employment rates. In addition, we include in table 6b comparable correlations for city-specific effects in earnings of self-employed individuals and city-effects of earnings for wage and salary employees.[16] A look at the entries, and a comparison of corresponding elements of table 5, yields two insights. First, the correlations for self-employment rates in tables 5a and 6a are nearly identical while the correlations for self-employment income in tables 5b and 6b are also close (though not as similar). That is, we learn that controlling for individual-specific attributes has essentially no effect on the cross-city correlations in self-employment rates and earnings. Accordingly, we focus on characteristics of the cities themselves. Second, and not surprisingly, the correlations for wage-salary earnings are uniformly higher than for self-employment rates (see table 6b), reflective of the greater idiosyncratic variation in the latter.

Our remaining task is to investigate the role of city characteristics in determining the racial patterns of self-employment. We begin by replicating the approach (in spirit, if not exact detail) of BB in table 7. Each column of the table displays the coefficient estimates for city-specific variables and regional dummy variables.[17] Consider, for example, the entries in the second column, which explore the variation in the self-employment rate for blacks. The entry in row five indicates that an increase in the average income in the metropoli-

---

16. Estimates of the city-specific effects for self-employment income and for wage-salary income were obtained by re-estimating equation 2, having substituted first in self-employment earnings and then again in earnings for wage workers.

17. Recall that we have already controlled for the characteristics of individuals in our first stage.

Table 5a. Correlation in Self-Employment Rates across Metropolitan Areas

Item	White	Black	Hispanic	Asian
White	1.000			
Black	0.411	1.000		
Hispanic	0.110	0.0574	1.000	
Asian	0.0812	0.0352	-0.0253	1.000

Source: Authors' calculation, Public Use Micro Sample of the 1990 Census.

Table 5b. Correlation in Self-Employment Earnings across Metropolitan Areas

Item	White	Black	Hispanic	Asian
White	1.000			
Black	0.4291	1.000		
Hispanic	0.1377	0.1386	1.000	
Asian	-0.0271	0.0295	0.2177	1.000

Source: Authors' calculation, Public Use Micro Sample of the 1990 Census.

Table 6a. Correlation in City-Specific Effects for Self-Employment

Item	White	Black	Hispanic	Asian
White	1.000			
Black	0.372	1.000		
Hispanic	0.101	0.070	1.000	
Asian	0.066	0.016	-0.038	1.000

Source: Authors' calculation, Public Use Micro Sample of the 1990 Census.

Table 6b. Correlation in City-Specific Effects for Self-Employment Earnings and Wage-Salary Earnings[a]

Item	White	Black	Hispanic	Asian
White	1.000			
	1.000			
Black	0.243	1.000		
	0.490	1.000		
Hispanic	0.283	0.206	1.000	
	0.538	0.227	1.000	
Asian	0.128	0.057	0.115	1.000
	0.472	0.200	0.340	1.000

Source: Authors' calculation, Public Use Micro Sample of the 1990 Census.
a. Correlations for self-employment earnings are above those for wage-salary earnings.

Table 7. Self-Employment and Minority Populations[a]

Item	White	Black	Hispanic	Asian
Constant	-0.0389	0.0801	0.0981	0.955
	(0.0118)[b]	(0.0234)	(0.0234)	(0.0463)
Percent metropolitan black	-0.0635	-0.000980	-0.0342	0.113
	(0.0263)	(0.0202)	(0.0789)	(0.119)
Percent metropolitan Hispanic	0.0550	0.0245	0.0262	0.645
	(0.0168)	(0.0338)	(0.0250)	(0.0441)
Percent metropolitan Asian	-0.0780	-0.0565	-0.0543	-0.131
	(0.0295)	(0.0444)	(0.0341)	(0.0985)
Metropolitan income x 10^{-6}	1.74	0.493	0.732	-6.84
	(0.719)	(0.822)	(1.34)	(2.86)
Middle Atlantic	0.144	0.0119	0.0185	0.462
	(0.00544)	(0.00639)	(0.00868)	(0.0224)
East-North Central	0.00955	0.00630	0.0150	0.00848
	(0.00538)	(0.00673)	(0.0113)	(0.0183)
West-North Central	0.0208	0.0194	0.000419	0.0172
	(0.00969)	(0.0139)	(0.0161)	(0.0289)
South Atlantic	0.0398	0.0237	0.0441	0.0487
	(0.00759)	(0.00637)	(0.0171)	(0.0235)
East-South Central	0.0315	0.0162	0.0460	0.0576
	(0.00717)	(0.00716)	(0.0224)	(0.0390)
West-South Central	0.0441	0.0228	0.0380	0.0235
	(0.00679)	(0.00696)	(0.0113)	(0.0300)
Mountain	0.0288	0.0121	0.0166	0.0105
	(0.00806)	(0.0158)	(0.0081)	(0.0242)
Pacific	0.0397	0.0368	0.0299	0.0263
	(0.00695)	(0.0114)	(0.00824)	(0.0463)
N	273	273	273	272

Source: Authors' calculation, Public Use Micro Sample of the 1990 Census.

a. Dependent variable is metropolitan-area fixed effect from linear probability model. See text. Linear probability model controls for a quartic in age, a set of education dummies (less than high school, high school dropout, some college, associate's degree, bachelor's degree, and graduate degree), a dummy indicating the respondent is disabled, a vector of marital status variables (divorced, widowed, separated, and never married), a dummy variable indicating the respondent is a veteran, and a vector of dummy variables indicating when the respondent immigrated to the United States. The omitted region is New England.

b. Huber-White standard errors shown in parentheses.

tan area raises the rate of black self-employment, but the coefficient is imprecisely estimated. Similarly, the entry in row 11 and column 3 indicates a statistically significantly higher rate of self-employment for Hispanics in the West-South Central region.

From the perspective of the BB hypothesis, of more direct interest are the estimates of the coefficients for the variables describing the racial composition of the metropolitan-area population. As shown, the black self-employment rate declines with a greater fraction of the population that is black (the estimate is –0.00109), rises with the fraction Hispanic (0.0245), and

Table 8. Self-Employment Incomes and Minority Populations[a]

	White	Black	Hispanic	Asian
Constant	7.82	11.1	7.18	9.64
	(0.0460)[b]	(0.158)	(0.135)	(0.199)
Percent metropolitan black	0.613	0.420	0.174	-0.704
	(0.0678)	(0.234)	(0.442)	(0.388)
Percent metropolitan Hispanic	0.275	0.418	0.0696	-0.0328
	(0.0570)	(0.250)	(0.0959)	(0.217)
Percent metropolitan Asian	0.0966	0.333	0.232	-0.0864
	(0.0864)	(0.314)	(0.161)	(0.403)
Metropolitan income x 10^{-6}	34.7	22.5	26.0	23.7
	(2.70)	(8.50)	(7.69)	(9.27)
Middle Atlantic	-0.00865	-0.0592	-0.0771	0.216
	(0.0194)	(0.152)	(0.0966)	(0.126)
East-North Central	-0.0612	-0.0297	0.0142	0.340
	(0.0224)	(0.102)	(0.105)	(0.131)
West-North Central	-0.0924	-0.129	-0.0797	0.0481
	(0.0359)	(0.123)	(0.0861)	(0.204)
South Atlantic	-0.0928	-0.0415	0.0553	0.184
	(0.0224)	(0.103)	(0.0948)	(0.154)
East-South Central	-0.105	-0.162	-0.103	0.236
	(0.0273)	(0.119)	(0.154)	(0.166)
West-South Central	-0.110	-0.169	-0.0790	0.233
	(0.0264)	(0.101)	(0.0820)	(0.153)
Mountain	-0.140	-0.288	-0.0893	0.0535
	(0.0383)	(0.123)	(0.0772)	(0.131)
Pacific	-0.0444	-0.141	-0.0386	0.0240
	(0.0219)	(0.114)	(0.0773)	(0.132)
N	273	246	229	245

Source: Authors' calculation, Public Use Micro Sample of the 1990 Census.

a. Dependent variable is metropolitan-area fixed effect from linear probability model. See text. Linear probability model controls for a quartic in age, a set of education dummies (less than high school, high school dropout, some college, associate's degree, bachelor's degree, and graduate degree), a dummy indicating the respondent is disabled, a vector of marital status variables (divorced, widowed, separated, and never married), a dummy variable indicating the respondent is a veteran, and a vector of dummy variables indicating when the respondent immigrated to the United States. The omitted region is New England.

b. Huber-White standard errors shown in parentheses.

falls with the fraction Asian (–0.0565), although none of these coefficient estimates is statistically significant at conventional levels. Put differently, the racial composition of the population has no statistically discernible effect on the fraction of blacks that are self-employed. This finding stands in contrast to the simple prediction of a consumer discrimination model that a larger fraction of blacks raises the size of the market, the return to self-employment, and the equilibrium number of self-employed blacks. Note, however, that the "simple" story may just be too simple. As our analytic framework makes clear, a priori the coefficient can take any sign or be equal to zero.[18]

18. See the coefficient on $\hat{\lambda}$ in equations A7 and A8 in appendix A.

Is this result unique to blacks? Examining the estimates in the remaining columns of the table suggests not. In no instance is the coefficient on the "own" minority variable positive and statistically significant. Indeed, the entire set of estimates displays little explanatory power, and no consistent story emerges from the sign patterns.

Given this, one would expect a comparable performance in the relationship between self-employment earnings and the composition of the population, which is the focus of table 8. A look at the table confirms this expectation. As with the propensity to choose self-employment, there is essentially no relationship between the importance of minority populations and the returns to self-employment.

To summarize, our use of the 1990 census to examine the simplest specifications of the relationship between consumer discrimination and self-employment among minorities yields little support for the hypothesis of Borjas and Bronars.[19] At the same time, our analytic approach suggests other avenues for these processes, and reflection suggests that it might be possible to sharpen the results by improving on several features of the econometric specification.[20]

To begin, the basic specification is devoid of any measure of agglomeration effects in urban areas. That is, there is no scaling for the size and economic clout of the minority community, city size, city area, or population density.[21] Instead, the specification in tables 7 and 8 relies on the *percentage* of members of a racial minority to proxy for the demand by consumers of the output of the self-employed. A more compelling specification would incorporate information on the purchasing power of these individuals, that is, would include information on minorities' incomes as well.[22] Such a specification is consistent with a long and increasingly active literature that has demonstrated that external economies of scale arising from various facets of city size and

19. Interestingly, our results do not differ so greatly from BB. Specifically, their investigation of the 1980 census did not display uniformly strong explanatory power from the racial composition variables. Instead, they focus on a selection-corrected earnings equation and highlight the racial patterns of self-selection into the self-employed sector. As noted earlier, given the difficulty of defending the precise parametric and distributional assumptions embedded in this approach, we choose a less restrictive framework.

20. One possibility is to differentiate between those businesses that rely on face-to-face contact—where the impact of discrimination may be higher—and those that may be conducted at a distance. In results not reported herein, numerous attempts to distinguish between "local" industries and "export" industries yielded no evidence of such a distinction.

21. Because city area is fixed, in both our model and our regressions, N will carry both scale effects and density implications.

22. See the role of $\hat{y}^B$ in appendix A.

Table 9. Minorities, Incomes, Agglomeration, and Self-Employment[a]

Item	White	Black	Hispanic	Asian
Percent black	-0.212	0.00301	-0.108	0.116
	(0.0398)	(0.0205)	(0.0863)	(0.135)
Percent Hispanic	-0.144	0.0277	-0.00903	0.0289
	(0.0408)	(0.0283)	(0.0349)	(0.0548)
Percent Asian	-0.122	-0.0326	-0.103	-0.0484
	(0.0381)	(0.0358)	(0.0468)	(0.0570)
Metropolitan income x 10^6	-23.2	-8.10	-20.1	-21.3
	(5.31)	(6.47)	(10.2)	(17.4)
Metropolitan income squared x 10^{10}	1.88	3.33	4.93	2.42
	(1.04)	(1.95)	(2.69)	(5.40)
Income of own racial group x 10^6	19.1	-2.04	7.27	11.3
	(3.36)	(1.93)	(2.61)	(2.25)
Log metropolitan population	-0.0112	-0.00320	0.0131	-0.0132
	(0.00254)	(0.00354)	(0.00518)	(0.0117)
Log metropolitan area	0.0807	0.00324	-0.00321	0.00500
	(0.00283)	(0.00385)	(0.00514)	(0.00908)
N	273	273	273	272

Source: Authors' calculation, Public Use Micro Sample of the 1990 Census.
a. Regressions also include intercept, dummy variables for Census region, and those described in notes to table 7.

composition affect productivity and growth in urban areas.[23] Presumably, these same considerations carry over to self-employment.

With this in mind, we present in tables 9 and 10 the estimates from an enhanced specification that augments the corresponding regressions in tables 7 and 8 with various variables designed to capture scale effects. Specifically, we include in the model the square of metropolitan-area income, the metro-politan-area income of the "own" racial minority—for example, income of blacks in the regression for blacks and so forth—the logarithm of metropolitan population, and the logarithm of the geographic size of the metropolitan area, the latter of which captures population density conditioned on population size.

Begin with the latter two variables. As one looks across the columns of table 9, one finds a statistically significant impact of population size on Hispanic self-employment (the estimate is 0.0131 with a standard error of 0.00518) and of metropolitan area on white self-employment (0.0807 with a standard error of 0.00283). But there is no consistent pattern of either sign or significance on either variable and, by implication, for population density. A similar result holds for a parallel examination of the role of these variables in

23. For example, Glaeser and others (1992); Ellison and Glaeser (1997); Henderson and others (1995); Henderson and Black (1999); Rosenthal and Strange (2000).

Table 10. Minorities, Incomes, Agglomeration, and Self-Employment Incomes[a]

Item	White	Black	Hispanic	Asian
Percent black	0.583	0.473	-0.266	-0.779
	(0.150)	(0.266)	(0.505)	(0.393)
Percent Hispanic	0.322	0.208	-0.0387	-0.103
	(0.172)	(0.233)	(0.153)	(0.238)
Percent Asian	-0.0298	0.0696	-0.311	-0.0831
	(0.131)	(0.385)	(0.204)	(0.320)
Metropolitan income x 10^6	40.8	-13.4	-27.4	107.5
	(20.4)	(61.0)	(47.8)	(60.7)
Metropolitan income squared x 10^{10}	-0.0138	5.59	6.53	-41.5
	(4.84)	(17.0)	(14.4)	(17.9)
Income of own racial group x 10^6	-14.0	38.8	45.8	51.5
	(13.5)	(20.4)	(15.3)	(7.36)
Log metropolitan population	0.0555	0.000742	0.0920	0.0239
	(0.0116)	(0.0338)	(0.0369)	(0.0351)
Log metropolitan area	-0.0292	-0.0563	-0.0922	-0.0260
	(0.0119)	(0.0400)	(0.0328)	(0.0407)
N	273	246	229	245

Source: Authors' calculation, Public Use Micro Sample of the 1990 Census.
a. Regressions also include intercept, dummy variables for Census region, and those described in notes to table 7.

explaining self-employment income in table 10. On the surface, these results seem to suggest that agglomerative spillovers have little systematic influence on self-employment. The consumer discrimination argument outlined earlier, however, suggests that agglomerative externalities likely influence race-specific self-employment outcomes that arise from the economic size of minority markets.[24] In table 9 observe that for whites, the coefficient on the "own-race" metropolitan per capita income is positive (19.1) and statistically significant, a result that is mirrored for the impact of the incomes of Hispanics (7.27) and Asians (11.3) on their self-employment rates. Only for blacks is the estimate insignificant (and also negative).

Our theory indicates that an increase in minority income should affect self-employment rates and self-employment earnings in the same direction. If increased purchasing power of a minority group should increase the earnings power of the minority entrepreneur of a given ability, it should also increase the number of entrepreneurs. In table 10 we examine the impact of the own racial group's income on self-employment earnings. Although the coefficient for whites (column 1) is negative and insignificant, in column 3 we see that

24. In terms of our modeling in appendix A, there is a role for $\hat{y}^B$ in addition to that of $\hat{N}$, and the theory suggests that their impact need not be the same.

an increase in the overall incomes of Hispanics raises the average earnings of their self-employed. Similarly, the coefficient for Asians (51.5) indicates a quantitatively stronger effect of the same type.

Comparison of the coefficients on metropolitanwide income (and its square) in tables 7 through 10 yields a revealing pattern that may help to explain these results. In tables 7 and 8, where race-specific income is omitted from the model, observe that metropolitan-area income has a positive influence on self-employment rates and income for different racial groups in nearly all instances, although these effects are generally significant only for self-employment income (table 8). In contrast, once race-specific metropolitan income is added to the model in tables 9 and 10, estimates of the influence of metropolitan-wide income become substantially weaker and typically not significant. Together, these results and those above are suggestive that the potential buying power of the own-race population plays an important role in determining self-employment, a finding consistent with the consumer discrimination analytics outlined earlier.

A difficulty with interpreting the results thus far in the context of our model is that they may reflect not only the effects identified in our models but also all features of the local labor market equilibrium that affect the allocation of labor between wage and salary jobs and the relative returns to these two spheres. For example, we have not paid explicit attention to local labor market policies, the industrial structure, or a myriad of other factors. One approach would be to include these variables as controls in our equations. The drawback, however, is the difficulty of both identifying the "right" list of regressors and matching these features to the available data. An alternative approach is to exploit available information on the *outcome* of the equilibrium, rather than its determinants. Our strategy, then, for clarifying the role of minority populations in determining racial self-employment and incomes is to use the dominant labor market group—whites—to serve as a baseline control for the equilibrium. We present in tables 11 and 12 the results of this strategy.

Specifically, we present in table 11 estimates in which the dependent variable is the *difference* between the minority self-employment rate (for example, Asian) and the white self-employment rate in each metropolitan area. The independent variables are the same as in previous tables. Focusing on the variables of interest, we continue to find that the relative presence of one's own race, as measured by percent of population, does not increase the fraction of minorities in self-employment. In contrast, however, the economic scale of the minority community, as measured by the own-race metropolitan area income,

Table 11. Minorities, Incomes, Agglomeration, and Self-Employment: Using Whites as Controls[a]

Item	Black	Hispanic	Asian
Percent black	-0.000454	-0.0269	0.223
	(0.0246)	(0.0859)	(0.127)
Percent Hispanic	-0.0712	-0.107	-0.0885
	(0.0262)	(0.0369)	(0.0550)
Percent Asian	-0.000276	-0.00453	-0.00740
	(0.0336)	(0.0408)	(0.0602)
Metropolitan income x 10^6	-8.31	-23.5	-31.3
	(6.39)	(11.1)	(18.8)
Metropolitan income squared x 10^{10}	1.20	4.34	3.96
	(1.88)	(3.00)	(5.90)
Income of own racial group x 10^6	3.60	8.97	10.1
	(1.67)	(3.07)	(2.37)
Log metropolitan population	-0.00146	0.00561	-0.0105
	(0.00368)	(0.00501)	(0.0112)
Log metropolitan area	0.00299	-0.00952	-0.00650
	(0.00475)	(0.00514)	(0.00878)
N	246	229	245

Source: Authors' calculation, Public Use Micro Sample of the 1990 Census.
a. Dependent variable is difference between minority self-employment rate and white self-employment rate. See notes to table 10.

does matter. In particular, the coefficient for own-race minority-group metropolitan income is positive and statistically significant for blacks (3.60), Hispanics (8.97), and Asians (10.1).

Table 12 presents similar differenced regressions based on the differential self-employment earnings of the minority groups versus whites. As for self-employment rates, observe that the differential rises with minority incomes for blacks (45.8), Hispanics (39.7), and Asians (47.0). In each case, the estimates are statistically significant. Together, these results and those above provide reasonably strong support for the idea that the economic scale of the minority market affects the ability of metropolitan areas to sustain minority entrepreneurs.

Our strategy of using whites to control for labor market features may not be successful if cyclical fluctuations affect racial groups differently. For example, white unemployment rates in a metropolitan statistical area (MSA) may reflect regional differences in business cycle effects. To the extent that whites benefit disproportionately during good times relative to minority groups, white self-employment outcomes should be more sensitive to business cycle effects than minorities'. Accordingly, it is possible that our minority income scale results could reflect unmeasured regional business cycle effects.

**Table 12. Minorities, Incomes, Agglomeration, and Self-Employment Income:
Using Whites as Controls[a, b]**

Item	Black	Hispanic	Asian
Percent black	-0.0237	-0.643	-1.19
	(0.273)	(0.514)	(0.402)
Percent Hispanic	-0.0644	-0.231	-0.287
	(0.236)	(0.156)	(0.249)
Percent Asian	0.122	-0.300	-0.0381
	(0.313)	(0.200)	(0.349)
Metropolitan income x 10^6	54.6	-51.4	73.8
	(62.0)	(52.0)	(61.3)
Metropolitan income squared x 10^{10}	8.46	6.82	-37.7
	(17.5)	(15.9)	(18.0)
Income of own racial group x 10^6	45.8	39.7	47.0
	(19.4)	(15.5)	(7.64)
Log metropolitan population	-0.0354	0.0476	-0.0292
	(0.0346)	(0.0375)	(0.0380)
Log metropolitan area	-0.0432	-0.0706	-0.00553
	(0.0399)	(0.0327)	(0.0428)
N	246	229	245

Source: Authors' calculation, Public Use Micro Sample of the 1990 Census.
a. See notes to table 11.
b. Self-employment earnings of minority group minus self-employment earnings of white.

To examine these issues, we augment the models in tables 11 and 12 with MSA-specific information on unemployment rates. Panel a of tables 13 and 14 present estimates for a subset of the coefficients from the expanded differenced regression models for self-employment rates and self-employment income. To conserve space and to focus attention on the coefficients of primary interest, only the coefficients on four of the variables are presented: own-race population share, income, unemployment rate, and the white unemployment rate.

Two important findings emerge from panel a of table 13 and table 14. Most important, minority own-race MSA income continues to be positive and significant in the self-employment propensity equation (table 13) for Hispanics and Asians, and for all three minority groups in the self-employment income equation (table 14). Thus our finding that economic scale of the minority community is important is robust with respect to the cyclical state of each MSA economy. Second, the MSA white unemployment rate has a positive and significant impact on minority-white self-employment rate gaps for all three minority groups (table 13). To the extent that local white unemployment rates reflect regional differences in the business cycle, these results are

Table 13. Minority Economic Scale, Unemployment, and Self-Employment: Using Whites as Controls[a]

Item	Black	Hispanic	Asian
		Panel A	
Percent own race	0.073	-0.0541	0.0337
	(0.0310)	(0.0359)	(0.0614)
Income of own race x 10^6	-1.27	10.0	12.4
	(2.94)	(2.72)	(2.38)
Unemployment rate own race	-0.00327	0.10248	0.11551
	(0.0704)	(0.1315)	(0.1310)
Unemployment rate white	0.65079	0.83129	0.94044
	(0.3134)	(0.3415)	(0.4817)
R^2	0.117	0.192	0.275
		Panel B	
Percent own race	0.180	0.223	0.158
	(0.083)	(0.128)	(0.170)
Income of own race x 10^6	-1.43	10.1	12.1
	(2.92)	(2.67)	(2.46)
Unemployment rate own race	0.03619	0.11911	0.12937
	(0.0847)	(0.1437)	(0.1545)
Unemployment rate white	1.16344	-1.49946	-1.33313
	(1.2193)	(1.7221)	(2.7862)
Percent own race x unemployment rate own race	-0.91824	-1.04586	-0.88605
	(0.58787)	(0.5895)	(4.0441)
Percent white x unemployment rate white	-0.53714	2.69149	2.69581
	(1.4819)	(2.1729)	(3.1775)
R^2	0.125	0.206	0.277
N	246	273	272

Source: Authors' calculation, Public Use Micro Sample of the 1990 Census.
a. See notes to table 11.

consistent with arguments that the white community benefits more in an upturn and, correspondingly, suffers more in a downturn.

In panel b of tables 13 and 14, we extend the robustness check to include as well the own-race unemployment rates interacted with the percent own-race (for the minority group) and the white unemployment rate interacted with the percent white in the MSA. In general, the interactive terms add little explanatory power to the model and, as such, do not change the basic conclusions above.

Thus far our discussion of minority economic scale has taken place without regard for the intracity location of the minorities. Put differently, is there any reason to suspect that our results on minority economic scale actually reflect regional differences in the degree of racial segregation in the different

Table 14. Minority Economic Scale, Unemployment, and Self-Employment Income: Using Whites as Controls[a]

Item	Black	Hispanic	Asian
		Panel A	
Percent own race	-0.282	-0.240	-0.019
	(0.310)	(0.177)	(0.361)
Income of own race x 10^6	57.6	42.2	50.7
	(20.7)	(17.9)	(7.82)
Unemployment rate own race	1.27087	0.43280	1.00074
	(0.8195)	(0.7175)	(0.5785)
Unemployment rate white	-4.74407	1.04011	-0.77094
	(2.6819)	(2.2334)	(2.3877)
R^2	0.095	0.0933	0.263
		Panel B	
Percent own race	-0.894	-0.049	0.270
	(1.045)	(0.673)	(0.922)
Income of own race x 10^6	59.5	42.4	49.9
	(20.2)	(18.3)	(7.89)
Unemployment rate own race	1.03404	0.48280	0.97749
	(1.0333)	(0.8058)	(0.6663)
Unemployment rate white	-5.90751	0.56997	-9.46161
	(15.1385)	(9.2348)	(11.6584)
Percent own race x unemployment rate own race	4.61158	-1.35267	1.62379
	(6.1527)	(3.8101)	(23.1789)
Percent white x unemployment rate white	0.96838	0.44885	10.39849
	(17.6985)	(11.7840)	(13.2366)
R^2	0.097	0.0937	0.264
N	246	229	245

Source: Authors' calculation, Public Use Micro Sample of the 1990 Census.
a. See notes to table 11.

MSAs (for reasons noted in the introduction)? To examine this possibility, we return in tables 15 and 16 to the baseline difference-regression models from tables 11 and 12. To the extent that highly segregated minority communities are isolated from broader economic opportunities available to the white majority—in part, perhaps, because of spatial mismatch—is it possible that segregation and not minority economic scale could be the driving force in determining differences across MSAs in minority-white differentials in self-employment outcomes?[25] To examine this issue, we augment the baseline models with a measure of the integration between each minority group and the white majority within the individual MSA.

25. For example, Kain (1968, 1992).

Table 15. Minority Economic Scale, Integration, and Self-Employment: Using Whites as Controls[a]

Item	Black	Hispanic	Asian
		Panel A	
Percent own race	0.0285	-0.0933	0.0156
	(0.0370)	(0.1065)	(0.1309)
Income of own race x 10^6	-1.74	11.1	12.8
	(3.39)	(4.00)	(2.59)
Integration rate of own race	-0.0097	-0.0190	0.0005
	(0.0193)	(0.0665)	(0.1019)
R^2	0.0705	0.155	0.2675
		Panel B	
Percent own race	-0.0641	-0.1011	-0.1465
	(0.0636)	(0.1033)	(0.1838)
Income of own race x 10^6	6.84	12.5	17.6
	(4.57)	(9.80)	(20.9)
Integration rate of own race	0.0734	0.0050	0.1014
	(0.0619)	(0.0935)	(0.1982)
Percent own race x integration own race	0.2923	0.0927	0.8222
	(0.1784)	(0.1584)	(0.6395)
Income own race x integration own race x 10^6	10.6	-1.54	-4.68
	(6.83)	(9.64)	(21.4)
R^2	0.1000	0.159	0.2694
N	253	253	253

Source: Authors' calculation, Public Use Micro Sample of the 1990 Census.
a. See notes to table 11.

In evaluating the possible role of racial segregation, we use a measure of how exposed the minority group is to the majority white non-Hispanic population. Our data are taken from Census Bureau calculations for 1990, our sample year.[26] Our selected measure of the degree of contact between the minority group and the white majority measures the extent to which the two groups share common residential areas. The index takes on a value of 1 when the minority community is fully integrated with the white majority, and a value of zero when the minority community is completely segregated.[27]

26. We obtained the index, along with several alternative indexes, from www.census.gov.
27. The interaction index measures the exposure of minority group members to members of the majority group as the minority-weighted average of the majority proportion of the population in each "standard" unit, in this case census tracts within a given MSA. As noted at the Census Bureau website from which the interaction index was obtained, "the interaction and isolation indices reported here are calculated with the non-Hispanic White population as the reference group rather than the total population (excluding the minority group of interest)." For that reason, 1 minus the integration index used here is equivalent to the Isolation index described in the literature on measures of racial segregation. See, for example, James and

Table 16. Minority Economic Scale, Integration, and Self-Employment Income: Using Whites as Controls[a]

Item	Black	Hispanic	Asian
		Panel A	
Percent own race	-0.5388	-0.8280	-0.8227
	(0.4783)	(0.6329)	(0.4963)
Income of own race x 10^6	53.6	45.3	46.5
	(22.9)	(23.9)	(8.72)
Integration rate of own race	-0.3727	-0.4115	-0.5377
	(0.4083)	(0.4477)	(0.4524)
R^2	0.0768	0.1039	0.2494
		Panel B	
Percent own race	-1.222	-1.0170	-0.9557
	(0.5844)	(0.6482)	(0.7857)
Income of own race x 10^6	15.4	33.9	105.4
	(54.0)	(59.9)	(79.2)
Integration rate of own race	-0.8141	-0.3112	-0.2451
	(0.4315)	(0.7276)	(0.7390)
Percent own race x integration own race	1.9473	1.6044	-2.4326
	(1.2514)	(1.0205)	(4.0353)
Income own race x integration own race x 10^6	47.4	11.7	-61.5
	(60.9)	(63.0)	(79.4)
R^2	0.083	0.1103	0.2512
N	228	212	229

Source: Authors' calculation, Public Use Micro Sample of the 1990 Census.
a. See notes to table 11.

How does integration affect our view of economic scale? In the top panels of tables 15 and 16 observe that the integration index is not significant for any of the minority groups in both tables. As would then be expected, minority MSA income continues to have a positive and significant effect on minority-white self-employment differentials, with the exception of blacks with regard to self-employment propensity in table 15.

It is possible, however, that the impact of integration on self-employment outcomes is sensitive to the scale of the minority population. To allow for this possibility, the lower panels of tables 15 and 16 interact our integration measure with the minority group's population share in the MSA and the minority group's MSA income. These variables also are generally not significant,

Taeuber (1985) and Massey and Denton (1988) for further discussion of various segregation measures in the literature, and Cutler, Glaeser, and Vigdor (1999) for a recent application of segregation measures to an analysis of black-white segregation in the United States during the 1900s.

although in table 16 integration appears to increase black self-employment income relative to whites. Once again, the restricted model is preferred and minority income of the MSA positively affects minority-white differences in self-employment outcomes.[28]

Conclusion

Using the 1990 Census, we have investigated the large spatial variation in self-employment and the return to self-employment, especially among minorities. Several findings emerge. First, there is substantial variation across metropolitan areas in the rates of self-employment, and earnings from self-employment, for blacks, Hispanics, and Asians. Second, the variation cannot be attributed to differences among the metropolitan areas in the individual attributes—age, education, immigrant status, marital status, and so on—of their populations. Neither can it be explained simply on the basis of location—there are not simply "good" places and "bad" places for the self-employed of all races.

Instead, we find that variation in self-employment and earnings is positively linked to minority-specific measures of economic scale—the purchasing power that minorities bring to the metropolitan-area market. This result is robust to a variety of specifications and controls for various alternative MSA attributes that might otherwise account for the finding, including minority and white MSA unemployment rates and the degree of MSA minority segregation. Our work provides support for the idea that the economic scale of the minority market affects the ability of metropolitan areas to sustain minority entrepreneurs. Moreover, this conclusion is consistent with models of self-

---

28. As a final set of robustness checks, the differencing strategy above can be taken one step further by examining difference in the "self-employment premium," earnings in self-employment relative to wage-salary work between minority and white populations. We compared estimates of the relative premium (a difference-in-difference regression); the results are reported in table B-4. Tables B-5 and B-6 further explore these patterns by presenting double-differenced regressions augmented first with the unemployment variables (table B-5) and then with the integration variable (table B-6). In each case, only the key estimates of interest are presented, while the remaining coefficients are not reported to conserve space. While intriguing, our conclusion is that double-differenced regressions strip away so much information that identification becomes difficult, especially given our relatively limited sample size. Hence we leave their interpretation to the reader.

employment in which consumer discrimination against minority entrepreneurs dampens minority self-employment opportunities.

Appendix A

As noted in the text, we seek a framework that illuminates the equilibrium determination of self-employment rates and earnings by race. At the same time, we wish to follow BB in highlighting the potential impact of discrimination on these outcomes. We begin by specifying the demand for products of the self-employed. For simplicity in exposition, we assume there are only two racial groups, whites (W) and blacks (B). Again, to make the presentation transparent, we assume that whites "discriminate" in the following sense: if the price of a product of a black self-employed individual is P, whites "perceive" the price to be αP, where $\alpha > 1$. Thus, faced with the choice between buying from a white entrepreneur and a black entrepreneur, both charging P, the white individual will choose to discriminate in favor of purchases from the white entrepreneur. For simplicity, we assume that blacks do not discriminate.

We assume that the per capita demand by blacks for the products of the self-employed is given by $D^B(P, y^B)$, where P is the relative price of the output of the self-employed (output of the wage-salary sector is the numeraire) and y^B is per capita income of blacks.[29] In contrast, whites initially consume from the white self-employed an amount given by $D^W_W(P, y^W)$. We assume, however, that they also purchase from blacks the per capita amount $D^W_B(\alpha P, y^W)$, where the demand specification reflects the higher perceived cost of these goods.[30]

The output of self-employed individuals depends on their ability, indexed by θ. For clarity, we assume that output equals ability; it is straightforward to extend the model to incorporate capital and other purchased inputs. We assume that ability is exogenously distributed among blacks and whites according to the density functions $f^B(\theta)$ and $f^W(\theta)$, respectively. The corresponding distribution functions are $F^B(\theta)$ and $F^W(\theta)$, where θ ranges from a lower bound of $\underline{\theta}$ to an upper bound of $\bar{\theta}$.

---

29. We assume that incomes per capita are exogenous. It would be straightforward—if tedious and cumbersome—to endogenously determine labor earnings and leave only capital income predetermined.

30. This specification follows Borjas and Bronars. BB specify the search-theoretic microfoundations of the equilibrium. Our approach captures the essence of the demand-side predictions but adopts a simpler framework.

Finally, we assume that the population of the metropolitan area, N, consists of N^W whites and N^B blacks. With these preliminaries, the demand for self-employed output matches the total supply when:

$$
\begin{aligned}
(A1) \quad & N^W\left\{D_W^W\left(P, y^W\right) + D_B^W\left(\alpha P, y^W\right)\right\} + N^B\left\{D^B\left(P, y^B\right)\right\} \\
& = N^W \int_{\theta^{W*}}^{\bar{\theta}} \theta f^W(\theta)d\theta + N^B \int_{\theta^{B*}}^{\bar{\theta}} \theta f^B(\theta)d\theta,
\end{aligned}
$$

where θ^{W*} is the ability level of the lowest-ability white individual who chooses to be self-employed. θ^{B*} is defined similarly.

The alternative to self-employment is a job in the wage and salary sector. We abstract from the labor-leisure decision and assume that all individuals supply their labor inelastically; thus the wage equals labor earnings as well, which we denote E. The labor market clears when E matches the marginal product of labor, which we assume is a function of aggregate wage-salary employment in the area. That is,

$$
(A2) \quad MP\left(N^W \int_{\underline{\theta}}^{\theta^{W*}} f^W(\theta)d\theta + N^B \int_{\underline{\theta}}^{\theta^{B*}} f^B(\theta)d\theta\right) = E.
$$

We assume individuals choose between the wage-salary sector and self-employment on the basis of their earnings. Specifically, an individual of ability θ will choose to be self-employed if $P\theta > E$, and vice versa. Accordingly, the marginal entrant to self-employment will be indifferent between sectors. By implication[31]

$$
(A3) \quad P\theta^{W*} = P\theta^{B*} = P\theta^* = E.
$$

The simultaneous solution to equations A1 to A3 determines the equilibrium allocation of labor between sectors (θ^*), earnings in the wage-salary sector (E), and the relative price of self-employed output (P).

Our interest is in the dependence of the equilibrium on the degree of discrimination (indexed by α), the size of the population, the relative sizes of the minority groups in the population, and the relative affluence of population subgroups. To do so, let λ denote the fraction of blacks in the total population, and let $\hat{\ }$ denote percentage changes. Differentiating equation A3 yields

$$
(A4) \quad \hat{P} + \hat{\theta}^* = \hat{E},
$$

31. The fact that the marginal entrant to self-employment will have identical ability, regardless of race, follows directly from our assumption that there is a single, identical product for the self-employed and could easily be generalized.

that is, percentage changes in wage-salary earnings and self-employment earnings must balance for the marginal entrant. Similarly, differentiating equation A2 leads to

(A5) $$A_0 \hat{N} + A_1 \hat{\lambda} + A_2 \hat{\theta}^* = \hat{E}$$

where

$$A_0 = \frac{MP'(\bullet)}{MP(\bullet)} N\left\{(1-\lambda)\left(F^W(\theta^*) - F^W(\underline{\theta})\right) + \lambda\left(F^B(\theta^*) - F^B(\underline{\theta})\right)\right\}$$

$$= \frac{MP'(\bullet)}{MP(\bullet)} N\left\{(1-\lambda)F^W(\theta^*) + F^B(\theta^*)\right\},$$

$$A_1 = \frac{MP'(\bullet)}{MP(\bullet)} N\lambda\left\{F^B(\theta^*) - F^W(\theta^*)\right\},$$

and

$$A_2 = \frac{MP'(\bullet)}{MP(\bullet)} N\theta^*\left\{(1-\lambda)F^W(\theta^*) + \lambda F^B(\theta^*)\right\}.$$

For future reference, we assume diminishing marginal productivity so that $A_0 < 0$ and $A_2 < 0$, that is, raising the number of wage-salary workers levels to lower earnings. The number can rise if the population gets large (and the share that is self-employed remains unchanged), or if the share of the population that is self-employed declines. A_1, however, depends upon the relative shapes of the skill distributions in the two populations. Without additional structure on the problem, it is of ambiguous sign. Note that if the skill distributions are identical, $A_1 = 0$ If, however, $F^B(\theta^*) > F^W(\theta^*)$ then $A_1 < 0$. In these circumstances, raising λ brings into the labor market more individuals without the skills to be self-employed. This raises the number of wage-salary workers and lowers earnings, other things being equal.

To complete the comparative statics, differentiate equation A1, yielding

(A6) $$B_0 \hat{P} + B_1 \hat{\alpha} + B_2 \hat{y}^w + B_3 \hat{y}^B + B_4 \hat{\lambda} = B_5 \hat{\theta}^* + B_6 \hat{\lambda},$$

where

$$B_0 = (1-\lambda)D_W^W \varepsilon_W^W + (1-\lambda)D_B^W \varepsilon_B^W + \lambda D^B \varepsilon^B,$$

$$B_1 = (1-\lambda)D_B^W \varepsilon_B^W,$$

$$B_2 = (1-\lambda)D_W^W \eta_W^W + (1-\lambda)D_B^W \eta_B^W,$$

$$B_3 = \lambda D^B \eta^B,$$

$$B_4 = \lambda \left[D^B - \left(D_W^W + D_B^W \right) \right],$$

$$B_5 = -\theta^* \left[\lambda \theta^* f^B(\theta^*) + (1-\lambda)\theta^* f^W(\theta^*) \right],$$

and

$$B_6 = \lambda \left[\int_{\theta^*}^{\bar{\theta}} \theta \left[f^B(\theta) - f^W(\theta) \right] d\theta \right].$$

In equation A6, ε_B^W denotes the price elasticity of D_B^W, ε_W^W denotes the price elasticity of D_W^W, ε^B denotes the price elasticity of D^B, and the η are the analogously defined income elasticities.

Assuming negative price elasticities and positive income elasticities, B_0, B_1, and B_5 are negative, B_2 and B_3 are positive, and the remainder are of ambiguous sign.

Intuitively, equation A6 reflects the balancing of demand and supply. On the demand side, increases in price depress the weighted average demand (B_0), increases in discrimination reduce demand by whites (B_1), and increases in incomes of whites raises demand for the output of the white self-employed (B_2). In addition, increases in the "economic clout" of minorities—as measured by the incomes per capita of blacks—raises the demand for the goods of self-employed minorities (B_3). Finally, to the extent that per capita purchases of self-employed goods is greater among blacks than whites, a shift toward a greater fraction of minorities will raise demand, and vice versa (B_4).

On the supply side, an increase in the skill requirement for self-employment lowers the supply (B_5), and increase in the fraction of minorities raises or lowers the supply of output by the self-employed according to whether minorities are, on average, more highly skilled than whites or less highly skilled than whites, respectively.

Collecting terms and solving for the changes in the endogenous variables yields the reduced form relationships in equations A7 to A9, which are the focus of our discussion.

(A7) $\quad \hat{\theta}^* = \dfrac{1}{B_5 - B_0(A_2 - 1)} \left\{ (B_0 A_0)\hat{N} + (B_0 A_1 + B_4 - B_6)\hat{\lambda} + B_1\hat{\alpha} + B_2\hat{y}^W + B_3\hat{y}^B \right\}.$

(A8) $\hat{E} = \dfrac{1}{B_5 - B_0(A_2 - 1)} \Big\{ (B_5 + B_0)\hat{N} + (A_1 B_5 + A_1 B_0 + A_2 B_4 - A_2 B_6)\hat{\lambda}$

$\qquad + (A_2 B_1)\hat{\alpha} + (A_2 B_2)\hat{y}^W + ((A_2 - 1)B_3)\hat{y}^B \Big\}.$

(A9) $\hat{P} = \dfrac{1}{B_5 - B_0(A_2 - 1)} \Big\{ (A_0 B_5)\hat{N} + (A_1 B_5 + (B_4 B_6)(A_2 - 1))\hat{\lambda}$

$\qquad + ((A_2 - 1)B_1)\hat{\alpha} + ((A_2 - 1)B_2)\hat{y}^W + ((A_2 - 1)B_3)\hat{y}^B \Big\}.$

How does discrimination affect the labor market? Begin with equation A7, which shows that an increase in α raises θ^*: an increase in discrimination lowers self-employment among blacks.[32] By extension, equation A8 reveals that additional discrimination lowers earnings. Note, however, that equation A9 shows that higher discrimination lowers P. In effect, despite the greater skills in the self-employed sector, the decrease in price dominates entrepreneurs' productivity and results in lower returns to the marginal entrant.

Unfortunately, discrimination is not observed, so there is no regression analogue to these comparative static relationships. Instead, we are able to, for example, examine the relationship between self-employment and the racial composition of the population. In our framework, this corresponds to the relationship between self-employment (θ^*), earnings (E), and prices (P), and the fraction of the population that is black λ. Examining (A7) reveals that the theory delivers no strong prediction regarding this relationship. Intuitively, changing the mix of whites and minorities affects both the mix of skills in population—a supply-side effect—and the mix of demand for self-employed products—a demand-side effect, with no clear prediction regarding which shift will dominate. The former is indicated by the presence of the parameters A_1 and B_6, while the latter are reflected in B_4. To see this most dramatically, notice that if the distributions of θ are identical in whites and blacks, $A_1 = B_6 = 0$. In this case, an increase in λ increases self-employment (lowers θ^*) if blacks buy more per capita from the self-employed than do whites ($B_4 > 0$). Of course, if they buy less, the reverse it true. Of course, if the spending patterns of whites and minorities are the same ($B_4 = 0$), then the races are interchangeable and λ has no effect.

---

32. Formally, it also lowers self-employment among whites. This stems directly from our assumption that the goods of white entrepreneurs and minority entrepreneurs carry the same market price—they are perfect substitutes. It is straightforward to relax this assumption.

The ambiguous effect of λ carries over to both E and P, as an examination of (A8) and (A9) reveals. Notice, however, that the same is not true of an alternative measure of the "importance" of minorities. Specifically, an increase in the purchasing power of minorities, y^B, unambiguously raises minority self-employment (see equation A7), the prices received by the self-employed (see equation A9), and their earnings (see equation A8).

Thus, in the context of a model of this type, a more stringent test for the presence of discrimination and its impact on self-employment is to use the economic scale of minorities, as opposed to their demographic importance alone.

Appendix B

Table B-1. Linear Probability Models for Self-Employment Rate[a]

Item	Whites	Blacks	Hispanics	Asians
Age	-0.010	-0.011	-0.012	-0.087
	(0.007)	(0.012)	(0.016)	(0.032)
Age squared x 10^{-3}	0.812	0.561	0.480	3.23
	(0.260)	(0.453)	(0.592)	(1.12)
Age cubed x 10^{-5}	-1.61	-0.670	-0.558	-4.91
	(0.403)	(0.707)	(0.934)	(1.81)
Age to the fourth x 10^{-7}	1.00	0.317	-0.147	2.57
	(0.228)	(0.403)	(0.538)	(1.03)
Less than high school	-0.012	-0.0008	-0.011	-0.040
	(0.002)	(0.002)	(0.002)	(0.005)
High school dropout	-0.0003	0.001	-0.002	-0.013
	(0.001)	(0.001)	(0.002)	(0.005)
Associate's degree	-0.007	0.006	0.001	-0.011
	(0.001)	(0.002)	(0.003)	(0.005)
Some college, no degree	0.013	0.006	0.012	-0.003
	(0.0008)	(0.001)	(0.002)	(0.004)
Bachelor's degree	0.009	0.012	0.019	-0.011
	(0.0008)	(0.002)	(0.003)	(0.005)
Graduate degree	0.052	0.048	0.081	-0.009
	(0.0010)	(0.002)	(0.003)	(0.004)
Divorced	-0.014	0.0005	-0.010	-0.030
	(0.0009)	(0.002)	(0.002)	(0.006)
Separated	-0.023	-0.004	-0.022	-0.037
	(0.0015)	(0.002)	(0.002)	(0.004)
Widowed	-0.032	-0.012	-0.009	-0.038
	(0.003)	(0.004)	(0.007)	(0.015)
Never married	-0.027	-0.008	-0.020	-0.045
	(0.0008)	(0.0012)	(0.002)	(0.003)
Veteran	-0.035	-0.012	-0.025	-0.049
	(0.0006)	(0.001)	(0.002)	(0.004)
Disabled	-0.037	-0.013	-0.025	-0.040
	(0.0010)	(0.001)	(0.002)	(0.005)
Immigrated 1987–90	-0.052	-0.003	-0.015	-0.056
	(0.004)	(0.005)	(0.003)	(0.005)
Immigrated 1985–86	-0.003	0.007	-0.011	-0.041
	(0.005)	(0.005)	(0.003)	(0.005)
Immigrated 1982–84	0.024	0.015	0.0001	-0.004
	(0.005)	(0.005)	(0.003)	(0.005)
Immigrated 1980–81	0.025	0.018	0.003	0.017
	(0.005)	(0.004)	(0.003)	(0.004)
Immigrated 1975–79	0.071	0.022	0.003	0.044
	(0.003)	(0.004)	(0.002)	(0.005)
Immigrated 1970–74	0.064	0.027	0.012	0.004
	(0.004)	(0.004)	(0.002)	(0.006)
Immigrated 1965–69	0.038	0.023	0.013	0.004
	(0.003)	(0.005)	(0.003)	(0.006)
Immigrated 1960–64	0.026	0.010	0.027	0.002
	(0.003)	(0.006)	(0.003)	(0.007)
Immigrated 1950–59	0.026	0.010	0.003	0.026
	(0.002)	(0.008)	(0.003)	(0.008)
Immigrated before 1950	0.026	-0.022	-0.006	0.022
	(0.004)	(0.015)	(0.005)	(0.014)
N	1,531,883	202,712	195,728	77,837

Source: Authors' calculation, Public Use Micro Sample of the 1990 Census.
a. Dependent variable is whether respondent is self-employed.

Table B-2. Self-Employment Earnings[a]

Item	Whites	Blacks	Hispanics	Asians
Age	0.156	-0.110	0.232	-0.005
	(0.062)	(0.259)	(0.171)	(0.294)
Age squared x 10^{-3}	-0.005	0.003	-0.007	0.001
	(0.002)	(0.009)	(0.006)	(0.010)
Age cubed x 10^{-5}	0.00008	-0.00003	0.0001	-0.0002
	(0.00003)	(0.0001)	(0.00010)	(0.0002)
Age to the fourth x 10^{-7}	0.000	0.000	0.000	0.000
	(0.000)	(0.000)	(0.000)	(0.000)
Less than high school	-0.179	-0.139	-0.222	-0.139
	(0.013)	(0.037)	(0.019)	(0.045)
High school dropout	-0.097	-0.102	-0.118	-0.107
	(0.008)	(0.027)	(0.020)	(0.042)
Associate's degree	0.103	0.100	0.059	0.030
	(0.010)	(0.041)	(0.031)	(0.041)
Some college, no degree	0.086	0.065	0.066	0.027
	(0.006)	(0.027)	(0.020)	(0.033)
Bachelor's degree	0.296	0.258	0.268	0.162
	(0.006)	(0.033)	(0.026)	(0.030)
Graduate degree	0.692	0.709	0.723	0.620
	(0.007)	(0.035)	(0.026)	(0.031)
Divorced	-0.244	-0.155	-0.207	-0.182
	(0.007)	(0.027)	(0.023)	(0.051)
Separated	-0.210	-0.204	-0.252	-0.222
	(0.013)	(0.030)	(0.023)	(0.041)
Widowed	-0.193	-0.077	-0.099	-0.252
	(0.025)	(0.072)	(0.065)	(0.125)
Never married	-0.376	-0.244	-0.270	-0.278
	(0.007)	(0.026)	(0.019)	(0.036)
Veteran	-0.007	-0.018	0.035	0.021
	(0.005)	(0.021)	(0.019)	(0.035)
Disabled	-0.428	-0.389	-0.345	-0.360
	(0.008)	(0.029)	(0.025)	(0.051)
Immigrated 1987–90	-0.476	-0.280	-0.366	-0.433
	(0.037)	(0.096)	(0.034)	(0.049)
Immigrated 1985–86	-0.258	-0.194	-0.248	-0.287
	(0.041)	(0.093)	(0.036)	(0.050)
Immigrated 1982–84	-0.152	-0.206	-0.189	-0.208
	(0.034)	(0.076)	(0.033)	(0.041)
Immigrated 1980–81	-0.142	-0.083	-0.136	-0.153
	(0.034)	(0.064)	(0.026)	(0.041)
Immigrated 1975–79	-0.104	0.005	-0.105	-0.103
	(0.020)	(0.059)	(0.024)	(0.036)
Immigrated 1970–74	-0.028	-0.069	-0.056	0.029
	(0.023)	(0.057)	(0.023)	(0.038)
Immigrated 1965–69	-0.004	-0.069	-0.024	0.002
	(0.022)	(0.067)	(0.025)	(0.044)
Immigrated 1960–64	0.010	0.101	0.035	0.029
	(0.022)	(0.101)	(0.025)	(0.056)
Immigrated 1950–59	0.021	-0.144	0.010	0.120
	(0.016)	(0.121)	(0.028)	(0.057)
Immigrated before 1950	0.074	0.116	-0.008	0.028
	(0.027)	(0.305)	(0.049)	(0.100)
N	196,995	9,544	15,451	9,529

Source: Authors' calculation, Public Use Micro Sample of the 1990 Census.
a. Dependent variable is the logarithm of the earnings of the self-employed.

Table B-3. Wage and Salary Earnings[a]

Item	Whites	Blacks	Hispanics	Asians
Age	0.691	0.116	0.256	0.355
	(0.018)	(0.062)	(0.054)	(0.091)
Age squared x 10^{-3}	-0.024	-0.004	-0.008	-0.010
	(0.0007)	(0.002)	(0.002)	(0.003)
Age cubed x 10^{-5}	0.0004	0.00009	0.0001	0.0001
	(0.00001)	(0.00004)	(0.00003)	(0.00005)
Age to the fourth x 10^{-7}	0.000	0.000	0.000	0.000
	(0.000)	(0.000)	(0.000)	(0.000)
Less than high school	-0.354	-0.275	-0.292	-0.313
	(0.004)	(0.011)	(0.006)	(0.016)
High school dropout	-0.216	-0.245	-0.192	-0.163
	(0.003)	(0.007)	(0.006)	(0.014)
Associate's degree	0.167	0.243	0.178	0.0196
	(0.003)	(0.010)	(0.009)	(0.014)
Some college, no degree	0.119	0.152	0.143	0.112
	(0.002)	(0.006)	(0.006)	(0.011)
Bachelor's degree	0.383	0.449	0.384	0.396
	(0.002)	(0.008)	(0.009)	(0.010)
Graduate degree	0.495	0.571	0.518	0.593
	(0.002)	(0.011)	(0.011)	(0.011)
Divorced	-0.276	-0.299	-0.247	-0.153
	(0.002)	(0.008)	(0.008)	(0.017)
Separated	-0.313	0.409	-0.380	-0.248
	(0.004)	(0.008)	(0.007)	(0.012)
Widowed	-0.217	-0.272	-0.314	-0.187
	(0.009)	(0.021)	(0.025)	(0.046)
Never married	-0.443	-0.464	-0.382	-0.293
	(0.002)	(0.006)	(0.005)	(0.009)
Veteran	-0.034	0.024	-0.083	0.020
	(0.002)	(0.006)	(0.006)	(0.011)
Disabled	-0.558	-0.547	-0.520	-0.449
	(0.003)	(0.009)	(0.010)	(0.019)
Immigrated 1987–90	-0.439	-0.394	-0.621	-0.729
	(0.010)	(0.024)	(0.010)	(0.013)
Immigrated 1985–86	-0.244	-0.209	-0.398	-0.554
	(0.013)	(0.024)	(0.010)	(0.014)
Immigrated 1982–84	-0.210	-0.145	-0.309	-0.443
	(0.012)	(0.021)	(0.010)	(0.013)
Immigrated 1980–81	-0.158	-0.157	-0.254	-0.350
	(0.013)	(0.019)	(0.008)	(0.013)
Immigrated 1975–79	-0.130	-0.052	-0.179	-0.217
	(0.009)	(0.018)	(0.007)	(0.012)
Immigrated 1970–74	-0.074	-0.023	-0.125	-0.113
	(0.009)	(0.018)	(0.008)	(0.013)
Immigrated 1965–69	-0.010	-0.016	-0.075	-0.079
	(0.009)	(0.021)	(0.009)	(0.015)
Immigrated 1960–64	-0.017	0.011	0.0009	0.006
	(0.008)	(0.030)	(0.010)	(0.020)
Immigrated 1950–59	0.017	0.009	0.005	0.027
	(0.006)	(0.037)	(0.018)	(0.022)
Immigrated before 1950	0.035	0.004	0.005	0.096
	(0.011)	(0.074)	(0.018)	(0.042)
N	1,218,309	153,312	157,005	59,770

Source: Authors' calculation, Public Use Micro Sample of the 1990 Census.
a. Dependent variable is the logarithm of the earnings of the wage and salary workers.

Table B-4. Minority Economic Scale and Self-Employment Income Premium Relative to Wage-Salary Income: Using Whites as Controls[a]

Item	Black	Hispanic	Asian
Percent own race	-0.0229	-0.158	0.152
	(0.273)	(0.212)	(0.422)
Income of own race x 10^6	9.40	23.5	15.6
	(25.2)	(21.6)	(7.86)
R^2	0.068	0.062	0.090
N	246	229	244

Source: Authors' calculation, Public Use Micro Sample of the 1990 Census.
a. See notes to table 11.

Table B-5. Minority Economic Scale, Unemployment, and Self-Employment Income Premium Relative to Wage-Salary Income: Using Whites as Controls[a]

Item	Black	Hispanic	Asian
	Panel A		
Percent own race	-0.473	-0.199	0.210
	(0.310)	(0.232)	(0.431)
Income of own race x 10^6	27.4	-93.1	18.5
	(23.9)	(61.2)	(8.14)
Unemployment rate own race	1.94	0.889	0.911
	(0.864)	(1.08)	(0.698)
Unemployment rate white	-8.415	1.172	0.460
	(2.51)	(2.82)	(2.99)
R^2	0.115	0.0750	0.100
	Panel B		
Percent own race	-1.277	0.645	0.0690
	(1.05)	(0.941)	(0.950)
Income of own race x 10^6	29.2	28.8	16.8
	(23.1)	(23.9)	(8.12)
Unemployment rate own race	1.69	0.953	0.550
	(1.10)	(1.21)	(0.772)
Unemployment rate white	-6.40	-8.63	-25.3
	(15.4)	(12.3)	(14.0)
Percent own race x unemployment rate own race	4.78	-1.73	30.4
	(6.44)	(4.71)	(22.6)
Percent white x unemployment rate white	-2.85	11.6	30.7
	(17.8)	(16.3)	(17.2)
R^2	0.118	0.0786	0.116
N	246	229	244

Source: Authors' calculation, Public Use Micro Sample of the 1990 Census.
a. See notes to table 11.

Table B-6. Minority Economic Scale, Integration, and Self-Employment Income Premium Relative to Wage-Salary Income: Using Whites as Controls[a]

Item	Black	Hispanic	Asian
	Panel A		
Percent own race	-0.217	-0.719	-1.42
	(0.500)	(0.918)	(0.618)
Income of own race x 10^6	21.3	33.5	20.6
	(29.9)	(33.5)	(8.45)
Integration rate of own race	-0.246	-0.346	-1.260
	(0.435)	(0.618)	(0.527)
R^2	0.0657	0.0758	0.109
	Panel B		
Percent own race	-0.140	-0.998	-2.12
	(0.746)	(0.890)	(0.909)
Income of own race x 10^6	-2.12	-7.38	93.3
	(53.9)	(89.5)	(96.0)
Integration rate of own race	-0.516	-0.493	-0.55
	(0.668)	(0.842)	(0.988)
Percent own race x integration own race	-0.328	1.78	1.04
	(1.55)	(1.26)	(4.29)
Income own race x integration own race x 10^6	31.3	43.4	-74.4
	(67.8)	(84.6)	(97.5)
R^2	0.0670	0.081	0.110
N	234	218	232

Source: Authors' calculation, Public Use Micro Sample of the 1990 Census.
a. Regressions also include intercept, dummy variables for Census region, and those described in notes to table 7.

Table B-7. List of Metropolitan Areas

Abilene, TX MSA
Akron, OH PMSA
Albany-Schenectady-Troy, NY MSA
Albuquerque, NM MSA
Alexandria, LA MSA
Allentown-Bethlehem, PA-NJ MSA
Altoona, PA MSA
Amarillo, TX MSA
Anaheim-Santa Ana, CA PMSA
Anchorage, AK MSA
Anderson, IN MSA
Anderson, SC MSA
Ann Arbor, MI PMSA
Anniston, AL MSA
Appleton-Oshkosh-Neenah, WI MSA

Asheville, NC MSA
Atlanta, GA MSA
Atlantic City, NJ MSA
Augusta, GA-SC MSA
Aurora-Elgin, IL PMSA
Austin, TX MSA
Bakersfield, CA MSA
Baltimore, MD MSA
Baton Rouge, LA MSA
Battle Creek, MI MSA
Beaumont-Port Arthur, TX MSA
Bellingham, WA MSA
Benton Harbor, MI MSA
Bergen-Passaic, NJ PMSA
Billings, MT MSA
Biloxi-Gulfport, MS MSA
Binghamton, NY MSA
Birmingham, AL MSA

Bloomington, IN MSA
Bloomington-Normal, IL MSA
Boise City, ID MSA
Boston, MA PMSA
Boulder-Longmont, CO PMSA
Bradenton, FL MSA
Brazoria, TX PMSA
Bremerton, WA MSA
Bridgeport-Milford, CT PMSA
Brockton, MA PMSA
Brownsville-Harlingen, TX MSA
Bryan-College Station, TX MSA
Buffalo, NY PMSA
Burlington, NC MSA

Table B-7. List of Metropolitan Areas, continued

Canton, OH MSA
Cedar Rapids, IA MSA
Champaign-Urbana-
  Rantoul, IL MSA
Charleston, SC MSA
Charlotte-Gastonia-Rock
  Hill, NC-SC MSA
Chattanooga, TN-GA MSA
Chicago, IL PMSA
Chico, CA MSA
Cincinnati, OH-KY-IN
  PMSA
Clarksville-Hopkinsville,
  TN-KY MSA
Cleveland, OH PMSA
Colorado Springs, CO MSA
Columbia, MO MSA
Columbia, SC MSA
Columbus, OH MSA
Corpus Christi, TX MSA
Dallas, TX PMSA
Danbury, CT PMSA
Danville, VA MSA
Davenport-Rock Island-
  Moline, IA-IL MSA
Dayton-Springfield, OH
  MSA
Daytona Beach, FL MSA
Decatur, AL MSA
Decatur, IL MSA
Denver, CO PMSA
Des Moines, IA MSA
Detroit, MI PMSA
Duluth, MN-WI MSA
Eau Claire, WI MSA
El Paso, TX MSA
Elkhart-Goshen, IN MSA
Erie, PA MSA
Eugene-Springfield, OR
  MSA
Fall River, MA-RI PMSA
Fayetteville, NC MSA
Fayetteville-Springdale, AR
  MSA
Flint, MI MSA
Florence, AL MSA
Florence, SC MSA
Fort Collins-Loveland, CO
  MSA
Fort Lauderdale-
  Hollywood-Pompano
  Beach, FL PMSA
Fort Myers-Cape Coral, FL
  MSA

Fort Pierce, FL MSA
Fort Wayne, IN MSA
Fort Worth-Arlington, TX
  PMSA
Fresno, CA MSA
Gainesville, FL MSA
Galveston-Texas City, TX
  PMSA
Gary-Hammond, IN PMSA
Grand Rapids, MI MSA
Greeley, CO MSA
Green Bay, WI MSA
Greensboro–Winston-
  Salem–High Point, NC
  MSA
Greenville-Spartanburg, SC
  MSA
Hagerstown, MD MSA
Hamilton-Middletown, OH
  PMSA
Harrisburg-Lebanon-
  Carlisle, PA MSA
Hartford, CT PMSA
Hickory-Morganton, NC
  MSA
Honolulu, HI MSA
Houma-Thibodaux, LA
  MSA
Houston, TX PMSA
Huntington-Ashland, WV-
  KY-OH MSA
Indianapolis, IN MSA
Jackson, MI MSA
Jackson, MS MSA
Jacksonville, FL MSA
Jacksonville, NC MSA
Jamestown-Dunkirk, NY
  MSA
Janesville-Beloit, WI MSA
Jersey City, NJ PMSA
Johnson City-Kingsport-
  Bristol, TN-VA MSA
Johnstown, PA MSA
Joliet, IL PMSA
Joplin, MO MSA
Kalamazoo, MI MSA
Kansas City, MO-KS MSA
Kenosha, WI PMSA
Killeen-Temple, TX MSA
Knoxville, TN MSA
Lafayette, LA MSA
Lafayette-West Lafayette,
  IN MSA
Lake County, IL PMSA

Lakeland-Winter Haven, FL
  MSA
Lancaster, PA MSA
Lansing-East Lansing, MI
  MSA
Las Cruces, NM MSA
Las Vegas, NV MSA
Lawrence-Haverhill, MA-
  NH PMSA
Lexington-Fayette, KY
  MSA
Lima, OH MSA
Lincoln, NE MSA
Little Rock-North Little
  Rock, AR MSA
Longview-Marshall, TX
  MSA
Lorain-Elyria, OH PMSA
Los Angeles-Long Beach,
  CA PMSA
Louisville, KY-IN MSA
Lowell, MA-NH PMSA
Lubbock, TX MSA
Macon-Warner Robins, GA
  MSA
Madison, WI MSA
Manchester, NH MSA
Mansfield, OH MSA
McAllen-Edinburg-Mission,
  TX MSA
Medford, OR MSA
Melbourne-Titusville-Palm
  Bay, FL MSA
Memphis, TN-AR-MS
  MSA
Merced, CA MSA
Miami-Hialeah, FL PMSA
Middlesex-Somerset-
  Hunterdon, NJ PMSA
Midland, TX MSA
Milwaukee, WI PMSA
Minneapolis-St. Paul, MN-
  WI MSA
Mobile, AL MSA
Modesto, CA MSA
Monmouth-Ocean, NJ
  PMSA
Monroe, LA MSA
Montgomery, AL MSA
Muncie, IN MSA
Nashua, NH PMSA
Nashville, TN MSA
Nassau-Suffolk, NY PMSA
New Bedford, MA MSA

Table B-7. List of Metropolitan Areas, continued

New Britain, CT PMSA
New Haven-Meriden, CT
 MSA
New London-Norwich, CT-
 RI MSA
New Orleans, LA MSA
New York, NY PMSA
Newark, NJ PMSA
Niagara Falls, NY PMSA
Norfolk-Virginia Beach-
 Newport News, VA
 MSA
Oakland, CA PMSA
Ocala, FL MSA
Odessa, TX MSA
Oklahoma City, OK MSA
Olympia, WA MSA
Omaha, NE-IA MSA
Orange County, NY PMSA
Orlando, FL MSA
Oxnard-Ventura, CA PMSA
Pascagoula, MS MSA
Pawtucket-Woonsocket-
 Attleboro, RI-MA
 PMSA
Pensacola, FL MSA
Peoria, IL MSA
Philadelphia, PA-NJ PMSA
Phoenix, AZ MSA
Pittsburgh, PA PMSA
Portland, OR PMSA
Providence, RI PMSA
Provo-Orem, UT MSA
Pueblo, CO MSA
Racine, WI PMSA
Raleigh-Durham, NC MSA
Reading, PA MSA
Redding, CA MSA
Reno, NV MSA
Richland-Kennewick-Pasco,
 WA MSA
Richmond-Petersburg, VA
 MSA
Riverside-San Bernardino,

CA PMSA
Roanoke, VA MSA
Rochester, MN MSA
Rochester, NY MSA
Rockford, IL MSA
Sacramento, CA MSA
Saginaw-Bay City-Midland,
 MI MSA
St. Cloud, MN MSA
St. Louis, MO-IL MSA
Salem, OR MSA
Salem-Gloucester, MA
 PMSA
Salinas-Seaside-Monterey,
 CA MSA
Salt Lake City-Ogden, UT
 MSA
San Antonio, TX MSA
San Diego, CA MSA
San Francisco, CA PMSA
San Jose, CA PMSA
Santa Barbara-Santa Maria-
 Lompoc, CA MSA
Santa Cruz, CA PMSA
Santa Fe, NM MSA
Santa Rosa-Petaluma, CA
 PMSA
Sarasota, FL MSA
Savannah, GA MSA
Scranton--Wilkes-Barre, PA
 MSA
Seattle, WA PMSA
Sharon, PA MSA
Sheboygan, WI MSA
Shreveport, LA MSA
South Bend-Mishawaka, IN
 MSA
Spokane, WA MSA
Springfield, IL MSA
Springfield, MO MSA
Springfield, MA MSA
Stamford, CT PMSA
State College, PA MSA
Stockton, CA MSA

Syracuse, NY MSA
Tacoma, WA PMSA
Tampa-St. Petersburg-
 Clearwater, FL MSA
Terre Haute, IN MSA
Toledo, OH MSA
Trenton, NJ PMSA
Tucson, AZ MSA
Tulsa, OK MSA
Tuscaloosa, AL MSA
Tyler, TX MSA
Utica-Rome, NY MSA
Vallejo-Fairfield-Napa, CA
 PMSA
Vancouver, WA PMSA
Vineland-Millville-
 Bridgeton, NJ PMSA
Visalia-Tulare-Porterville,
 CA MSA
Waco, TX MSA
Washington, DC-MD-VA
 MSA
Waterbury, CT MSA
Waterloo-Cedar Falls, IA
 MSA
Wausau, WI MSA
West Palm Beach-Boca
 Raton-Delray Beach, FL
 MSA
Wichita, KS MSA
Wichita Falls, TX MSA
Williamsport, PA MSA
Wilmington, DE-NJ-MD
 PMSA
Wilmington, NC MSA
Worcester, MA MSA
Yakima, WA MSA
York, PA MSA
Youngstown-Warren, OH
 MSA
Yuba City, CA MSA
Yuma, AZ MSA

Comment

Bruce Fallick: The paper attempts to test the intuitively appealing hypothesis that consumer discrimination lowers the return to self-employment by reducing the size of the effective market for minority entrepreneurs. Hence, self-employment among a minority group should be more common in locations that are relatively free of this limitation, that is, in areas where members of that same minority group constitute a large market.

However, this idea is, so to speak, a "negative" version of consumer discrimination—customers prefer not to do business with members of a particular group. I suggest two alternative hypotheses that focus on how racial minority economic clout can improve entrepreneurs' access to capital. First, "positive" consumer discrimination helps minorities in areas with high own-minority populations to overcome capital constraints by providing a large eager market. Second, a large local own-minority population makes more minority-specific capital available, possibly through informal networks.

Whichever hypothesis one chooses, the authors present evidence that minority self-employment is related to the aggregate incomes of the local own-minority population. At first glance, these results support the notion that consumer discrimination is a large part of the story. However, on a closer look, the results give me pause.

First, in table 9 in the paper the coefficient on own-group income is much larger for whites than it is for the other groups. This is troubling, because whites are the group that one would expect to suffer the least from consumer discrimination. Perhaps large white incomes facilitate self-employment for all groups, but the regressions do not speak directly to this possibility. Why not include income for every group in each regression?

Second, even if one writes off the white coefficient in table 9 as spurious and concentrates on the "difference from whites" regression in table 11, the coefficient for blacks is much smaller than those for Hispanics or Asians. I would expect blacks to suffer most from customer discrimination, at least the "negative" version put forward by the authors.

Consequently, I find the authors' results unconvincing. There are, I think, ways to investigate the importance of consumer discrimination further. One tack might be to examine how much of the regional disparity in self-employment rates is accounted for by differences in the relative importance of industries in which one would not expect to see a great deal of consumer discrimination. I did not have the 1990 census handy, but I did have some CPS files. For 1994, removing workers in agriculture, public administration, and the military from the sample made a considerable difference in the relative self-employment rates of various regions. For example, removing these industries shifts the West North Central region from having a considerably higher self-employment rate than the Mid-Atlantic region to having about the same rate.

In the course of this exercise, I noticed that the variation in self-employment rates by race in my CPS sample was similar to that reported in the paper, but the variation by region was not. For example, in the paper's census sample, the Northeast (which I assume are the New England states) had a below-average rate of self-employment; in my CPS sample this region's rate was above the average. Furthermore, the regional patterns in the CPS varied sufficiently between 1994 and 1999 to raise some concerns about how robust the correlations in the paper may be across time.

On the econometric side, I see no need to shy away from logits or probits. One can have the benefits without large computational costs either by estimating equation 11 by logit or by making the unit of observation the metropolitan area rather than the individual and running logistic regressions on the percentage of the employed who are self-employed.

Finally, two points about definitions in the data. First, I assume that the self-employment rate used in the paper is defined as the number of self-employed workers divided by the number of people employed. To the extent that self-employment is an alternative for those who have difficulty finding jobs, it is not clear that the number employed is the appropriate denominator. Second, the measure of self-employment used includes only the unincorporated self-employed. My calculations from the CPS indicate that racial disparities are greater if one includes self-employed workers who have incorporated their businesses.This makes me worry that results from the unincorporated sample may be biased by the selection into incorporated versus unincorporated.

References

Black, Dan. 1995. "Discrimination in an Equilibrium Search Model." *Journal of Labor Economics* 13 (April): 308–33.

Blanchflower, David G. 2000. "Self-Employment in OECD Countries." Working Paper 7486. Cambridge, Mass.: National Bureau of Economic Research (January).

Borjas, George J., and Stephen G. Bronars. 1989. "Consumer Discrimination and Self-Employment." *Journal of Political Economy* 97 (June): 581–605.

Bruce, Don. 1999. "Effects of the United States Tax System on Transitions into Self-Employment." Syracuse University, Center for Policy Research (September). Mimeo.

Card, David, and Alan Krueger. 1992. "Does School Quality Matter? Returns to Education and the Characteristics of Public Schools in the United States." *Journal of Political Economy* 100 (February): 1–40.

Carrasco, Raquel. 1997. "Transitions to and from Self-Employment in Spain: An Empirical Analysis." Working Paper 9710. Madrid: Centro De Estudios Monetarios y Financieros.

Cowling, Marc, and Peter Mitchell. 1997. "The Evolution of U.K. Self-Employment: A Study of Government Policy and the Role of the Macroeconomy." *The Manchester School LXV* (September): 427–42.

Cutler, David M., Edward L. Glaeser, and Jacob L. Vigdor. 1999. "The Rise and Decline of the American Ghetto." *Journal of Political Economy* 107 (June): 455–506.

Ellison, G., and Edward Glaeser. 1997. "Geographic Concentration in U.S. Manufacturing Industries: A Dartboard Approach." *Journal of Political Economy* 105 (October): 889–927.

Evans, David S., and Boyan Jovanovic. 1989. "An Estimated Model of Entrepreneurial Choice under Liquidity Constraints." *Journal of Political Economy* 97 (August): 808–27.

Fairlie, Robert W., and Bruce D. Meyer. 1996. "Ethnic and Racial Self-Employment Differences and Possible Explanations." *Journal of Human Resources* 31 (Fall): 757–93.

Gabriel, Stuart A., and Stuart S. Rosenthal. 1996. "Commutes, Neighborhood Effects, and Earnings: An Analysis of Racial Discrimination and Compensating Differentials." *Journal of Urban Economics* 40 (July): 61–83.

Georgellis, Yannis, and Howard J. Wall. 1999. "Gender Differences in Self-Employment: Panel Evidence from the Former West Germany." Working Paper 99-008B. Federal Reserve Bank of St. Louis (January). Mimeo.

Glaeser, Edward L., and others. 1992. "Growth in Cities." *Journal of Political Economy* 100 (December): 1126–52.

Green, Shelley, and Paul Pryde. 1990. *Black Entrepreneurship in America*. Transaction Publishers.

Harhoff, D., K. Stahl, and M. Waywood. 1998. "Legal Form, Growth and Exit of West German Firms—Empirical Results for Manufacturing Construction, Trade, and Service Industries." *Journal of Industrial Economics* 46 (December): 453–88.

Henderson, J. V., and D. Black. 1999. "A Theory of Urban Growth." *Journal of Political Economy* 107 (April): 252–83.

Henderson, J. V., A. Kuncoro, and M. Turner. 1995. "Industrial Development in Cities." *Journal of Political Economy* 103 (October): 1067–85.

Holtz-Eakin, Douglas, Harvey S. Rosen, and Robert Weathers. 2000. "Horatio Alger Meets the Mobility Tables." *Small Business Economics* 14 (June): 243–74.

Holtz-Eakin, Douglas, and Thomas Dunn. 2000. "Financial Capital, Human Capital, and the Transition to Self-Employment: Evidence from Intergenerational Links." *Journal of Labor Economics* 18 (April): 282–305.

Holtz-Eakin, Douglas, David Joulfaian, and Harvey S. Rosen. 1994. "Entrepreneurial Decisions and Liquidity Constraints." *Rand Journal of Economics* 25 (Summer): 334–47.

James, David R., and Karl E. Taeuber. 1985. "Measures of Segregation." In *Sociological Methodology 1985*, edited by Nancy Tuma, 1–32. Jossey-Bass.

Johansson, Edward. 2000. "Self-Employment and Liquidity Constraints: Evidence from Finland." *Scandinavian Journal of Economics* 102 (June): 123–34.

Kain, John. 1968. "Housing Segregation, Negro Employment, and Metropolitan Decentratalization." *Quarterly Journal of Economics* 82 (May): 175–97.

——. 1992. "The Spatial Mismatch Hypothesis: Three Decades Later." *Housing Policy Debate* 3 (2): 371–462.

Massey, Douglas S., and Nancy A. Denton. 1988. "The Dimensions of Residential Segregation." *Social Forces* 67 (December): 281–315.

Meyer, Bruce. 1990. "Why Are There So Few Black Entrepreneurs?" Working Paper 3537. Cambridge, Mass.: National Bureau of Economic Research (December).

Pfeiffer, E., and W. Pohlmeier. 1992. "Uncertainty, and the Probability of Self-Employment." *Recherche Economiques de Louvain* 58 (3-4): 265–81.

Robson, Martin T. 1997. "The Relative Earnings from Self and Paid Employment: A Time-Series Analysis for the UK." *Scottish Journal of Political Economy* 44 (November): 502–18.

Rosenthal, Stuart S., and William C. Strange. 2000. "Geography, Industrial Organization, and Agglomeration." Working Paper. Syracuse University, Center for Policy Research (April).

Taylor, Mark P. 1996. "Earnings Independence of Unemployment: Why Become Self-Employed?" *Oxford Bulletin of Economics and Statistics* 58: 253–66.

Yuengert, Andrew. 1996. "Left-Out Capital and the Return to Capital and Labor in Self-Employment." Unpublished manuscript. Pepperdine University (August).

Zax, Jeff. 1990. "Race and Commutes." *Journal of Urban Economics* 28 (November): 336–49.